'This book disrupts simplistic ideas about student enga
neoliberal stone to reveal questions of power at the hea
the university. It does exactly what it claims: advances student engagement and
invites the reader to take a critical, reflective and challenging stance about a concept
that has become a buzzword. I recommend it highly'.

Prof Tansy Jessop NTF, Pro Vice-Chancellor for Education,
University of Bristol (UK)

'This book provides a much-needed, in-depth exploration of the context of student engagement in higher education today, and makes a powerful case for why
we should continuously be reflecting on our current practices. It is both a detailed
discussion of the current academic debates at play, while remaining an accessible
resource for anyone interested in ensuring the success of student engagement'.

Livia Scott, Students' Union Community and Projects Officer, Wonkhe

'Anyone who has attempted to innovate their practice with students, run a student
feedback workshop, or engage students as partners will know that there are numerous
challenges. This edited collection draws together practitioners from across the field
who discuss these challenges up-front, offering innovative recommendations and
flexible practice to ensure students are truly included. There are important questions
to be continuously addressed in our universities relating to inclusivity and equality
opportunities to engage, and this book is a great starting point for colleagues looking
to engage students within their area of the modern university'.

Prof Claire Hamshire NTF, Vice President (Europe), International Society for
the Scholarship of Teaching and Learning & Head of International,
Manchester Metropolitan University (UK)

'This is an excellent volume, timely and comprehensive, which explores the variety
of contexts for student engagement in today's HE landscape. Building on existing
works, it continues to make the case for student engagement as a crucial focus for
HE institutions, but the collection also problematises student engagement, challenging assumptions and investigating barriers. This critical dimension is a key
strength of the collection. The recommendations for improving practice which
emerge from its chapters are invaluable'.

Prof Stephen McVeigh, Chair of Researching, Advancing and Inspiring Student
Engagement (RAISE) (2019–22) & Associate Dean – Education,
Swansea University (UK)

'The book frames students clearly as invested members of the university community,
and emphasises the importance of knowing about and embedding student engagement
in all aspects of university life and work. Threaded through the book is the consistent
message that each student is a unique learner who needs, in fact deserves, individual
attention, and the task of achieving this is explored and explained in different contexts'.

Dr Rachel Forsyth PFHEA, Editor in Chief of the Student Engagement in
Higher Education Journal & Project Leader, Lund University (Sweden)

Advancing Student Engagement in Higher Education

Providing a selection of critical pieces on the key challenges and debates in student engagement in higher education, this edited collection of sector-leading, scholarly informed critical reflections is designed to consider and build upon what can be done to advance student engagement.

By problematising student engagement practice, this book explores how to strengthen policies, recognise the issues and create solutions to overcome barriers and tensions. It considers topics such as diversity, accessibility, representativeness, evidencing impact, data analytics, the campus estate and the impact of COVID-19. The contributors provide lessons learned and knowledge from the field to make practice with students more considered and robust for the challenges ahead in the post-pandemic university.

Moving beyond endorsing student engagement and offering best practice to critically reflect on and challenge our engagements with students in contemporary higher education, this book is ideal reading for all those developing education, course leaders and heads of academic departments, as well as anyone interested in advancing student engagement in their higher education setting.

Tom Lowe is a Senior Lecturer in Higher Education at the University of Portsmouth (UK) and the Chair of Researching, Advancing and Inspiring Student Engagement (RAISE).

The Staff and Educational Development Series

Written by experienced and well-known practitioners and published in association with the Staff and Educational Development Association (SEDA), each book in the series contributes to the development of learning, teaching and training and assists in the professional development of staff. The books present new ideas for learning development and facilitate the exchange of information and good practice.

Series Editor: James Wisdom

Titles in the series:

Understanding and Developing Student Engagement
Edited by Colin Bryson

Advancing Practice in Academic Development
Edited by David Baume and Celia Popovic

Developing Intercultural Practice
Academic Development in a Multicultural and Globalizing World
David Killick

Delivering Educational Change in Higher Education
A Transformative Approach for Leaders and Practitioners
Edited by Jackie Potter and Cristina Devecchi

A Handbook for Student Engagement in Higher Education
Theory into Practice
Edited by Tom Lowe and Yassein El Hakim

Supporting Course and Programme Leaders in Higher Education
Practical Wisdom for Leaders, Educational Developers and Programme Leaders
Edited by Jenny Lawrence, Sue Morón-García, Rowena Senior

Developing Expertise for Teaching in Higher Education
Practical Ideas for Professional Learning and Development
Edited by Helen King

Advancing Student Engagement in Higher Education
Reflection, Critique and Challenge
Edited by Tom Lowe

For more information about this series, please visit: www.routledge.com/SEDA-Series/book-series/SE0747

Advancing Student Engagement in Higher Education

Reflection, Critique and Challenge

Edited by Tom Lowe

Routledge
Taylor & Francis Group

LONDON AND NEW YORK

Designed cover image: © Getty Images

First published 2023
by Routledge
4 Park Square, Milton Park, Abingdon, Oxon OX14 4RN

and by Routledge
605 Third Avenue, New York, NY 10158

Routledge is an imprint of the Taylor & Francis Group, an informa business

British Library Cataloguing-in-Publication Data
A catalogue record for this book is available from the British Library

ISBN: 978-1-032-19868-2 (hbk)
ISBN: 978-1-032-22250-9 (pbk)
ISBN: 978-1-003-27178-9 (ebk)

DOI: 10.4324/9781003271789

Typeset in Galliard
by Taylor & Francis Books

Contents

Illustrations

Contributors

Sophia Abbot is a doctoral student in Higher Education at George Mason University (Virginia, USA). She has participated in and studied students as partners practices for the last decade.

Talia Adams is the Vice President of Education and Lincoln Students' Union where she represents the academic interests of all students at the University of Lincoln to ensure their academic and wider student experience is the best it can be.

Dr Liz Austen is Head of Evaluation and Research (Student Experience, Teaching and Learning) at Sheffield Hallam University (UK) and Visiting Professor at Staffordshire University (UK). Her role includes research and evaluation within higher education, focused on improving student experiences.

Dr Sarah Bayless is Senior Lecturer in Psychology at the University of Winchester (UK). Her research interests are in Developmental and Cognitive Psychology, and aspects of Student Experience, Learning and Teaching.

Zoheir Beig is currently the Manager of the School of Arts and Humanities at the Royal College of Art (UK). He completed the PG Cert Student Engagement in Higher Education at the University of Winchester and previously worked at University of the Arts London.

Dr Hazel Brown is Head of the School of Sport, Health and Community at the University of Winchester (UK).

Prof Alison Cook-Sather is Mary Katharine Woodworth Professor of Education at Bryn Mawr College and Director of the Teaching and Learning Institute at Bryn Mawr and Haverford Colleges, USA.

Eddie Corr is the Data for Student Success Executive at Maynooth University (Ireland). His research interests include learning analytics and student success; extra-curricular activity and belonging; and developing student partnership practices.

Jim Dickinson is an Associate Editor at higher education policy website Wonkhe (UK), taking a particular interest in the student experience, university governance, and regulation – and leading Wonkhe's work with students' unions.

Dr Mollie Dollinger is the Senior Lecturer, Learning Futures at Deakin University (Australia). Her research interests include participatory design, equity and inclusion, and work-integrated learning.

Alan Donnelly is a Lecturer in Student Engagement, Evaluation and Research at Sheffield Hallam University (UK). Alan has experience of designing and implementing research and evaluation approaches on institutional and sector-wide projects.

Dr Harriet Dunbar-Morris PFHEA, NTF, Dean of Learning and Teaching and Reader in Higher Education, provides leadership in the enhancement of the student experience, champions the student voice, and ensures student engagement in Portsmouth's activities.

Katja Eftring recently graduated from the Environmental Engineering programme at Lund University (Sweden). She has been a student representative throughout her studies, and has coordinated student participation in the course evaluation process as a part of the student union at the Faculty of Engineering.

Madalene George is a Student Engagement Coordinator at University of Worcester (UK) Library Services. In her role, Madalene helps lead the development of Library Services' student engagement and impact strategies.

Maisha Islam is the Student Engagement Research and Projects Coordinator at the University of Winchester (UK), whilst also working towards a professional doctorate in Education.

Dr Alison Jaquet is the Associate Director, Student Engagement and Success at the University of the Sunshine Coast (Australia), and has championed innovative, learning-centred practice at universities for over 15 years.

Dr Naomi King is a Research Associate in Psychology at Oxford Brookes University (UK). Her research interests are in Applied Social Psychology, and she specialises in qualitative methods.

Jia Yi Loh is a 2021 graduate of the Bryn Mawr College Department of Literatures and Education Program, USA. A Naval Officer, Jia Yi is a continual student and practitioner of learner-forward education in both academic and professional capacities.

Dr Cassie Violet Lowe is a Senior Teaching Associate in the Centre for Teaching and Learning at the University of Cambridge (UK).

Tom Lowe is a Senior Lecturer in Higher Education at the University of Portsmouth (UK) and the Chair of Researching, Advancing and Inspiring Student Engagement (RAISE).

Dr Tanya Lubicz-Nawrocka is an Academic Development Partner at the University of Stirling (UK). She recently completed PhD research at the University of Edinburgh (UK), regularly publishing and presenting on curriculum co-creation and partnership.

Prof Jenny Marie is the Head of Academic and Learning Enhancement at the University of Greenwich (UK), focusing on educational strategy and policy. She previously led UCL's partnership scheme, UCL ChangeMakers.

Maria Moxey is a Teaching Fellow in Student Engagement at the University of Winchester (UK), where she is the Programme Leader for the Masters in Student Engagement in Higher Education.

Emily Parkin is a student engagement practitioner experienced in partnership and widening participation. She currently works at Northumbria University leading initiatives to support the success and progression of underrepresented students.

Dr Keith Parry is Head of Department in the Department of Sport and Event Management at Bournemouth University (UK).

Nathaniel Pickering is a Senior Lecturer in Student Engagement, Evaluation and Research at Sheffield Hallam University (UK). His role includes research and evaluation within higher education with a particular focus on widening participation and social justice.

Dr Clare Rathbone is a Senior Lecturer at Oxford Brookes University (UK). Her research, funded by an ESRC Future Research Leaders grant, explores autobiographical memory and self concepts.

Torgny Roxå is an Associate Professor at Lund University (Sweden), and for 35 years has been an academic developer. His research is focused upon strategic change in academic teaching cultures, significant networks and microcultures. He has taught at several professional development activities for academic developers in Sweden and internationally.

Dr Stuart Sims is an Associate Professor of Higher Education Learning & Teaching at the University of Greenwich. He previously led the University of Winchester's partnership-based Student Fellows Scheme.

Dr Zachery Spire is a Student Services Officer at Stanford University and a visiting lecturer at the University of Winchester. His research focuses on universities, student residential accommodation and student engagement.

Dr Terrell L. Strayhorn is a Professor of Hight Education and Women's, Gender & Sexuality Studies at Illinois State University (USA), where he also directs the PhD programme in the Department of Educational Administration & Foundations (EAF).

Dr Louise Taylor Bunce is a Principal Lecturer Student Experience at Oxford Brookes University (UK) and National Teaching Fellow. She specialises in student identities and anti-racist learning and teaching.

Rosie Tressler OBE is CEO of Student Minds, the UK's charity for student wellbeing and mental health. Awarded an OBE for her higher education work, Rosie is also a Trustee for the Mental Health Foundation.

Fatima Umar is the Team Lead for Student Success at the Lahore University of Management Sciences (Pakistan). Her interests include programme development and implementation for diverse student populations.

Simon Varwell is Senior Development Consultant at sparqs, Scotland's national agency for student engagement. He is a graduate of the University of Winchester's Masters in Student Engagement in Higher Education.

Kate Walsh is the Student Representation and Development Officer at the Flinders University Student Association (Australia). She has extensive experience in student engagement nationally and was the inaugural Project Manager for Student Voice Australia.

Acknowledgements

My greatest thanks to James Wisdom for his time supporting and mentoring me during this publication, as well as Prof Catherine Bovill, Prof Mike Neary, Liz Dunne, Dr Jill LeBihan and Prof Colin Bryson for sharing their thoughts on student engagement with me over the last decade. Finally, my greatest thanks to my wife Cassie for her continued support with my endless projects.

Foreword

Rosie Tressler OBE, CEO Student Minds (UK)

It is an honour to introduce an edited book that has been so thoughtfully and comprehensively developed, and by a group of professionals and academics that I greatly admire. I first met the collection's editor, Tom Lowe, several years ago, whilst preparing to speak at a conference about digital in higher education. I was immediately struck by how collaborative Tom was as a member of a growing student engagement community. I knew he was a real expert in the theory of student engagement, yet he immediately made me feel like my opinions and experiences – which were practical, messy and not always successful – mattered.

I was invited by Tom and the fabulous RAISE committee (who represent a network of staff and students in higher education who work or have an interest in the research and promotion of student engagement) to one of their conferences some months later. I'll admit that I had no idea how developed the student engagement professionals sector was. As I wandered around the fascinating poster presentations I was blown away to learn of hundreds of professionals who truly valued the 'how' and 'student voice' in universities. As someone who'd cut my teeth as a Students' Union Officer, it made me so happy to see so many places in our sector where the idea of co-production with students is a given – seen as 'how it should be' and not as an inconvenience.

At that conference I reflected on how student engagement work is at times difficult and undervalued, and how my own understanding had evolved from being transactional (adding quotes from students into papers to back up what I thought!) to being authentic, inclusive and meaningful, with thanks to a decade of learning alongside our Student Advisory Committee, Student Minds colleagues and the wider sector. Being generous, coaching types though, the RAISE crowd made our team feel like our co-production toolkits and examples of student-led projects were inspirational.

What people like Tom and the student engagement community are able to help the people around them feel is 'agency'. They often disrupt typical power dynamics, and build people up to feel like they can influence their own lives and beyond. This is why they are so good at what they do. As someone who works across education and mental health, I know how much life, or rather certain systems or individuals, can really knock our agency out of us. Most of us will know how it feels to be told what to do, think or feel, cultures that are fixated on tradition and hierarchies. So when we are shown the real respect that what we do, think and feel matters too, it is incredibly powerful for all involved.

A few months after the RAISE conference in late 2019, I'd see all of that learning and encouragement well put to use! Before the winter break, Student Minds (UK) published quality standards for universities on mental health, called the University Mental Health Charter. Following deep engagement with students and university professionals – we set out all that should be done within an institution to create thriving university communities – from how we teach, to the accommodation we provide, the support we offer, to the ways our leaders and community work together. And then just a few months later we would all see our understanding of student engagement tested further, responding to the COVID-19 pandemic.

As we all know, during the pandemic, students tried to learn and make friends through online spaces like Zoom, but research showed that students have been lonelier than the rest of us adults. Students also lost much-needed part-time jobs, many had housing and money issues, and students from minoritised groups likely had even more barriers to engagement. In response, at Student Minds we launched Student Space – dedicated, relevant support for mental health during this difficult time. Thousands of students have been helped, or helped each other, through Student Space so far – supported to deal with grief, or manage difficult symptoms, to find people who understand their experiences. Both the University Mental Health Charter and Student Space have shown our team and partners just how critical it is to genuinely listen and have an authentic student engagement mindset – we haven't got everything right, but we have certainly picked up the mantle set out in the first chapter – and are being critically reflective as we go.

It has been a tough few years in this sector; people have worked incredibly hard, and we have to be realistic that there are more challenges ahead. I hope though, with what we've all been through these recent years, more of us can see the opportunities we have for learners and educators, universities, students' union and their range of partners, to establish better ways of working together. Together we can get past suspiciousness, the 'fear of stepping on toes' and focus on creating cultures and a community that is caring and healthy together. Indeed, the more I think about the challenges facing society and higher education today, the more I keep coming back to this word, agency.

For higher education professionals, our job in the face of the climate breakdown, racial injustice and a multitude of social issues and inequalities surely has to be to ensure that every person who comes through our institutions' doors will leave us feeling like they truly have the agency to make positive contributions in our society and to build agency with others. The current and next generation of students will quite rightly expect it, and I think this timely collection of chapters will come to be regarded as the core handbook on how we facilitate this together.

Chapter 1

Advancing student engagement in higher education

The need for reflection, critique and challenge

Tom Lowe

Introduction

In an ever-developing higher education (HE) context, taking time to research, discuss and develop student engagement is crucial to ensuring that our institutions remain student-centred. With regard to developing student success and improving learning and teaching in HE, there is an increasing focus on student engagement both within and alongside the curriculum (Tight, 2020; Quaye, Harper and Pendakur, 2019; Lygo-Baker, Kinchin, and Winstone, 2019). As best practice for enhancement, engaging students in educational development has flourished, with an international movement towards: new co-design practices (Bovill, 2020); methods to gain student feedback (Lowe and Bols, 2020); research projects about students' experiences (Buckley et al., 2021, and Kahu, Picton, and Nelson, 2020, are recent examples); and students' taking on roles such as partners and reviewers (Bryson, 2016; Owen, 2013). These together work towards developing education for the betterment of all stakeholders (Snijders et al., 2020, Lowe and El Hakim, 2020, and Dunne, 2017, offer summaries of student engagement in educational development practice). There continues to be great momentum in such student engagement areas as student voice, student–staff partnership, extra-curricular activity and learner analytics, all with significant potential outcomes impact upon, for example, satisfaction, retention and employability (Adams, 2023; Abbot, 2023; Corr, 2023; Beig, 2023). Working with our students to develop education has become the norm in many institutions at both policy and curriculum levels. However, as sector-wide rhetoric continues to emphasise value for money, it is now even more important to be critically reflective about what student engagement practices we are implementing at our institutions. An international community of scholarship has emerged, advocating, exploring and developing HE student engagement. This publication is timely in its provision of reflections, critique and challenge to student engagement agendas in order to advance practice and to be more inclusive of a diverse student body; its authors remain committed to the values of student engagement, even in the context of an increasingly marketised sector. Each of these chapters reflects on a theme for development within the student engagement discourse and the book as a whole offers recommendations for best practice from a field of scholars with specific expertise.

DOI: 10.4324/9781003271789-1

As an outcome of the powerful marketisation effect upon the HE sector of several nations and, in particular, of the United Kingdom, North America and Australia, the task of implementing engagement has fallen on all levels of their HE institutions, not just on educational developers and students' unions: now, management/administrators, course leaders, student services and careers advisers and, most recently, 'student experience/engagement' professionals are all prioritising student engagement (Chapter 17 – George, 2023). Ensuring that students have an engaging HE experience is, increasingly, critically measured by government-led metrics and national surveys that are shared with prospective future students and emphasise learning, retention and outcomes (Chapter 2 – Bayless, 2023 – expands upon this). These metrics then influence the promotion of business models prioritising both expansion and retention, for student numbers relate strongly to university finances. Despite this metrics-driven approach within our institutions, we must remain student-centred and committed to the values of engagement by working with students, listening to them and researching how best to engage them. It is between the metric-driven agendas (Chapter 25 –Lowe and Parkin, 2023) and the morally driven values that seek to develop HE for students and staff in partnership (Chapter 16 – Cook-Sather and Loh, 2023) that enthusiasts for engagement practices sit. Communities of practice have arisen, creating sources of knowledge about engagement practice – such as those that discuss the pragmatics of engaging students in shaping the student experience – so that HE providers now demand conferences, staff development opportunities and educational journals to foster the growth of these activities in their institutions. Recognising the complexity involved and the issues and the inevitable consequent tensions, this publication adds to a growing discourse about student engagement in contemporary HE and offers recommendations from experience in the field.

This book follows the previous SEDA edited collection, *A Handbook for Student Engagement in Higher Education: Theory into Practice* (Lowe and El Hakim, 2020), which offered an international set of case studies, theoretical perspectives and student accounts; it explored and evidenced why a focus on student engagement in educational developments is crucial for university enhancement and best practice. This collection, going beyond endorsing student engagement and offering best practice case studies, critically reflects upon and challenges our assumptions about our engagements with students in contemporary HE. Although there are plenty of innovatory engagement strategies, institutions do still face challenge and have more to do. With their critical perspectives, the authors here seek to strengthen institutional focus and effort. Their chapters analyse obstacles and barriers and make relevant, achievable recommendations. They cover such significant matters as diversity and race, learner analytics, learning from COVID-19, the space of the campus estate, the student role (as consumer, partner and producer in HE) and activities beyond the classroom (Chapters 7, 11 and 18: Taylor Bunce, Rathbone and King, 2023; Dickinson, 2023b; Spire, 2023). This publication includes both student and staff chapters authored by published HE professionals and academics worldwide. On account of both theoretical and policy-inspired agendas to engage students as partners, rather than as customers or passive learners, universities globally must continue to prioritise engagement to enhance their experiences (Chapters 15 and 21: Abbot, 2023; Walsh and Jaquet, 2023).

Student engagement in contemporary HE

This collection aims to be inclusive of wider definitions of student engagement in HE. When they embark upon a project, study or discussion relating to student engagement in our institutions, colleagues and students alike face the same challenge: to define what is – and is not – 'student engagement'. Though this publication is not immune to this debate, the editor felt it important to welcome wider areas of focus within engagement, in order to speak to a more diverse audience and so, alongside more traditional chapters focusing on the curriculum and learning, there are chapters relating to more contemporary definitions, such as the co-curricular student voice space, wider emotional engagement (such as belonging) and behavioural engagement now, in our digital age, largely measured online through analytics. Creating an inclusive definition framework for 'student engagement' to serve as an introduction to such a broad collection is a tricky task. Trowler's (2010) literature review on student engagement is useful, when adapted as in Figure 1.1. Trowler's literature review found three main themes within the student engagement discourse: emotional engagement (feelings, thoughts and experiences), cognitive engagement (learning and wider curriculum) and behavioural (physical activities such as attendance and digital activities as small as clicks and downloads). These Trowler themes still work more than a decade later, except that they do not cover a now major area of student engagement literature included in this collection: student engagement in educational developments, such as co-design, students as partners and student voice areas. The model below is thus adapted to embrace them.

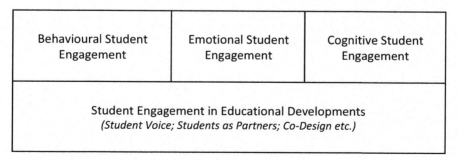

Figure 1.1 Themes of student engagement
Adapted from Trowler (2010)

Why include students in the development of education?

Engaging students as more fully invested members rather than merely as learners is critical to the continued development of student-centred learning and success in modern universities and colleges (Chapter 6 – Dunbar-Morris, 2023 – offers a leadership perspective). Students in HE are more than capable adults, with rich life experiences that are often untapped sources of innovation and insight, and are uniquely positioned to support the development of institutions. Students make up 80–90% of our HE communities, yet student representatives are still in the minority – and often alone – on our management boards and academic committees, utterly outnumbered by seasoned administrators in the staff territory of the boardroom. Though HE institutions are centred upon knowledge and research, when it comes to educational development, their students, in spite of having real, first-hand experience as recipients of what is on offer, usually have little or no voice in the planning of interventions, are not involved in any analysis and may expect to be consulted only for retrospective commentary on whatever initiative they've been subjected to. Staff opinion – powerfully influential – about curriculum or wider provision development is frequently prefaced by the faux authority of the hackneyed "When I was a student…", which in fact depends on an HE experience quite unlike that of current students. Generation Z is being educated at a time when poor mental health is increasing, when universities are hyper-dependent on digital delivery (the more so because of the pandemic, itself uniquely disruptive and challenging) and when, for some nations, rising tuition fees (Chapter 14 – Dollinger, 2023) are having previously unheard-of effects on individual student lives. It is instructive to consider that elected students' union presidents and vice presidents may serve for only two years after they graduate, with their student experience being deemed no longer relevant to that of current undergraduates.

Certainly, HE institutions must do everything possible to engage students in the development of education: university administrators and teaching staff must keep clearly in mind that students who voluntarily commit three or four years to study – for the sake of pursuing knowledge, of gaining a relevant qualification and of making themselves employable in a very financially constrained world – deserve the greatest support for their learning and ultimate success… and the best support comes from enabling them to participate in improving HE provision (see Chapter 10 – Eftring and Roxå, 2023).

Critical reflective practice in student engagement in HE

"We learn by doing and realising what came of what we did" (1938, cited in Rolfe, Jasper and Freshwater, 2011, p.34). To focus on student engagement in HE is increasingly becoming a more mainstream activity in this sector and derives from several agendas: the original development of learning (Chickering and Gamson, 1987), the improvement of student retention (Yorke and Longden, 2004), the creation of a feeling of belonging (Strayhorn, 2018; Thomas, 2012) and the provision of opportunities for co-design, partnership or student voice (Bovill, 2017). National systems have come into being, supporting and practising student representation on committees from course to university; metric-focused institutions now invest staggering sums in student engagement dashboards, in order to monitor success indicators (Parnell et al., 2018). As discussed above, although definitions of the term vary enormously, 'student engagement' in its broadest sense (whether relating to behaviour, support, emotional attachment, learning or student feedback) is now core business to HE. Institutions may now even go as far as to present themselves as 'champions', 'leaders' or 'experts' in their defined areas of student engagement, with research and exploratory studies becoming areas of work and perhaps its own professional area (Varwell, 2022). However, although engagement practices, approaches and related research findings have been celebrated globally, it is important not just to promote the cause evangelically; we must also "problematize the issues" and reflect critically on the engagement innovations as they are developed (Bryson, 2014, p.17).

Reflective practice in the study of one's own experience is highly regarded as a valuable approach towards the making of meaning, the development of theory and the continuous improvement of practice (Jasper, 2003). Educational developers have long encouraged academics to exercise reflective practice in relation to their teaching, after examples set by health professionals, pre-tertiary educators and social services (Trelfa, 2021). This chapter argues that reflective practice tools should be developed for those practising and championing innovation in student engagement, if improvement is to continue. Reflection is a "social and political responsibility", because we are often in a position of authority, "questioning and changing the way we work" (Bolton and Delderfield, 2013, p.13); it should underpin how we engage students, create student voice opportunities and engage with staff; it should govern how we assess areas for development, identify and replicate good practices, create new theories, become more aware of our own activities and more inclusive in ourselves, our practices and our communities (Rogers, 2002), where "[i]t is important to look outside as well as inside for viable change ideas and solutions... the most successful changes are the result of a team effort in which people learn together" (Dunne, 2017, pp.325–326). Tools and frameworks have also been developed to assess our practice concerning student engagement in decision-making; Chapter 24 examines the value of frameworks for student engagement (Varwell, 2023).

Development themes for exploration

So, we must develop student engagement, but what challenges remain and what themes should we address? Although 'successful' ventures may well be taking place, we must continue to adopt a critically constructive approach in order to ensure that our practices are welcoming of diverse voices and are inclusive and accessible. The following sections, if not an exhaustive coverage of the topics covered in this collection, do highlight major themes for our consideration.

Recognising power

Although not all readers will be managers, budget holders or established HE career professionals, all HE staff must understand that their positions imbue them with "power, whether discussed or left unspoken, is always a factor in [student–staff] interactions" and therefore with the responsibility to recognise how that may adversely influence their work with students (Matthews, 2017, p.3). This power imbalance between staff and students may prevent the latter from having any control over the nature and scope of projects or even from choosing what part they will play in those activities. If our choices for students create barriers to the engagement of some of them, we can hardly be said to have done well by them. For example, our selection of a particular technology-enhanced platform to support student discussion via smart phones in a lecture theatre might create opportunities for some students with appropriate technology to engage at a higher level, but limit or prohibit participation by those without it, so alienating them. Or if, in a discussion about students' social lives, we thoughtlessly skew the conversation to the on-campus experience, only those who are resident on site are likely to find it meaningful; the topic is far less accessible for commuting students. We must also, as engagement practitioners, be acutely alert to how students perceive us because of our titles, whether lecturer, project officer or manager; it is incumbent upon us to be proactive in minimising such barriers and establishing spaces of trust where students feel their voices will be respected and heard. Depending on where in the world the institution is, such negative effects of power imbalance will vary, with greater or lesser demand on our initiative and ability to alleviate them. Finally, we should not ignore the potential barriers of time, place and language when we run engagement projects; our empowered choice of rooms and times of day for meetings and of the language we use to advertise activities (as explored in Chapters 8, 12 and 13) may prove to be very disconcerting indeed for some students, for example if they find themselves asked to speak confidently when they are, for the first time ever, in traditional staff territory, such as a boardroom (Lowe and Lowe, 2023) – for some an uncomfortable, unfamiliar space, laden with notions of power, hierarchy and permissions (Marie and Sims, 2023; Lubicz-Nawrocka, 2023).

Diversity: whom are you engaging?

The benefits of engaging students in the development of education are many and the possible opportunities wide, including curriculum, quality assurance and general provision (Brand and Millard, 2019). Often, such initiatives involve students in developmental work, from research study (for example, answering surveys) to taking a more active driver role, say as a student partner on a curriculum development project or as a member of a committee. All of these enhance the learning experience of students and are rightly celebrated. Yet here, too, we must cast an appraising eye over which students do what and whether we need to counter any demographic bias that may, for some, limit accessibility, remembering that we have the power to resolve perceived difficulty. Student-led transformation and enhancement, informed by students' own experiences, may be enshrined in the institutional rationale for working with students on educational development, but if only some engage, the range of relevant voices and experiences may be limited. For example, since most student committee roles at any level are voluntary, it is those not tied to work or caring responsibilities who are able to engage. Furthermore, the fact that many engagement opportunities rely on success in democratic elections excludes many students who lack the confidence to enter the process. Finally, those who do this are often already highly engaged with the institution, perhaps in a place of comfort or belonging, which gives them the confidence to question university practice. Such selection processes favour students with high social capital and confidence, so militating against an inclusive cross-section of voices and experiences to inform practice. As institutions aim to achieve equal opportunity of education for all students, we must address the likely imbalance between the confident and privileged majority and the others, who represent the greatest diversity and whose voices we need to hear. Chapters 4 and 5 offer a fuller discussion about whom we are engaging (Umar, 2023; Islam, 2023).

Accessibility: how are you engaging?

To expand on diversity issues and matters of student demographics, it is also important to reflect on the logistical and operational practicalities of our student engagement opportunities, which are inextricably linked to how diverse the body of students who can engage may be. As highlighted above, time commitment – and this may be considerable – is a major consideration for students. Many providers build in payment, bursary or other reward schemes to unlock time, but these, although empowering in some ways, can change the motivation for student participation from development to employment – additionally making the university coordinator more of an employer, a position with its own power implications. As already discussed, time, time of day and location should figure prominently in terms of likely inclusion or exclusion. Language and other cultural barriers may limit take-up. For example, if an opportunity emphasises 'lobbying for change', we should ask whether this might put off students content with the current offer or those who do not wish to go against the grain and challenge those in positions of power. Equally, university jargon, such as 'academic quality development', may mean little to most students. Finally, the recruitment processes for student engagement roles require further critical scrutiny, for many roles, such as committee representatives, are accessed by election or are filled from an already established pool of elected students (Lowe and Lowe, 2022) using traditional application forms favouring those with social privilege who have already been immersed in application practices (O'Shea, 2018). Just because an opportunity to engage with university development is open to all does not mean it is necessarily inclusive (Chapters 4, 8 and 9 – Umar, 2023; Lowe and Lowe, 2023; Adams, 2023).

Representativeness

After conversations about accessibility, the diversity of those we are engaging and the social, cultural and physical barriers that may limit participation comes discussion of 'representativeness'. Questions about whose voices are being heard in forums made up of so-called 'representatives' have led to the examination of just how representative they are. Bols (2017, p.84) highlights that there "has been a perception that student representatives are primarily drawn from particular demographics of students" and perhaps this means that the usual suspects and 'super engaged' students are being heard, while more diverse, non-traditional student voices are being left out (Bryson and Callaghan, 2021). The challenge of engaging a wider student representative body beyond the volunteer (Dickinson, 2022a) is difficult to overcome when the title of 'student representative' itself suggests a democratically elected and accountable individual. Unfortunately, after the initial election, the democracy ends and the very confident student with high social capital becomes part of the development system. This is even more pertinent when, as the previous collection in this series concludes, increasing numbers of students engaged in educational developments are selected following application and interview (at best) as opposed to being elected as a representative at all (Lowe and Lowe, 2022; Lowe and Bols, 2020). Therefore, many institutions are moving beyond the traditional lone student representative on the committee model and instead are moving towards larger student advisory groups, in an attempt to gain a greater diversity of perspectives. However, it is not clear how empowered these students are beyond consultation (Dollinger and Vanderlelie, 2019). Finally, it is one matter to question just how representative of an entire student body one student committee member may be; quite another is the increasing evidence of the influence over educational development of social media campaigns by groups of students or even individuals, in a medium where voices are not just heard, but overheard – and therefore potentially over-represented – and so offer a picture of the student experience that is lacking in true diversity.

Evaluating impact

The massification of the HE sector and subsequent metrics-driven agendas demanding indicators of 'success' with demonstrable impact created a performance-based and target-governed financial environment inextricably tied to student numbers: the more students retained, the more future income secured. In many nations, the metrics have moved beyond retention to other measurable areas of 'student success', such as academic achievement, satisfaction and employment post-graduation. Many of these measures are based upon, or have their roots within, student engagement, meaning that those engaging students on the ground in HE are increasingly working towards targets, where students become less like individuals, but, instead, numbers as part of a wider system. In the UK, institutions have been asked: "in partnership with their student body, define, promote, monitor and evaluate the range of opportunities to enable all students to engage in quality assurance and enhancement processes" (UKSCQA and QAA, 2018, p.4), in order to ensure that all students – no matter what their background – succeed, as measured against targets (Office for Students, 2022).

Evaluating the impact of engagement interventions, such as a new support scheme, or a new enhancement, is often extremely difficult, if one seeks to prove a causal relationship for such reporting. First, as highlighted above, students are all individuals whose tremendous diversity of backgrounds, learning preferences and many other variables interact with their experiences during their studies. So, to prove that an intervention – such as a new referencing workshop at the start of a semester – had an impact on grades is likely to be an exercise hampered by limitations, particularly if it is conducted without several repeat studies and a control group (this with its own ethical concerns). Nevertheless, such interventions are commonly expected to be so measured (Chapter 2 – Austen, Pickering and Donnelly, 2023). Those familiar with research methods scholarship will know the difficulties associated with these agendas, yet, increasingly, surveys and outcomes are bringing more funding, exposure and support for engagement interventions – though, it has to be admitted, with the increased accountability that comes with these promises for impact.

Measuring engagement

Increasing reliance on metrics for student engagement is often correlated with the new learning analytics data systems now quite common in institutions which focus on student retention (Beig, 2023). Because of universities' application to the learning setting of tried-and-tested customer analytical management systems, assessing a particular form of student engagement through spreadsheets has never been easier – and it's a far cry from the basic pre-1900s class register. These measures of student engagement draw upon behavioural engagement indicators, not just in terms of student attendance, but also of the vast array of digital engagements students make, such as library use, engagement with the virtual learning environment and accessing of wider student services. These analytical platforms have very useful capabilities, for example for assessment of students' engagement *en masse* and for enabling us to offer critical support to students who may be at risk of dropping out or have become, according to the analytics data, less engaged (Foster and Siddle, 2020). We still have to accept, however, that the future of student engagement measures through learning analytics is uncertain, as the technology continues to advance, offering increasingly complex algorithms and touchpoints of data sources to measure behaviour and so, potentially, to indicate students' future outcomes more clearly.

Despite the apparent advantages of the leaner analytics tools, these systems employed to measure student engagement present challenges. As witnessed in the wider consumer world, data privacy and security issues dominate modern life and students are understandably likely to want a say in how their data is used, so raising concerns about institutional trust (Jones et al., 2020). Universities experimenting with such data must take care to gain approval from students for the use of their data, something which before now has been subsumed unspecifically by the more general 'terms and conditions' of being a student (Wintrup, 2017). There is also little opportunity to opt out and, in most cases, students are completely unaware of how their data is being used, discussed and analysed. The counter argument is attempting to give students ownership and full view of their data, so allowing them to gamify and track their 'student engagement score', opting out if they so choose, although the approach is not yet clear (O'Donoghue, 2022). Alongside the student perspective, institutions might fall foul of stereotyping students on the basis of their demographic, which, when combined with analytics software, could lead to erroneous or misleading assumptions and assessments of the likelihood of a certain student outcome. If not managed appropriately, this might lead to discrimination, micro-aggressions and homogenising of certain student groups. Finally, students' being assigned a 'student engagement score' could create an impression of – or a label for – them as a concrete indication of their future success or likelihood of failure, all as a result of their behavioural engagement measures. Further issues become obvious when one considers the variety of ways students can be seen as engaging in their university experience. The analytics tools cannot provide an accurate well-rounded picture of a student's *emotional* engagement, for example. Behavioural activities that fall outside the software's measures, such as a student's membership of a course-based society, fail to provide a full picture of students' engagement. The direct conclusions drawn from these systems should be seen as just one perspective of a student's engagement and never the full or conclusive assessment of a student's learning experience at a provider institution.

Belonging

In many discussions relating to creating engaging spaces, practices and services in HE, the debate often comes back to belonging: having a 'sense of belonging', or feeling part of the community, is integral – as students certainly found to be the case during the pandemic – to their satisfaction with and attachment to the university (Corr, 2023; Strayhorn, 2023; Moxey, 2023). Now that the digital world has penetrated much further into daily life and certainly into education, the question of how to ensure, support and facilitate students' belonging through communities remains a challenge to be resolved (Pownall, Harris and Blundell-Birtill, 2022). Debate about student engagement in learning spaces is not new, yet, thanks to COVID-19, the physical classroom and the campus more widely are under scrutiny as institutions try to support accessibility and flexibility, in a delicate balance with preventing isolation and following through with promises about particular student experiences associated with university life. The discourse of belonging permeates this publication, as do the complementary topics of ensuring students not only belong, but also have the sense that they matter to all staff. As the sector continues to evolve and change, the need to manage, meet and match students' expectations is ever greater. Instead of asking for students' feedback at the end of an experience, out of the altruistic desire to make the next cohort's experience better, we should be aiming to tease out their responses from the very outset of co-design of our institutional provision, so that they, and not just the following cohorts, can enjoy the benefits of enhanced learning experiences that have come about because of their involvement.

COVID-19

The sector literature has no shortage of papers endorsing 'blended', 'synchronised', 'a-synchronous' and 'flipped' learning. However, the precise nature and balance of future hybrid at-home/on-campus higher education has yet to be confirmed. The benefits for a personalised mixture of both have received much endorsement (Bearman, Ajjawi and O'Donnell, 2022; Kalaichelvi and Sankar, 2021; Singh, Steele and Singh, 2021), but where students have been engaged, the view is mixed, with some students wishing for a return to face-to-face and increasing feelings of isolation – similar perhaps to staff members' mixed views on returning to face-to-face teaching. The global pandemic features in many chapters, where perhaps as higher education traditionally relies heavily on face-to-face interactions, the social distancing measures of 2020–22 created significant shifts and chaos for student engagement. Acting as a magnifier for all of the tensions in society, higher education sectors globally had their stresses tested by the pandemic, whether that being an over-reliance on a physical campus estate, the technology skills and wealth of students and staff, or the speed in which students can be engaged in decision making, the global pandemic was perhaps the greatest quick-to-emerge catalyst for rethinking and developing students' engagement in higher education.

Looking forward – communities of critical practice

Student engagement has enjoyed the attention of HE developers for decades, perhaps because it makes them look with new eyes at how students learn. The authors of these chapters were asked to be clear, for the benefit of readers, about just what they understand by the term 'engagement'. Students are part of the whole context of university, not just of one aspect, and, alongside engagement activities, they have a complex range of experiences. Within such a context, this chapter has shown that we must continue to pursue a reflective and critical approach to student engagement, together with appropriate research and scholarship. By standing on the shoulders of others and creating communities of dialogue, we may achieve much, much more, to the benefit of all students from all backgrounds. Whether we talk informally or interact in the more formal settings of conferences, reading groups and committee meetings, we must continue to make space for constructive critical interaction.

Many of the reflections of this collection derive from the work of the University of Winchester (UK) Masters in Student Engagement in Higher Education (Moxey et al., 2022). This part-time blended learning programme for HE colleagues ran from 2018 until 2022 from the institution's Centre for Student Engagement, where over 70 students came together with sector theorists to debate, critique, research and advance student engagement in a mutually supportive academic cohort. The programme featured a module entitled 'Critically Reflecting on Student Engagement' and some of the graduates of the programme have written up their final assessments into chapters in this collection (Bayless, 2023; Varwell, 2023; Beig, 2023; Corr, 2023). Critical communities of practice like these cohorts have catalysed our thinking, as have important national networks such as the SEDA (Staff Educational Developers Association), RAISE Network (Researching, Advancing and Inspiring Student Engagement), the *International Journal of Students as Partners* (IJSaP) and Student Voice Network Australia.

As you read the chapters here, you may wish to keep in mind critical questions like those outlined below as you consider your own student engagement contexts. Some of these questions may not yet have answers for the sector, let alone for a specific university, but it is nevertheless important that we keep challenging ourselves and sharing solutions and recommendations when they are discovered. The chapters which follow certainly do go a long way to exploring the implications of the questions and offer recommendations and best practice from the field.

Questions to prompt critical reflection of student engagement

1   Who are the students you are engaging with in your context and what characteristics do they have in common?
2   Who are the students you are engaging with less in your context and what characteristics do they have in common?
3   Are your engagement methods accessible to some student characteristics more than to others?
4   Are there any structural, cultural and language barriers to engagement faced by students you are engaging with less in your context?
5   How representative are your students you engage in student voice and partnership activities, compared to the wider student body?
6   Are those students engaged in student voice and partnership activities in your context empowered? Or are staff in control and students without – or with less – power?
7   Are your students full and equal partners or are easier routes taken to engage students in the development of education?
8   How do you measure student engagement in your context? And... does that measure give a true representation of all of the student engagement occurring?
9   How do you evidence 'success' in your student engagement activities?

10 What is the balance of agenda behind your student engagement in educational development activity, between push factors for marketisation and pull factors for enhancement?

11 How robust are your student engagement activities to crises, such as the COVID-19 pandemic?

12 How much do your values of education, pedagogy and service align with the main ways you engage with students?

References

Abbot, S., 2023. Student–instructor partnerships for curricular justice. In: Lowe, T. (ed) *Advancing Student Engagement in Higher Education: Reflection, Critique and Challenge*. Abingdon: Routledge.

Adams, T., 2023. How to engage students in your educational developments – a student leader's view. In: Lowe, T. (ed) *Advancing Student Engagement in Higher Education: Reflection, Critique and Challenge*. Abingdon: Routledge.

Austen, L., Pickering, N. and Donnelly, A., 2023. Researching and evaluating student engagement – a methodological critique of data gathering approaches. In: Lowe, T. (ed) *Advancing Student Engagement in Higher Education: Reflection, Critique and Challenge*. Abingdon: Routledge.

Bayless, S., 2023. Challenges and tensions for student academic engagement practices in contemporary UK higher education. In: Lowe, T. (ed) *Advancing Student Engagement in Higher Education: Reflection, Critique and Challenge*. Abingdon: Routledge.

Bearman, M., Ajjawi, R. and O'Donnell, M., 2022. Life-on-campus or my-time-and-screen: Identity and agency in online postgraduate courses. *Teaching in Higher Education*. https://doi.org/10.1080/13562517.2022.2109014

Beig, Z., 2023. Learning analytics in higher education: The ethics, the future, the students. In: Lowe, T. (ed) *Advancing Student Engagement in Higher Education: Reflection, Critique and Challenge*. Abingdon: Routledge.

Bols, A.T.G., 2017. Enhancing student representation. *The Journal of Educational Innovation, Partnership and Change*, 3(1), p.81. doi:10.21100/jeipc.v3i1.585.

Bolton, G. and Delderfield, G., 2013. *Reflective Practice: Writing and Professional Development*. London: Sage Publications.

Bovill, C., 2020. *Co-Creating Leaning and Teaching: Towards Relational Pedagogy in Higher Education*. St Albans: Critical Publishing.

Bovill, C., 2017. A framework to explore roles within student-staff partnerships in higher education: Which students are partners, when and in what ways? *International Journal for Students as Partners*, 1(1), pp.1–5. https://doi.org/10.15173/ijsap.v1i1.3062

Brand, S. and Millard, L., 2019. Student engagement in quality in UK higher education: More than assurance? In: Tanaka, M. (ed) *Student Engagement and Quality Assurance in Higher Education*. Abingdon: Routledge. https://doi.org/10.4324/9780429025648-4

Bryson, C., 2016. Engagement through partnership: Students as partners in learning and teaching in higher education. *International Journal for Academic Development*, 21(1), pp.84–86. https://doi.org/10.1080/1360144x.2016.1124966

Bryson, C., 2014. *Understanding and Developing Student Engagement*. Abingdon: Routledge.

Bryson, C. and Callaghan, L., 2021. A whole cohort approach to working in partnership between students and staff: Problematising the issues and evaluating the outcomes. *Student Engagement in Higher Education Journal*, 3(2), pp.176–196.

Buckley, K., Stone, S., Farrell, A.M., Glynn, M., Lowney, R. and Smyth, S., 2021. Learning from student experience: Large, higher education classes transitioning online. *Irish Educational Studies*, 40(2), pp.399–406. https://doi.org/10.1080/03323315.2021.1916566

Chickering, A.W. and Gamson, Z.F., 1987. Seven principles for good practice in undergraduate education. *AAHE Bulletin*, 3, p.7. https://doi.org/10.1016/0307–4412(89)90094–0

Cook-Sather, A. and Loh, J.Y., 2023. Embracing student agentic engagement and enacting equity in higher education through co-creating learning and teaching. In: Lowe, T. (ed) *Advancing Student Engagement in Higher Education: Reflection, Critique and Challenge*. Abingdon: Routledge.

Corr, E., 2023. Recognising the hidden impact of extra-curricular activity on student engagement and success. In: Lowe, T. (ed) *Advancing Student Engagement in Higher Education: Reflection, Critique and Challenge*. Abingdon: Routledge.

Dickinson, J., 2022a. It's time we gave students credit for helping out. Wonkhe. Available at: https://wonkhe.com/blogs/its-time-to-give-students-credit-for-helping-out/ (accessed: 29 August 2022).

Dickinson, J., 2023b. The problem with student engagement during Covid-19. In: Lowe, T. (ed) *Advancing Student Engagement in Higher Education: Reflection, Critique and Challenge*. Abingdon: Routledge.

Dollinger, M., 2023. Critical challenges to support Generation Z learners. In: Lowe, T. (ed) *Advancing Student Engagement in Higher Education: Reflection, Critique and Challenge*. Abingdon: Routledge.

Dollinger, M. and Vanderlelie, J., 2019. Developing and enacting student governance and leadership training in higher education: A practice report. *Student Success*, 10(2), pp.59–65. https://doi.org/10.5204/ssj.v10i2.1309

Dunbar-Morris, H., 2023. Authentic leadership for student engagement. In: Lowe, T. (ed) *Advancing Student Engagement in Higher Education: Reflection, Critique and Challenge*. Abingdon: Routledge.

Dunne, E., 2017. Concluding thoughts on the REACT Programme. *The Journal of Educational Innovation, Partnership and Change*, 3(1), pp.320–329.

Dunne, E., 2016. Design thinking: A framework for student engagement? A personal view. *Journal of Educational Innovation, Partnership and Change*, 2(1). http://dx.doi.org/10.21100/jeipc.v2i1.317.

Eftring, K. and Roxå, T. 2023. Student evaluation of courses – co-creation of meaning through conversations: Insights from the student perspective. In: Lowe, T. (ed) *Advancing Student Engagement in Higher Education: Reflection, Critique and Challenge*. Abingdon: Routledge.

Foster, E. and Siddle, R., 2020. The effectiveness of learning analytics for identifying at-risk students in higher education. *Assessment and Evaluation in Higher Education*, 45(6), pp.842–854. https://doi.org/10.1080/02602938.2019.1682118

George, M. 2023. Defining, delivering and evaluating student engagement in a professional service in higher education: A case study of a student engagement team in an academic library. In: Lowe, T. (ed) *Advancing Student Engagement in Higher Education: Reflection, Critique and Challenge*. Abingdon: Routledge.

Islam, M., 2023. Equality and diversity in our student engagement practice: Radical possibilities to reaching racial and religious equity in higher education. In: Lowe, T. (ed) *Advancing Student Engagement in Higher Education: Reflection, Critique and Challenge.* Abingdon: Routledge.

Jasper, M., 2003. *Beginning Reflective Practice.* Cheltenham: Nelson Thornes.

Jones, K.M., Asher, A., Goben, A., Perry, M.R., Salo, D., Briney, K.A. and Robertshaw, M. B., 2020. "We're being tracked at all times": Student perspectives of their privacy in relation to learning analytics in higher education. *Journal of the Association for Information Science and Technology*, 71(9), pp. 1044–1059. https://doi.org/10.1002/asi. 24358

Kahu, E.R., Picton, C. and Nelson, K., 2020. Pathways to engagement: A longitudinal study of the first-year student experience in the educational interface. *Higher Education*, 79(4), pp.657–673. https://doi.org/10.1007/s10734-019-00429-w

Kalaichelvi, R. and Sankar, J.P., 2021. Pedagogy in post-COVID-19: Effectiveness of blended learning in higher education. *Asian EFL Journal*, 28(3.1), pp.86–109.

Lowe, C. and Lowe, T., 2023. Accessibility to student engagement opportunities: A focus on 'hard to reach' universities. In: Lowe, T. (ed) *Advancing Student Engagement in Higher Education: Reflection, Critique and Challenge.* Abingdon: Routledge.

Lowe, T. and Bols, A., 2020. Higher education institutions and policy makers. In: Lowe, T. and El-Hakim, Y. (eds) *A Handbook for Student Engagement in Higher Education.* Abingdon: Routledge. https://doi.org/10.4324/9780429023033-26

Lowe, T. and El Hakim, Y. 2020. *A Handbook of Student Engagement: Theory into Practice.* Abingdon: Routledge.

Lowe, T. and Lowe, C., 202. Perceptions of the challenges and effectiveness of students on internal quality assurance review panels: A study across higher education institutions. *All Ireland Journal of Higher Education*, 14(1). https://ojs.aishe.org/index.php/aishe-j/article/view/641

Lubicz-Nawrocka, T., 2023. To what extent can we really make students partners in neoliberal universities? In: Lowe, T. (ed) *Advancing Student Engagement in Higher Education: Reflection, Critique and Challenge.* Abingdon: Routledge.

Lygo-Baker, S., Kinchin, I.M. and Winstone, N.E. (eds), 2019. *Engaging Student Voices in Higher Education: Diverse Perspectives and Expectations in Partnership.* Cham: Springer.

Marie, J. and Sims, S., 2023. Control, freedom and structure in student–staff partnerships. In: Lowe, T. (ed) *Advancing Student Engagement in Higher Education: Reflection, Critique and Challenge.* Abingdon: Routledge.

Matthews, K.E., 2017. Five propositions for genuine students as partners practice. *International Journal for Students as Partners*, 1(2). doi:10.15173/ijsap.v1i2.3315.

Moxey, M., 2023. Placing sport at the heart of the university community: A critical reflection on sports club membership and what it means for student engagement from a Bourdieusian perspective. In: Lowe, T. (ed) *Advancing Student Engagement in Higher Education: Reflection, Critique and Challenge.* Abingdon: Routledge.

Moxey, M., Lowe, T., Bovill, C., Bryson, C., Neary, M., LeBihan, J., Islam, M., Green, P. and Marie, J., 2022. The postgraduate certificate and master's in student engagement in higher education: A professional development opportunity to critically examine and influence research, policy and practice. *All Ireland Journal of Higher Education*, 14(1), pp.1–13.

O'Donoghue, K., 2022. Learning analytics within higher education: Autonomy, beneficence and non-maleficence. *Journal of Academic Ethics.* https://doi.org/10.1007/s10805-021-09444-y

O'Shea, S., 2018. Equity and students as partners: The importance of inclusive relationships. *International Journal for Students as Partners*, 2(2), pp.16–20. https://doi.org/10.15173/ijsap.v2i2.3628

Office for Students, 2022. *New OfS Conditions to Raise Quality Bar and Tackle Grade Inflation*. Available at: www.officeforstudents.org.uk/news-blog-and-events/press-and-media/new-ofs-conditions-to-raise-quality-bar-and-tackle-grade-inflation/ (accessed: 16 August 2022).

Owen, D., 2013. Students engaged in academic subject review. In: Dunne, E. and Owen, D. (eds) *Student Engagement Handbook: Practice in Higher Education*. Bingley: Emerald Group Publishing.

Lowe, T. and Parkin, E., 2023. So what and what next? Concluding thoughts on advancing student engagement. In: Lowe, T. (ed) *Advancing Student Engagement in Higher Education: Reflection, Critique and Challenge*. Abingdon: Routledge.

Parnell, A., Jones, D., Wesaw, A. and Brooks, D.C., 2018. *Institutions' use of data and analytics for student success: Results from a National Landscape Analysis*. EDUCAUSE. Available at: https://library.educause.edu/resources/2018/4/institutions-use-of-data-and-analytics-for-student-success (accessed: 16 May 2021).

Pownall, M., Harris, R. and Blundell-Birtill, P., 2022. Supporting students during the transition to university in COVID-19: Five key considerations and recommendations for educators. *Psychology Learning and Teaching*, 21(1), pp.3–18. https://doi.org/10.1177/14757257211032486

Quaye, S.J., Harper, S.R. and Pendakur, S.L. (eds), 2019. *Student Engagement in Higher Education: Theoretical Perspectives and Practical Approaches for Diverse Populations*. Abingdon: Routledge.

Rodgers, C., 2002. Defining reflection: Another look at John Dewey and reflective thinking. *Teachers College Record*, 104(4), pp.842–866. https://doi.org/10.1177/016146810210400402

Rolfe, G., Jasper, M. and Freshwater, D., 2011. *Critical Reflection in Practice*. Basingstoke: Palgrave Macmillan.

Singh, J., Steele, K. and Singh, L., 2021. Combining the best of online and face-to-face learning: Hybrid and blended learning approach for COVID-19, post vaccine, and post-pandemic world. *Journal of Educational Technology Systems*, 50(2), pp.140–171. https://doi.org/10.1177/00472395211047865

Snijders, I., Wijnia, L., Rikers, R.M. and Loyens, S.M., 2020. Building bridges in higher education: Student–faculty relationship quality, student engagement, and student loyalty. *International Journal of Educational Research*, 100, p.101538. https://doi.org/10.1016/j.ijer.2020.101538

Spire, Z., 2023. University estates: From spaces to places of student engagement. In: Lowe, T. (ed) *Advancing Student Engagement in Higher Education: Reflection, Critique and Challenge*. Abingdon: Routledge.

Strayhorn, T.L., 2023. Widening the aperture on college students' sense of belonging: A critical ecological perspective. In: Lowe, T. (ed) *Advancing Student Engagement in Higher Education: Reflection, Critique and Challenge*. Abingdon: Routledge.

Strayhorn, T.L., 2018. *College Students' Sense of Belonging: A Key to Educational Success for All Students*. Abingdon: Routledge.

Taylor Bunce, L., Rathbone, C. and King, N., 2023. Students as consumers: A barrier for student engagement? In: Lowe, T. (ed) *Advancing Student Engagement in Higher Education: Reflection, Critique and Challenge*. Abingdon: Routledge.

Thomas, L. 2012. *Building Student Engagement and Belonging in Higher Education at a Time of Change: A Summary of Findings and Recommendations from the What Works? Student Retention and Success Programme.* London: Paul Hamlyn Foundation. Available at: http://lizthomasassociates.co.uk/commuter_students.html (accessed 16 May 2021).

Tight, M., 2020. Student retention and engagement in higher education. *Journal of Further and Higher Education,* 44(5), pp.689–704. https://doi.org/10.1080/0309877x.2019.1576860

Trelfa, J., 2021. 'Getting to the soul': Radical facilitation of 'real world' learning in higher education programmes through reflective practice. In Morley, D.A., and Jamil, M.G. (eds) *Applied Pedagogies for Higher Education.* Cham: Palgrave Macmillan. https://doi.org/10.1007/978-3-030-46951-1_13

Trowler, V., 2010. *Student Engagement Literature Review.* Higher Education Academy. Available at: www.heacademy.ac.uk/system/files/studentengagementliteraturereview_1.pdf (accessed: 16 May 2021).

UKSCQA and QAA, 2018. *Student Engagement Advice and Guidance Theme, UK Quality Code for Higher Education.* United Kingdom Standing Committee for Quality Assessment and Quality Assurance Agency for Higher Education.

Umar, F., 2023. There is not one student experience: Our learner journeys as individuals. In: Lowe, T. (ed) *Advancing Student Engagement in Higher Education: Reflection, Critique and Challenge.* Abingdon: Routledge.

Varwell, S., 2023. Valhalla and Nirvana: Views of Arnstein's Ladder of Citizen Participation in further and higher education. In: Lowe, T. (eds) *Advancing Student Engagement in Higher Education: Reflection, Critique and Challenge.* Abingdon: Routledge.

Varwell, S., 2022. *A Professional Standards Framework for Student Engagement.* Wonkhe. Available at: https://wonkhe.com/blogs/a-professional-standards-framework-for-student-engagement/ (accessed: 15 August 2022).

Walsh, K. and Jaquet, A., 2023. Towards inclusive student partnership: Challenges and opportunities for student engagement in the Australian context. In: Lowe, T. (ed) *Advancing Student Engagement in Higher Education: Reflection, Critique and Challenge.* Abingdon: Routledge.

Wintrup, J., 2017. Higher education's panopticon? Learning analytics, ethics and student engagement. *Higher Education Policy,* 30(1), pp.87–103. https://doi.org/10.1057/s41307-016-0030-8

Yorke, M. and Longden, B., 2004. *Retention and Student Success in Higher Education.* London: McGraw-Hill Education.

Chapter 2

Researching and evaluating student engagement

A methodological critique of data-gathering approaches

Liz Austen, Nathaniel Pickering and Alan Donnelly

Introduction

This chapter begins by exploring the research and evaluation landscape in which the concept and measures of student engagement exist. This introductory critique outlines some of the problems in current practices and then provides two examples of data gathering which we suggest have lost their institutional purpose: the Module Evaluation Questionnaire and the UK Engagement Survey.[1] We ask that the methodological limitations of routine data gathering, beyond student engagement research, are considered. Both approaches were recently evaluated by academics located within a central directorate to ensure they were fit for purpose and were meeting prescribed objectives. This is the asserted approach, in comparison to the annual adoption of student engagement data gathering without critique. The chapter concludes with recommendations for developing good research and evaluation practices.

Why does the higher education sector research and evaluate student engagement?

Student engagement, via the scholarship of teaching and learning, is now recognised internationally as a research domain with a growing evidence base (Aparicio et al., 2021). This co-exists alongside a measurement and monitoring function of student engagement data; as a competitive measure of institutional quality/success via retention and withdrawal rates and a mandate for evaluating policies and practices to generate institutional change (Dismore et al., 2019).

Aparicio et al.'s (2021) analysis of student engagement research themes can be interpreted as 'engagement with an activity/intervention', 'types of engagement', and 'engagement measurement'. Articles discussing 'engagement with' are often pedagogical, such as focusing on 'completed' or 'chosen' elements of active learning (see Alonso-Nuez et al., 2021) but also include engagement in institutional processes such as surveys or student evaluations of teaching. To enable effective student feedback, evaluation and research, students also need to be *engaged with* the evidence gathering approach. Building on Bryson's (2014)

DOI: 10.4324/9781003271789-2

definitions, institutions and sector bodies are routinely interested in research data which shows how many students are 'being engaged' to align with outcome measures and sector benchmarks, whilst students and practitioners are interested in the evaluation of strategies which ensure students are 'engaging'. All types of research in this domain require student voices as evidence and distinct methods of data gathering may be required. The blurred distinctions between research, evaluation and student feedback adds complexity to this engagement space (Austen, 2020). These symbiotic connections risk confusing the purpose of data gathering where a clear rationale for researching and evaluating student engagement is not observed. This is complicated further by whether the outcomes for students or the outcomes for the institution are the primary objective of initiatives designed to enhance student engagement. To this end, a fuller discussion of student engagement as an outcome is needed.

Is engagement a student outcome?

Austen et al.'s (2021) integrative literature review of access, retention, attainment and progression interventions that claim a demonstrable impact on student outcomes concluded that student engagement was a peripheral theme in the evidence.[2] The literature reviewed either omitted student engagement, or framed it as intangible, intermediary or predictive in nature (e.g. attendance leads to engagement which leads to persistence). Few studies connected medium-term student engagement with longer-term student outcomes and none of the sources discussed the impact of students as co-producers, co-designers.

Wilson et al. (2019, p. 1931) suggest "there is still much to learn about the linkage between engagement programmes, effects, and outcomes in Higher Education", noting the abundance of student voices data on experience and engagement, but a lack of evidence on the factors which are affecting them. In addition, the "academy also needs to evidence the direct link between specific student engagement initiatives and learning gain" and "how and why interventions work" (Wilson et al., 2019, p.1931). Wilson et al. (2019) advocate for student engagement to be conceptualised as a behaviour change activity, which would position it as an intermediate outcome in a theory of change. A behaviour change may be increased attendance, for example, grounded by the assumption that class attendance correlates with student success. Holec and Marynowski (2020) sought to use changes in engagement as an intermediate outcome and contributing factor to increased attainment. Using quasi-experimental action research and a student engagement survey as the main data collection tool, they explored whether student engagement was improved when the learning environment and pedagogy were changed. They found that the active learning classroom contributed to higher student self-reported engagement than the traditional classroom. However, they did not continue the evidence trajectory to include longer-term impact on grades.

The trajectory of evidence connecting engagement with retention, attainment and progression outcomes presents a gap in research and evaluation. Austen et al.

(2021) suggested that data confidence and accessibility, time bound funding, the duration and scope of institutional projects, and a desire for quick wins can focus on short-term impact and limit the analysis of longer-term outcomes. Wilson et al. (2019) also advocate for more practical resources for developing a measure of student engagement as behavioural change.

A dominant quantitative student outcome focus often excludes student engagement evidence due to the interpretivist basis of this knowledge. "Research investigating alternative forms of engaging the student voice has developed in the formidable shadow of increasingly powerful institutional drive for quantifiable data" (Darwin, 2021, p.230) and as such is at odds with the "ideological demands for more quantifiable evaluative forms" (Gibbs et al., 2017 in Darwin, 2021, p.266). However, there are good examples of qualitative explorations of engagement. For example, Trinidad et al. (2020) explored pedagogical and assessment strategies by asking students during interviews which practices were engaging (liked or enjoyed) and which practices were effective (impact on learning), and published their results. An extension of this work to include attainment outcomes could be possible and highlights how subjective engagement measures in the short/medium term could be connected with objective effective measures in the longer term in a change-based evaluative process. This would extend the exploration of 'engagement with' research to an impact focus.

How diverse are student voices within student engagement research and evaluation?

Austen et al. (2021) also highlight the lack of research evidence on the impact of interventions and engagement initiatives on distinct student groups, beyond a description of sample characteristics. This omission risks overlooking how "persistent social inequalities affect student success" (Tzafea, 2021 p.1). An impressionistic analysis of one volume in a leading student engagement journal indicated that student engagement initiatives reported as co-production, co-design and co-research tended to discuss the benefits for small numbers of engaged students (Sambell et al. 2021; Yates and Oates, 2021; Dunstone, 2021). The characteristics of participants were often (but not always) reported, however they were rarely discussed unless the intervention was targeted in nature. Sometimes, activities aimed to engage a diverse student cohort in an institution-wide project, but only a subject/course focus was the defining student characteristic (Dunbar-Morris, 2021). Bryson and Callaghan (2021) attempted to overcome the acknowledged assumptions between engagement and 'social capital', by promoting a 'whole class' approach to address inclusion and self-selection. Whilst this provided a compelling rationale, the impact of the whole class intervention for different student groups was not measured or discussed.

In the student evaluation of teaching literature, diversity in voices is often framed by what students say (bias and balance of power) rather than who they are (sample composition). Darwin (2021, p.227) suggests that "more developed analytical frameworks to authentically interact with the diverse range of student perspectives (such as collaborative forms of research) becomes essential to the success of this form of evaluative engagement".

The utility of the standardised student survey

This discussion highlights some of the complexity surrounding the purpose, method, outcome and sample of student engagement research and evaluation. In the student engagement research domain, methodology will be critiqued during collaborative design, ethical approval and peer review. This level of critique is less likely to occur with routine institutional data gathering, such as institutional student surveys. In this space, it is easy to proceed uncritically, repeat the comfortable or follow sector trends without setting local, institutional objectives. Clarity of objectives is essential.

Standardised surveys are commonly used across the sector and by institutions in higher education research, particularly for large-scale projects, due to their capacity to capture significant volumes of data with relative ease and efficiency compared to other methods. However, engagement from students via high response rates are necessary for the potential of these surveys to be fulfilled, and institutions can have "unrealistic expectations" about students' engagement with institutional processes (Lowe and Bols, 2020, p.274). In reality, student engagement in many surveys tends to be low, which can affect the accuracy of the data and lead to concerns of representation (Klemenčič and Chirikov, 2015). There are many reasons why students may opt out of completing a survey, such as: being asked to complete multiple survey requests, often within a short time span; a lack of personal salience in the topic; or other competing priorities at the point of receiving the invite (Stein et al., 2021).

Another criticism of surveys in higher education relates to the aspects of institutional practice and student behaviour that are measured. It has been argued that "standardised surveys imply an established (fixed) standard of process or outcome against which institutions are evaluated and need to demonstrate conformity" (Klemenčič and Chirikov, 2015, p.370). This also brings into question who determines what should be measured. Pownall (2020) highlights that this process often excludes the input of students, leading to narrow conceptualisations of student engagement in higher education which "fail to acknowledge diversity of experience" and that overlook the possibility that "student community's engagements and successes do not always fit into rigid, quantifiable outcomes" (p.252).

Proponents of surveys highlight their ability to track changes in student views, experiences and behaviour over time, as well as their ability to capture data at various levels and for differences to be examined across student groups, disciplines and even institutions. However, the logic underpinning some of these arguments has been challenged. Research has highlighted the range of contextual and extraneous factors that can influence student responses in surveys, which has led to doubts about the reliability and validity of the data (e.g. Hornstein, 2017). There is also the risk of staff misinterpreting results and attaching too much importance to differences in numerical data which are minor, statistically non-significant and decontextualised (Boysen, 2017). At a course level, the ability of surveys to provide meaningful comparisons can also be poor, in part due to many courses having small sample sizes (Buckley, 2019). These points are not intended to dissuade researchers or practitioners from using a survey in their research or evaluation activities, but to be mindful of its limitations and to check that it is the most appropriate method for their own context.

This chapter now presents two case studies of routine standardised student survey at one post-92 higher education institution in England. One is a critique of the Module Evaluation Questionnaire and the other is a critique of the national UK Engagement Survey. Both sources of data provide insights into student engagement, exploring engagement with teaching and learning, engagement with institutional processes, types of engagement and engagement measurement.

Case study 1: Institutional Module Evaluation Questionnaire

Background: It is commonplace for students in higher education institutions to be asked to provide their perspectives on their learning and teaching experiences on individual modules (credited units of study), usually towards the end of their delivery, via a questionnaire. The design of module evaluation questionnaires (MEQs) are usually specific to each institution, with the questions used often developed 'in-house' or aligned with those used in course-level national student experience surveys. Students can expect to complete multiple MEQs during each year of study.

In this case study, a post-1992 university based in England has used an institution-wide MEQ since 2014/15. A set of objectives were created at the point of its inception, which primarily consisted of helping to improve the content and teaching of modules, fulfil responsibilities for quality and standards and for capturing and responding to students' perspectives. There had previously been limited systematic monitoring of these objectives to determine if, and how well, these objectives were being met.

Evaluation approach: An institutional review of the MEQ was carried out by applying principles of process and impact evaluation to assess the extent to which it was meeting its original aims. An evaluation team was established to conduct the work and a steering group was formed that represented all key user groups, including students, to promote objectivity and avoid bias (Parsons, 2017). This project sought to engage students and staff members in the evaluation process to address the absence of student and other stakeholder involvement in evaluation practices in teaching and learning identified across the sector (Klemenčič and Chirikov, 2015). The starting point of the review was to develop a logic model, which sets out how an initiative will achieve its outcomes, using reflections of the group and available evidence from the institution and the sector. Further data was collected with module leaders, other staff and student representatives through interviews and focus groups.

Findings and learning: Co-creating the logic model has helped to create a shared understanding of the factors that can help or hinder the success of the MEQs and identified unvoiced assumptions about its operation. Initially, it was necessary for the steering group to establish whether its original aims were complementary or whether its diverse purposes across multiple stakeholders had resulted in tensions or trade-offs. Given its design and focus, the MEQ was arguably in closer alignment with quality assurance, and serving the needs of the institution, rather than with module-level quality enhancement processes or student engagement purposes. The types of questions asked, such as those exploring how satisfied students were with aspects of their experience, have previously been deemed to provide only limited insight into the ways in which module content and teaching can be improved (Arthur, 2020). The timing of MEQs, at the end of a module's delivery, is compatible with the need to inform review processes but it is too late to fulfil the aims of making improvements to modules and for demonstrating to students how their concerns have been responded to.

Institutional data showed approximately one-third of eligible students completing at least a single MEQ in the 2020/21 academic year. This resulted in low response rates meaning some, but not all, students were engaged as information providers (Varwell, 2021). There was variation in the extent that results or actions taken were consistently reported back to students, while the low volumes of data, alongside concerns about its representativeness, limited the opportunities for MEQs to be used for any of their intended purposes. Furthermore, there is a risk of creating distrust, rather than engagement, if expectations are set but not fulfilled (Shah et al., 2017).

Considering its challenges in fulfilling both its quality assurance and enhancement purposes, it has been advocated that the purpose of MEQs should adopt a more narrow and concentrated focus, such as being more closely aligned with practices on programmes and students' learning (Borch, 2021) or on partnership work between staff and students (Stein et al., 2021). It is important that the purpose is shaped and shared by all stakeholder groups, and various levels of student involvement are possible. Academics and students could be afforded more discretion over the focus of MEQs by designing their own questionnaire, or individual questions, to help capture data for local contexts (Bamber, 2011; Wiley, 2019). This would build on existing work within the institution where students have engaged in cognitive interviews to assess their interpretation of questions and provide feedback on the content of the MEQ. Rather than being "engaged in their educational experience as individuals" (Lowe and Bols, 2020, p.279), MEQs could be used to involve staff and students in a process of collective problem solving, with responses being collected anonymously prior to an in-class group discussion to explore key points and identify shared actions.

Case study 2: UK Engagement Survey

Background: The UK Engagement Survey (UKES), which is based on the American National Survey of Students Engagement (NSSE) and is delivered by

Advance HE in the UK, is a powerful tool that provides insight into how students use the resources provided in higher education to enhance and engage in their learning (Kandiko Howson and Buckley, 2017). UKES offers an alternative to transactional satisfaction student surveys that focus on inputs; instead, UKES focuses on outputs which enable an understanding of the impact of inputs to be captured and allows outcomes such as learning gain to be measured. It not only provides institutional data on how students are engaging in their studies but provides students with an opportunity to assess and reflect on their own behaviour, progress and engagement in their studies (Lowe et al., 2019). The case study HEI has run UKES annually since 2014 with foundation year and undergraduate students that are not included in the National Student Survey[3] (NSS), a UK-wide annual survey which explores final-year undergraduate students' opinions and satisfaction with their higher education experience at the end of an undergraduate course. Given the pressures on resources created by COVID-19, it was necessary to review a number of activities to ensure they were delivering on their intended outcomes.

Evaluation approach: A process evaluation was adapted to assess if UKES had been effectively implemented and was delivering on certain outputs (Parsons, 2017; Silver, 2004). This type of evaluation allows the investigator to assess the "fidelity and quality of implementation" and "clarify causal mechanisms and identify contextual factors associated with variation in outcomes" (Moore et al., 2015, p.1). Drawing on existing evidence and informal meetings with key stakeholders within the institution, UKES performance was assessed against four delivery outputs:

1   Provides evidence for enhancement and evaluation of the student experience
2   Provides comprehensive and robust institutional data
3   An indicator of future NSS performance
4   Access to sector benchmarking on student engagement

This evaluation was focused on how the institution had used and implemented UKES; it is not an assignment of quality or validity of UKES as a survey tool, which is already well established in the academic literature, especially in relation to its precursor NSSE (Kandiko and Matos, 2013).

Findings and learning

The intention was that UKES results could support enhancement at a course, department and institutional level. However, there was limited evidence that data from UKES has been used for enhancement or evaluation of the student experience. Staff usage of the Tableau reports that continued the survey's results showed a marked decrease over the last three years, with some academic departments not accessing the results at all over that time. This decline in use coincided with the need for course teams to formally respond to UKES results in internal quality processes. The feedback from stakeholders suggested that there was a plethora of competing student voice mechanisms, and it was challenging to use and address them all. While UKES had been used in the university's TEF (Teaching Excellence and Student Outcomes Framework) submission, there was no evidence of it being used to evaluate other institution-wide initiatives. Stakeholders felt that this survey lacked the nuances of context or institutional cultural aspects that have helped shape these programmes. While Advance HE offers the opportunity to add institution-specific questions, the case study institution already used this space to align UKES with the NSS.

The second delivery output aimed to use UKES to create comprehensive and robust institutional data about students excluded from the NSS. While the case study university achieved some of the highest UKES response rates of participating institutions it was still below 20% most years. As well as the low response rate there were several issues that brought into question the robustness and validity of data. Firstly, the sampling criteria had evolved over time to reflect the institution's changing student body and course provision. Secondly, the data becomes increasingly unreliable as it is broken down into subsets, with many courses not meeting the internal publication thresholds, meaning each year the makeup of courses reporting results changes. In addition, results would fluctuate significantly each year because of the low response rate and variable sample. Thirdly, the self-selecting census sampling approach meant that certain groups were overrepresented in the data, such as female students, students on health courses and mature students, which has the potential to skew the data. This sampling approach also limits the statistical tests that can be undertaken. All these challenges mean that year-on-year trend analysis becomes problematic or even inadvisable.

The NSS has come to dominate as a measure of student satisfaction in the UK and institutions are keen to provide any pre-emptive insight into how they might preform in the future (Kandiko Howson and Matos, 2021). The case study institution incorporated key NSS questions into UKES in the hope that it could provide early indications about NSS performance and provide data that can be triangulated across the institution to identify emerging trends or issues on a course so they could be addressed before the students completed the NSS. However, the large differences in response rates between UKES and the NSS at an institutional and course level mean that it is impossible to draw any reliable conclusions or predictions about how an institution or course might perform in the NSS. Including the NSS questions also made UKES much longer which impacted on the completion rates of the overall survey. While it is advisable to triangulate data, the purpose and limitation of triangulation needs to be clearly understood. Institutions should also avoid overreliance on measures such as the NSS as they are often a poor representation of a student's learning and teaching experience (Langan and Harris, 2019).

Finally, one of the promoted advantages of UKES is that Advance HE will produce sector-benchmarked reports that will help institutions contextualise their results and compare their performance against other providers. The first issue with benchmarking relates to the changeability of the other institutions participating in this optional survey. This changeability means an institution's position could rise or fall in a benchmark group not because its results have gotten better or worse but because the institutions in a grouping have changed. The second and perhaps the most fundamental issue is with the student population included in the survey by each provider. Advance HE's only guidance is that a student must be on at least a 60-credit course and all other sampling decisions are open to 'interpretation' by providers. There is the potential for great variability in the sample across the sector and therefore not comparing like for like; for instance, the case study institution is one of the few providers that includes foundation year students in their sample. This problem is then compounded by how institutions choose to group courses together for the benchmarking reports. Some institutions pre-determine which subjects a course belongs to, while others let students self-identify their subject group. This approach is very problematic and jeopardises the quality of the data for comparison purposes.

In conclusion, the evidence suggests that the delivery outputs were not being met, so the decision was taken to pause running the UKES, while the institution reflected on how this useful engagement tool can be used more strategically to support other student voice mechanisms. When UKES was first delivered at this institution, there were no other consistent quantitative data sources that could provide insights into the non-NSS student experience; however, this is no longer the case, as other mechanisms have superseded the need for UKES in this space. Nonetheless, it is felt UKES could have real value in helping institutions understand the experience of students experiencing additional barriers to their success and progression in higher education.

Recommendations for good research/evaluation practice

Critique the status quo of engagement data gathering: Scrutinise the purpose, focus, sample and measures used to avoid uncritical acceptance or adoption. Collecting data that does not meet its stated objective or is underutilised is an unethical approach. Disrupt the use of surveys as a default method across the sector and within institutions, as students' experiences, and mode of delivery, become increasingly diversified. Reimagine how surveys are delivered through randomised sampling approaches, targeting surveying and clear reporting of outcomes that lead to action.

Encourage reflection beyond 'research methods' to 'evaluative thinking': Reaffirm the importance of 'why' in data gathering decision making rather than 'when' and 'how'. Focus on the purpose of research/evaluation rather than preoccupation with specific methods or data collection instruments.

Involve students in the research/evaluation process to develop the rationale, outcomes and method: Apply the same co-production lens utilised for engagement initiatives to engagement research and evaluation. At the point of designing an activity/intervention, acknowledge the agendas or interests of each user group to help avoid any tensions or misunderstandings and develop points of consensus.

Apply 'Theory of Change' (Dent et al., 2022) principles to connect engagement activity/interventions (behaviour change) and the intermediate outcomes and longer-term impact: Ensure that any assumptions made are supported by evidence and highlight any areas of weakness or gaps in knowledge.

Measure impact on individuals and specific demographic groups rather than just whole cohorts: Explore the impact of an activity/intervention on each participant by collecting data for individual students. This data can be aggregated to measure the impact on specific demographic sub-groups. In cases where numbers of participants are low, strategies should be implemented to protect the anonymity of individuals.

Do not be afraid to stop doing something, or to make changes, if it is not working: Evaluation has been described as focusing on "both proving and improving" (Moore, Banerjee and Myhill, 2019, p.48), which means that inconclusive or negative results are also helpful for informing decisions. Consider the ethics of persisting with an activity/intervention. A clear rationale and plan of what you are doing and why is essential.

Ensure that there are opportunities for staff at all levels of an institution to strengthen their capacity building in relation to research and evaluation: Build knowledge and understanding of the key concepts and stages to enable a critique. Ensure there are sufficient opportunities and resources for support.

Notes

1 www.advance-he.ac.uk/knowledge-hub/tags/teaching-and-learning/student-experien ce-and-outcomes/uk-engagement-survey-ukes
2 This research limited the search strategy to empirical and causal evidence.
3 www.thestudentsurvey.com/

References

Alonso-Nuez, M.J., Gil-Lacruz, A.I. and Rosell-Martínez, J., 2021. Assessing evaluation: Why student engages or resists to active learning? *International Journal of Technology and Design Education*, 31(5), pp.1001–1017. https://doi.org/10.1007/s10798-020-09582-1.

Aparicio, G., Iturralde, T. and Maseda, A., 2021. A holistic bibliometric overview of the student engagement research field. *Journal of Further and Higher Education*, 45(4), pp.540–557. https://doi.org/10.1080/0309877X.2020.1795092.

Arthur, L., 2020. Evaluating student satisfaction – restricting lecturer professionalism: Outcomes of using the UK national student survey questionnaire for internal student evaluation of teaching. *Assessment and Evaluation in Higher Education*, 45(3), pp.331–344. https://doi.org/10.1080/02602938.2019.1640863

Austen, L., 2020. The amplification of student voices via institutional research and evaluation. In: Lowe, T., and El Hakim, Y. (eds) *A Handbook of Student Engagement: Theory into Practice*. Abingdon: Routledge. https://doi.org/10.4324/9780429023033–16

Austen, L., Hodgson, R, Heaton, C., Pickering, N. and Dickinson, J., 2021. *Access, Retention, Attainment and Progression: An Integrative Review of Demonstrable Impact on Student Outcomes.* Available at www.advance-he.ac.uk/knowledge-hub/access-retention-attainment-and-progression-review-literature-2016-2021 (accessed 7 January 2022).

Bamber, V., 2011. Self-evaluative practice: Diversity and power. In Saunders, M., Trowler, P. and Bamber, V. (eds) *Reconceptualising Evaluation in Higher Education: The Practice Turn.* London: McGraw-Hill Education.

Borch, I.H., 2021. *Student Evaluation Practice: A Qualitative Study on How Student Evaluation of Teaching, Courses and Programmes Are Carried Out and Used.* PhD thesis, The Arctic University of Norway. Available at: https://munin.uit.no/bitstream/handle/10037/21920/thesis.pdf?sequence=2&isAllowed=y (accessed: 17 January 2022).

Boysen, G.A., 2017. Statistical knowledge and the over-interpretation of student evaluations of teaching. *Assessment and Evaluation in Higher Education,* 42(7), pp.1095–1102. https://doi.org/10.1080/02602938.2016.1227958

Bryson, C., 2014. Clarifying the concept of student engagement. In: Bryson, C. (ed) *Understanding and Developing Student Engagement.* Routledge: London.

Bryson, C. and Callaghan, L., 2021. A whole cohort approach to working in partnership between students and staff: Problematising the issues and evaluating the outcomes. *Student Engagement in Higher Education Journal,* 3(2), pp.176–196. Available at: https://sehej.raise-network.com/raise/article/view/1023/776 (accessed: 7 January 2022).

Buckley, A., 2019. How much are your NSS results really telling you?Wonkhe. Available at: https://wonkhe.com/blogs/how-much-are-your-nss-results-really-telling-you/ (accessed: 13 January 2022).

Darwin, S., 2021. The changing topography of student evaluation in higher education: Mapping the contemporary terrain. *Higher Education Research and Development,* 40(2), pp.220–233. https://doi.org/10.1080/07294360.2020.1740183

Dent, S., Mountford-Zimdars, A. and Burke, C., 2022. *Theory of Change: Debates and Applications to Access and Participation in Higher Education.* Bingley: Emerald Group Publishing.

Dismore, H., Turner, R. and Huang, R., 2019. Let me edutain you! Practices of student engagement employed by new lecturers. *Higher Education Research and Development,* 38(2), pp.235–249. https://doi.org/10.1080/07294360.2018.1532984

Dunbar-Morris, H., 2021. Co-creating a student charter. *Student Engagement in Higher Education Journal,* 3(2), pp.26–34. Available at: https://sehej.raise-network.com/raise/article/view/1033 (accessed: 7 January 2022).

Dunstone, K., 2021. Newcomer to expert practitioner: Identifying emerging communities of practice in extra-curricular student engagement activities in art and design. *Student Engagement in Higher Education Journal,* 3(2), pp.17–25.

Holec, V. and Marynowski, R., 2020. Does it matter where you teach? Insights from a quasi-experimental study on student engagement in an active learning classroom. *Teaching and Learning Inquiry,* 8(2), pp.140–164. https://doi.org/10.20343/teachlearninqu.8.2.10

Hornstein, H.A., 2017. Student evaluations of teaching are an inadequate assessment tool for evaluating faculty performance. *Cogent Education,* 4(1). https://doi.org/10.1080/2331186X.2017.1304016

Kandiko Howson, C. and Buckley, A., 2017. Development of the UK engagement survey. *Assessment and Evaluation in Higher Education*, 42(7), pp.1132–1144. https://doi.org/10.1080/02602938.2016.1235134

Kandiko Howson, C. and Matos, F., 2021. Student surveys: Measuring the relationship between satisfaction and engagement. *Education Sciences*, 11, p.297. https://doi.org/10.3390/educsci11060297

Kandiko Howson, C. and Matos, F., 2013. *Engagement for Enhancement: Full Qualitative Testing Report of a UK Survey Pilot*. York: Higher Education Academy. Available at: www.heacademy.ac.uk/sites/default/files/resources/Engagement_for_enhancement_Cognitive_interviewing.pdf (accessed: 14 January 2022).

Klemenčič, M. and Chirikov, I., 2015. How do we know how students experience higher education? On the use of student surveys. In Curaj, A., Matei, L., Pricopie, R., Salmi, J. and Scott, P. (eds) *The European Higher Education Area: Between Critical Reflections and Future Policies*. Cham: Springer. https://doi.org/10.1007/978-3-319-20877-0_24

Langan, A.M. and Harris, W.E., 2019. National student survey metrics: Where is the room for improvement? *Higher Education*, 78, 1075–1089. https://doi.org/10.1007/s10734-019-00389-1

Lowe, C., Sims, S. and Winter, J., 2019. Going beyond metric-driven responses to surveys: Evaluating uses of UKES to support students' critical reflection on their learning gain. *Higher Education Pedagogies*, 4(1), pp.448–461. https://doi.org/10.1080/23752696.2019.1672359

Lowe, T. and Bols, A., 2020. Higher education institutions and policy makers: The future of student engagement. In: Lowe, T., and El Hakim, Y. (eds) *A Handbook of Student Engagement: Theory into Practice*. Abingdon: Routledge. https://doi.org/10.4324/9780429023033-26

Moore, G.F., Audrey, S., Barker, M., Bond, L., Bonell, C., Hardeman, W. and Baird, J., 2015. Process evaluation of complex interventions: Medical Research Council guidance. *BMJ: British Medical Journal*, 350. doi:10.1136/bmj.h1258.

Moore, J., Banerjee, P. and Myhill, D. (2019) *Evaluating the Standards of Outreach: Final Project Report and Self-Assessment Toolkit for the Office for Students*. Available at: www.officeforstudents.org.uk/media/f2424bc6-38d5-446c-881e-f4f54b73c2bc/using-standards-of-evidence-to-evaluate-impact-of-outreach.pdf (accessed: 16 May 2021).

Parsons, D., 2017. *Demystifying Evaluation: Practical Approaches for Researchers and Users*. Bristol: Policy Press.

Pownall, M., 2020. Who defines success in higher education? A student perspective on the future of student engagement. In: Lowe, T., and El Hakim, Y. (eds) *A Handbook of Student Engagement: Theory into Practice*. Abingdon: Routledge. https://doi.org/10.4324/9780429023033-24

Sambell, K., Brown, S. and Adamson, E., 2021. Engaging with feedback processes in workplace settings: Using student expertise to co-create resources to foster first-year students' feedback literacy development. *Student Engagement in Higher Education Journal*, 3(2), pp.54–73. Available at: https://sehej.raise-network.com/raise/article/view/1025 (accessed: 7 January 2022).

Shah, M., Cheng, M. and Fitzgerald, R., 2017. Closing the loop on student feedback: The case of Australian and Scottish universities. *Higher Education*, 74(1), pp.115–129. https://doi.org/10.1007/s10734-016-0032-x

Silver, H., 2004. *Higher Education and Policy-Making in Twentieth-Century England*. Abingdon: Routledge.

Stein, S.J., Goodchild, A., Moskal, A., Terry, S. and McDonald, J., 2021. Student perceptions of student evaluations: Enabling student voice and meaningful engagement. *Assessment and Evaluation in Higher Education*, 46(6), pp.837–851. https://doi.org/10.1080/02602938.2020.1824266

Trinidad, J.E., Ngo, G.R., Nevada, A.M. and Morales, J.A., 2020. Engaging and/or effective? Students' evaluation of pedagogical practices in higher education. *College Teaching*, 68(4), pp.161–171. https://doi.org/10.1080/87567555.2020.1769017

Tzafea, O., 2021. Examining the relationship between student's engagement and socio-economic background in higher education. *Student Engagement in Higher Education Journal*, 3(2), pp.141–157.

Varwell, S., 2021. Models for exploring partnership: Introducing sparqs' student partnership staircase as a reflective tool for staff and students. *International Journal for Students as Partners*, 5(1), pp.107–123. https://doi.org/10.15173/ijsap.v5i1.4452

Wiley, C., 2019. Standardised module evaluation surveys in UK higher education: Establishing students' perspectives. *Studies in Educational Evaluation*, 61, pp.55–65. https://doi.org/10.1016/j.stueduc.2019.02.004

Wilson, C., Broughan, C. and Marselle, M., 2019. A new framework for the design and evaluation of a learning institution's student engagement activities. *Studies in Higher Education*, 44(11), pp.1931–1944. https://doi.org/10.1080/03075079.2018.1469123

Yates, E. and Oates, R., 2021. "It's nice to know you might make a difference": Engaging students through primary research as an authentic assessment. *Student Engagement in Higher Education Journal*, 3(2), pp.35–53. Available at: https://sehej.raise-network.com/raise/article/view/1040 (accessed: 7 January 2022).

Chapter 3

Challenges and tensions for student academic engagement practices in contemporary UK higher education

Sarah Bayless

Student engagement (SE) has become closely tied to notions of quality and evaluation of UK higher education (HE). "The provider engages students individually and collectively in the development, assurance and enhancement of the quality of their educational experience" (QAA, 2018, p.3). Such external promotion and guidance sets out expectations for the way in which student engagement (including representation and governance) is implemented, and highlights the need for its monitoring and evaluation. While the most commonly perceived motivations for student engagement "practices" are for enhancement of the student experience, it is necessary to acknowledge different ideologies, perspectives and motivations that have an effect on SE initiatives (Freeman, 2013). One key driver has been the change to the HE funding system (Browne, 2010). The introduction of higher tuition fees in England has had a profound impact on our evaluation of HE practices and the policies that shape them. The introduction of higher tuition fees has contributed to a shift in students' identities, positioning students as consumers, damaging their identity as learners and their academic performance (Bunce et al., 2016). Student consumer orientation tends to lead to extrinsic rather than intrinsic approaches to learning, and is often accompanied by a minimisation of effort. Similarly, academic difficulty is conflated with the nature of provision rather than investment of personal effort. A key issue with such a mindset is that instant gratification and short-term goals tend to be favoured, and experiences which are undesirable or insufficiently engaging are considered as irrelevant and not 'value for money' (e.g. see Tomlinson, 2017). This identity as discerning consumer is promoted through university rankings and league tables and perhaps further (magnified) by surveys and evaluations such as the National Student Survey (NSS; annual UK-wide survey of student satisfaction managed by the Office for Students, the independent regulator of HE). This is one reason why these are commonly considered critically for their simplification of the student experience and the relationship between outcome metrics and quality of learning and teaching (York et al., 2014). Recent government discourse around 'low value courses' (Dickinson, 2021) in the run-up to the response to Sir Philip Augar's 2019 Review for the UK Government increasing focus on graduate salary data is likely to further compound these issues. Additionally, the Office for Students HE register and the

DOI: 10.4324/9781003271789-3

recently introduced "B" conditions (Office for Students, 2022), in particular the planned Condition B3 around student outcomes, adds to tensions for HE providers to justify the value of their courses.

Although the marketisation of HE is considered a key driver for the shift in HE landscape, it is necessary to acknowledge other important influences. Universities are educating a much wider and more diverse population of students than they did in the 1990s and early 2000s (Gibbs, 2010). With this expansion of HE into a more diversified context comes the responsibility to adapt practices to support students from all backgrounds and abilities who choose to engage with HE (Office for Students, 2018). Furthermore, the representation of students and student voice is not restricted to the UK HE landscape, or countries which implement HE fees, but is characteristic of other European (Klemenčič, 2012), and worldwide HE institutions (e.g. Coates, 2005; Yin and Wang, 2016). It is widely acknowledged that it is necessary to consider the efficacy of HE practices for all demographics of students, and to what extent the collective student voice is successful in representing this diverse population.

"Students bring more to higher education than their A-level scores. It is likely that their cultural capital, their aspirations, self-confidence and motivations all influence their performance and interact with teaching and course design variables" (Gibbs, 2010, p.18).

Due to practical constraints, representation of those whose voices are important because of the barriers they face (traditionally referred to as hard to reach, or the unengaged) may not be achieved. These are students for whom pedagogic practices are not well suited, or who are time and/or resource limited, and for such reasons are unable to take on or are not selected for representational roles. This runs the risk of selective representing, a selective perspective and the voice being heard speaking about others, not for them (Weller and Mahbubul, 2019), an issue which is increasingly recognised in efforts to advance Decolonising the Curriculum agendas in higher education institutions (HEIs) (Charles, 2019).

Weller and Mahbubul (2019) discuss students' role in the evaluative process, as well as in the active implementation of quality enhancement. While this has noble aims at its heart, there are some concerns to be considered for the spectrum of roles students may personify: from mere sources of survey data (by which policies may be shaped primarily to achieve more positive survey scores, rather than as a genuine response to improve student experience), through to active change agents (which have the power to shape governance, policy and pedagogy in ways that might be beneficial or harmful in the longer term). Frankham (2017) highlights an example where use of survey scores and reactive practice based on metrics was unsuccessful. One institution reacted to low UK NSS (2016) scores on "personal development" with increased resources and provision of employability-related content. This did not lead to improved student satisfaction, in part because the implementations made by the institution were misaligned with the responses (which students did not interpret as being employment-related).

Despite such examples serving as a reminder to avoid articulating activities to speak directly to NSS (or other metrics) in order to improve scores, there are examples where the feedback through large-scale surveys such as the NSS has had some value in focusing or prioritising improvements to aspects of the student experience. An important example is the role of feedback in student learning. While the utility of feedback and its optimisation for effective student learning has long been acknowledged as important for learning gain (Hattie and Timperley, 2007), it has received wider and more focused prominence in recent years (Winstone and Nash, 2016). One area of NSS scores with persistently low scores is the feedback category (HEA, 2013). Winstone and colleagues have developed a toolkit to improve the provision and utilisation of feedback which is based and grounded in relevant literature and empirical research (Winstone and Nash, 2016). Despite the apparent success of this approach in improving feedback delivery and student engagement with feedback, this context highlights an important issue. Metrics such as the NSS seem to reinforce a transmission view which depicts a linear process from educator or expert to novice (Nicol, 2010). Furthermore, a performativity approach to quality in HE strengthens the trend towards a recipience of services, and the delivery of such services, which is promoted by the consumerist HE culture (Nash and Winstone, 2017). With feedback being traditionally perceived as the responsibility of the educator, the task of engaging students to utilise it is particularly difficult. For example, Deeley and Bovill (2017) point out that increased staff–student partnerships increase intrinsic motivations, so it is necessary to challenge expectations and perceptions around feedback practice to improve its effectiveness, and for students to engage with it. A proactive recipience of feedback is required which necessitates self-regulation, goal setting, assessment literacy as well as engagement and motivation for it to be effective (Winstone et al., 2017).

The above example relating to feedback practices is important as it outlines how the focus on pedagogical developments and improvements may be prioritised as a result of metrics and evaluation. However, it also highlights the importance of engagement extending into partnership practices, and how these affect roles and responsibilities between staff and students (Healey and Healey, 2018). There is a comprehensive body of evidence to promote the benefits of partnership approaches, but in practice there are still a number of barriers to overcome. As already mentioned, there is a challenge of representation (Weller and Mahbubul, 2019), but additionally there is the difficulty of multiple and poorly defined roles, responsibilities and power relationships. As illustrated by the example of promoting best feedback practice, there is an inherent power relationship between academic staff and students, especially in situations where student work is evaluated and graded, in which students assume a more submissive role. Partnership is encouraged in many settings (e.g. Lowe et al., 2017) and can have beneficial outcomes at many levels of practice (programme, faculty, institution). However, introducing a partnership approach and a feeling of collaborative construction of learning is perhaps most difficult in a feedback or evaluation setting.

An area of pedagogical development that has seen successful partnership approaches both in the UK and internationally is in programme and curriculum design and redevelopment (e.g. Garaway, 2018; Marquis et al., 2016; Barrineau et al., 2016) The programme redevelopment described by Case et al. (2016) outlines a successful example of student engagement and partnership in practice, enhancing the student experience and outcomes (retention, completion, degree classifications). However, Case et al. describe the difficulties characteristic of such large-scale changes. These include the side effects of consumer-oriented HE, the diversification of student demographics and needs. A specific focus of their discussion is the national drivers of changes to SE practices which, they argue, may not always be well grounded in evidence. Adding to these challenges are the responsibilisation of staff through monitoring and initial reticence from staff who are implementing proposed changes and affected by them (Case et al., 2016). Acknowledging the challenges for academic staff is important as staff are key to implementing enhancement interventions and programmes. Sutton (2015) has discussed the multiple roles of academic staff who are often faced with the tension between the role of educator and service provider. Similarly Wong and Chiu (2019) used interview data to describe the evolving perceived identities of academic staff. Their findings echo the research describing the shift in learning attitudes amongst students (Bunce et al., 2016) and identify changes to teaching practices to accommodate them. For instance, students seem take a more pragmatic approach to their studies with the primary motivation of obtaining a job after graduation instead of also becoming a scholar of their subject. This shift seems to be accompanied with a reluctance to invest too much time in activities that do not have an immediate or obvious goal (such as passing an assignment). Many lecturers mentioned under-prepared students as a challenge (see also Grove, 2017), and that they mitigated this by providing handouts summarising key materials, and set bite-size readings (blogs, rather than articles and textbooks). While this supports lower-achieving and under-prepared students, and appears to represent a better 'service provision', it does have an undesirable side effect of lowering the expected standards for critical analysis, reading and thinking independently. Excessive support may also reinforce lower levels of effort, increase student reliance and decrease the development of independence and skills (Wood and Su, 2017).

As Case et al. (2016) point out, these changes to pedagogical practices are concerning if they are driven by expressions of student dissatisfaction and metrics such as NSS and the Teaching Excellence Framework (TEF). While feeling entertained is not in conflict with intellectual learning (Arthur, 2009), it seems that students often express dissatisfaction at challenging course material and assignments (Frankham, 2017). Adjusting for this dissatisfaction risks diminishing the intellectual content and challenge of HE, and the benefits that developing skills to engage with such challenges bring. Some suggest such adjustments may contribute to the phenomenon of grade inflation (Bachan, 2017). This is particularly worrying in light of emphasis on graduate employability and adds to the tensions associated with the impending OfS Condition B3 (Office for Students, 2022). There seems a need to anchor changes in pedagogic practices to evidence (as in the case of feedback practices, Winstone et al., 2017), rather than making reactive adjustments to teaching practices in order to improve student satisfaction and engagement in the short term. It is necessary to take a longer-term approach to adjusting best practice and challenging some of the unhelpful learning attitudes that are characteristic of contemporary fee-paying students.

The sector faces a challenge if it risks allowing national drivers of change (metrics, performativity agenda) to shape practices that are not well theoretically or empirically grounded. Although there is a large body of research that suggests that engaged students learn better (see Coates, 2005), the difficulty often arises at the point of finding a one-size fits all definition of 'engaged'. As Macfarlane and Tomlinson (2017) point out, there is a lot of research that is concerned with the effectiveness of student engagement initiatives, linking engagement with positive outcomes such as higher retention, attendance and degree results. However, they highlight that the study of SE remains under-theorised (Kahn, 2014), that methodologies often are lacking in rigour (few longitudinal studies, positionality of the researchers who are evaluating SE initiatives, often within their own institution), and that publication bias results in an under-representation of studies of less successful initiatives.

A principal difficulty relates to the lack of clear definition, and therefore a cloudy interpretation of what metrics are measuring. SE is often discussed in the context of student experience (e.g. Kuh, 2010). For a more orderly understanding of the term it can be helpful to distinguish the pedagogical and political (student voice) aims. In the pedagogical perspective, distinct aims relate to 1) improving student motivations to learning and studying, and 2) the participation of students in quality enhancement and assurance (e.g. QAA, 2018). In North American, Australasian and most European literature SE is understood to refer primarily to pedagogical practices that increase intrinsic motivation, improve learning attitudes and performance and engagement in individual learning (Buckley, 2014; Trowler, 2010). In this context, SE is typically framed as a constructivist notion, assuming behavioural and affective elements and which are necessarily active and visible (Gourlay, 2017). For example, Coates (2007) includes "active learning", "communication", "collaboration", "enriching experiences" and "feeling legitimised" in their definition of SE. While the first three can be well captured by standardised questionnaires, it is the phenomenological aspects of a student's experience captured by the final two descriptors that are more difficult to measure in a survey. This is problematic as they represent perhaps the richest reflection of students' experiences. However, effective engagement does not necessarily need to be visible, or measurable, so there is some concern about how well the outcome metric reflects the process. This is challenging, especially when these metrics are designed to capture process-level quality to inform the effectiveness of a course, or HEI (Senior et al., 2017). There is a risk to conflating satisfaction with learning experiences that are designed to capture rigour, and high-quality learning. However, the political aims of the SE movement (student voice, empowerment) are often considered as a democratic necessity to the positioning of students as consumers.

There is a lack of convincing evidence that the SE movement that conflates SE as defined by engagement in individual learning with the definition that encompasses citizenship and student voice is necessarily counteracting the effects of consumer-oriented HE. While the former has documented clear benefits for student retention, completion rates and quality of learning, there is little to suggest that focusing on student governance and voice for its political aims is beneficial for improving learners' intrinsic motivation, self-efficacy and positive learning attitudes (beyond perhaps the learning experiences of the individuals involved) which are affected by consumer-oriented HE (Bunce et al., 2016). It could be argued that the increased performativity related to SE activities inadvertently serves to intensify a consumer focus. Especially given the emphasis on student satisfaction, and a perceived lack of justification for less popular aspects of study, such as challenge, rigour and engaging with activities that may not be directly or perceivably linked to outcomes (e.g. assignments). It is, furthermore, unclear to what extent these initiatives do help to include under-represented students, or those who don't engage in visible or traditional ways (Macfarlane and Tomlinson, 2017). Some go as far as questioning whether feedback surveys are intended to improve students' experiences, or merely used to increase fees (see NUS boycott of NSS, Fazackerley, 2016).

Students expect economic returns from their HE experience – importantly, a degree that offers a beneficial position in the labour market (see Holligan and Shah, 2017) and increasingly the value of different degrees is measured against outcome metrics such as those in OfS Condition B3. This reflects the neo-liberal ideology that underscores current HE landscapes, an orientation that is focused on economic values, and a consumer-driven objective. It also neglects to recognise the student (graduate) voice in the perceived or experienced value of the degree, potentially undermining that voice by placing emphasis solely on employability metrics (Cheng et al., 2021). A further concern is that the increasing quantification of graduate outcomes, and focus on these, may exacerbate student's anxiety related to transition out of HE (Cage et al., 2022) and may impact motivation and engagement in study by promoting a defeatist mindset. There seems, however, to be a profound misalignment between the skills and characteristics that are desired or sought after by employers, and the expectations and attitudes that are reinforced by a 'dilute' or linear learning experience that many academics describe as necessary to 'satisfy' their students (Frankham, 2017). This expectation is one that is driven by extrinsic motivation, assignment success and a discomfort to engage in activities that are designed to be challenging or don't have direct assessment objectives. This is an important area for future investigation: examining the pedagogical value in the apparently reactive shifts in teaching and learning practices instigated by a desire to improve returns on government evaluations (NSS, TEF). It is necessary to determine whether adjustments, such as providing reading summaries in place of original and longer articles, affects students' development of critical thinking skills, research skills and the ability to extract key information from different media, and whether it reinforces disengagement rather than engagement with study. One way to address this may be to more actively engage teaching staff in this process of evaluative practice, since they are often responsible for conceiving and implementing strategies to improve SE and, by proxy, student satisfactions and outcomes. As illustrated in (Wong and Chiu, 2019), academic staff perceive the necessity to adjust their teaching and adapt to changing expectations, but don't seem to feel that these adjustments are necessarily pedagogically justified. Similarly, Case et al. (2016) describe some reticence amongst staff about changes to practice, and the responsibility for improving metrics that is placed upon staff.

Traditionally held hierarchical structures in HE are increasingly re-defined (Cook-Sather et al., 2014), with an important and justified emphasis on greater equity between staff and students. However, this can leave academic staff uncertain of their role, and undervalued for their expertise (Jarvis et al., 2016). This shift is neatly articulated by Holligan and Shah (2017):

> Under the British elite system of higher education of the mid 20th century, the professional integrity of academics was 'the paramount guarantor of quality' (Williams, 1997: 287) but in contemporary higher education, this intellectual authority appears to have shifted to students as determiners of the 'quality of the student experience'.
>
> (p.116)

With increasing staff workloads (Kenny and Fluck, 2014) and some risk inherent in engaging in substantial changes to provision (Bryson and Furlonger, 2018) it is necessary to avoid alienating staff through excessive emphasis on performativity, and the challenges that accompany the nurturing of student voice, especially when this is articulated in damaging or unconstructive ways (The Guardian, 2015). Perhaps it is worth not only celebrating students' expertise by experience, but also nurturing instructors' expertise by scholarship of a subject. Rather than expecting a passive acceptance and internalisation of some radical changes to long-held power structures, pedagogical approaches and practices, it may be in HEIs' best interest to provide deliberate and targeted support and training to staff about dealing with the new challenges that are arising from the shifting HE landscape. Revisiting long-held concepts in occupational psychology for strategies of improving engagement of students and staff (Bakker et al., 2015), and positive psychology for improving resilience and functioning (Donaldson et al., 2015), may provide a useful theoretical and empirical grounding for future SE initiatives.

To ensure a long-term favourable effect of the SE movement, it seems necessary to manage the expectations of both staff and students in their roles and responsibilities. It is necessary for HEI management to adequately support staff to be able to adapt to the modern HE landscape, while preserving important pedagogical principles. Additionally it is essential to manage students' expectations and attitudes around proactive approaches to learning promoting the longer-term benefits of engaged personal learning to ensure good value for money, learning gain (McGrath et al., 2015), and the chance to build a fulfilling and valuable career.

References

Arthur, L., 2009. From performativity to professionalism: Lecturers' responses to student feedback. *Teaching in Higher Education*, 14(4), pp.441–454. https://doi.org/10.1080/13562510903050228

Augar, P., 2019. *Independent Panel Report to the Review of Post-18 Education and Funding*. London: HMSO.

Bachan, R., 2017. Grade inflation in UK higher education. *Studies in Higher Education*, 42 (8), pp.1580–1600. https://doi.org/10.1080/03075079.2015.1019450

Bakker, A.B., Sanz Vergel, A.I., Kuntze, J., 2015. Student engagement and performance: A weekly diary study on the role of openness. *Motivation and Emotion*, 39, pp.49–62. https://doi.org/10.1007/s11031-014-9422-5

Barrineau, S., Schnaas, U., Engström, A., and Härlin, F., 2016. Breaking ground and building bridges: A critical reflection on student–faculty partnerships in academic development. *International Journal for Academic Development*, 21(1), pp.79–83. doi:10.1080/1360144X.2015.1120735.

Browne, J., 2010. *Securing a Sustainable Future in Higher Education*. London: Department of Business Innovation and Skills. Available at: https://assets.publishing.service.gov.uk/government/uploads/system/uploads/attachment_data/file/422565/bis-10-1208-securing-sustainable-higher-education-browne-report.pdf (accessed: 6 January 2022).

Bryson, C. and Furlonger, R., 2018. A shared reflection on risk in trying to work with students in partnership. *Teaching and Learning Together in Higher Education*, 24. https://repository.brynmawr.edu/tlthe/vol1/iss24/8

Buckley, A., 2014. How radical is student engagement? (And what is it for?) *Student Engagement and Experience Journal*, 3(2), pp.1–23. http://dx.doi.org/10.7190/seej.v3i2.95

Bunce, L., Baird, A. and Jones, S., 2016. The student-as-consumer approach in higher education and its effects on academic performance. *Studies in Higher Education*. doi:10.1080/03075079.2015.1127908.

Cage, E., James, A.I., Newell, V., and Lucas, R., 2022. Expectations and experiences of the transition out of university for students with mental health conditions. *European Journal of Higher Education*, 12(2), pp.171–193. doi:10.1080/21568235.2021.1917440.

Case, S., Ugwudike, P., Haines, K., Harris, K. and Owen, J., 2016. The Swansea Student Engagement Project: Students and staff as partners in programme review and enhancement. *Enhancing Learning in the Social Sciences*. https://doi.org/10.11120/elss.2014.00027.

Charles, E., 2019. Decolonizing the curriculum. *Insights*, 32(1), p.24. http://doi.org/10.1629/uksg.475

Cheng, M., Adekola, O., Albia, J.C. and Cai, S., 2021. Employability in higher education: A review of key stakeholders' perspectives. *Higher Education Evaluation and Development*, 16(1), pp.16–31. doi:10.1108/HEED-03-2021-0025.

Coates, H., 2007. A model of online and general campus-based student engagement. *Assessment and Evaluation in Higher Education*, 32(2), pp.121–141. https://doi.org/10.1080/02602930600801878

Coates, H., 2005. The value of student engagement for higher education quality assurance. *Quality in Higher Education*, 11(1), pp.25–36. https://doi.org/10.1080/13538320500074915

Cook-Sather, A., Bovill, C. and Felten, P., 2014. *Engaging Students as Partners in Teaching and Learning*. San Francisco, CA: Jossey-Bass.

Deeley, S., and Bovill, C., 2017. Staff-student partnership in assessment: Enhancing assessment literacy through democratic practices. *Assessment and Evaluation in Higher Education*, 42, pp.625–644. doi:10.1080/02602938.2015.1126551.

Department of Business, Innovation and Skills (BIS), 2011. *Higher Education: Students at the Heart of the System*. London: Department for Business, Innovation and Skills. www. gov.uk/government/uploads/system/uploads/attachment_data/file/32409/ 11-944-higher-education-students-at-heart-of-system.pdf (accessed 6 January 2022).

Dickinson, J., 2021. What did Williamson say at HEPI conference?Wonkhe. Available at: https://wonkhe.com/wonk-corner/what-did-williamson-say-at-hepi-conference/ (accessed: 6 January 2022).

Donaldson, S.I., Dollwet, M. and Rao, M.A., 2015. Happiness, excellence, and optimal human functioning revisited: Examining the peer-reviewed literature linked to positive psychology. *The Journal of Positive Psychology*, 10(3), pp.185–195. doi:10.1080/ 17439760.2014.943801.

Fazackerley, A., 2016. Universities and NUS plan boycott of flagship teaching rankings. Available at: www.theguardian.com/education/2016/nov/22/universities-nus-boycott-teaching-excellence-framework-tuition-fees (accessed: 6 January 2022).

Frankham, J., 2017. Employability and higher education: The follies of the 'productivity challenge' in the Teaching Excellence Framework. *Journal of Education Policy*, 32(5), pp.628–641. doi:10.1080/02680939.2016.1268271.

Freeman, R., 2013. Student engagement in practice: Ideologies and power in course representation systems. In Dunne, E. and Owen, D. (eds) *The Student Engagement Handbook: Practice in Higher Education*. Bingley: Emerald. https://doi.org/10.4324/ 9780429023033-6

Garaway, C., 2018. How we raised our NSS feedback and assessment scores by 26% in three years. UCL. Available at: www.ucl.ac.uk/teaching-learning/case-studies/2018/apr/ how-we-raised-our-nss-feedback-and-assessment-scores-26-three-years (accessed: 6 January 2022).

Gibbs, G., 2010. *Dimensions of Quality*. York: HEA.

Gourlay, L.J., 2017. Student engagement, 'learnification' and the sociomaterial: Critical perspectives on higher education policy. *Higher Education Policy*, 30(1), pp.23–34. doi:10.1057/s41307–41016–0037–0031.

Grove, J., 2017. *THE Teaching Survey 2017: Results and Analysis*. Available at: www.tim eshighereducation.com/features/the-teaching-survey-2017-results-and-analysis. (accessed: 7 January 2022).

The Guardian, 2015. My students have paid £9,000 and now they think they own me. *Guardian Online*. Available at: www.theguardian.com/higher-education-network/ 2015/dec/18/my-students-have-paid-9000-and-now-they-think-they-own-me (accessed: 6 January 2022).

Hattie, J. and Timperley, H., 2007. The power of feedback. *Review of Educational Research*, 77(1), pp.81–112. doi:10.3102/003465430298487.

Healey, M. and Healey, R.L., 2018. "It depends": Exploring the context-dependent nature of students as partners' practices and policies. *International Journal for Students as Partners*, 2(1). https://doi.org/10.15173/ijsap.v2i1.3472.

Higher Education Academy (HEA), 2013. *HEA Feedback Toolkit*. York: HEA.

Holligan, C. and Shah, Q., 2017. Global capitalism's Trojan Horse: Consumer power and the National Student Survey in England. *Power and Education*, 9, pp.114–128. https://doi.org/10.1177/1757743817701159

Jarvis, J., Clarke, K., Dickerson, C. and Stockwell, L., 2016. Student–staff partnership in learning and teaching. *Link*, 2(2). www.herts.ac.uk/link/volume-2,-issue-2/student-staff-partnership-inlearning-and-teaching

Kahn, P.E., 2014. Theorising student engagement in higher education. *British Educational Research Journal*, 40(6), pp.1005–1018. https://doi.org/10.1002/berj.3121

Kenny, J.D.J. and Fluck, A.E., 2014. The effectiveness of academic workload models in an institution: A staff perspective. *Journal of Higher Education Policy and Management*, 36 (6), pp.585–602. doi:10.1080/1360080X.2014.957889.

Klemenčič, M., 2012. Student representation in Western Europe: Introduction to the special issue. *European Journal of Higher Education*, 2(1), pp.2–19. https://doi.org/10.1080/21568235.2012.695058

Kuh, G.D., 2010. *High-Impact Educational Practices: What They Are, Who Has Access to Them and Why They Matter*. Washington, DC: American Association for Colleges and Universities.

Lowe, T., Shaw, C., Sims, S., King, S. and Paddison, A., 2017. The development of contemporary student engagement practices at the University of Winchester and Winchester Student Union. *International Journal for Students as Partners*, 1(1). https://doi.org/10.15173/ijsap.v1i1.3082

Macfarlane, B. and Tomlinson, M., 2017. Critiques of student engagement. *Higher Education Policy*, 30(1), pp.6–21. https://doi.org/10.1057/s41307-016-0027-0023

Marquis, E., Puri, V., Wan, S., Ahmad, A., Goff, L., Knorr, K., Vassileva, I. and Woo, J., 2016. Navigating the threshold of student–staff partnerships: A case study from an Ontario teaching and learning institute. *International Journal for Academic Development*, 21(1), pp.4–15. doi:10.1080/1360144X.2015.1113538.

McGrath, C.H., Guerin, B., Harte, E., Frearson, M. and Manville, C., 2015. *Learning Gain in Higher Education*. Santa Monica, CA: RAND Corporation. Available at: www.hefce.ac.uk/media/HEFCE,2014/Content/Pubs/Independentresearch/2015/Learning, gain,in,HE/Learning_gain.pdf (accessed: 6 January 2022).

Nash R.A. and Winstone N.E., 2017. Responsibility-sharing in the giving and receiving of assessment feedback. *Frontiers in Psychology*, 8. doi:10.3389/fpsyg.2017.01519.

Nicol, D., 2010. From monologue to dialogue: Improving written feedback processes in mass higher education. *Assessment and Evaluation in Higher Education*, 35, pp.501–517. doi:10.1080/02602931003786559.

Office for Students, 2022. *New OfS Conditions to Raise Quality Bar and Tackle Grade Inflation*. Available at: www.officeforstudents.org.uk/news-blog-and-events/press-and-media/new-ofs-conditions-to-raise-quality-bar-and-tackle-grade-inflation (accessed: 29 August 2022).

Office for Students, 2020. *Outcome Performance Measures, Key Performance Measure 16*. Available at: www.officeforstudents.org.uk/about/measures-of-our-success/outcomes-performance-measures/employers-think-that-graduates-are-equipped-with-the-required-skills-and-knowledge/ (accessed: 22 July 2022).

Office for Students, 2018. *The Regulatory Framework for Higher Education in England*. Available at: www.officeforstudents.org.uk/advice-and-guidance/regulation/the-regulatory-framework-for-higher-education-in-england/ (accessed: 7 January 2022).

Quality Assurance Agency for Higher Education (QAA), 2018. *The Revised UK Quality Code for Higher Education*. Available at: https://qaa.ac.uk/quality-code (accessed: 6 January 2022).

Senior, C., Moores, E. and Burgess, A.P., 2017. "I can't get no satisfaction": Measuring student satisfaction in the age of a consumerist higher education. *Frontiers in Psychology*, 8, p.980. doi:10.3389/fpsyg.2017.00980.

Sutton, P., 2015. A paradoxical academic identity: Fate, utopia and critical hope. *Teaching in Higher Education*, 20(1), pp.37–47. https://doi.org/10.1080/13562517.2014.957265

Tomlinson, M., 2017. Student engagement: Towards a critical policy sociology. *Policy in Higher Education*, 30, pp.35–52. https://doi.org/10.1057/s41307-016-0035-3

Trowler, V., 2010. *Student Engagement Literature Review*. York: HEA. Available at: www.advance-he.ac.uk/knowledge-hub/student-engagement-literature-review (accessed: 6 January 2022).

Weller, S. and Mahbubul, A., 2019. The student role in quality: From data source to partner and back again? In: Ellis, R. and Hogard, E. (ed) *Handbook of Quality Assurance for University Teaching*. Oxford: Routledge. https://doi.org/10.4324/9781315187518-16

Winstone, N.E. and Nash, R.A., 2016. *The Developing Engagement with Feedback Toolkit (DEFT)*. Available at: www.heacademy.ac.uk/knowledge-hub/developing-engagement-feedback-toolkit-deft (accessed: 7 January 2022).

Winstone, N.E., Nash, R.A., Parker, M. and Rowntree, J., 2017. Supporting learners' agentic engagement with feedback: A systematic review and a taxonomy of recipience processes. *Educational Psychologist*, 52, pp.17–37. doi:10.1080/00461520.2016.1207538.

Wong, B. and Chiu, Y.-L.T., 2019. Let me entertain you: The ambivalent role of university lecturers as educators and performers. *Educational Review*, 71(2), pp.218–233. doi:10.1080/00131911.2017.1363718.

Wood, N. and Su, F., 2017. What makes an excellent lecturer? Academics' perspectives on the discourse of 'teaching excellence' in higher education. *Teaching in Higher Education*, 22(4), pp.451–466. doi:10.1080/13562517.2017.1301911.

Yin, H. and Wang, W., 2016. Undergraduate students' motivation and engagement in China: an exploratory study. *Assessment and Evaluation in Higher Education*, 41(4), pp.601–621. doi:10.1080/02602938.2015.1037240.

Yorke, M., Orr, S. and Blair, B., 2014. Hit by a perfect storm? Art and design in the National Student Survey. *Studies in Higher Education*, 39, pp.1788–1810. doi:10.1080/03075079.2013.806465.

There is not one student experience

Our learner journeys as individuals

Fatima Umar

When you grow up in a South Asian household, after your parents, the next entity it is essential to show utmost respect to is one's teachers. This respect growing up meant little things like standing up when teachers enter the classroom, never calling them just by their name, never arguing because, in the back of our minds, they are always supposed to be right. I was a star pupil at school thus perhaps it was easy to not notice the lapses in my teachers' pedagogical practices, essentially because they worked for me. It was only when I entered higher education and I found myself struggling in calculus that I first reflected on pedagogy. I did not understand why the class was at a pace that I could not keep up with and wondered why the teacher would not slow down and spend longer on the basics. "Do the 150 other students all know what's going on?" I asked myself. To cope with this I relied on online video content and tutorials conducted by the teaching assistants, essentially feeling that I must take ownership of my own learning. At this point, I was forced to reflect on the importance of teaching styles and I began selecting classes where I felt like I could really connect with the professor. But then again, I was still looking essentially for a homogeneous pedagogical style that simply worked for me. It was not until my graduate degree in education that I began to realize that instead of the student trying to find the professor that works for them, the professor should be finding ways to connect with the diverse learners in their classroom.

My cohort in the MPhil Education, Leadership and Management program was a unique combination of students with varying ages, socioeconomic backgrounds, language proficiency levels, learning styles, life circumstances, motivators, etc. Most of all, each individual was there to fulfill an individual need, which could range from building their résumé to get a better job, shifting professional fields, giving back to their community, freshening up a rusty mind, or merely trying to find their true calling. While many of these variations probably existed at the undergraduate level, an intimate cohort of 45 perhaps served as a microcosm for the larger undergraduate batch size. With this class I found the faculty switching between English and Urdu, eager to really hear what those from different backgrounds brought to the room. Even though most of the curriculum with its extensive English assignments was not very inclusive, you could see snippets of

DOI: 10.4324/9781003271789-4

inclusive pedagogical application. This involved some faculty members switching primary deliverables to creating models of what you wish to portray instead of written submissions. But one significant strategy was clubbing diverse students together for class projects. While not all these groups always worked in perfect harmony, this did offer richer experiences where in many cases students could pick up things from each other's skill set and enhance their own. While this experience was reassuring that these strategies do help more students to evolve with the classroom, I did not feel it was enough.

My belief that pedagogical practices need to be centered around the students more than the curriculum was further strengthened when I was assigned a project in my 'School Effectiveness' course, where the crux was to create tailored and deeply contextualized educational development interventions for real-world school. Under this project, I designed a language expansion program for primary-level students with autism. The learners I observed all had their favored learning styles and environments, leading to different comfort levels with their use of vocabulary. Furthermore, any major changes in routine impacted how they felt about coming into a learning environment. Hence, my educational development project utilized color coding, personalized storytelling and the utilization of different senses to expand vocabulary. The students were thus able to bring aspects of their own private world and tell custom stories which helped increase their language ability. Adopting this new pedagogical technique was not that difficult for the teachers who were eager to ensure all students could enhance their skills. This helped me realize that at all ages it is necessary to alter the thought process around teaching and learning practices. Right now, many teachers in Pakistan, often due to pressure from school administration, parental expectations, time-consuming activities and general culture, deem it their duty to ensure students get an 'A' with students indulging in 'deep learning' being a much more secondary objective. I have generally felt that a lot of this stems from not indulging in reflective practices to improve the current state. After my positive experience in this class, I was selected to work as a teaching assistant with the new cohort. As the entire class worked with diverse schools from around the city focusing on diverse projects, I realized, being closer to the students' experiences, that assessing their work would need to happen in a very subjective and thoughtful manner. Thus, along with the faculty member, I encouraged an open-door policy where students could discuss in-depth the pace of their specific work, share their struggles, delays in progress, innovative ideas, implications of diverse group dynamics etc. Learning about these experiences allowed for assessment to occur more holistically on individual progress rather than a specific set standard to achieve.

I indulged in my own reflective experience when I worked with the Learning Institute at the Lahore University of Management Sciences to collaborate with a faculty member to design a course. The faculty member was from the business degree whereas I was a budding educationist. The course was meant to be introductory to expose learners to disruptive technologies. My journey with the faculty member to devise this curriculum was a rather interesting one. I believed I was entering this space staying consciously aware of the needs of the students the course would address. But I was unaware of the limitations that my own values as a student would bring to this space. While I had ideas for what could be useful for the students, I struggled to voice them to my faculty partner due to my own values, where I did not think I could negotiate with her to alter her plans. During this experience, I again returned to that status as a student who would place a teacher on the highest pedestal without questioning them. It was only when I reflected on my own experience that I was able to understand how students need to contribute to pushing the faculty member to create a more inclusive environment. When I did put forward my opinion the instructor was eager to hear me out, as she thought there could be no better representation of the student stakeholder than a student themselves. Once discussion was free-flowing, we embarked on a project which included creating a diverse range of assignments to cater to different learners with reflective components to focus on the individual learners. These were powerful conversations and they helped me reflect on the informational asymmetries between students and faculty members that need to be minimized so each can better understand the other's needs. Our negotiation involved us discussing how the introductory course we were designing would welcome a range of students from various backgrounds, some with exemplary quantitative skills, while others might have better verbal skills, thus the way we assessed our class could not just keep in mind one type of student. As a result, the course we designed included the mathematical models the faculty member felt were essential, but this content was complemented by watching relevant films from mainstream cinema to develop a passion and an ability to visualize disruptive technologies. This experience helped me understand that course syllabi do not have to be compromised, but rather can be supported to enhance student experience.

I think my various personal and professional experiences helped me realize how behaviors in a classroom are a manifestation of a lifetime of learning behaviors both on the teacher and the student side. It is necessary for relearning to occur within the classroom, so both these stakeholders must negotiate their needs and support each other to create an inclusive and conducive environment. The classroom must find a way to transform all its entrants into a better, more informed version of themselves before releasing them back into the world. To enable the classroom to do so, the faculty members must maintain an open, accessible door policy where the student feels safe and empowered enough to partake in taking decisions for their own learning. This also helps faculty members, who would not have to teach in a classroom ignorant of student needs; rather it creates an atmosphere where these needs are embraced and fulfilled.

Chapter 5

Equality and diversity in our student engagement practice

Radical possibilities to reaching racial and religious equity in higher education

Maisha Islam

"Who will speak out for the public good of higher education if its members do not? Who will speak out for students, like me, if we do not speak out for ourselves? Who will create avenues for students to speak out if we in academe do not invite them to speak?" (Quaye, 2005, p.306).

Here it is, you may think. The quintessential chapter on equality and diversity, terms that are a staple part of UK higher education (HE). However, before thinking that you are well acquainted with these debates and issues, that you know the data and have heard it all before, it is important to remain humble in our shared endeavour to ensure *equitable* experiences and outcomes for all students and staff. With topics such as race, class and gender (i.e. the three 'diversity heavyweights') having dominated practice in educational development, one would assume that their related inequalities would be fully realised, and that fast-paced progress would have been made in dismantling the structures that have worked against minoritised and underrepresented students in HE. Such structures at both the macro- (e.g. systemic racism) and micro-level (e.g. unequal power differentials) have resulted in several disparities we see in the experience and outcomes of our diverse student bodies.

Among them in the UK include: around 100,000 Muslim students forgoing or self-funding a university education due to lacking alternative student finance (Muslim Census, 2021); a long-standing degree-awarding gap in the proportion of racially minoritised students[1] receiving a 2:1 or first class honours degree (Codiroli Mcmaster, 2021); financial hardships experienced by international students (Office for Students, 2020); institutional policies excluding student parents (Moreau, 2016); a burgeoning student mental health crisis that puts certain student groups at higher risk (e.g. LGBTQ+ students) (Neves and Hillman, 2017); an increased likelihood of drop-out for students disclosing a disability (Hubble and Bolton, 2021); and those from economically disadvantaged backgrounds being less likely to attend selective institutions where they stand to gain better social mobility outcomes (The Sutton Trust, 2021). Inequities such as these are prevalent across wider, if not all, international HE landscapes, from indigenous students in Australia (Gore et al., 2017) to rural and economically disadvantaged students in China (Xie, 2015), and Black and Latinx students in the United States of America (Galindo, 2021).

DOI: 10.4324/9781003271789-5

Such disparities set the precedent as to why areas related to equality and diversity are important to critically reflect upon, and fundamentally why it is important to consider diversity in our student engagement practices and conceptualisations of 'the student experience'. Universities are often motivated to do this by various 'push' factors (e.g. Access and Participation Plans mandated by the regulator of English Higher Education, the Office for Students) and 'pull factors' (e.g. ensuring accessibility and all students' ability to thrive in HE) (Lowe and El-Hakim, 2020). Whilst many have therefore looked to embed a focus on student engagement as a democratising force that improves student retention, success and progression, to what extent do student engagement in educational development initiatives (e.g. student–staff partnership projects, student representation, feedback mechanisms etc.) perpetuate inaccessible HE systems that cater towards those already privileged (Mercer-Mapstone and Bovill, 2019)?

Felten (2020) argues that a persistent and significant tension existing within research and practice related to student engagement includes how its construction assumes generic students, ignoring how student identities impact learning and experiences. Terms such as 'the student experience' have rightly been critiqued (Lowe and El-Hakim, 2020) as they imply a singular, 'gold standard' experience that is often conflated to young, White, middle-class, campus-based students immersed in a drinking culture, i.e. 'authentic' and 'traditional' student hallmarks. This fails to recognise the multiplicity of varied students' experiences, perpetuating the myth of 'traditional students' which then becomes problematic and damaging, not only to the way in which it informs the service provisions invested in by universities and student unions but also in the perceptions of 'legitimate' and normative students (Sykes, 2021).

Where terms such as 'hyper/super diversity' have been used in relation to student bodies (Atherton and Mazhari, 2018), the binary conceptualisations of 'traditional'/'non-traditional' students and limited descriptions of 'the student experience' are no longer relevant in contemporary HE. Sabri (2011) poignantly asserts that despite the totemic status that the notion of 'the student experience' plays within the sector, conceptualisations of the term are often taken-for-granted, shallow and disembodied. This is partly due to public and institutional policies assuming that students' educational experiences are predicated on factors irrespective of their class, gender, race, religion etc.

Acknowledging the diversity of students' experiences therefore means looking in *and* beyond the learning and teaching sphere; students' engagements with their universities are embodied at micro- and macro-level sites and so what contributes to 'student success' and sense of belonging must encompass a more holistic outlook (Islam, Burnett and Collins, 2021). This requires reflection upon the variety of institutional structures that further marginalise those diverse and minoritised students. Contextualising the constraints students face by their *intersectional* identities thus becomes important as student experience discourses have largely been historically shaped by marketised motivations rather than moral imperatives to serve and support minoritised student groups.

The context in which this chapter seeks to explore engaging with and for diverse students in HE takes place in the recent resurgence of Black Lives Matter (BLM) – a movement which seeks to advance racial justice but is also intersectional at its core. This chapter therefore offers a critical reflection on the place of race and religion together (a grossly under-researched area), within student engagement research and wider HE practices and literature. Despite certain governmental rhetoric threatening to stifle racial progress under the guise of protecting academic freedom (Dickinson, 2022) or deem focus on race and intersectional issues as 'culturally irrelevant' (Elzas, 2021) and 'divisive' (Greene, 2022), HE institutions display a strong commitment to listening and meaningfully working in partnership with their students on such matters. Nevertheless, there are still feats to climb in integrating religion and belief in educational research, national and institutional policy, as well as realising the part it plays in 'the student experience' (Sabri, 2017). This chapter hopes to highlight the need for significantly more work to address less emphasised components of diversity, namely religious oppression (Obear, 2012), and how these considerations must become further embedded in our student engagement and educational development practices if we are truly to remain accessible and achieve greater parity in the voices that are represented – for it is our duty to speak with and elevate these voices.

The rise and fall of race equality in HE – a year like no other

The 2020–2021 academic year took place in the context of the COVID-19 pandemic and other major socio-political events. Where the pandemic shifted almost the entirety of our everyday lives online, it was impossible to not know the name George Floyd or witness his nine-minute execution (Hill et al., 2020). It was here we saw the beginnings of a truly global conversation and resistance both for and against racial equality. This increased exposure further revealed the true extent of racism, be it through the disproportionate rate of COVID-19 fatalities impacting communities of colour (Office for National Statistics, 2020) to the vulnerabilities further exposed to students of colour (Singh, 2020). Within UK HE, we saw a dichotomy of perspectives in relation to governmental rhetoric and sector practice when looking at race equality.

Figure 5.1 represents the oxymoronic nature of HE's responses and approaches to dealing with race equality. Universities across the sector were prompted to (or pressured by their students) to (re)commit their efforts of enacting change. This included applying for Race Equality Charter[2] marks and confronting their historically oppressive cultures and histories (Advance HE, 2021), to acknowledging the existence of institutional racism in very public ways (Mohdin, 2021) and national commitments to taking anti-racist approaches (Advance HE, 2020b). Truly, "we are now seeing a much more systematic and detailed examination of inequities associated with 'race' and racism across the HE sectors" (Dacosta et al., 2021, p.6).

In contrast to the sector's bold messaging, UK governmental rhetoric has downplayed the existence of institutional racism (Commission on Race and Ethnic Disparities, 2021) and has specifically targeted universities that apply for nationally

May-June 2020
- Black Lives Matter (BLM) protests, largely driven by young people and students, are seen to be the largest form of anti-racism protest since the abolition of slavery (Mohdin, Swann and Bannock, 2020).
- UK universities make public statements to show support for the BLM movement (Dunn, 2020).

August 2020
- Landmark commitment from all 19 colleges and 26 universities within Scotland supporting a declaration to tackle racism (Advance HE, 2020b).

October 2020
- Equalities Minister, Kemi Badenoch states that the Conservative government 'stands unequivocally against Critical Race Theory' (UK Parliament, 2020).

November 2020
- Universities UK release guidance for universities to tackle racial harassment on campus, following an Equality and Human Rights Commission report (2019) revealing widespread racism.
- Vice-Chancellor of the University of East Anglia, Prof. David Richardson declares that all UK universities are institutionally racist (Universities UK, 2020).

February 2021
- Minister of State for Universities, Michelle Donelan likens decolonisation of the curriculum to a form of censorship (Stubley, 2021).
- Department for Education release a policy paper for the intended Higher Education (freedom of speech) Bill, citing decolonising the curriculum as a 'contested political ideology' that interferes with academic freedom (Department for Education, 2021).

March 2021
- Launch of the controversial Commission on Race and Ethnic Disparities Report, stating that institutional racism does not exist and calls for abolishing the term 'BAME' (Commission on Race and Ethnic Disparities, 2021).

April 2021
- BBC Three airs documentary 'Is Uni Racist?' where journalist Linda Adey explores the accounts of students who have experienced racism on UK campuses and the inadequacy of reporting mechanisms (Adey, 2021).

Figure 5.1 Key activities for race equality in UK HE during 2020–2021

recognised schemes which demonstrate their voluntary commitment towards racial equity, e.g. working to 'decolonise' their curriculum (Dickinson, 2022). Decolonising the curriculum broadly relates to actively assessing teaching, learning and representation in curricula; reflecting on pedagogical practice used; and ultimately interrogating and challenging unequal social structures that we see constantly being reproduced (Liyange, 2020). Such explicit opposition risks a chilling effect on universities' efforts towards decolonisation – despite only a fifth actively supporting a curriculum reform that acknowledges the influence of colonialism (Batty, 2020). Specifically targeting decolonising the curriculum movements as impinging on academic freedom not only overrepresents its current influence but discourages universities taking this path less travelled. Also troubling is the implicit message that this sends to students of colour at the heart of these movements, finally feeling empowered to use their voice.

It is clear that BLM not only empowered students to consider how these issues can be considered in future policy and practice, but also brought students and staff collectively to do this (Phoenix et al., 2020). In a space where much of this activity garners hope via the transgressing of hierarchical structures, too much hope may be misguided and even naïve. For example, the 2021 UK Student Academic Experience Survey included, for the first time, questions on how students perceived their institution's commitment on race equality (Neves and Hewitt, 2021), where Black and Chinese students were markedly less confident in their university's efforts. Nonetheless, as Freire states, "it is imperative that we maintain hope even when the harshness of reality may suggest the opposite" (Freire, 1997, p.106). Hope emerges in not only the normalisation of language and efforts towards anti-racism but also how much of this is (and can be traced back to) the efforts largely driven by students.

Reviving the master's toolkit? The use of partnership to serve racial equity

"It's the students – they are what help me survive. When I hear their stories, when I see the changes we have made, I know I can take on the next battle" (Kezar, 2008, p.434).

All students want an education that is relevant to them; an education that is connected to their experience in which they feel they have an active stake in not only their learning and teaching setting but also in wider society (hooks, 1994). Systemic issues such as degree-awarding gaps between White and racially minoritised students suggest that this type of relevant and liberatory education is not being fulfilled for students of colour – be it from a sense of alienation, to a curriculum that does not speak to the issues that are of importance (National Union of Students, 2011; Mann, 2001).

When given avenues to have a voice and their experiential knowledge utilised, we truly see students' excellence and expertise (Rodríguez and Brown, 2009). A compendium of work showcasing this includes the special edition issue of the *Journal of Educational Innovation, Partnership and Change* – 'Enriching BAME Staff–Student Partnerships in Higher Education'.[3] This collection presents examples of racially minoritised students working together with staff to create systemic change, both across disciplines and across the Atlantic. For example, noting a lecturer's inability to diagnose skin conditions on darker skin and a racially derogatory comment made by a medical actor, Anthony-Okeke et al. (2021) describe embedding a more racially inclusive curriculum, stating that student–staff partnership was integral to bringing a renewed equality and diversity focus within their School of Pharmacy in the United Kingdom. Work like this has garnered international attention, as exemplified by Mukwende, Tamony and Turner's (2020) book *Mind the Gap*, which had its humble beginnings via a student–staff partnership grant at St. George's, University of London (UK). Promisingly, these projects have the potential to create tangible change to not only curricula but also in racialised health disparities.

The effects of student–staff partnership not only empower racially minoritised students, but those staff involved to realise the extent to which racial prejudice and indifference to the experiences of students of colour are embedded into universities. For example, Barefoot et al. (2019) reflect on critical incidents encountered as staff led change to eliminate their degree-awarding gap between White and racially minoritised students. Even those staff occupying marginalised identities can uncover certain 'blind spots' and learn from students' insights (e.g. methodological and experiential standpoints), as shown in Islam and Valente's

(2021) critical dialogue reflecting on a partnership project investigating Asian students' university experiences in the UK (see also Islam, 2021b). Changes brought about through collective student–staff work serve as powerful reminders of why such partnerships are so worthwhile.

These examples present an archetypal form of student–staff partnership that, when done right, can engender more inclusive and equitable practices (Felten et al., 2013). Yet, student–staff partnership approaches are susceptible to further reproducing inequality – after all, to what extent can the master's tools dismantle the masters' house? (Lorde, 1984). Thus, whilst the practice of student–staff partnership represents a transformative disruption to traditional hierarchical structures (Mercer-Mapstone and Abbot, 2020a), does it accommodate equity work? Particularly considering 'diversity' is rarely the starting point for many partnerships (Varnham, 2017); conditions under which partnerships occur may not always be preferential for students (Martens et al., 2019); limited strategies or understanding of what it means to be inclusive of both student and staff diversity are apparent (Mercer-Mapstone, Islam and Reid, 2019); and difficulties arising when seeking to retain social justice aims when scaling student–staff partnership models (Peters and Mathias, 2018). Here, we turn attention to a much less considered vector of diversity – religion and belief. If we are to adopt an orientation whereby student–staff partnership and wider student engagement in educational development practices can still be regarded as 'locations of possibility' empowering all students and staff, be it through increased accountability or agency (Cates, Madigan and Reitenauer, 2018), how is this serving religiously minoritised students and their battles?

The rarity of religion in student engagement

"If diversity work is meant to become a part of larger endeavours to promote social justice, it should embrace a wider conceptualization and practice of diversity" (Shalabi, 2014, n.p.).

It seems UK HE follows the rules of 'dinner party' conversations by neglecting to talk about religion and religious students. In a data-driven landscape, the fact that UK universities were mandated to return data on religion and belief only since 2017/18 (Advance HE, 2018) is telling of the place of faith in HE. Despite over half of the UK student population identifying with some sort of religion/belief (Advance HE, 2020a), there is a false guise of universities being secular spaces (Aune and Stevenson, 2017). Looking specifically at Muslim students, systemic issues related to their experiences are clear in the UK and internationally, with university spaces characterised as discriminatory and exclusionary (Hopkins, 2011), lacking in accommodation to religious provisions (Chen, Tabassum and Saeed, 2019) and regarding their Muslim students as 'suspect communities' (Kyriacou et al., 2017).

As a sector, we are aware of the ways in which such negative academic and social experiences of racially minoritised students manifest into systemic inequalities such as degree-awarding gaps, lack of a sense of belonging and low levels of ethnic diversity amongst staffing bodies (Broecke and Nicholls, 2007; Universities UK and National

Union of Students, 2019). Recent literature illustrates similar trends with Muslim students in the UK, with less than two-thirds being awarded a 2:1 or first class honours degree (Codiroli Mcmaster, 2020); over 40% of Muslim students feeling unable to use their student voice (National Union of Students, 2018); and implications on how Muslim students feel a sense of belonging (Universities UK, 2021). Despite this evidencing how religion can and does affect students' engagement, participation and outcomes, we are currently doing little to acknowledge and respond to this emerging 'Muslim degree-awarding gap' (Gholami, 2021) and the wider integration of religious students in student experience-related activities. For example, it was only in 2021 that the University of Winchester's (UK) Student Advisory Council (a student representation consultative body to the Executive Leadership Team) approved a post for a 'religiously minoritised' student representative. There is another conversation to be had if similar positions are apparent and available in other universities. Therefore, to what extent do student representation systems reflect the wider student body (Bols, 2017)?

Limited available research suggests that when interfaith cooperation and religious diversity training is promoted, Muslim students are less likely to perceive their university environments as hostile, suggesting that institutional change meaningfully impacts this experience (Cole, Ahmadi and Sanchez, 2020). Opportunities such as student–staff partnership enhancement or research projects which focus on Muslim experiences are one way of allowing students to produce counter-hegemonic narratives that view Muslims as 'disengaged' (Afran, Bibi and Seal, 2016), allowing Muslim students to be active change agents to improving social and academic experiences. Exemplifying this are student-led projects, including a University of Leeds (UK) student experience research placement project investigating faith and its impact on student success (Abdulmula, 2021) and institutional policy recommendations to promote equitable university experiences for Muslim students at King's College London (UK) and Newman University (UK) (Yafai, Khan and Anwar, 2015; Shaffait, 2019).

Akin to the actions of students of colour, when provided with opportunity, resource and staffing support, Muslim students are also able to thrive and make positive social change transcending the university space. This includes the student-led Ramadan Tent Project that went international in its aims to encourage cross-community cohesion and understanding (SOAS, 2014), or how Muslim students at Syracuse University (USA) continued to provide religious and wellbeing support to their students during COVID-19 (Muslim Student Life, 2021). Further national and institutional precedence to supporting Muslim student experience (see Universities UK, 2021), sense of belonging and student voice (Islam, 2021a) can then only seek to improve equity aims, recognise the heterogeneity of students' experiences and lead to less alienating environments.

Turning transitions into transformations

This chapter demonstrates the positive transitions made to embed greater equity and inclusion within UK HE and its related student engagement initiatives. At a time where more universities demonstrate the 'institutional readiness' to commit to such issues (see Jones-Devitt et al., 2017), I offer recommendations to ensuring these transitions can result into the transformations we seek for racially and religiously diverse student bodies in an ever-evolving HE landscape. These are outlined below as; Define; Decolonise; and Defend.

Define

If umbrella terms such as 'student engagement' require clear definitions before embarking on student engagement-related projects (Lowe and El-Hakim, 2020), so too must terms such as 'diversity' and 'inclusivity' if they are to effectively redress sector-wide inequities. Despite these terms appearing as principles and values underpinning partnership working (see Healey et al., 2014; Varnham, 2017), they should not be employed as buzzwords when referenced in student engagement practices – particularly where it has been highlighted that these terms have not equally served all markers of diversity (e.g. religious students in HE) or the heterogeneity and intersectionality present within these groups (e.g. the acronym 'BAME' – Black, Asian and minority ethnic, diluting the experiences and oppressions encountered by South Asian Muslim students in HE).

Decolonise

Practices of decolonisation draw parallels to the ethos of student engagement. If decolonisation offers alternate ways of thinking about the world (i.e. away from Eurocentric and colonial perspectives) and diverse forms of praxis (Bhambra, Gebrial and Nişancıoğlu, 2018), it aligns to various student engagement practices that intentionally oppose the status quo (Guitman and Marquis, 2020). However, where power asymmetries have been identified in these practices (Felten et al., 2013), there is a fear that expansion of socially just learning and teaching and student engagement in educational development practices will continue to be concentrated at senior levels and with those in already privileged social locations who exercise performative allyship and passive anti-racism without actually crediting, empowering or authentically listening to the minoritised students (and staff) this work concerns.

In this context, partnership operates in the form of a two-person rowboat. If driven by marketised rather than moral imperatives, a privileged staff member can invite a minoritised student on board but does not provide them with an oar. With one oar doing all the steering, it can only go around in circles or aimlessly move away from its intended destination. Partnership, and by extension allyship (Mercer-Mapstone and Abbot, 2020b), requires the student to be given an oar in order to guide the rowboat hoping to reach its destination of equity.

When engaging with/for racially and religiously diverse students, practitioners should be encouraged to decolonise their own practice and utilise existing methodologies and theoretical perspectives which have served underrepresented and historically marginalised communities. This may include the use of Critical Race Theory to examine the pervasive, taken-for-granted nature that Whiteness (Rollock and Gillborn, 2011) or 'Christian privilege' (Ahmadi, Cole and Lee, 2020) hold within student representation mechanisms, or using Participatory Action Research to empower students of colour to be change agents at *all* levels of engagement (Rodríguez and Brown, 2009). Importantly, when we invite students into doing equity work, measures must be taken to ensure they are safeguarded as it is inevitable that difficulties will be encountered when operating in largely White, secular spaces. Are staff partners themselves representative of diverse student bodies? Are they equipped to deal with the emotional labour and trauma encountered by student partners? We must reflect upon these critical avenues to not further compound existing inequalities – such considerations have implications for the way in which a student truly belongs in these partnerships (Islam and Valente, 2021).

Defend

Finally, where certain governmental and institutional rhetoric has attempted to disregard decolonialisation efforts or downplay the importance of issues related to race and religion in HE, there must be a collective resistance to subvert such narratives. Following BLM in 2020, racially minoritised students have been given a larger platform to speak and have their experiences heard and validated; the same must apply for religious students. Not opening our spaces to these rarely privileged voices has resulted in an indifference we have shown to our diverse student bodies and the climates we ask them to learn in. This inhibits our ability to create a 'sticky campus' for all, implicitly suggesting to minoritised groups that their ideas for change are invalid, with repercussions for the way in which they are inclined to engage and made to feel they belong (Shalabi, 2014). For staunch student engagement practitioners, continue to defend the necessity of resources being put into this work; to diversify institutional committees, structures, representation mechanisms; and enact policies that speak to the needs of racially and religiously diverse students – we (the oppressed) have fought for this for too long, and we are tired.

Notes

1 The term 'racially minoritised' has been used as the author's preferred terminology to denote those belonging to Black, Asian and minority ethnic backgrounds. In using the term, the author emphasises how processes and structures have positioned these groups as a minority, but acknowledges the limitations and contentions drawn when using broad and collective language.
2 The Race Equality Charter mark is a voluntary national scheme which recognises universities' efforts to improve representation in, success from and progression within UK Higher Education specifically for Black, Asian and minority ethnic students and staff.
3 Edited by K. Sum, S. Walker and S. Knight. Available at: https://journals.studentengagement. org.uk/index.php/studentchangeagents/issue/view/75

References

Abdulmula, H., 2021. *Faith and Student Success*. University of Leeds. Available at: https:// teachingexcellence.leeds.ac.uk/research/student-success-and-belonging-research-group/ student-research-experience-placements/project-faith-and-student-success/ (accessed: 24 December 2021).

Adey, L., 2021. *Is Uni Racist? Black and Ethnic Minority Students Allege Mishandling of Racism Complaints*. BBC Three. Available at: www.bbc.co.uk/bbcthree/article/ 1c314b3c-c895-4566-9b92-d9d3a1acb079 (accessed: 20 September 2021).

Advance HE, 2021. *Black Lives Matter and the Student Voice*. Available at: www.advance-he. ac.uk/knowledge-hub/black-lives-matter-and-student-voice (accessed: 3 July 2021).

Advance HE, 2020a. *Equality in Higher Education: Statistical Report 2020*. Available at: www.advance-he.ac.uk/knowledge-hub/equality-higher-education-statistical-report-2020 (accessed: 23 May 2021).

Advance HE, 2020b. *We Stand United Against Racism*. Available at: www.advance-he.ac. uk/we-stand-united-against-racism#declaration (accessed: 20 September 2021).

Advance HE, 2018. *Religion and Belief: Supporting Inclusion of Staff and Students in Higher Education and Colleges*. Available at: www.advance-he.ac.uk/knowledge-hub/ religion-and-belief-supporting-inclusion-staff-and-students-higher-education-and (accessed: 24 December 2020).

Afran, A., Bibi, A. and Seal, M., 2016. *Islam, Participation and Public Life in Birmingham, Newman Student–Staff Partnership*. Available at: https://newmanssp.wordpress. com/2016/07/12/scp-1-islam-participation-and-public-life-in-birmingham/ (accessed: 26 September 2021).

Ahmadi, S., Cole, D. and Lee, B., 2020. Engaging religious minority students. In: Quaye, S.J., Harper, S.R., and Pendakur, S.L. (eds) *Student Engagement in Higher Education: Theoretical Perspectives and Practical Approaches for Diverse Populations* (3rd edn). New York: Routledge.

Anthony-Okeke, A., Baddoo, H., Boardman, H., Fynn-Famodun, R.A., George, R., Anne Irorere, O., Osoba, R., Oweh, K., Paul, G. and Vanderpuye, V., 2021. Reforming a United Kingdom school of pharmacy to promote racial inclusion via a student–staff partnership project. *Journal of Educational Innovation, Partnership and Change2*, 7(1). https://journa ls.studentengagement.org.uk/index.php/studentchangeagents/article/view/1029

Atherton, G. and Mazhari, T., 2018. *Preparing for Hyper-Diversity: London's Student Population in 2030*. Available at: www.accesshe.ac.uk/resources/publications-research-rep orts/ (accessed: 23 December 2021).

Aune, K. and Stevenson, J., 2017. *Religion and Higher Education in Europe and North America*. Abingdon: Routledge.

Barefoot, H.C., Ghann, N., St John, J. and Yip, A., 2019. How did the work impact me? Reflections of the researchers and facilitators of BME success projects. *Compass: Journal of Learning and Teaching*, 12(1). https://doi.org/10.21100/compass.v12i1.937

Batty, D., 2020. Only a fifth of UK universities say they are 'decolonising' curriculum. *The Guardian*. Available at: www.theguardian.com/us-news/2020/jun/11/only-fifth-of-uk-universities-have-said-they-will-decolonise-curriculum (accessed: 20 September 2021).

Bhambra, G.K., Gebrial, D. and Nişancıoğlu, K., 2018. *Decolonising the University*. London: Pluto Press.

Bols, A.T.G., 2017. Enhancing student representation. *The Journal of Educational Innovation, Partnership and Change*, 3(1), p.81. doi:10.21100/jeipc.v3i1.585.

Broecke, S. and Nicholls, T., 2007. *Ethnicity and Degree Attainment*. Research Report No. RW92. Available at: https://dera.ioe.ac.uk/6846/1/RW92.pdf (accessed: 21 June 2020).

Cates, R.M., Madigan, M.R. and Reitenauer, V.L., 2018. "Locations of possibility": Critical perspectives on partnership. *International Journal for Students as Partners*, 2(1), pp.33–46. doi:10.15173/ijsap.v2i1.3341.

Chen, B., Tabassum, H. and Saeed, M.A., 2019. International Muslim students: Challenges and practical suggestions to accommodate their needs on campus. *Journal of International Students*, 9(4), pp.933–953. doi:10.32674/jis.v9i3.753.

Codiroli Mcmaster, N., 2021. *Ethnicity Awarding Gaps in UK Higher Education in 2019/ 20*. Available at: www.advance-he.ac.uk/knowledge-hub/ethnicity-awarding-gaps-uk-higher-education-201920 (accessed: 11 December 2021).

Codiroli Mcmaster, N., 2020. *Research Insight: Religion and Belief in UK Higher Education*. Available at: www.advance-he.ac.uk/knowledge-hub/research-insight-religion-and-belief-uk-higher-education (accessed: 31 March 2020).

Cole, D., Ahmadi, S. and Sanchez, M.E., 2020. Examining Muslim student experiences with campus insensitivity, coercion, and negative interworldview engagement. *Journal of College and Character*, 21(4), pp.301–314. doi:10.1080/2194587X.2020.1822880.

Commission on Race and Ethnic Disparities, 2021. *Commission on Race and Ethnic Disparities: The Report – March 2021*. Available at: www.gov.uk/government/publications/ the-report-of-the-commission-on-race-and-ethnic-disparities (accessed: 20 September 2021).

Dacosta, C., Dixon-Smith, S. and Singh, G., 2021. *Beyond BAME: Rethinking the Politics, Construction, Application, and Efficacy of Ethnic Categorisation – Stimulus Paper*. Available at: https://drive.google.com/file/d/1jb0k6kk1jv0jIC8ldePJatAcKNL1vrsU/view? usp=sharing (accessed: 3 July 2021).

Department for Education, 2021. *Higher Education: Free Speech and Academic Freedom*. Available at: www.gov.uk/official-documents (accessed: 3 July 2021).

Dickinson, J., 2022. Michelle Donelan fires a big new shot at the sector in the culture wars. Wonkhe. Available at: https://wonkhe.com/wonk-corner/michelle-donelan-fires-a-big-new-shot-at-the-sector-in-the-culture-wars/ (accessed: 27 July 2022).

Dunn, O., 2020. *UK Universities' Response to Black Lives Matter*. Available at: https:// halpinpartnership.com/debate/halpin-sector-report-uk-universities-response-blm (accessed: 20 September 2021).

Elzas, S., 2021. Academics under fire for studying race and racism in colour-blind France. RFI. Available at: www.rfi.fr/en/france/20210325-studying-race-and-racism-in-uni versalist-colour-blind-france-islamo-leftism-islamo-gauchisme-academia-paris (accessed 27 July 2022).

Equality and Human Rights Commission, 2019. *Tackling Racial Harassment: Universities Challenged*. Available at: www.equalityhumanrights.com/sites/default/files/tackling-racial-harassment-universities-challenged.pdf (accessed 27 July 2022).

Felten, P., 2020. Critically reflecting on identities, particularities and relationships in student engagement. In: Lowe, T. and El-Hakim, Y. (ed) *A Handbook for Student Engagement in Higher Education*. Abingdon: Routledge. https://doi.org/10.4324/ 9780429023033-13

Felten, P., Bagg, J., Bumbry, M., Hill, J., Hornsby, K., Pratt, M. and Weller, S., 2013. A call for expanding inclusive student engagement in SoTL. *Teaching and Learning Inquiry*, 1(2), pp.63–74. doi:10.20343/teachlearninqu.1.2.63.

Freire, P., 1997. *Pedagogy of the Heart*. New York: Continuum.

Galindo, C., 2021. Taking an equity lens: Reconceptualizing research on Latinx students' schooling experiences and educational outcomes. *The ANNALS of the American Academy of Political and Social Science*, 696(1), pp.106–127. https://doi.org/10.1177/00027162211043770

Gholami, R., 2021. Critical race theory and Islamophobia: Challenging inequity in higher education. *Race Ethnicity and Education*. doi:10.1080/13613324.2021.1879770.

Gillborn, D., 2008. *Racism and Education: Coincidence or Conspiracy?* Abingdon: Routledge.

Gore, J., Patfield, S., Fray, L., Holmes, K., Gruppetta, M., Llyod, A., Smith, M. and Heath, T., 2017. The participation of Australian Indigenous students in higher education: A scoping review of empirical research, 2000–2016. *The Australian Educational Researcher*, 44, pp.323–355. doi:10.1007/s13384-017-0236-9.

Greene, P., 2022. *Teacher Anti-CRT Bills Coast to Coast: A State By State Guide*. Forbes. Available at: www.forbes.com/sites/petergreene/2022/02/16/teacher-anti-crt-bills-coast-to-coast-a-state-by-state-guide/?sh=44db366d4ff6 (accessed: 27 July 2022).

Guitman, R. and Marquis, E., 2020. A Radical Practice? In: Mercer-Mapstone, L. and Abbot, S. (ed) *The Power of Partnership: Students, Staff, and Faculty Revolutionizing Higher Education*. Elon, NC: Centre for Engaged Learning. https://doi.org/10.36284/celelon.oa2

Healey, M., Flint, A. and Harrington, K., 2014. *Engagement through Partnership: Students as Partners in Learning and Teaching in Higher Education*. York: Advance HE. Available at: www.advance-he.ac.uk/knowledge-hub/engagement-through-partnership-students-partners-learning-and-teaching-higher (accessed: 25 April 2020).

Hill, E., Tifenthaler, C., Triebert, C., Jordan, D., Willis, H. and Stein, R., 2020. How George Floyd was killed in police custody. *The New York Times*. Available at: www.nytimes.com/2020/05/31/us/george-floyd-investigation.html (accessed: 20 September 2021).

hooks, b., 1994. *Teaching to Transgress: Education as the Practice of Freedom*. New York: Routledge.

Hopkins, P., 2011. Towards critical geographies of the university campus: Understanding the contested experiences of Muslim students. *Transactions of the Institute of British Geographers*, 36(1), pp.157–169. www.jstor.org/stable/23020847

Hubble, S. and Bolton, P., 2021. *Support for Disabled Students in Higher Education in England, Number*. Available at: https://commonslibrary.parliament.uk/research-briefings/cbp-8716/ (accessed: 23 December 2021).

Islam, M., 2021a. *Building Belonging: Developing Religiously Inclusive Cultures for Muslim Students in Higher Education*. Available at: www.advance-he.ac.uk/knowledge-hub/building-belonging-developing-religiously-inclusive-cultures-muslim-students-higher (accessed: 24 December 2021).

Islam, M., 2021b. *Disaggregating the BAME Degree-Awarding Gap: Understanding and Exploring the 'Asian' Student Experience*. doi:10.13140/RG.2.2.19843.63525.

Islam, M. and Valente, I., 2021. A critical dialogue reflecting on the potentials of black, Asian and minority ethnic student–staff partnerships. *Journal of Educational Innovation, Partnership and Change*, 7(1). doi:10.21100/JEIPC.V7I1.1037.

Islam, M., Burnett, T.-L. and Collins, S.-L., 2021. Trilateral partnership: An institution and students' union collaborative partnership project to support underrepresented student groups. *International Journal for Students as Partners*, 5(1), pp.76–85. doi:10.15173/ijsap.v5i1.4455.

Jones-Devitt, S., Austen, L., Chitwood, L, Donnelly, A., Feam, C., Heaton, C., Latham, G., LeBihan, J., Middleton, A., Morgan, M., Parking, H.J. and Pickering, N., 2017.

Creation and confidence: BME students as academic partners... but where were the staff? *Journal of Educational Innovation, Partnership and Change*, 3(1), pp.278–285. http://dx.doi.org/10.21100/jeipc.v3i1.580

Kezar, A., 2008. Understanding leadership strategies for addressing the politics of diversity. *The Journal of Higher Education*, 79(4), pp.406–441. doi:10.1080/00221546.2008.11772109.

Kyriacou, C., Reed, B.S., Said, F. and Davies, I., 2017. British Muslim university students' perceptions of Prevent and its impact on their sense of identity. *Education, Citizenship and Social Justice*, 12(2), pp.97–110. doi:10.1177/1746197916688918.

Liyange, M., 2020. *Miseducation: Decolonising Curricula, Culture and Pedagogy in UK Universities*. Oxford: Higher Education Policy Institute. Available at: www.hepi.ac.uk/wp-content/uploads/2020/07/HEPI_Miseducation_Debate-Paper-23_FINAL.pdf (accessed: 27 July 2022).

Lorde, A., 1984. The Master's Tools Will Never Dismantle the Master's House. In *Sister Outsider: Essays and Speeches*. Berkeley, CA: Crossing Press. https://doi.org/10.1163/9781848881051_028

Lowe, T. and El-Hakim, Y., 2020. An introduction to student engagement in higher education. In: Lowe, T. and El-Hakim, Y. (eds) *A Handbook for Student Engagement in Higher Education*. Abingdon: Routledge.

Mann, S.J., 2001. Alternative perspectives on the student experience: Alienation and engagement. *Studies in Higher Education*, 26(1), pp.7–19. doi:10.1080/03075070020030689.

Martens, S.E., Sprujit, A., Wolfhagen, I.H.A.P., Whittingham, J.R.D. and Dolmans, D.H.J.M., 2019. A students' take on student–staff partnerships: Experiences and preferences. *Assessment and Evaluation in Higher Education*, 44(6), pp.910–919. doi:10.1080/02602938.2018.1546374.

Mercer-Mapstone, L. and Abbot, S., 2020a. *The Power of Partnership: Students, Staff, and Faculty Revolutionizing Higher Education*. Elon, NC: Centre for Engaged Learning.

Mercer-Mapstone, L. and Abbot, S., 2020b. Things that make us go hmmm. In: Mercer-Mapstone, L. and Abbot, S. (eds) *The Power of Partnership: Students, Staff, and Faculty Revolutionizing Higher Education*. Elon, NC: Centre for Engaged Learning.

Mercer-Mapstone, L. and Bovill, C., 2019. Equity and diversity in institutional approaches to student–staff partnership schemes in higher education. *Studies in Higher Education*. doi:10.1080/03075079.2019.1620721.

Mercer-Mapstone, L., Islam, M. and Reid, T., 2019. Are we just engaging 'the usual suspects'? Challenges in and practical strategies for supporting equity and diversity in student–staff partnership initiatives. *Teaching in Higher Education*. doi:10.1080/13562517.2019.1655396.

Mohdin, A., 2021. UK universities are institutionally racist, says leading vice-chancellor. *The Guardian*. Available at: www.theguardian.com/education/2021/apr/28/uk-universities-are-institutionally-racist-says-leading-vice-chancellor (accessed: 20 September 2021).

Mohdin, A., Swann, G. and Bannock, C., 2020. How George Floyd's death sparked a wave of UK anti-racism protests. *The Guardian*. Available at: www.theguardian.com/uk-news/2020/jul/29/george-floyd-death-fuelled-anti-racism-protests-britain (accessed: 20 September 2021).

Moreau, M.-P., 2016. Regulating the student body/ies: University policies and student parents. *British Educational Research Journal*, 42(5), pp.906–925. doi:10.1002/berj.3234.

Mukwende, M., Tamony, P. and Turner, M., 2020. *Mind the Gap: A Handbook of Clinical Signs in Black and Brown Skin*. London: St. George's University of London. Available at: www.blackandbrownskin.co.uk/mindthegap (accessed: 14 November 2021).

Muslim Census, 2021. *Levelling Up Unequal Access to University Education, Muslim Census*. Available at: https://muslimcensus.co.uk/unequal-access-to-university-education (accessed: 14 November 2021).

Muslim Student Life, 2021. *Muslim Student Life in the Changing World, Syracuse University*. Available at: https://surface.syr.edu/cgi/viewcontent.cgi?article=1004&con text=msl (accessed: 26 September 2021).

National Union of Students, 2018. *The Experience of Muslim Students in 2017–18*. Available at: www.nusconnect.org.uk/resources/the-experience-of-muslim-students-in-2017-18 (accessed: 25 January 2020).

National Union of Students, 2011. *Race for Equality: A Report on the Experiences of Black Students in Further and Higher Education*. Available at: www.nus.org.uk/en/news/ra ce-for-equality (accessed: 13 June 2020).

Neves, J. and Hewitt, R., 2021. *Student Academic Experience Survey 2021*. Available at: www. advance-he.ac.uk/knowledge-hub/student-academic-experience-survey-2021 (accessed: 3 July 2021).

Neves, J. and Hillman, N., 2017. *Student Academic Experience Survey 2017*. Available at: www.hepi.ac.uk/wp-content/uploads/2017/06/2017-Student-Academic-Experience-Survey-Final-Report.pdf (accessed: 23 December 2021).

Obear, K., 2012. Reflections on our practice as social justice educators: How far we have come, how far we need to go. *Journal of Critical Thought and Praxis*, 1(1), pp.30–52.

Office for National Statistics, 2020. *Why Have Black and South Asian People Been Hit Hardest by COVID-19?* Available at: www.ons.gov.uk/peoplepopulationandcomm unity/healthandsocialcare/conditionsanddiseases/articles/whyhaveblackandsouthasianp eoplebeenhithardestbycovid19/2020-12-14 (accessed: 20 September 2021).

Office for Students, 2020. *Supporting International Students*. Available at: www.officefor students.org.uk/publications/coronavirus-briefing-note-postgraduate-research-students/ (accessed: 20 September 2021).

Peters, J. and Mathias, L., 2018. Enacting student partnership as though we really mean it: Some Freirean principles for a pedagogy of partnership. *International Journal for Students as Partners*, 2(2), pp.53–70. doi:10.15173/ijsap.v2i2.3509.

Phoenix, A., Amesu, A., Naylor, I. and Zafar, K., 2020. Viewpoint: "When black lives matter all lives will matter" – a teacher and three students discuss the BLM movement. *London Review of Education*, 18(3), pp.519–523. doi:10.14324/LRE.18.3.14.

Quaye, S.J., 2005. Let us speak: Including students' voices in the public good of higher education. In: Kezar, A., Chambers, A.C. and Burkhadt, J.C. (eds) *Higher Education for the Public Good: Emerging Voices from a National Movement*. San Francisco, CA: Jossey-Bass.

Rodríguez, L.F. and Brown, T.M., 2009. From voice to agency: Guiding principles for participatory action research with youth. *New Directions for Youth Development*, 123, pp.19–34. doi:10.1002/yd.312.

Rollock, N. and Gillborn, D., 2011. *Critical Race Theory, British Educational Research Association Online Resource*. Available at: www.bera.ac.uk/publication/critical-race-theory-crt (accessed: 24 September 2020).

Sabri, D., 2017. Do religion and belief have a place in "the student experience"? in Aune, K. and Stevenson, J. (eds) *Religion and Higher Education in Europe and North America*. Abingdon: Routledge.

Sabri, D., 2011. What's wrong with "the student experience"? *Discourse*, 32(5), pp.657–667. doi:10.1080/01596306.2011.620750.

Shaffait, H., 2019. *Inclusivity at University – Muslim Student Experiences*. Available at: www.kcl.ac.uk/geography/assets/kcl-sspp-muslim-policy-report-digital-aw.pdf (accessed: 24 September 2020).

Shalabi, N., 2014. Toward inclusive understanding and practice of diversity: Directions for accommodating Muslim and other religious minoritized students on university campuses. *Journal of Critical Thought and Praxis*, 2(2). https://doi.org/10.31274/jctp-180810-19

Singh, G., 2020. *Supporting Black, Asian Minority Ethnic (BAME) Students during the COVID-19 Crisis*. Shades of Noir. Available at: https://shadesofnoir.org.uk/supporting-black-asian-minority-ethnic-bame-students-during-the-covid-19-crisis/ (accessed: 27 October 2020).

SOAS, 2014. *Award-Winning Student-Led Ramadan Tent Project Goes International*. Available at: www.soas.ac.uk/news/newsitem93700.html (accessed: 26 September 2021).

Stubley, P., 2021. Universities minister compares 'decolonisation' of history to 'Soviet Union-style' censorship. *The Independent*. Available at: www.independent.co.uk/news/education/education-news/history-curriculum-university-michelle-donelan-culture-war-b1808601.html (accessed: 20 September 2021).

The Sutton Trust, 2021. *Universities and Social Mobility: Summary Report*. Available at: www.suttontrust.com/our-research/universities-and-social-mobility (accessed: 23 December 2021).

Sykes, G., 2021. Dispelling the myth of the "traditional" university undergraduate student in the UK. In Brooks, R. and O'Shea, S. (eds) *Reimagining the Higher Education Student: Constructing and Contesting Identities*. Abingdon: Routledge. https://doi.org/10.4324/9780367854171-6

UK Parliament, 2020. *Black History Month, UK Parliament*. Available at: https://hansard.parliament.uk/commons/2020-10-20/debates/5B0E393E-8778-4973-B318-C17797DFBB22/BlackHistoryMonth (accessed: 20 September 2021).

Universities UK, 2021. *Tackling Islamophobia and Anti-Muslim Hatred: Practical Guidance for UK Universities*. Available at: www.universitiesuk.ac.uk/what-we-do/policy-and-research/publications/tackling-islamophobia-and-anti-muslim (accessed: 24 December 2021).

Universities UK, 2020. *Tackling Racial Harassment in Higher Education*. Available at: www.universitiesuk.ac.uk/what-we-do/policy-and-research/publications/tackling-racial-harassment-higher (accessed: 20 September 2021).

Universities UK and National Union of Students, 2019. *Black, Asian and Minority Ethnic Student Attainment at UK Universities: #ClosingTheGap*. Available at: www.universitiesuk.ac.uk/policy-and-analysis/reports/Documents/2019/bame-student-attainment-uk-universities-closing-the-gap.pdf (accessed: 20 January 2020).

Varnham, S., 2017. *Creating a National Framework for Student Partnership in University Decision-Making and Governance: Principles*. Available at: www.uts.edu.au/sites/default/files/article/downloads/toolkit%20291117.pdf pdf (accessed: 16 May 2021).

Xie, A., 2015. Chinese education and society toward a more equal admission? Access in the mass higher education era. *Chinese Education and Society*, 48(3), pp.157–162. doi:10.1080/10611932.2015.1095614.

Yafai, T., Khan, B. and Anwar, S., 2015. *Muslim Students Experiences in a Catholic University*. Available at: https://newmanssp.wordpress.com/2015/07/09/sap-9-muslim-students-experiences-in-a-catholic-university (accessed: 26 September 2021).

Chapter 6

Authentic leadership for student engagement

Harriet Dunbar-Morris

Introduction

This chapter will describe how, as Dean of Learning and Teaching at the University of Portsmouth (UK), I employ an authentic leadership approach, both to facilitate connected decision-making across the university to deliver an excellent student learning experience, and to promote, encourage and advocate student engagement. Through experience gained undertaking partnership-working with students on large-scale institutional change initiatives, I will set out, from my experience, some of the practical ways in which authentic leadership can, I feel, be instrumental in ensuring student engagement, and the sorts of challenges it can help to address. The examples which will be presented include how a university committee can be refocused to function as a student–staff research group, and how institutional change, such as curriculum revision, tackling awarding gaps, or the development of blended learning during the COVID-19 pandemic, can be implemented in partnership with students. The challenges that I feel authentic leadership helps me to address, and which are considered here, are those of amplifying and valuing the student voice, which advances student engagement, and of ensuring *whole team*-working to the benefit of student learning and students' experience of higher education (HE). This includes working with, and innovating around, issues which make people uncomfortable, and innovating and ensuring engagement in condensed timescales and when students are unavailable.

Authentic leadership

My leadership approach is described by Bill George as 'authentic leadership': "People of the highest integrity, [...] who have a deep sense of purpose and are true to their core values, who have the courage to build their companies to meet the needs of all their stakeholders" (George, 2003). In a university setting, as I explained when invited by the Students' Union Elected Officer at that time to give my 'Personal Reflections on Leadership' at her 'Women in Leadership' event, I believe there is room for 'authentic leaders', who are genuine, moral, character-based leaders; who put students at the heart of what they do, and clearly set out the expectations of providing a university education.

DOI: 10.4324/9781003271789-6

An authentic leader "objectively analyse[s] all relevant data before coming to a decision. Such leaders also solicit views that challenge their deeply held positions"; they are "especially interested in empowering their followers to make a difference" (Walumbwa et al., 2008).

An authentic leader, therefore, is ideally suited to ensuring and championing student engagement in educational development. This leadership approach means being clear about one's values, but also deliberately taking a step back to allow others the space to develop their voice, and the scope of projects, and then to enable both of these to be developed in genuine partnership.

My leadership, as Dean of Learning and Teaching, is concerned with keeping students and staff focused on what we are trying to achieve – together. The objective is to make a difference to students' experience of HE. Specifically, to enhance it: by working with people and data of all kinds, to understand what works, and what does not work so well, for students, and which then informs and shapes our joint endeavours to change things for the better for the students and their experience of HE. Absolutely key to this is ensuring the centrality and equality of the student voice, among the other voices in the room.

The elements which make up authentic leadership (self-awareness; balanced processing; relational transparency; internalised moral perspectives; see Figure 6.1 for the model), particularly the 'balanced processing of information', allow leaders to use the scientific method: observation; reason; experiment. In other words, gathering data, triangulating, understanding, and acting upon data, and importantly, for leaders with responsibility for teaching, learning and the student

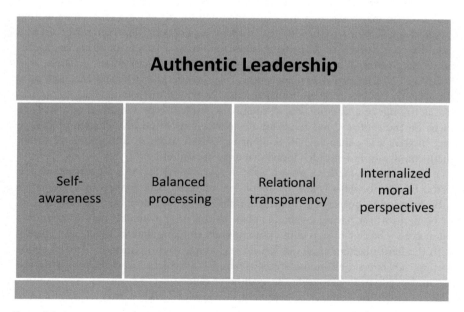

Figure 6.1 Authentic leadership attributes

experience, working with students as partners. Not only as the NUS advocate, but because in my view it is vital to invest "students with the power to co-create, not just knowledge or learning, but the higher education institution itself" (NUS, 2012, p.8). However, that is not as easy to achieve as it is to type and indeed hold as an ideal.

Student Experience Committee as a research group

One of the challenges we face in our institutions is to go beyond simply listening to students, and then telling them why we will not, or cannot, make changes; which means that students are likely to disengage from our feedback processes (Lowe and Bols, 2020). Student engagement happens when we actually value and act upon their views and opinions, about their course and about how the institution enables them to make the most of their time with us (Fletcher, 2017). Another challenge is amplifying the student voice in a formal setting, among other sometimes strident voices. It can be challenging to ensure that everyone acts as a singular team – working together to enhance the student experience.

As an example, in order to make full use of student-generated data sources, and to ensure that students perceived that their views and opinions were valued, I refocused a university committee that I chair to function as a student–staff research group.

This means in practice that our Student Experience Committee adopted a data-driven research approach (Dunbar-Morris, 2021b). Going beyond simply gathering student feedback, committee members employ it as a source of evidence which enables us to take a research-informed approach for developing and implementing practical applications to benefit the student experience. The committee takes a data-driven approach to identifying areas for focus: a variety of available institutional data (internal and external; quantitative and qualitative) are collated, analysed, and conclusions drawn each year, to prioritise and drive enhancements for the student experience in the forthcoming year(s). In my role as chair, my objective is to engage and empower all members (student representatives and staff) to focus on the *evidence*, and to adopt a role as agents of positive change in addressing matters and enhancing the student experience at an *institutional level*, rather than simply raising issues for individual areas to address.

I should say something about what I mean by data. Although perhaps it is better to describe what is not data here. For example, data as anecdotal evidence is subjective, often hearsay and usually unreliable. Instinct and, yes, experience too, or opinion, whilst having a valuable place in analysing evidence, may sometimes – often even – be out of step with contemporary thinking and attitudes, and at odds with the hard mathematical and logical reasoning, void of emotion – that I allude to here. Of course, all inputs are considered – all voices heard, but *hard data* is key and needs to sit alongside the qualitative data.

I call on all the committee members to consider a wide variety of data, and to draw conclusions based on the sum of all the data, whether it is their data or if it comes from other sources. I foster 'balanced processing of information' and encourage the data-driven approach which amplifies our continual enhancement methodology undertaken in partnership with students at Portsmouth (as described in models of HE quality management, see for example Brookes and Becket, 2007). I invite all members to present data and suggest enhancement projects. Ensuring that the student voice is amplified through the data sources, via the student representatives and their input, and in the co-created projects which ensue – this is, I believe, student engagement in action. The students are engaged as active members of the committee and the resulting projects; student data is key evidence, so students who give feedback are more likely to engage in the feedback process, because they feel that their views and opinions are *valued* and *acted upon*.

Thinking back to the challenges of ensuring student engagement through working together as one team, and the amplification of the student voice to ensure student engagement – as an authentic leader, I have designed the functioning of the committee to address these. All members of the committee are equal, including the chair and especially the student representatives, and we all have one objective: to enhance the student experience, for which we all bring data, all analyse, and all propose projects in which any of us may be involved. As an authentic leader, one allows oneself to be challenged by other people's views, and one allows and enables the data to do the talking. This is what happens in the Student Experience Committee. There is no top-down approach; the decisions are community-agreed, based upon evidence.

Regarding the challenge of students disengaging from our feedback processes if they do not feel it is taken seriously; I actively signal the value of the student voice by the importance I place on the student-generated data sources. I highlight the centrality and equality of the student voice in the central role held by student representatives in the consideration of the data and the action we take as a result.

Charrettes for co-creating solutions

Another challenge for student engagement is when we have to deal with addressing a 'difficult' issue. Perhaps that might be something which is difficult to understand, or it might be something which makes us or someone else feel uncomfortable. One such issue is the awarding gap between graduates of different ethnicities. Students have differing awarenesses of the awarding gap, and there is, or has been, some hesitancy about how to explain the gap and the data to students. Staff also have differing understandings of the gap and how to talk to students about it. As a leader I want, and indeed need, to be able to work in partnership with students and staff to come up with innovative solutions to address the issue, and as an authentic leader I have some tools that I can bring to bear which will help me to do that.

This brings me on to my second example of authentic leadership for student engagement – the use and further development of the 'Sandpit' model which had been developed to 'proof of concept' level by the University Alliance (UK) for use in innovative course design.[1] I have renamed it the 'Charrette' approach at Portsmouth – as Charrettes have long been used as collaborative workshop sessions which bring people together to rapidly design solutions to issues; notably in the 1970s in America related to the transition to racial integration in schools, and which was depicted in the 2019 film *Best of Enemies*. Charrettes are most often used in design and planning, but are frequently used in educational settings (Carlson et al., 2021). I employ Charrettes as a co-creation mechanism to enable students and staff to work together to develop projects and initiatives to address the awarding gap between students of different ethnicities by making changes in curricula or classrooms (Dunbar-Morris and Williams, 2021). Student and staff teams (where the staff are both from professional services and academics) are brought together to design a solution to a *challenge* (participants having undertaken some pre-reading and having understood the data in relation to the challenge).

In the first place it is important that the core values and moral perspective are unmistakeable for all. This is part of being an authentic leader, but it is absolutely key to addressing an issue which makes people feel uncomfortable, or unsure, or unwilling to engage. In the Charrette, the facilitators make it clear to student and staff attendees that we have an awarding gap (at the appropriate level at which the participants will be focusing, university, course, etc.) and that this is not acceptable. We also make it plain that this is not about a deficit on the part of students, and that we must examine what we do in our curricula and classrooms.

Secondly, everyone participating has to have a shared understanding of the issue being addressed. As an authentic leader my answer to this is 'balanced processing of information' – gathering relevant data and evidence that everyone digests before the Charrette. The student members of the Charrette could also input their own experience and perceptions of what actually happens in their courses and classrooms to the discussions. But, as above, they first of all have to feel comfortable that they will be listened to and that the issue and their experience are valid.

One of the other challenges, which some of the Students' Union Elected Officers have raised with me at different times over recent years, and which is particularly relevant to this example, is that they feel that in some situations they do not feel able to represent all of the student body.

So how does one implement the Charrette model in a university setting to actually make a difference to a student's experience?

Firstly, we ran a university-level Charrette which centred on ways to improve significantly the attainment of students with a particular focus on black students and males from the most deprived areas, as highlighted in our institutional-level data. The morning session included action planning for 'quick wins' that would be achievable by the end of our first Teaching Block. The afternoon session focused on more strategic planning for the following academic year or beyond. In all cases action plans are developed complete with evaluation plans for the proposed activities, enhancements or changes. The students and staff who took part in the first university-level Charrette could then become part of the 'ripple down' for

Charrettes at more local levels (faculty, department, course) with more specific and therefore bespoke solutions for subjects and students.

Charrettes have now been run at university, faculty and department levels. Examples of solutions which have been developed include assessment design, and elements of personal tutoring which were fed into the new Personal Tutoring and Development Framework which we launched in June 2020 (Dunbar-Morris, 2022). Work continues on the transition to HE and developing an ongoing sense of belonging which were longer-term actions and are some of our extended university-level projects.

The students who were invited to take part in the first Charrette were those who had expressed an interest in the area of the awarding gap and belonged to the then student network of black and minority ethnic (BAME) students. This was set up in partnership with the Students' Union Elected Officer (representative) at that time. In later Charrettes, more students from across the wider university were involved, and the BAME Ambassadors, later renamed PGM (people of the global majority) Ambassadors, took an active interest in certain faculties.

While the Elected Officers indicated that they do not feel they can represent all students, it was also important not to place an expectation on students from minoritised ethnicities that they were there to speak for a grouping of students, or to 'educate' staff or other students.

The active involvement of students who wish to participate is very important, and they need to have some understanding of the issues. However, learning can occur for both staff and students before and during the Charrette, and innovation comes from the open exchange of ideas from all participants.

The role of the authentic leader is to create a space where: co-creation can occur; solutions are based on evidence; and all voices are equal. No-one must feel that their view is not welcome, but there will always be a focus on developing community-agreed achievable solution(s). Similar to the challenge of consultation in the sector, not all ideas or views will be accepted for development, and there is a need for groups within the Charrette to be brought to that understanding. The authentic leader has a great deal of work to do during a Charrette to ensure true co-creation is being undertaken, and which results in realistic achievable changes. It is a challenge worth attempting though, because ensuring whole-team innovation on an issue, like the awarding gap, results in better solutions and better student, and indeed staff, engagement.

Student engagement in institutional change

As an institution we are very proud of our student partnership work. We have developed an approach to student engagement and co-creation that has proved successful in institutional change projects, where we actively champion the role of students as 'active collaborators' (Dunne in Foreword to Dunne and Zandstra, 2011, p.4), and work with them as active partners in their HE experience (see, for examples, Bovill and Felten, 2016; Healey et al., 2014), particularly when they are well-planned in advance and carried out in a fairly stable context with reasonable timescales.

We developed our Curriculum Framework and its annexes, including the Personal Tutoring and Development Framework, by implementing a model of co-creation in partnership with students (Dunbar-Morris et al., 2019). Similarly, we partnered with our students to develop our Blended and Connected approach to learning and teaching for the 2020/21 academic year in light of the COVID-19 pandemic (Armellini et al., 2022). Another project (Dunbar-Morris, 2021a) – to co-create a charter which staff and students felt they could 'sign up to' and to help students achieve the Hallmarks of the Portsmouth Graduate (a set of graduate attributes) – was developed using a co-creation workshop process which brought together a range of students, and deliberately drew upon those who do not engage with the Students' Union, academic staff, and professional services staff. As described in Dunbar-Morris et al. (2019) we have a long history of co-construction with students, having co-constructed our Education Strategy and Hallmarks before setting out to re-design our taught curricula. We made use of the Students' Union's strong and robust network to collect feedback from multiple sources at the start of the journey and throughout the process. We also included them in the formal project mechanisms such as the steering group and operational groups. Student voice data fed into the project at various points and we provided tools for course teams to work with students on changes that they were making.

In all of these co-created projects I worked to ensure that students were part of the vision-setting, decision-making, and the feedback processes, i.e. full student engagement. As a senior leader I am in a very fortunate position; I can insist that projects are set up with student representation, that data is sourced, and that consultation is carried out that places the student at the centre of what we are trying to do. All of my cross-institutional, large-scale projects have a lead Associate Dean and a Students' Union Elected Officer on the membership. Where possible I source students from the wider student body to join the groups, and if not, and in any case, I ensure that the Elected Officer facilitates the input of student views and opinions into the project.

Usually there is plenty of time to plan and organise these large-scale change projects and take the time to ensure good communication and consultation with all stakeholders. However, the development of an approach to learning and teaching during the COVID-19 pandemic was challenging. For everyone in the sector it was challenging to develop learning and teaching for the start of the academic year at a time when students were finishing their assessments and then absent over the summer. How do you engage students when they are not here? By which I mean how do you engage students both with learning and with the design of the learning approach? Yet, once again, I think authentic leadership did help, even if everything had to be carried out in a very compressed timescale and in a period when students were not readily accessible.

So how do you plan a rapid pivot to Blended and Connected Learning during a pandemic and ensure student engagement in the process? The challenge of course is to continue to ensure that students are involved in the vision-setting, decision-making, and feedback processes.

Like everywhere else I am sure, we set up a workstream structure with some clear objectives about what we wanted to achieve in some very short timescales. The Learning and Teaching Workstream (LTW) which I led, and its sub work-strands, had Students' Union staff and Elected Officer members. In the LTW we also set out to have a clear view of what we were trying to achieve, so we developed together the principles of our Blended and Connected (B&C) approach. While we could not take the time to consult widely on these, as we might have done in other projects, we did include in our principles the need for B&C learning to be staff and student partnership-centred. Meaning that the B&C learning and teaching would be co-created as time allowed and passed.

One key area of focus was to compel student engagement with learning, taking into consideration that they might be in a variety of different locations, at home, on campus, in halls, in private student housing. During the development of our B&C approach we kept in mind: "Good teaching is inextricably intertwined with good curriculum design, which is about planning and aligning what to teach, how to teach and how to assess so that students experience coherent learning" (Hunt and Chalmers, 2012); and "Pedagogy, curricula and assessment are designed and delivered to engage students in learning that is meaningful, relevant and accessible to all" (Hockings, 2010).

We adopted a pedagogically founded, technically supported approach to this, which saw staff prepare a range of resources for students to engage with, in a consistent, weekly template on the virtual learning environment, online, prior to face-to-face, interactive, sense-making sessions. Other workstrands were focused on how the developments needed to take account of the different groups of students, and create a sense of belonging, build resilience, and prepare students for a new experience. Staff and students developed online modules and resources to support students with online learning and to develop their resilience and wellbeing.

It is no surprise perhaps that one of the first things I asked the LTW to do, through one of its workstrands, was to triangulate existing data and evidence on what works. Then, we were able to ask academic staff to work with student voice data we already had, and good practice from our distance learning and digital offerings. Subsequently, working with the Students' Union, we set up a panel of students (drawn from across the university, mirroring the staff champion network we had in place as one of our workstrands) to call upon to discuss proposals, and to act as a sounding board. We also planned evaluation. We further developed a survey instrument that investigates students' sense of belonging and surveyed the student body several months after B&C learning had begun. Additionally, we planned to use existing course and module surveys which are designed to probe students' satisfaction with the learning experience and resources. In addition, the Students' Union worked with us to provide data through their surveys of students. Finally, I led a QAA-funded collaborative project with three other UK universities:

'Differing Perceptions of Quality of Learning', which provided quantitative and qualitative data on students' experience of B&C learning (Dunbar-Morris et al., 2021).

There might not have been as much time as usual to engage students in the early development of B&C learning, but as an institution we have continued with B&C learning, and the student voice has fed into the refining of it. One of the practical examples of that is our co-written paper with a student, which is based on analysis of student comments about B&C learning (Armellini et al., 2022). Therefore, in a real loop both for the student voice and for this chapter, we were well-placed to continue our scientific method approach about enhancing the student experience, and bring the data to the Student Experience Committee and thus carry on our continual enhancement.

Using the authentic leadership approach, i.e. focusing on data and evidence with a joint understanding of what we were trying to achieve, working in partnership with students and staff, albeit in different ways, and to compressed timescales, I believe the LTW was successful at producing full student engagement in the way it involved students in the vision-setting, decision-making and feedback processes. It was certainly a whole-team approach. Moreover, student feedback has shown that many students did engage very effectively with their learning as shown by quotes from students in the Differing Perceptions of Quality of Learning research (Dunbar-Morris et al., 2021):

> I liked the mixture of both online and face-to-face. The online saved time in terms of travel to and from university [which is] approx. 2 hours. However, the face-to-face was good for group discussions and having debates. After the pandemic and going forward, it would be beneficial to students and teachers to continue with both teaching methods.
>
> (Student survey response)

> Independent learning gives me time to reflect on the module, research and collate evidence that allows me to produce work for assessment. Without independent learning I would not have the necessary time to research or to recap on learning to make sure that I have fully understood the concept at hand. Independent learning allows me to explore in detail the subjects that are being taught.
>
> (Student, ethnic background not known, Health Sciences, focus group)

Concluding comments

I think of my role as a champion for student learning and students' experience of HE, so it is not surprising that I am an advocate for student engagement, co-creation, and partnership working. I am all too aware that this is not the case for all staff in any institution. However what authentic leadership provides is permission to say that this is important to me, and this is why I do what I do, and why I ask you to join with me to achieve certain things. It gives me a call to arms. It also allows me, for the benefit of student learning and student experience, to work in collaboration across boundaries, and to ignore those boundaries too. The key thing for me is that it enables me to do more than I could do on my own, because it enables community agreement on projects and community ownership and leadership of projects. The case is made for a project by research and evidence, a team coalesce around the objective, and then things really start to happen, and always it is with and for students.

Note

1 www.unialliance.ac.uk/2017/10/19/the-tea-sandpit

References

Armellini, A., Dunbar-Morris, H., Barlow, A. and Powell, D. 2022. Student engagement in blended and connected learning and teaching: A view from students. *Student Engagement in Higher Education Journal*, 4(2), pp.165–181.

Bovill, C. and Felten, P. 2016. Cultivating student–staff partnerships through research and practice. *International Journal for Academic Development*, 21(1). https://doi.org/10. 1080/1360144x.2016.1124965

Brookes, M. and Becket, N. 2007. Quality management in higher education: A review of international issues and practice. *The International Journal for Quality and Standards*, 1, pp.1–37.

Carlson, E.R., Craigo, L., Hoontis, P.P., Jaffe, E., McGee, L. and Sayegh, J., 2021. Creating a Charrette process to ignite the conversation on equity and inclusion. *Community College Journal of Research and Practice*, 45(8), pp.608–618. https://doi.org/ 10.1080/10668926.2020.1756534

Dunbar-Morris, H. 2021a. Co-creating a student charter. *Student Engagement in Higher Education Journal*, 3(2), pp.26–34.

Dunbar-Morris, H. 2021b. Using a committee as a student staff partnership research group to implement data-driven, research-informed practical applications to benefit the student experience. *Journal of Academic Development and Education*, 13, pp.65–74.

Dunbar-Morris, H., 2022. Developing an effective institutional personal tutoring and development framework to support student success. In: Lochtie, D., Stork, A. and Walker, B.W. (ed) *The Higher Education Personal Tutor's and Advisor's Companion*. St Albans: Critical Publishing.

Dunbar-Morris, H. and Williams, M., 2021. *Sandpits for BAME success*. AdvanceHE Annual Conference 2021, online.

Dunbar-Morris, H., Ali, M., Brindley, N., Farrell-Savage, K., Sharp, L., Sidiropoulou, M. P., Heard-Laureote, K., Lymath, D., Nawaz, R., Nerantzi, C., Prathap, V., Reeves, A., Speight, S., and Tomas, C. 2021. *Analysis of 2021 Differing Perceptions of Quality of Learning (Final Condensed Report)*. Quality Assurance Agency for Higher Education. Available at: https://sites.google.com/port.ac.uk/qaa-bame-enhancementproject?pli=1 (accessed: 3 January 2023).

Dunbar-Morris, H., Barlow, A. and Layer, A. 2019. A co-constructed curriculum: A model for implementing total institutional change in partnership with students. *Journal of*

Educational Innovation Partnership and Change, 5(1). https://doi.org/10.21100/jeipc.
v5i1.926

Dunne, E. and Zandstra, R., 2011. *Students as Change Agents – New Ways of Engaging with Learning and Teaching in Higher Education*. Available at: https://dera.ioe.ac.uk/14767 (accessed: 16 May 2021).

Fletcher, A.F., 2017. *Student Voice Revolution: The Meaningful Student Involvement Handbook.* CommonAction Publishing.

George, B., 2003. *Authentic Leadership Rediscovering the Secrets to Creating Lasting Value.* San Francisco, CA: Jossey-Bass.

Healey, M., Flint, A. and Harrington, K., 2014. *Engagement through Partnership: Students as Partners in Learning and Teaching in Higher Education.* York: HEA.

Hockings, C., 2010. *Inclusive Learning and Teaching in Higher Education: A Synthesis of Research.* Available at: www.advance-he.ac.uk/knowledge-hub/inclusive-learning-and-teaching-higher-education-synthesis-research (accessed: 16 May 2021).

Hunt, L. and Chalmers, D., 2012. *University Teaching in Focus.* Abingdon: Routledge.

Lowe, T. and Bols, A., 2020. Higher education institutions and policy makers: The future of student engagement. In: Lowe, T. and El-Hakim, Y. (eds) *A Handbook for Student Engagement in Higher Education.* Abingdon: Routledge. https://doi.org/10.4324/9780429023033-26

National Union of Students (NUS), 2012. *A Manifesto for Partnership.* Available at: www.nusconnect.org.uk/resources/a-manifesto-for-partnership (accessed: 16 May 2021).

Walumbwa, F.O., Avolio, B., Gardner W., Wernsing, T. and Peterson, S. 2008. Authentic leadership: Development and validation of a theory-based measure. *Journal of Management*, 34, 89–126. https://doi.org/10.1177/0149206307308913

Students as consumers

A barrier for student engagement?

Louise Taylor Bunce, Clare Rathbone and Naomi King

Introduction

The marketisation of higher education (HE) in several countries in the Global North, including England, the United States of America and Australia, has transformed students into consumers, and HE institutions (HEIs) into service providers. In this neoliberal model of HE, the cost of education has been transferred away from governments onto individual students, who are now protected by consumer law and sector regulations (e.g., the Office for Students in the UK). Although marketisation is intended to drive down tuition fee costs and improve teaching quality by increasing competition, the extent to which this has been achieved is debatable. For example in England, UK, in the first year that students were charged the full cost of tuition (2012), almost all HEIs charged the maximum fees (Bolton, 2018) (£9000, equivalent to approx. US$11,600 or €9,900). Furthermore, teaching quality is difficult to measure, and is typically assessed via student satisfaction or experience surveys which have questionable reliability and validity (Lenton, 2015). Many educators have expressed legitimate concerns about the impacts of marketisation, both on students' attitudes and behaviours relating to studying and educators' experiences of teaching (Jabbar et al., 2017; King and Bunce, 2020; Rolfe, 2002; Wong and Chiu, 2019). Students may be more likely to view their degree as a means to an end – with the end being a high-paying career – rather than as a process of intellectual growth and development. They may expect to be 'served' rather than challenged, and if they are not satisfied, this will reflect badly on HEIs in their feedback and evaluations of provision (Delucchi and Korgen, 2002). Consequently, some staff may feel pressured to engage in 'safe teaching' methods that involve simplistic assessment of pre-specified content, in order to reduce the risk of student complaints about challenging content and improve student satisfaction metrics (Naidoo and Jamieson, 2005, p.275).

The notion of students as consumers of their education has, once again, been in the spotlight during the pandemic caused by COVID-19. The pandemic led to campus closures in the UK in March 2020, and a switch to online learning and teaching which extended (to varying degrees depending on institution) into the academic years 2020–21 and 2021–22. Some students questioned whether they

DOI: 10.4324/9781003271789-7

were receiving value for money during this time, demanding tuition fee reductions and refunds owing to their inability to engage with physical campus services. When the UK government debated one such student petition[1] on this issue, they concluded that as long as the HEI was maintaining academic standards and delivering a high-quality education online, there was no cause for refunds. Understandably, students were frustrated by this decision, but it provides an example of students using their consumer voice and the potential power that this has in the sector (Bunce, 2019; Lygo-Baker et al., 2019).

What is a student 'consumer'?

The characteristics associated with students acting as 'consumers' of their education have been described by Saunders, and subsequently measured in his Customer Orientation Scale (2015). Saunders argued that student consumers may feel a sense of entitlement, for example feeling entitled to receive a degree because they are paying for it. They may also have a more passive approach to learning, believing that it is their lecturers' responsibility to make sure that they pass their course, and think that grades are more important than learning. They may also be more likely to view their degree primarily as a path to highly paid employment. The Customer Orientation Scale comprises 18 statements to which students rate their level of agreement on a 5-point scale, where 1 = agree strongly and 5 = disagree strongly, e.g., 'If I'm paying for my college education, I'm entitled to a degree', 'I only want to learn things in my courses that will help me in my future career', and 'The main purpose of my college education should be maximising my ability to earn money'. Saunders (2015) gave the scale to more than 2,500 students at a university in the Northeast of the United States of America, during the summer before their course began. He found that the mean consumer score was 3.32 (SD = 0.64), and almost one-third (29%) of students held some level of consumer orientation, although a strong consumer orientation was only seen in 9% of students. As these students were assessed at the start of their course, we do not know to what extent levels of consumer orientation may have changed during their time studying. However, a study using an adapted version of this scale for students studying in England, UK, with students across all years, found a similar mean score of 3.47 (SD = 0.85) (reversed here for equivalency) (Bunce et al., 2017). That study also examined whether there were differences in consumer orientation across year of study, and did not find any difference (they compared first year students with students combined across other years). Thus, it seems that in both studies, a significant minority of students were willing to express attitudes and beliefs that are commensurate with behaving like a consumer of their education (see also Finney and Finney, 2010; Haywood et al., 2011; Nixon et al., 2011; Tomlinson, 2014, 2017; White, 2007).

Impact of students identifying as consumers on engagement

While it is right that students should expect to receive a high-quality education in exchange for their tuition fees, behaving as consumers will not necessarily enable them to develop critical skills that they will need as graduates. Students who identify as consumers display a range of attitudes and behaviours that are not conducive to learning (Bunce and Bennett, 2021; King and Bunce, 2020) or achieving higher grades (Bunce et al., 2017). For example, Bunce et al. (2017) found a negative correlation between consumer orientation and academic performance. To explore further the impact of a consumer orientation on learning engagement, Bunce et al. (2017) developed a 20-item scale of learner identity, designed to assess attitudes and behaviours associated with intellectual engagement and approaches to studying. Students responded to statements on a 7-point scale, where 0 = strongly disagree and 6 = strongly agree, e.g., 'I want to expand my intellectual ability' and 'I think of myself as being at university to learn'. The study also measured academic performance by asking students to report their most recent mark for an assessed piece of work. The mean learner identity score was quite high at 4.77 (SD = 0.61), whereas the consumer score was substantially lower at 2.53 (SD = 0.85). This means that, on average, students tended to have a reasonably strong learner identity, which positively correlated with academic performance, and a weak consumer identity, which negatively correlated with academic performance. Bunce et al. (2017) then examined the mediating impact of a consumer identity on the relation between learner identity and academic performance. They found that a consumer identity negatively impacted the relation between a learner identity and academic performance, whereby a weaker learner identity was associated with lower academic performance, in part because it was associated with a stronger consumer identity. The authors suggested that a learner identity may 'compete' with a consumer identity; for example, where consumer identity is strong, the impact of a strong learner identity on academic performance may be reduced.

In a follow-up study, Bunce and Bennett (2021) further explored the potential impact of a consumer orientation on engagement with learning. They reasoned that student consumers may be more likely to engage with their studies in a superficial way, that is, by adopting a surface approach to learning, which is characterised by shallow processing of material with a focus on knowledge reproduction rather than understanding. In contrast, they may be less likely to adopt a deep approach to learning, which involves an active intention to draw meaning and understanding from material and to engage with it critically (Marton and Säljö, 1976). This reasoning was supported by data from almost 600 students, showing that a stronger consumer orientation was associated with more surface and less deep approaches to learning, which was associated with lower academic performance (see also Bliuc et al., 2011).

Thus far, this chapter has considered the extent to which students identify as consumers and the potential impact on engagement in terms of students' learner identities, approaches to learning and academic performance. While these studies tell us about the *average* student, they do not, however, tell us much about any one individual student. To find out more about individual students in terms of the relative strengths of learner and consumer identities, we take another look at some data from our most recent survey (as published in Bunce and Bennett, 2021). Looking at individuals can tell us about the types of students at HEIs as categorised in terms of whether they have 1) weak or strong learner identities, and 2) weak or strong consumer identities. The two identity dimensions, alongside their strength (strong or weak) can combine to create four 'types' of student, e.g., one type would have a strong learner identity and a strong consumer identity (referred to here as the Striver). We will present the numbers of each type of student from our data, before exploring the demographic and psychological characteristics of students within each of the four types that may impact engagement. A description and summary of the four types of student can be seen in Table 7.1.

For this chapter, we analysed data from 780 students studying at HEIs in England, UK, as collected by Bunce and Bennett (2021), to explore the numbers of students within each of these four categories. We considered a weak identity to be below the scale mid-point (<3.00, where 1 = strongly disagree and 5 = strongly agree), and a strong identity to be equal to or above the scale mid-point (≥3.00). As can be seen in Table 7.2, a sizeable minority of students had a strong consumer identity (340, 44%), although only 33 (4%) students also had a weak learner

Table 7.1 A description of the four types of student based on the strength of their learner and consumer identities.

		Learner Identity	
		Strong	Weak
Consumer Identity	Strong	**Strivers** enjoy studying but are focused on learning material perceived as relevant for a specific career	**Consumers** view their degree as a financial investment for a career and expect good grades for minimal effort
	Weak	**Thinkers** gain a deep level of satisfaction from studying and are not especially driven by career ambitions	**Undecided** students are not particularly engaged with learning and may be uncertain about the value of their chosen subject

Table 7.2 The number of students categorised as belonging to one of four student types based on the strength of their learner and consumer identities.

		Learner Identity		
		Strong	Weak	Total
Consumer Identity	Strong	Striver 307 (39%)	Consumer 33 (4%)	340 (44%)
	Weak	Thinker 411 (53%)	Undecided 29 (4%)	440 (56%)
	Total	718 (92%)	62 (8%)	780 (100%)

identity (Consumer), with the majority of them having a strong learner identity (Strivers) (307, 39%). The majority of individual students (411, 53%) were Thinkers, whereby they had a strong learner identity and a weak consumer identity. These data suggest that approximately half of our students are how we might traditionally define them – as Thinkers with strong learner identities – but that means that approximately half of our students are expressing other student types. Somewhat reassuringly, only a minority of students expressed a strong consumer identity and weak learner identity (Consumer).

What is intriguing is the rather large number of students (39%) who were Strivers – with strong learner identities as well as strong consumer identities. On the one hand, attitudes and beliefs associated with these two identities seem to be at odds with one another, for example simultaneously holding the views that 'I want to expand my intellectual ability' (learner) and 'For me, it is more important to get a good grade in a course than it is to learn the material' (consumer). This supports the idea that learner and consumer identities may compete (Bunce et al., 2017), creating internal conflict and being detrimental to learning. It also reflects the findings of Tomlinson's (2014, 2017) research, in which the majority of 68 UK undergraduate students participating in focus groups or interviews expressed mixed and ambivalent views towards the consumerism of HE. Tomlinson (2017) observed how tensions "emerged between adopting a more proactive level of engagement in the learning processes, where levels of personal investment are drawn upon, and more passive forms of consumerism during periods of relative disengagement" (p.460); he attributed this partly to a clash between students' own views of HE as an opportunity for learning and self-development, and their perceptions of being socially positioned as 'consumers' by HEIs, wider media and policy discourses.

On the other hand, however, learner statements such as 'I take notes during class' and 'I make good use of my study time' may not conflict with consumer statements such as 'I only want to learn things in my courses that will help me in my future career'. Strivers may have a strong motivation for learning as well as high career aspirations, which work together to promote proactive engagement. A study by Brooks et al. (2020) examined undergraduate students' views of the purpose of HE by analysing data from 295 students in 54 focus groups conducted across Denmark, England, Germany, Ireland, Poland and Spain. While the most common perception was that HE prepared them for the labour market, others frequently mentioned personal growth and enrichment (e.g., gaining new knowledge and/or developing new skills) and contributing to societal development and progress. This range of perceived purposes, which could align with students' own motivations and goals, does not seem incompatible; a student with ambitious aims for their career could, for example, also have high levels of engagement in learning due to a passion for their subject and a desire to develop strong skills for entering employment. In other words, while Strivers and Thinkers may differ in their aspirations (i.e., level of focus on future career), they may be similar in that they put in much effort and adopt deep approaches to learning (Marton and Säljö, 1976). To further understand characteristics of Strivers, and how these might affect engagement, we looked at some of the demographic and psychological characteristics of this group.

Before doing so, it is important to bear in mind a few caveats to this data. First, they were collected from a voluntary survey, thus they are unlikely to be wholly representative of the student population despite the large numbers involved. Second, it is likely that we found fewer students in the Consumer category than may be true in reality, because students with a strong consumer identity and weak learner identity may be less inclined to take part in a voluntary study that did not offer financial gain. Also, the number of students in the Undecided category may be lower than in reality because they may be experiencing a general lack of motivation to engage with voluntary research.

Characteristics of Strivers

To understand the potential impact of the student type Striver (strong learner and consumer identities) on engagement, we examined some of the characteristics that may differentiate them from other student types (using data collected by Bunce and Bennett, 2021). These characteristics include gender, age, ethnicity, year group, grade goal (i.e., desired grade, grade aspiration), academic attainment, approaches to learning (deep and surface), participation in their course as a student representative or similar, and course (dis)satisfaction, measured as the extent to which they complain about their course on a 1–5 scale (see Taylor Bunce et al., 2021).

First, there was no statistical difference between Strivers and other student types according to ethnicity, with a similar proportion of white students being categorised as Strivers compared with students from other ethnic groups. There was also no difference according to year group, with a similar proportion of students being categorised as Strivers in their first year versus students from other year groups (see Table 7.3). However, there were statistical differences on all other variables we looked at.

In terms of gender and age, there were more males (54%) and a higher proportion of mature students (26%) in the Striver category than in any other category. Another difference was in grade goal (measured as a 1st class goal versus other); 40% of Strivers had a first-class grade goal, which was more similar to Consumers (39%) than Thinkers (47%). In terms of self-reported level of academic attainment, Strivers reported slightly lower attainment than Thinkers, but higher attainment than Consumers and Undecided students (see Table 7.3).

To explore how engaged Strivers were in their learning, we looked at the extent to which they adopted deep and surface approaches to learning. Using the 20-item revised two-factor Study Process Questionnaire (Biggs et al., 2001), Strivers scored high on the deep approach to learning scale (3.74, min 1, max 5), which was a similar level to Thinkers (3.81) and significantly higher than Consumers and Undecided students (at 2.93 and 2.94 respectively). In terms of surface approach to learning, Strivers scored 2.79, which was significantly more than Thinkers (2.25) but significantly less than Consumers (3.35).

Table 7.3 The proportion (Gender, Age, Grade Goal, Course rep.), percentage (Attainment), or mean (and standard deviations) (Approaches to learning, Complaining) of each characteristic for the four different student types.

	Student Types			
	Strivers	Thinkers	Consumers	Undecided
* Gender: Male	54	31	39	45
* Age: Mature students	26	19	12	10
* Grade goal: 1st class	40	47	39	24
* Attainment	66.45 (12.30)	68.13 (9.06)	64.04 (10.64)	64.75 (10.03)
** Deep approach to learning	3.74 (.71)	3.81 (.72)	2.93 (.91)	2.94 (.81)
** Surface approach to learning	2.79 (.93)	2.25 (.95)	3.35 (.85)	3.19 (.81)
** Course representative	31	24	9	7
** Complaining	2.86 (.99)	2.48 (.89)	2.70 (.88)	2.59 (.95)

For the approaches to learning and complaining scales, the minimum score was 1 and the maximum score was 5. Attainment was out of 100. The association with student types / differences among student types were significant * p <.05, ** p <.001

In terms of course participation, a similar proportion of Strivers and Thinkers were engaged in extra-curricular roles within their HEI, namely that of a course representative (31% and 24% respectively), whereas only a small proportion of Consumers were course representatives (9%). Finally, we looked at the extent to which each type of student was (dis)satisfied with their course, as measured by the frequency with which they made complaints about it. Strivers appeared to be the least satisfied, with a higher frequency of complaining (2.86) (min 1, max 5), and this level of complaining was most similar to Consumers (2.70). In contrast, Thinkers complained significantly less than Strivers (2.48).

Conclusions and implications for pedagogic practice

In general, Strivers shared some important characteristics with Thinkers, notably, they were more likely to take a deep approach than a surface approach to learning, and they were more likely to be engaged in their course by being course representatives. However, they also shared some characteristics associated more strongly with Consumers, namely experiencing less satisfaction by making a higher frequency of complaints about their course, and they were somewhat less likely to have a 1st class grade goal than Thinkers. In terms of academic attainment, there was no significant difference between Strivers and Thinkers, or between Strivers and Consumers. Taken together, these data suggest that identifying as a consumer *to some extent* is not necessarily a barrier to engagement when this identity is accompanied by a strong identity as a learner.

Although these identities may create some tensions for these students some of the time (Bunce et al., 2017; Tomlinson, 2014, 2017), our data suggest that Strivers are, nonetheless, engaged in their learning and engaged in their course, for example by being course representatives. In contrast, students who have a strong consumer identity and a weak learner identity (Consumers) seem less engaged than Strivers: they are less likely to adopt a deep approach to learning, more likely to take a surface approach, and are unlikely to be course representatives. Although Strivers express a relatively high frequency of complaints, we might speculate that the motivation behind the complaints, and the nature of complaints, is qualitatively different to those of Consumers. For example, given that almost one-third of Strivers were course representatives, they may have communicated legitimate concerns based on their own and other students' experiences, rather than unreasonable discontent based on consumer-like expectations (e.g., 'I deserve a better grade because I'm paying tuition fees'). Future research might explore these issues.

Given the challenging nature of the current UK job market, it may even be the case that Strivers are better prepared than other student types for entering the workplace. According to a report by the Chartered Management Institute (2021), many UK employers believe that graduates lack crucial workplace skills (e.g., flexibility and adaptability, initiative and self-direction, digital skills), and many students feel unprepared for graduate employment. While Thinkers may flourish in an academic environment, it is possible that they are less capable than Strivers in terms of preparing for life beyond HE. It could be, for example, that Strivers have lower grade goals and slightly lower academic attainment than Thinkers because they engage more in career-related activities (e.g., work experience and professional networking).

Ultimately, as educators, our goal is to motivate and engage our students, albeit as Thinkers or Strivers, and to minimise the extent to which students identify solely as the Consumer type. To this end, we have developed a teaching resource, freely available at www.brookes.ac.uk/SIIP, which provides material to run a 90-minute workshop. In the workshop, students and educators collaborate to develop a shared social identity as members of their discipline, which research shows improves engagement and attainment (see e.g., Bliuc et al., 2011). First, students self-assess the strength of their identities as learners and consumers to establish their student type. Next, they learn about the research on the impacts of learner and consumer identities before engaging in discussions designed to build their social identities as student learners in their disciplines. Details of the workshop are described in Table 7.4.

Research behind developing a shared social identity

Haslam (2017), following Dewey (1916), argued that education is undeniably a form of group behaviour involving social processes, and that it "centres on the capacity for individuals to participate in self-development through more or less

Table 7.4 Key elements of the workshop with suggested format and timings.

Identities workshop for small groups

- Students complete self-assessment questionnaire ('Student profiler quiz') to establish strength of learner and consumer identities and discover their student 'type' (15 minutes)
- Educator presents PowerPoint slides provided, describing the four student types and the impacts of identities on learning (15 minutes)
- In break-out groups students engage with discussion questions (35 minutes)
- Educator leads a plenary to co-create with students a summary of attitudes and behaviours that support learning, in order to create a shared social identity as an 'X student', where X = name of discipline (20 minutes)
- Students and educator complete relevant feedback form to evaluate their experience of the workshop (5 minutes)

constructive engagement with instructors and instructional systems" (pp.19–20). When people are encouraged to interact in ways that enhance their sense of shared social identity, this generally serves to increase their social engagement and subsequently their wellbeing and intellectual performance (Haslam, 2017). This social identity approach views learners not as isolated individuals, but as individuals who are influenced by others around them. It also suggests a role for educators in supporting (or challenging) identities that facilitate (or inhibit) learning and engagement. Educators have the capacity to do this by creating time and space in the learning environment to discuss and debate with students (Whannell and Whannell, 2015). With these issues in mind, the teaching resource was designed to enable students to develop a shared social identity as members of their discipline to enhance their engagement and academic success.

Initial feedback from the workshop has been positive, and it has already been adopted by several educators nationally. One student said: "It helps you understand yourself better, your motivations, and perhaps even help[s] explain why you do well or not that well in your course". So why not give it a try with your students? As educators we have a duty to nurture students' natural motivation for growth and development, and counteract the damaging narrative of students being solely consumers of their higher education.

Note

1 The petition was entitled "Require universities to partially refund tuition fees for 20/21 due to Covid-19", https://petition.parliament.uk/petitions/324762

References

Biggs, J., Kember, D. and Leung, D.Y., 2001. The revised two-factor study process questionnaire: R-SPQ-2F. *British Journal of Educational Psychology*, 71(1), pp.133–149. https://doi.org/10.1348/000709901158433

Bliuc, A.M., Ellis, R.A., Goodyear, P. and Hendres, D.M., 2011. The role of social identification as university student in learning: Relationships between students' social identity, approaches to learning, and academic achievement. *Educational Psychology*, 31(5), pp.559–574. https://doi.org/10.1080/01443410.2011.585948

Bolton, P., 2018. *Tuition Fee Statistics* (HC Briefing Paper 917). London: House of Commons. Available at: https://commonslibrary.parliament.uk/research-briefings/sn00917 (accessed: 12 January 2022).

Brooks, R., Gupta, A., Jayadeva, S. and Abrahams, J., 2020. Students' views about the purpose of higher education: A comparative analysis of six European countries. *Higher Education Research and Development*, 40(7), pp.1–14. https://doi.org/10.1080/07294360.2020.1830039

Bunce, L., 2019. The voice of the student as a 'consumer'. In: Lygo-Baker, S., Kinchin, I. M. and Winstone, N.E. (ed) *Engaging Student Voices in Higher Education: Diverse Perspectives and Expectations in Partnership*. Cham: Palgrave Macmillan. https://doi.org/10.1007/978-3-030-20824-0_4

Bunce, L. and Bennett, M., 2021. A degree of studying? Approaches to learning and academic performance among student 'consumers'. *Active Learning in Higher Education*, 22(3), pp.203–214. http://dx.doi.org/10.1177/1469787419860204

Bunce, L., Baird, A. and Jones, S.E., 2017. The student-as-consumer approach in higher education and its effects on academic performance. *Studies in Higher Education*, 42(11), pp.1958–1978. https://doi.org/10.1080/03075079.2015.1127908

Chartered Management Institute, 2021. *Work Ready Graduates: Building Employability Skills for a Hybrid World*. Available at: www.managers.org.uk/wp-content/uploads/2021/09/employability-skills-research_work-ready-graduates.pdf (accessed: 12 January 2022).

Delucchi, M., and Korgen, K., 2002. "We're the customer – we pay the tuition": Student consumerism among undergraduate sociology majors. *Teaching Sociology*, 30(1), pp.100–107. https://doi.org/10.2307/3211524

Dewey, J. 1916. *Democracy and Education: An Introduction to the Philosophy of Education*. New York: Macmillan.

Finney, T.G. and Finney, R.Z., 2010. Are students their universities' customers? An exploratory study. *Education + Training*, 52(4), pp.276–291. https://doi.org/10.1108/00400911011050954

Haslam, S.A., 2017. The social identity approach to education and learning: Identification, ideation, interaction, influence and ideology. In: Mavor, K.I., Platow, M.J. and Bizumic, B. (ed) *Self and Social Identity in Educational Contexts*. Abingdon: Routledge. https://doi.org/10.4324/9781315746913

Haywood, H., Jenkins, R. and Molesworth, M., 2011. A degree will make all your dreams come true: higher education as the management of consumer desires. In: Molesworth, M., Scullion, R. and Nixon, E. (ed) *The Marketisation of Higher Education and the Student as Consumer*. Abingdon: Routledge. https://doi.org/10.4324/9780203842829

Jabbar, A., Analoui, B., Kong, K. and Mirza, M., 2017. Consumerisation in UK higher education business schools: Higher fees, greater stress and debatable outcomes. *Higher Education*, 76(1), pp.85–100. https://doi.org/10.1007/s10734-017-0196-z

King, N. and Bunce, L., 2020. Academics' perceptions of students' motivation for learning and their own motivation for teaching in a marketized higher education context. *British Journal of Educational Psychology*, 90(3), pp.790–808. https://doi.org/10.1111/bjep.12332

Lenton, P., 2015. Determining student satisfaction: An economic analysis of the National Student Survey. *Economics of Education Review*, 47, pp.118–127. https://doi.org/10.1016/j.econedurev.2015.05.001

Lygo-Baker, S., Kinchin, I.M., and Winstone, N.E., 2019. *Engaging Student Voices in Higher Education: Diverse Perspectives and Expectations in Partnership*. Cham: Palgrave Macmillan.

Marton, F. and Säljö, R., 1976. On qualitative differences in learning: I – Outcome and process. *British Journal of Educational Psychology*, 46, pp.4–11. https://doi.org/10.1111/j.2044-8279.1976.tb02980.x

Naidoo, R. and Jamieson, I., 2005. Empowering participants or corroding learning? Towards a research agenda on the impact of student consumerism in higher education. *Journal of Education Policy*, 20(3), pp.267–281. https://doi.org/10.1080/02680930500108585

Nixon, E., Scullion, R. and Molesworth, M., 2011. How choice in higher education can create conservative learners. In: Molesworth, M., Scullion, R. and Nixon, E. (ed) *The Marketisation of Higher Education and the Student as Consumer*. Abingdon: Routledge. https://doi.org/10.4324/9780203842829

Rolfe, H., 2002. Students' demands and expectations in an age of reduced financial support: The perspectives of lecturers in four English universities. *Journal of Higher Education Policy and Management*, 24(2), pp.171–182. https://doi.org/10.1080/1360080022000013491

Saunders, D.B., 2015. They do not buy it: Exploring the extent to which entering first-year students view themselves as customers. *Journal of Marketing for Higher Education*, 25(5), pp.1–24. https://doi.org/10.1080/08841241.2014.969798

Taylor Bunce, L., Bennett, M. and Jones, S.E., 2021. *Complaining, Approaches to Learning, and Academic Achievement in Undergraduates: A Social Identity Approach*. Manuscript submitted for publication.

Tomlinson, M., 2017. Student perceptions of themselves as 'consumers' of higher education. *British Journal of Sociology of Education*, 38(4), pp.450–467. https://doi.org/10.1080/01425692.2015.1113856

Tomlinson, M., 2014. *Exploring the Impact of Policy Changes on Students' Attitudes and Approaches to Learning in Higher Education*. Available at: www.heacademy.ac.uk/system/files/resources/Exploring_the_impact_of_policy_changes_student_experience.pdf (accessed: 12 January 2022).

Whannell, R. and Whannell, P., 2015. Identity theory as a theoretical framework to understand attrition for university students in transition. *Student Success*, 6(2), pp.43–53. https://doi.org/10.5204/ssj.v6i2.286.

White, N.R., 2007. 'The customer is always right?' Student discourse about higher education in Australia. *Higher Education*, 54(4), pp.593–604. https://doi.org/10.1007/s10734-006-9012-x

Wong, B. and Chiu, Y.L.T., 2019. Let me entertain you: The ambivalent role of university lecturers as educators and performers. *Educational Review*, 71(2), pp.218–233. https://doi.org/10.1080/00131911.2017.1363718

Chapter 8

Accessibility to student engagement opportunities

A focus on 'hard-to-reach' universities

Cassie Violet Lowe and Tom Lowe

Introduction

Student engagement, in the context of practices which engage students outside the curriculum but within their roles as students in higher education, continues to spread across the sector as a means of best practice for student development and educational enhancement to create a more meaningful curriculum and supportive student experience. These practices include engaging students in: extra-curricular partnership or voice activities (Millard and Evans, 2021; Bols, 2020); student support and transition initiatives (Pownall, Harris and Blundell-Birtill, 2022); roles which enable students to develop professionally and/or personally (Tran, 2015); election of student representatives in various forms (McStravock, 2022). Case studies of practice and research in the growing field of student engagement and students as partners (Matthews and Dollinger, 2022; Healey and Healey, 2018; Dunne, 2016) have proliferated. In the period 2015–17, three United Kingdom (UK) universities were funded to explore the accessibility and impact of such opportunities with 16 collaborative partner universities from across the UK (Lowe and Dunne, 2017). A key component of the project sought to understand which students were engaging in these student engagement development opportunities and whether the demographic characteristics of the students participating in these initiatives reflected the wider university student body and their diversity at each institution (Sims, Luebsen and Guggiari-Peel, 2017). In this vein, the project was part of the wider international sector growth in working with students to enhance their educational experience and focus on understanding which students were engaging and, therefore, whose voices were being heard (Mercer-Mapstone and Bovill, 2020; O'Shea, 2018).

These questions led to examining more closely the characteristics of the students engaging in these opportunities in relation to the wider demographic diversity of the institution, in order to understand in what ways race, gender, class, sexuality, age and ability affect students' access to such opportunities. Importantly, the project sought to explore what interventions can be actioned to begin the process of dismantling barriers to engagement for a diversity of students, who often have an intersectional experience of many of these characteristics and can

DOI: 10.4324/9781003271789-8

face greater challenges to student engagement opportunities (Mercer-Mapstone, Islam, and Reid, 2021; Bindra et al., 2018). Aligned with movements in individual national governments, their public bodies and private businesses to increase accessibility, there is a need to ensure that initiatives undertaken to encourage wider voices into the enhancement process are open to scrutiny and critical reflection. These participation and representation opportunities, although founded upon values of equality and liberation (Healey, Flint and Harrington, 2014; NUS, 2012), must ensure that they are not unintentionally (at least where it cannot be avoided) creating barriers to certain demographic groups and that opportunities work towards greater accessibility, so that a greater diversity of voices may be heard. This chapter will discuss critically the major barriers to engagement and highlight some considerations for practitioners in improving the accessibility of student engagement in educational development activities, in order to support the development of student engagement initiatives at institutions worldwide.

The REACT Project (Realising Engagement through Active Culture Transformation), funded by the Higher Education Funding Council for England (HEFCE), sought to explore the relationship between student engagement, attainment and retention. Alongside this, it also aspired to understand more fully which students were less likely to engage and why. This was with particular reference to the notion of 'hard-to-reach' students and how they could be better engaged (Shaw et al., 2017). The term 'hard to reach' will be returned to in the concluding section. On this note, the project concluded: "If we are to resist a consumerist, transactional approach to Higher Education and work with students as partners then these opportunities cannot fall exclusively to the 'easy to reach' and that is a responsibility that must be addressed on an institutional scale" (Shaw et al., 2017, p.32). Furthermore, the project equally asserted:

> the right to choose your own level and form of engagement as a student should be protected. The responsibility of the institution is to offer inclusive practices, this implies better understanding of what motivates people to be engaged and strong communication in order to allow students to make informed choices to engage or not.
>
> (Shaw et al., 2017, p.33)

With this in mind, this chapter will explore a variety of potential barriers faced by students and offer some approaches – a by no means exhaustive stock – for how these might be addressed for the purposes of engaging students in extra- and co-curricular opportunities (such as the student voice and student partnership activities discussed in this edited collection). Extant are several studies exploring students' motivations to engage in higher education; these outline differing perspectives and approaches – from socio-cultural context to structural and psycho-social influences – which can be explored to develop student engagement both within and alongside the curriculum (Kahu, 2013). This chapter will make practical recommendations for colleagues, so that a greater diversity of students than at present may be able to make an informed choice about an achievable personal level of engagement in practices beyond the curriculum, in preference to a situation in which only the traditional, often time-rich and financially privileged, minority finds it easy or possible to engage.

Students – who are they?

University students are often indiscriminately stereotyped with no regard for their individuality or personal views: it is often the case, whether in committee meetings or in the public media, that students are too frequently misrepresented as one homogeneous mass, thinking or feeling alike and having the same values, contexts and needs; that they have a single voice. Such misguided generalisations create barriers to student engagement in all institutions. The student body is in fact hugely diverse and each individual in it passes through university with unique requirements and experiences. Though we happily accept that each of us is unlike everyone else, students are often thoughtlessly lumped together as if they all have the same past experiences, identical educational journeys and common ambitions. It is often assumed that all students devote most of their time, energy and thinking to their studies – this view in keeping with entrenched perceptions of the traditional university student: a scholar who can attend university full time and is utterly committed to personal education. However, most modern students do not fit this stereotype: many, at any given time, juggle multiple obligations (jobs, family, caring responsibilities, extra-curricular opportunities etc.) and along the way face substantial barriers of time and money.

Higher education professionals, for the most part, appreciate this diversity in the student body and recognise the individual student as a complex composition of personal past and present experiences, commitments and aspirations; as someone with a unique story and an individual set of life events that shapes personal time at university. Consequently, educators and engagers of students, if they are to be able to accommodate such a wide variety of needs, must be prepared to be adaptable and to create appropriately flexible opportunities for students to learn and develop. Sadly, educational initiatives and methods to engage students still tend to fall back on the assumption that if an opportunity is open to all students it must be accessible to all students; that they all have the opportunity to engage because anyone can apply (Lowe and Lowe, 2022). As Mercer-Mapstone and Bovill highlight, just because an opportunity is 'open to all' does not mean it's accessible to all (Mercer-Mapstone and Bovill, 2020). We must therefore discuss more fully what this means, exploring some of the key considerations for making a student engagement opportunity more accessible to the varied needs and individual responsibilities of the diverse student body. Student engagement has been shown to be important in many ways to students' experience and their development (Pereira, Vassil and Thompson, 2020; Lubicz-Nawrocka, 2018; Garwe, 2015) and we must continue to reflect on what has worked well, what has increased engagement or what has enabled students who have previously encountered barriers to engage. This chapter will explore how we might proceed with initiatives that will promote accessibility to engagement for students in all their diversity. It will explore barriers to engagement and methods for inclusion, as well as explore some of the ways practitioners can create more opportunities that are truly accessible to all.

Recognition of time

Those students managing paid employment alongside their university studies may find it impossible to access an extra-curricular activity with a strict schedule of contact time. Necessity may well dictate whether such students can channel their energies into anything that impinges on time already allocated to pursuing their studies and to working to support themselves – and sometimes families, too. These time and financial barriers to engagement means inequality and, inevitably, feelings of alienation. Depending on the nature of the activity (for examples, a research or peer-support scheme may differ from a sporting opportunity), one possible solution to this might be to explore supportive payment for the initiative, perhaps by hourly contracts or a bursary. Realistically, not all extra-curricular activities would qualify, but institutions do need to approach engagement holistically and attempt to address particular needs and provide at least some openings to those students whose circumstances result in unfortunate discrimination. Diversity in the opportunity offer portfolio would also help to remove possible barriers.

Engagement opportunities with financial recognition of time are often the positions for students to act as co-researchers (Marie, 2020; Lowe and Sims, 2020) or participate in quality assurance processes – for example as student reviewers or panel members (Lowe and Lowe, 2022) – or activities for developing employability skills (Moxey and Simpkin, 2021). Making opportunities accessible to more students by recognising individuals' time, contributions and effort and targeting financial support accordingly would be preferable to using payment as a blanket incentive. However, whilst this strategy might seem to be the key to enabling all students to participate (ignoring for a moment the obvious financial implications for the institution and assuming all student engagement initiatives could so function) – it is important to note that financial recognition for the opportunity may, ironically, create other barriers. For example, it is worth highlighting that not all payment schemes are accessible to certain international students, who may have visa restrictions; in the UK, there are also visa rules relating to student incomes/bursaries and what type of activity qualifies for this payment method. Furthermore, we should not lose sight of the inherent power structure created through a payment scheme, as students may consider themselves to be employees of the institution and feel an obligation to behave or use their voice in a certain way. This may be of concern if the opportunity is reliant on the honesty of the student's voice, in such cases as student academic/course representatives or students working as partners in a project or research initiative (LeBihan, Lowe, Marie, 2018). Bursary schemes may go some way towards dealing with this issue, as students can be made aware that this does not mean that they are 'employed' per se, but are provided with financial support in recognition of their efforts. Yet once again it is important, for the purposes of this chapter, to draw attention to the fact that bursary schemes, though effective in some respects, can lead to a poor hourly rate, depending on the hours students are committing to an opportunity. For example, one student might take much longer than another to read and scrutinise the documentation for a quality assurance opportunity, even though each is being paid the same bursary. Whilst financial recognition can help some students to engage in opportunities and enable them to apportion their time to achieve participation, it is equally important to be mindful of how it may also alienate other students and change the working relationship with students. Individual institutions must therefore consider this option in line with their student demographic, the type of opportunity, their wider portfolio of opportunities and what can be done to mitigate the issues accompanying financial recognition.

The setting of the engagement – time, place, space

The mass move to online education during the COVID-19 pandemic brought with it many challenges, but also some opportunities to venture into previously unexplored modes of delivery, to test and make new discoveries about what works to enable greater – or more varied – participation. Staff across the sector, tasked with engaging students, faced this and boldly sought alternative routes for connecting with students, trying new technological solutions to achieve the aims of their initiatives and to ensure that students were still able to engage. Through these experimental modes of delivery for extra-curricular student engagement initiatives, many practitioners have discovered possible positive steps towards participation. Instead of an opportunity requiring a student to travel to attend a meeting in a physical location – with implications of cost and clash with personal responsibilities – the same student can attend the meeting virtually, or even asynchronously, in less time and with no outlay, so disposing of potential barriers to involvement. We can learn much from reflecting on these recent developments, as their very exploration of new territories of digital engagement challenges the ways of thinking of the status quo. We must therefore continue to question our current practice, rather than uncritically assume that it is our modes of engagement that need to be adapted. This is not to say that every initiative has to be moved online, but judicious appraisal of where the digital route could increase accessibility (i.e., physical location no longer vital) could be very helpful. You might run a session as a hybrid event or you could mix in-person and online events/meetings/sessions across the year.

To take this further, if there are physical in-person events associated with an extra-curricular opportunity, careful consideration of their nature and location could eliminate potential barriers to some students. For example, social or networking events that contain alcoholic beverages might alienate students who, for a host of reasons, might not be able to or might not want to attend (Islam, Lowe and Jones, 2018). Sensitive prior scrutiny and more thoughtful planning would allow for a variety of activities to cater for and so encourage attendance by a diversity of students: alcohol-free 'world cafés' for networking events would certainly help to address this barrier. The allocated room or space must also be physically accessible to all students and any materials provided must adhere to inclusivity guidelines, with neurodiversity in mind. Meticulous preparation will not ignore the possible risk to successful participation of the time designated for the occasion: students may well have conflicting caring, family, job or cultural responsibilities that require them to be off-campus and/or otherwise engaged. Avoidance of rigid scheduling of meetings and events at the same time or on the same day (such as evening activities only) and provision of alternative opportunities to engage would assist participation and include students whose absence would be a great loss to everyone involved. A training event or meeting during a weekday could be repeated one evening; digital solutions may also be possible, especially if sessions can be recorded. And if repeats within a week don't work, the strategy of varying days and times throughout the year could include those who might miss out. It is true, of course, that you may face scheduling conflicts outside your control (e.g., a team sport might need a specific location that has to be shared with other groups, with consequent restrictions to time); the coordinator of an activity might have personal responsibilities limiting availability. Overall, the setting of the engagement – the time, space and location – deserves the astute analysis of potential barriers to some students.

The perception of relevance – use of language

A factor influencing a student's interest in an engagement opportunity – if it isn't mandatory – and constituting a potential barrier to participation is often the language used to present the activity, which may determine whether the student deems it relevant to personal needs and desirable as an experience. The way something is described is powerfully related to which students engage, according to how useful they see it to be and to whether they feel they *can* engage. For example, an employability scheme advertised as having an application and interview process may immediately put some students off or suggest to them that they cannot engage without a well-written curriculum vitae and that they must have prior experience to apply. However, these are exactly the students whom the hypothetical initiative seeks to engage (those without experience who are looking to gain some and those hoping to understand how to write a strong application). The language of our communication is thus highly influential and merits our shrewd consideration of its likely effect. We might opt, say, for more informal expression or call the interview a 'recruitment fair', encouraging students to feel that it is something for all and not just for those who have already honed their employability skills and have well-crafted applications. Often it can be useful to highlight exactly what qualities students need to have to apply for a scheme, which can be as simple as asking for 'a willingness to learn and develop'.

To provide another example, the first author of this chapter was the lead editor for the student research journal and student–staff editorial board at a previous institution. The advertisement for students to apply to join the journal editorial panel presented the post as a developmental opportunity for anyone with an interest in the work of the journal (rather than just those with previous editorial experience); it made it clear that no prior experience was required and that a short expression of interest would be judged on enthusiasm for journal reviewing, the editorial process, publishing and giving constructive feedback to peers, as well as reading a wide variety of research in various subject areas across the institution. It would be enthusiasm and understanding of the journal itself that would guide the decision, rather than any previous experience as an editor. Having thus changed the language and given much more explicit information about the criteria for judgement, not to mention having adjusted the application process to an online Microsoft Form instead of a more formal email, we saw applications for the panel grow from 7 to 21 and then, this year, to 50.

To turn to consider the language used in student engagement opportunities more broadly, if an initiative is branded as 'making change' rather than enhancing or developing practice, it might seem intimidating or unusual to some students who perceive change as criticism and who may not be used to having their voices heard (Ahmadi, 2021). Another consideration might be the language relating to payment, as already mentioned, but framed here as affecting the perceived relevance of an opportunity. Higher-education-specific terminology, or jargon, is also a barrier, being language with which the student may not be familiar (Mann, 2001), and institutions are riddled with it – relating to processes, committees, documentation, titles and procedures, many of which draw from the ecclesiastical foundations of traditional European institutions. It is almost always completely foreign to students and is likely to alienate them from the moment they arrive. Therefore, as staff, although our own familiarity with these terms can make them seem clear and direct, we must empathise with our target audience of students and avoid alienating them with unnecessary confusion and complication in such adverts as these.

Using more direct and accessible language can break down such barriers and, further, using attractive language to market opportunities, such as outlining the impact students can have in the role, can widen participation. For example, describing an opportunity as one that 'scrutinises course documentation in line with quality assurance procedures for (re)validation' is likely not to be understood beyond experienced student academic representatives or elected student presidents and, therefore, may fail, in all its mystery, to attract; indeed, it is more likely to repel, so that students do not apply and their voices are never heard. Such jargon may make some students feel, being unfamiliar with university process and policies, that they would not be able to perform well in the role, when their very naivety about university procedures produces original, objective and hugely valuable critical insights to influence such significant effects as course innovations. Finally, our willingness to continue to review communication strategies – to ensure that they are effective and do not alienate some students through the channels employed – will have a beneficial effect on engagement.

Reflexively developing student engagement

The discussion in this chapter outlines several areas for practitioner reflection, so as to enhance the accessibility of student engagement initiatives. This chapter seeks to help coordinators identify previously unconsidered possible barriers to participation and offers some practical steps towards improving access. Key is to ensure that a diversity of students can be heard and participate in the range of opportunities – if they choose to, rather than having the decision made for them by what could have been avoidable barriers. This is not to suggest that every opportunity needs to be so flexible that the coordinator is running several events a week at multiple times in various settings and paying each attendee! Instead, it is to place all the targeted areas above in the context of a continuing effort to make student engagement opportunities accessible to the greatest number of students. Beyond increasing the reach of our opportunities, we have a moral obligation to ensure that all students may engage in extra-curricular activities that will benefit their development in many ways. We now outline further recommendations for those tasked with overcoming such barriers as we have discussed.

The cornerstone of any successful student engagement opportunity is a commitment to reflective practice. It is important that the initiative is under continuous critical evaluation to ensure it remains fit for purpose and accessible. One way this might be conducted is through working with a student to research and evaluate the initiative in partnership, to explore where improvements can be made (Lowe et al., 2017). Colleagues need not feel unsupported in undertaking evaluation or research into their initiatives, as there are many networks globally that focus on sharing best practice and helping fellow practitioners to overcome challenges, such as the RAISE Network,[1] SEDA,[2] Student Voice Australia[3] and ISSOTL.[4] Whilst the evaluative processes might at first appear onerous, once they become embedded in the annual cycle of a scheme, they become part of the culture and expectations. They shape a future-focused outlook and ensure that the development of the initiative is in line with student feedback. This research-informed reflection will yield better results for the student engagement opportunity in question, such as a greater diversity of students being able to engage and practice being continuously reviewed for its accessibility. This recommendation also does not prescribe how to undertake evaluation or opportunities to review practice; they need not always be through written means and can instead be conducted through facilitated conversations with students and with some informal activities built into the annual cycle. This could also be actioned through engaging students' voices in the early stages of planning new developments. Conducting critical reflection each year will allow schemes to evolve and progress to suit evolving higher education environments and changing student cohorts, so in turn supporting accessibility and a greater diversity of students each year.

As has been outlined above, there is not one approach to suit every student; neither is there one solution to the same scheme at every university, as institutions are also unique in their portfolios, size, student body and procedures. There is no one-size-fits-all approach to making student engagement initiatives accessible. Taking some of the approaches outlined in this chapter – and many of the other chapters in this edited collection – will start to catalyse the development of the student engagement opportunity in question and invite you to reflect critically on practice so that you can work towards a scheme that enables a greater diversity of participation. It might be that, alongside continuous review, you consider a more targeted approach to your practice to increase the access to a group of students, whose voices may be absent in the current initiative. It is the authors' hope that these strategies may offer some insight into understanding the barriers some students face and provide some practical steps forward to addressing them. Though structure often provides student engagement initiatives with clear boundaries and guidelines, it can also limit participation; so, where flexibility can be offered, it is worthwhile exploring how these moments of flexibility can be built into the cycle of events and activities. This can be through recording trainings, offering multiple sessions at various times, and promoting the opportunity in different ways to attract a variety of students.

A 'hard-to-reach' university: concluding thoughts

This chapter began by drawing upon the HEFCE-funded REACT project, which was tasked with exploring the so-called 'hard-to-reach' students in student engagement activities. This chapter has critically examined such activities and would therefore suggest that the term 'hard to reach' is better placed as a term associated with the university itself, as there are many barriers students might face to their participation, some of which are under the institution's control. When applied to students, the term suggests a rigid centrality of privileged staff, in a place where students must engage in traditional ways, rather than asking staff to rethink the practices of the university. It places the onus on the students when the barriers faced are too often under the university's control. What this chapter has made clear is that it is in fact not the students who are 'hard to reach', but, rather, that it is the university's initiatives that might be (often unintentionally) inaccessible for many reasons, as outlined above: 'hard-to-reach' universities, not 'hard-to-reach' students! The 'hard-to-reach university' as a perspective focuses the deficit on where the university should develop further, rather than suggesting it is the students who should be overcoming barriers to their engagement. It is with this realignment of the responsibility for access to engagement opportunities that the focus can be shifted to exploring and dismantling barriers, so that a greater diversity of students may engage in a greater variety of opportunities. This chapter offers many areas for reflection and suggests practical solutions, but the list is not exhaustive and there are in train further ways of developing student engagement initiatives, many of which are outlined in other chapters within this collection.

Higher education institutions are often known for their siloed thinking, lack of collaborative approaches to problem-solving, and a sense of privileged tradition. Without taking a critical and reflexive approach to understanding student engagement practices more holistically to explore barriers to access, they will continue to privilege the same students. Seidman emphasises that students will often only come to university education once in their lives and it is an educational route that they cannot simply retake like a driving test (Seidman, 2012). It is therefore the responsibility of a university to ensure that it remains focused on how to tackle barriers to participation, so that increasingly diverse students can all choose their level of engagement with the university's activities, rather than having this decision made for them by encountering barriers to their access.

Notes

1 Researching, Advancing and Inspiring Student Engagement (RAISE) Network: www.raise-network.com/
2 Staff Educational Developers Association (SEDA): www.seda.ac.uk/
3 Student Voice Australia: https://studentvoiceaustralia.com/
4 International Society for the Scholarship of Teaching and Learning (ISSOTL): https://issotl.com/

Reference

Ahmadi, R., 2021. Student voice, culture, and teacher power in curriculum co-design within higher education: An action-based research study. *International Journal for Academic Development.* https://doi.org/10.1080/1360144x.2021.1923502

Bindra, G., Easwaran, K., Firasta, L., Hirsch, M., Kapoor, A., Sosnowski, A., Stec-Marksman, T. and Vatansever, G., 2018. Increasing representation and equity in students as partners initiatives. *International Journal for Students as Partners*, 2(2), pp.10–15. https://doi.org/10.15173/ijsap.v2i2.3536

Bols, A., 2020. The changing nature and importance of student representation. In: Lowe, T. and El-Hakim, Y. (eds) *A Handbook for Student Engagement in Higher Education.* Abingdon: Routledge. https://doi.org/10.4324/9780429023033-6

Dunne, E., 2016. Design thinking: A framework for student engagement? A personal view. *Journal of Educational Innovation, Partnership and Change*, 2(1). http://dx.doi.org/10.21100/jeipc.v2i1.317

Garwe, E.C., 2015. Student voice and quality enhancement in higher education. *Journal of Applied Research in Higher Education*, 7(2), pp.385–399. https://doi.org/10.1108/jarhe-05-2014-0055

Healey, M. and Healey, R., 2018. 'It depends': Exploring the context-dependent nature of students as partners practices and policies. *International Journal for Students as Partners*, 2(1), pp.1–10.

Healey, M., Flint, A. and Harrington, K., 2014. *Engagement through Partnership: Students as Partners in Learning and Teaching in Higher Education.* York: Higher Education Academy. Available at: www.heacademy.ac.uk/system/files/resources/engagement_through_partnership.pdf (accessed: 16 May 2021).

Islam, M., Lowe, T. and Jones, G., 2018. A 'satisfied settling'? Investigating a sense of belonging for Muslim students in a UK small-medium Higher Education Institution. *Student Engagement in Higher Education Journal*, 2(2), pp.79–104.

Kahu, E.R., 2013. Framing student engagement in higher education. *Studies in Higher Education*, 38(5), pp.758–773. https://doi.org/10.1080/03075079.2011.598505

LeBihan, J., Lowe, T. and Marie, J., 2018. Considerations of the challenges, conflicts and competitions when expanding student–staff partnerships across an institution: Perspectives from three UK universities. *Journal of Learning and Teaching in Higher Education*, 1(2), pp.173–180. https://doi.org/10.29311/jlthe.v1i2.2954

Lowe, T. and Lowe, C., 2022. Perceptions of the challenges and effectiveness of students on internal quality assurance review panels: A study across higher education institutions. *All Ireland Journal of Higher Education*, 14(1). https://ojs.aishe.org/index.php/aishe-j/article/view/641

Lowe, C. and Sims, S., 2020. On the origin of Student Fellows: Reflections on the evolution of partnership from theory to practice. In: Lowe, T. and El-Hakim, Y. (eds) *A Handbook for Student Engagement in Higher Education*. Abingdon: Routledge. https://doi.org/10.4324/9780429023033-17

Lowe, T. 2019. The exclusive campus bubble: The best and worst feature of campus universities. In: Krčmář, K. (ed) *The Inclusivity Gap*. Inspired by Learning.

Lowe, T. and Dunne, E., 2017. Setting the scene for the REACT programme: Aims, challenges and the way ahead. *The Journal of Educational Innovation, Partnership and Change*, 3(1), pp.24–39. http://dx.doi.org/10.21100/jeipc.v3i1.678

Lowe, T., Shaw, C., Sims, S., King, S. and Paddison, A., 2017. The development of contemporary student engagement practices at the University of Winchester and Winchester Student Union. *International Journal for Students as Partners*, 1(1). https://doi.org/10.15173/ijsap.v1i1.3082

Lubicz-Nawrocka, T.M., 2018. Students as partners in learning and teaching: The benefits of co-creation of the curriculum. *International Journal for Students as Partners*, 2(1), pp.47–63.

Mann, S., 2001. Alternative perspectives on the student experience: Alienation and engagement. *Studies in Higher Education*, 26(1), pp.7–19. https://doi.org/10.1080/03075070020030689

Marie, J., 2020. Empowering students to enhance education at their university. In: Lowe, T. and El-Hakim, Y. (eds) *A Handbook for Student Engagement in Higher Education*. Abingdon: Routledge. https://doi.org/10.4324/9780429023033-19

Matthews, K.E. and Dollinger, M., 2022. Student voice in higher education: The importance of distinguishing student representation and student partnership. *Higher Education*. https://doi.org/10.1007/s10734-022-00851-7

McStravock, K., 2022. We cannot be who we cannot see – Exploring the extent to which Students' Union officers can be truly representative of an increasingly diverse student body. *All Ireland Journal of Higher Education*, 14(1). https://ojs.aishe.org/index.php/aishe-j/article/view/617

Mercer-Mapstone, L. and Bovill, C., 2020. Equity and diversity in institutional approaches to student–staff partnership schemes in higher education. *Studies in Higher Education*, 45(12), pp.2541–2557. https://doi.org/10.1080/03075079.2019.1620721

Mercer-Mapstone, L., Islam, M. and Reid, T., 2021. Are we just engaging 'the usual suspects'? Challenges in and practical strategies for supporting equity and diversity in student–staff partnership initiatives. *Teaching in Higher Education*, 26(2), pp.227–245. https://doi.org/10.1080/13562517.2019.1655396

Millard, L. and Evans, R., 2021. Listening for retention: Enabling student success through partnering with the student voice. In Shah, M., Kift, S. and Thomas, L. (eds) *Student Retention and Success in Higher Education*. Cham: Palgrave Macmillan. https://doi.org/10.1007/978-3-030-80045-1_8

Moxey, M. and Simpkin, E., 2021. Harnessing the potential of extracurricular opportunities to enhance graduate employability in higher education. *Journal of Learning Development in Higher Education*, 21. https://doi.org/10.47408/jldhe.vi21.631

National Union of Students (NUS), 2012. *A Manifesto for Partnership*. Available at: www.nusconnect.org.uk/resources/a-manifesto-for-partnership (accessed: 16 May 2021).

O'Shea, S., 2018. Equity and students as partners: The importance of inclusive relationships. *International Journal for Students as Partners*, 2(2), pp.16–20.

Pereira, J.V.B., Vassil, J.C. and Thompson, R.E., 2020. Students as partners in an Australian medical program: Impact on student partners and teachers. *International Journal for Students as Partners*, 4(2), pp.110–121.

Pownall, M., Harris, R. and Blundell-Birtill, P., 2022. Supporting students during the transition to university in COVID-19: Five key considerations and recommendations for educators. *Psychology Learning and Teaching*, 21(1), pp.3–18. https://doi.org/10.1177/14757257211032486

Seidman, A., 2012. *College Student Retention: Formula for Student Success* (ACE Series on Higher Education). Aberdeen: ACE.

Shaw, C., Humphrey, O., Atvars, T. and Sims, S., 2017. Who they are and how to engage them: A summary of the REACT systematic literature review of the 'hard to reach' in higher education. *The Journal of Educational Innovation, Partnership and Change*, 3(1), pp.51–64. http://dx.doi.org/10.21100/jeipc.v3i1.685

Sims, S., Luebsen, W. and Guggiari-Peel, C., 2017. Exploring the role of co-curricular student engagement in relation to student retention, attainment and improving inclusivity. *The Journal of Educational Innovation, Partnership and Change*, 3(1), pp.93–109. http://dx.doi.org/10.21100/jeipc.v3i1.605

Sims, S., King, S., Lowe, T. and El Hakim, Y., 2016. Evaluating partnership and impact in the first year of the Student Fellows Scheme. *Journal of Educational Innovation, Partnership and Change*, 2(1). http://dx.doi.org/10.21100/jeipc.v2i1.257

Sims, S., Lowe, T., Barnes, G. and Hutber, L., 2014. The Student Fellows Scheme: A partnership between the University of Winchester and Winchester Student Union. *Educational Developments*, 15(3), pp.7–10. Available at: www.seda.ac.uk/resources/files/publications_188_Ed%20Devs%2015.3%2OFINAL.pdf (accessed: 31 July 2022).

Tran, T.T., 2015. Is graduate employability the 'whole-of-higher-education-issue'? *Journal of Education and Work*, 28(3), pp.207–227. https://doi.org/10.1080/13639080.2014.900167

Chapter 9

How to engage students in your educational developments

A student leader's view

Talia Adams

Introduction

More than ever, the importance of student engagement in educational developments is encouraged as good practice in higher education. This is ensured in England by the requirement from overseeing bodies such as Office for Students (England's higher education regulator) to create high-value learning experiences and the accountability universities are held to by their students' unions. However, arguably the motivation for enhancing student engagement should stem from the positive outcomes of having strong student engagement, such as greater relationships between students and staff, and enhancements in learning and teaching (Bovill, 2020). With varying definitions and forms of student engagement in educational development present in our field, we must be careful to prioritise meaningful active student engagement to avoid tokenistic approaches. It is important to understand the different reasons why students may engage, before highlighting the ideal approaches to student engagement in educational developments. In this chapter, I will proceed to highlight several example activities whilst considering the limitations and recommendations for best practice.

Why do students engage in educational developments?

Firstly, it is important to understand why students engage in educational developments. Personality is one of the largest variables for why students may or may not engage with feeding back on educational developments (Zhang, Chen, and Xu, 2020). Conscientiousness has been identified as a significant personality trait in student engagement (Qureshi et al., 2016). Other factors include altruism, which is often a reason why students want to feedback and engage in developments as it will benefit others (John-Matthews et al., 2020). This means a varied approach to match varying students' personalities is needed to capture as many voices in educational developments as possible. Secondly, it is important to consider variance in students' availability. For example, many students are balancing a full-time degree, often part-time work and everything in-between, therefore time is valuable, so students need to know how feeding back is going to have impact

DOI: 10.4324/9781003271789-9

and often, how long activities will take. If it is not a monetary value or an instantaneous gain such as a freebie, which should not be underestimated, we must show students how their time spent feeding back is worthwhile. The National Student Survey[1] (UK) nationally highlights a lower score for students knowing how feedback is acted on which has been shown across the sector, therefore there is a need to show students the impact of student feedback. With the knowledge that their feedback is valuable due to visible positive change that benefits themselves and others we are more likely to draw on prosocial behaviour and feeding back will be more embedded. Another aspect when engaging students in educational developments to be mindful of is drawing on the same groups of students for the benefit of the project. For example, we must take care to reach out to underrepresented students to address the challenges universities need to unpick such as decolonising the curriculum. Giving students an opportunity to get involved to co-create important educational developments is different to targeting student groups as a 'tick-box' exercise to meet requirements of student consultation. In summary, when we approach engaging students in educational developments, our preliminary thoughts should be around engaging a range of students, supporting those who do engage and how we are going to exhibit to students their involvement makes a positive impact.

Student engagement practices

As a student representative and now as a student leader, I have observed more traditional in-person methods of student engagement in educational developments seeing both their strengths and weaknesses. Some of these methods were supported by digital mechanisms which can be beneficial in an increasingly digital world, but there are some cautions to be aware of. Increased use of digital methods were trialled through the COVID-19 pandemic and highlighted how these digital methods could help reach a wider range of students at a distance. Traditional methods usually rely on in-person, campus-based opportunistic approaches, such as feedback forums and/or student–staff committees, which only capture limited students who are present on campus. Looking ahead to a post-COVID-19 world, it is important to take the benefits of digital formats and partner this with traditional ideas to gain a breadth of student engagement, and not return to favouring on-campus-only activities. In the chapter ahead, I will be highlighting examples of ways students can be actively engaged in educational developments whilst referencing the challenges of each showing how a multi-faceted approach is usually optimal. I will also highlight the ways digital methods can be harnessed and explored in our more blended higher education. These digital methods allow us to meet individual differences and preferences more readily whilst being able to understand our students as individuals better than ever before. The approaches outlined will include those that students' unions may lead on, ones that would stem from university staff members and where together partnered practices can be used.

Student Representative Hubs

Students' unions are the hubs for collecting feedback and representing students. These forums are not exclusive to students' unions, however where possible institutions should support and elevate the work done by students' unions in driving student engagement. An example of gaining student feedback at Lincoln Students' Union is at 'Rep Hubs' (forums) where all our elected and recruited academic course representatives from across the institution come together to discuss various topics including educational developments. The ideal aim of these hubs is to have a representative sample of students to reflect what the wider student body believes. We split our student representatives into the four colleges to help the focus of conversations and to mimic focus group sessions. In this space students can give their thoughts and we can collect their feedback for wider university conversations, as a valuable forum that is repeated across an academic year. However, once a student feels their time and contribution has gone to waste the interest decreases. Therefore, if we capture student academic representatives' ideas and show them how that is impacting university life, they are more likely to continue to engage. However, it must be recognised that drawing on student academic representatives is capturing the thoughts of the most engaged voices. Whilst it is incredibly important to elevate and empower our student academic representatives who aim to help all students be heard, we cannot stop there when approaching feedback for educational developments. We must therefore consider how else we can get students to contribute to educational developments through additional activities, highlighted below.

School Action Events

Another way that Lincoln Students' Union has helped support schools in bringing students together to feedback is through 'School Action Events'. The purpose of these events is to engage a wide range of students and staff members to come together to gain mass feedback on desired themes. The goal is to give all students the opportunity to attend so their voice can be heard which is commonly paired with community and social elements of bringing school communities together. These could be run by schools independently of the students' unions; however they work well as a partnered event with invested interest from both students' union and university. Additionally, to student academic representatives, extra-curricular student academic societies (such as the History Society) are invited and present, further helping to start conversations, and having staff ready to listen to students makes students feel more heard. The feedback areas brought to these action events have been around themes such as improving assessments and feedback. This type of event allows autonomy in how feedback is collected to suit the students within different schools, which is important as one size does not fit all for each school. There is also an opportunity to reach a wider range of voices to complement academic representative feedback from both staff and students. The main challenge of this event is the initial engagement of getting students to attend a voluntary event. One way to address this is incentivising attendance, for example a free lunch. A consistent approach from staff members highlighting the importance of the event and encouraging students to go can have a more positive impact than first realised. Whilst requiring considerable planning, buy-in from staff involved and the encouragement of student attendance, School Action Events can have extremely positive outcomes for involving student engagement in educational developments.

Pop-up events

To address the challenge of low student attendance to physical events, another method that has been used at Lincoln Students' Union is feedback pop-up events in and around different university buildings. The purpose of these pop-ups are to gain student feedback through a completely opportunistic approach to try to capture students' feedback, especially from students who would not always engage with other feedback methods, in return for a small incentive. One example of pop-ups includes being based in different university buildings across the week where we managed to collect 200 pieces of feedback through our online anonymous feedback application (discussed below) in return for an advent calendar near Christmas. Our request for feedback was about the broad student experience in December, but it can also be more directed towards educational developments which we did at another point in the spring through a short survey on assessment feedback in return for a chocolate Easter egg. This is where partnerships with students' unions' support can be positively utilised for engaging students in educational developments. Another method we have previously trialled for collecting feedback is commissioning an ice cream truck and giving students an item of their choice for free in return for their feedback. These short opportunistic feedback opportunities can field a high response rate in less than an hour. Whilst some may try to move away from incentivisation I can reassure when students are rewarded for taking their time to feedback the experience is more positive. Making feeding back more convenient by catching students in between classes can also remove a barrier, which we should be keen to take advantage of, as well as reducing the number of online surveys. Whilst this takes up more staff time compared to sending out an online survey, you still recruit a perhaps more random field of participants and this can provide a more well-rounded approach to educational developments. These types of large-scale feedback methods are good practice for a broad view on high-level directions for educational developments, where more focused consultation with students on committee can follow.

Lecturer and module evaluations

Subject-specific feedback gained through in-person lectures can be effective due to students being present and feeling there is an expectation to complete the feedback before leaving. The way in which feedback is collected in a teaching session should be carefully thought through, as asking in front of a full class could easily lead to the most confident speaking out or students feeling obliged to give feedback the lecturer would agree with. To help increase the likelihood of a variety of student respondents to surveys, it is important to ensure students feel able to feedback honestly. Historically, encouraging students to complete a module/unit feedback survey, which at Lincoln we know as module evaluations, has had the best completion rates when the time to complete the evaluation is within teaching time rather than in the students' valuable spare time. This is a shift seen across the sector where students are less willing or able to give up their time for free, which is a hindrance in engaging students in educational developments outside of core contact time, or surveys getting lost in email traffic. Making time for feedback requests in lectures can be a great way to get focused insight, but where possible pre-empting the questions to allow students time to think is best practice. However, surveys can be hit by attrition rates where if students are asked for too much they will disengage. Another aspect that has emerged is a concern around feeding back critically or negatively, and this being perceived to impact students negatively, for example harsher marking on the student who gives that feedback. Whilst this should not be a legitimate possibility, it is important to acknowledge this could be a barrier for students giving feedback honestly. We should ensure we reassure students with the intentions of feedback to help encourage their response and use online methods such as polling platforms to allow students to give anonymous feedback. Additionally in some situations, it may be more appropriate for the lecturer (staff member) to leave the room and the student academic representatives or students' union leaders to gather the feedback, particularly on sensitive topics. Fostering a safe open environment from the start of modules is key in engaging students in educational developments.

Online feedback application

As we move towards a more digitally orientated higher education, we can also look at capturing students' voices through digital mediums, a possibility which has only been accelerated by the COVID-19 pandemic. At Lincoln Students' Union we have an online feedback application, 'Coursemate', which is an anonymous internal online submission form for anyone who wants to give feedback, which is then passed on to the relevant student academic representative to raise on behalf of the student. For some students having their name attached to their feedback can be a barrier for giving it, therefore feedback is anonymous, so students can be more comfortable raising their points. A similar mechanism is the anonymous virtual learning environment discussion board which can be added to some course sites allowing more specific feedback to an individual course or module.

University meetings

Many of the previously outlined aspects can be facilitated in a hybrid approach between face to face and online, which also applies to student engagement in university meetings, committees and boards. It is important to involve student academic representatives in meetings where educational developments are being discussed. Involvement in university meetings gives students the platform to be considered as a partner, a voting member of those committees, as equals to the staff members present. When given committee papers under discussion in advance and the space to be part of the discussion, students can make more informed decisions and offer an invaluable learner input from a current student perspective. There are challenges, however, such as avoiding students becoming passive members of committees and maintaining consistent engagement through agendas. Also, the logistics of meetings can bring different benefits, as face-to-face meetings can allow a more personal atmosphere, while online meetings can be more convenient and inclusive, with additional ways to contribute such as text 'chat bars'. Where I have seen the most successful student engagement (online or in-person) is through thematic discussions. Ideally staff and academic representatives will collectively identify topics that they want discussed in their school-, college- or university-level meeting. Having a part in directing the conversations increases the student's ownership which elicits higher investment and therefore engagement. Examples which cover and go beyond educational developments to the wider student experience have included student–staff communications, assessment feedback practices and student career readiness. Overall thematic discussions can work when directing educational projects with students at the heart. Supporting student academic representatives in deciding the agenda is beneficial, as no student is an expert in university committees prior to their role. I believe we underestimate how valuable it is to understand the experience of important meetings for students new to our institutional committees, especially when considering most staff members present are ten years or more into their careers! Student involvement in committees needs to have three levels of consideration, including: 1) levelling up student knowledge so students are prepared to engage; 2) involving students in meeting content and design; and 3) allowing a space for student curiosity in agenda items to explore and expand on points.

Student written submissions

Following the 2022 consultation of the UK Teaching Excellence Framework[2] where a student written submission on the student experience at that institution is included, we should think about how we professionalise the way students give their feedback for reporting purposes. At Lincoln for Periodic Academic Reviews, a student written submission type process is carried out which allows students to have ownership over the feedback they submit to the review panel. With this type of work, students are supported to collect feedback and submit a more professional report. The fact the report is sent directly to the panel also means it is independently reviewed, which is reassuring for the students who put the work in to make their suggestions. The student engagement process gives engaged students more experiences and skills to add to their employability portfolio, as a tangible report-writing experience beyond their degree. It may be that we take time to professionalise students in certain areas, allowing them to take ownership in their engagement in educational developments but also gain expertise on a certain part of the report. By emphasising the skills gained in such activities, students can perceive additional value for their time which helps address the earlier discussed issues.

Teaching and learning panels

The COVID-19 pandemic added another dimension to consider in our approach to student engagement which is important to acknowledge. Higher education was catapulted into an uncertain position where teaching had to be more dynamic and flexible, where digital engagement methods were attempted through trial and error. I believe the challenge of online student engagement was underestimated and pedagogy has required reframing since returning to face-to-face. There are some examples of effectively engaging students online which could still be used in a hybrid world that are now being evaluated. One project to oversee these evaluations and assessments developed at the University of Lincoln (UK) were the Teaching and Learning Panels. The panels were run between Lincoln Academy of Learning and Teaching (LALT) and Lincoln Students' Union to provide students the opportunity to make suggestions on proposals from academics and professional services during the pandemic. The proposals would range from asking for student insight in the beginning of a project to help determine approaches, through to evaluative sessions to understand what should be done next based on students' feedback. Originally the panels were to inform blended learning practices, but developed to include a wider range of topics as the year progressed. Students were recruited through the students' union's promotion of the opportunity, and to thank students for their contribution, they were given a gift voucher for attending each panel. The student panels acted as focus groups to 'temperature check' and gain development pointers for projects at the university. To ensure the engagement was student focused, a number of students who were interested were trained to chair the panels. An environment was created where students were in greater control of the proceedings and felt their time and input was worthwhile because of the appreciation they received. Whilst the sustainability at scale of paying students for contributing is still debated (Lowe and Lowe, 2022), we found that there was a greater range of students who got involved (i.e. not just student academic representatives) which may have been due to the monetary incentive. As many of these meetings were taking place online, we found the online chat function was advantageous as it provided an opportunity for students who were not as comfortable speaking to give their feedback. At points we were gaining double the amount of feedback in the same timeframe, due to both verbal and written feedback during the meeting. Having a space where trained students led by an informed student chair on planned topics allowed rich discussion that was beneficial to those who brought the proposals. This more structured approach using students as consultants through panels could provide greater engagement in educational developments.

How should authentic student engagement be approached?

By recognising different students will feel more comfortable engaging in educational developments in different ways, we should be dynamic in the approaches taken to gain student engagement. With the knowledge that students are often time-poor, we must consider the value students will gain from engaging in educational developments, whether that is change implementation, opportunities to gain skills or reward. Through COVID-19, we learnt to realise the value of face-to-face engagement, as well as learning how digital mechanisms can enhance our previously face-to-face-reliant approaches. We must ensure we are preparing students to be in an informed position to be able to engage in educational developments, whether that is in a meeting, during a designated panel, or in a consultant-related role. Looking forward, we should aim to empower student academic representatives by helping their visibility, developing their skills and making them feel valued in educational developments. In addition, we should trust and empower the wider student body by giving students diverse options to engage and offer professionalised academic opportunities which will positively impact their future careers. The aim is to make student engagement in educational developments inclusive. With this in mind, focus should be on providing accessible opportunities, elevating those who grasp opportunities and avoiding targeting students based on tokenistic need. The above will not result in perfect student engagement; however, it will provide foundational ideas to create an embedded culture which in time can lead to having more students meaningfully engaged in educational developments.

Notes

1 Available at: www.officeforstudents.org.uk/advice-and-guidance/student-information-and-data/national-student-survey-nss/
2 About the TEF: www.officeforstudents.org.uk/advice-and-guidance/teaching/about-the-tef

References

Bovill, C., 2020. Co-creation in learning and teaching: The case for a whole-class approach in higher education. *Higher Education*, 79(6), pp.1023–1037. https://doi.org/10.1007/s10734-019-00453-w

Bovill, C., Cook-Sather, A., Felten, P., Millard, L. and Moore-Cherry, N., 2016. Addressing potential challenges in co-creating learning and teaching: Overcoming resistance, navigating institutional norms and ensuring inclusivity in student–staff partnerships. *Higher Education*, 71(2), pp.195–208. http://dx.doi.org/10.1007/s10734-015-9896-4

John-Matthews, J.S., Robinson, L., Martin, F., Newton, P.M. and Grant, A.J., 2020. Crowdsourcing: A novel tool to elicit the student voice in the curriculum design process for an undergraduate diagnostic radiography degree programme. *Radiography*, 26, pp. S54–S61. https://doi.org/10.1016/j.radi.2020.04.019

Lowe, C. and Lowe, T. 2022. Accessibility to student engagement opportunities: A focus on 'hard-to-reach' universities. In: Lowe, T. (ed) *Advancing Student Engagement in Higher Education: Reflection, Critique and Challenge*. Routledge: London.

Qureshi, A., Wall, H., Humphries, J. and Balani, A.B., 2016. Can personality traits modulate student engagement with learning and their attitude to employability? *Learning and Individual Differences*, 51, pp.349–358. https://doi.org/10.1016/j.lindif.2016.08.026

Zhang, X., Chen, G. and Xu, B., 2020. The influence of group Big-Five personality composition on student engagement in online discussion. *International Journal of Information and Education Technology*, 10(10), pp.744–750. https://doi.org/10.18178/ijiet.2020.10.10.1452

Chapter 10

Student evaluation of courses – co-creation of meaning through conversations

Insights from the student perspective

Katja Eftring and Torgny Roxå

Introduction

Bovill and Wollmer (2020) argue that much can be gained from involving students in evaluation of courses and teaching. They emphasise student engagement in the meaning-making and interpreting process, which arguably is at the core of any evaluation. Students, they argue, can bring a unique perspective to the table and thereby benefit both the practice being evaluated as well as the students' personal development and learning. At the heart of this, we argue, is the conversation between students and teachers that occurs when they sit face to face and jointly try to make sense of what has happened in a course.

In this text we describe a faculty-wide system for evaluation of courses, and especially how students, teachers and programme coordinators meet in order to collaboratively make sense of 'the numbers' and free text answers provided in course evaluation. What we want to highlight are the feelings and experiences students perceive as they prepare for this meeting, but also how a student union has organised support and structures in order to scaffold students as they shoulder the responsibility offered to them.

This chapter describes the organisational contexts and the system for student evaluation of courses at Lund University (Sweden). The focus is the meeting, 'the conversation', at the core of the evaluative process. The second author of this text has participated in many such conversations, first as a student representative and then as heading the organisation within the student union responsible for recruiting, training and supporting students for this task. Furthermore, she has also authored a recent report investigating in detail how different branches of the student organisation value this meeting and how they prepare themselves for the encounter. The aim here is to forward the students' perspective on and experiences from meetings with academic teachers with the purpose of collaboratively making sense of course evaluations.

Context and the course evaluation system

The 'foundation' of the course evaluation system at the Faculty of Engineering at Lund University (LTH) is the Course Experience Questionnaire (CEQ)

DOI: 10.4324/9781003271789-10

(Warfvinge et al., 2022). The CEQ (Ramsden, 2005) reports on aspects that are important for the student experience and perception of a course, as well as factors that encourage either a deep or a surface approach to learning. One important part of the CEQ-form used at LTH is the two open questions at the end, where students can, in their own words, describe what they thought were the best parts of the course and what should be improved. The entire process is visualised in Figure 10.1.

Since 2003, this evaluation form has been used to evaluate all courses at LTH. The form is sent out by email to all students that have participated in the course in question. Students have around three weeks to fill it out. Although the CEQ is the basis for the course evaluation, the questionnaire is only the first step in the course evaluation process at LTH (see Figure 10.1 above). When the electronic form is closed, different branches of the student union (also known as 'student councils') are given access to the free text answers in a digital platform. The branches review the answers to the open-ended questions in order to make sure there are no irrelevant or potentially offensive comments, while still making sure that the students' feedback remains clear. This work is guided by a written framework provided by the student union (Eftring, 2021; Eftring and Roxå, 2021). After the reviewing and subsequent editing is done, the free text answers are compiled together with general course information and statistics from the CEQ into a so-called 'working report'. The working report is sent out to the relevant parties, i.e. the student councils, course responsible teacher and the programme coordinator. The working report is then used as a material in the next and most central part of the process: the evaluation meeting (also known as the CEQ-meeting). After the meeting, the three parties summarise the conversation during the CEQ-meeting independently. These summaries are then included in the evaluation *end report*, which is sent out to all course participants as well as the course teacher, programme coordinator, the head of the department concerned and the branches of the student union which have been involved. The end reports are also made available on a website accessible to all students and teachers at LTH.

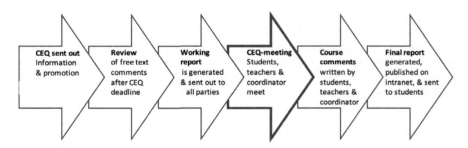

Figure 10.1 A schematic description of the course evaluation process at LTH
Adapted from Eftring (2021)

The CEQ-meeting and preparations

In this section of the text, we focus on the CEQ-meeting and explain experiences gained from those, using predominantly a student perspective. The section starts with a vignette that offers a situational experience of these meetings. The following text summarises the experiences gained from interviews with student councils about the process, personal experiences and the atmosphere of these meetings (Eftring, 2021).

Vignette

Two students are waiting outside the small conference room of the department. They squeeze their computers to their chests, shuffle their feet and exchange quiet comments. The meeting they are about to take part in concerns a mandatory course in the second year of their education, which is central to the programme, but which has been problematic for several years. The teacher is a respected professor at the department and has been responsible for the course for many years, but little has changed in the course despite recurring criticism from the students. Last year the evaluation meeting did not lead anywhere, and all parties left the meetings dissatisfied.

The course teacher and the programme coordinator arrive, and they all enter the conference room. A few pleasantries are exchanged as everyone settles down and sets up their notes and computers. The students look at each other and nod. They have met earlier in the day to discuss what to say and in which order, everything to maximise the chances of getting the point across in regard to the students' opinions without creating a conflict and locking horns with the teacher. They know that the response rate for the course has been comparatively low, something which may reduce the chances of getting the teacher to truly listen. They have tried to prepare arguments to counteract this as well.

Preparing for the meeting

Going to CEQ-meetings can be stressful for students. It is hard to escape the image of students sitting on one side of the table laying out complaints about the course they just attended while the teacher is sitting on the other side of the table, listening and becoming increasingly defensive. This, however, is rarely the case. Instead, most meetings are constructive in an atmosphere of mutual respect and commitment. So, even though exceptions to this exist, in general the meetings are appreciated by both students and teachers (Åkerman, 2020; Eftring, 2021).

One part of the explanation for this is to be found in the way the student representatives prepare themselves for the meeting. All branches of the student union have slightly different but well-established processes for the preparation. The first step, as mentioned above, to reduce the risk of conflict is the manual review of the students' free text comments from the evaluation questionnaire. Already in this step the students need to find the sweet spot between eliminating harsh comments and making sure that the criticism and suggestions are clear to the reader. The student union has set up general guidelines for reviewing the comments, in order to align the work of the different branches. But despite this, it is sometimes difficult to know where to draw the line, and some comments might be perceived as unjust by the teacher.

According to the study by Eftring (2021), all branches of the student union have their meeting representatives read through the working report before the meeting in order to be prepared for any critical discussion topics. If the representatives are new to the process, the head of the branch or another experienced representative will also provide information on how the meetings work and what to expect from them. Some branches also have their meeting representatives discuss the contents of the working report before the meeting. It is a way to prepare the students but also a way to prioritise the material and decide what is important to put forward in relation to the course in question. Sometimes the preparation is easy, and the discussion at the evaluation meeting does not need specific planning, but in other cases the criticism from the course participants can be more severe or harsh. During these situations the tactics can also be discussed, since the evaluation meetings are slightly more delicate than usual, and it is important to formulate the critique in a way that leads to change. The aim is to create a meeting atmosphere that is constructive and leads to serious conversations about how to improve the course. After all, the teacher has most likely invested a lot of time and effort in the course and it can feel deeply personal having all that work questioned and criticised. The students need to strike a perfect balance between being clear and straightforward, without expressing themselves in a way that can be perceived as offensive and thereby risking a confrontational situation. Sometimes it is almost like a form of art to get difficult points and critique across without provoking a defensive response.

Even though the experiences are similar throughout the LTH student union's different branches, they all work independently from each other and have developed variations in their routines, e.g. in how much the leader of the specific branch engages and how they recruit students for the meetings. Some branches elect 'temporary' representatives per course, while others elect representatives for one or more academic years of the programme. Common for all, though, is to strive for preparing students who have first-hand experience of the course and to have students be as prepared as possible before the meeting since the degree of preparation and experience of the individual student participating will affect the outcome of the meeting.

The meeting

Most meetings take about 40 minutes per course and are held during the lunch break. At some programmes several courses are discussed at the same time, and then the meetings may last longer. Generally, students are offered a central role, e.g. it is common in the CEQ-meetings that the students are asked to lead the conversation. In some meetings the programme coordinator acts as a chairperson, distributing the speaking turns and leading the discussion, but also in these situations the students' rundown of the feedback is often the central topic. This arrangement improves the position of the students in a situation where the power relationships may otherwise be rather unequal. Commonly, the students start by summarising what they have prepared to put forward and then a discussion follows. Not only the results from the survey to students are discussed, but also other topics can be brought to the table if they are found to be relevant for the discussion. For example, the student council or the teacher may have performed a sort of mid-course evaluation, and the results from this can be brought up at the CEQ-meeting.

Issues related to response rates are often talked about in the CEQ-meetings, since an important issue concerns how relevant various points of view are. Here students can draw on their preparation before the meeting, since other sources and the students' own experience can be used to 'fill in the gaps' and compensate for a low response rate. And, after all, some issues can indeed be important even though only one student has mentioned it in the open-ended comments. The intent of the meeting is to discuss how the course can be improved, not necessarily how to comply with a majority. Teachers also report in other investigations that even though the response rate is low they sometimes assign meaning to single comments, simply because they are useful and add to the quality of the course (Roxå and Bergström, 2013). Thus, it is not simply the proportion of students that has answered that determines the quality in these conversations; rather it is how meaningful the conversation is in relation to the development of the course in focus.

The CEQ-meeting is not a meeting where formal decisions are made. Instead, the students, the teacher and the programme coordinator independently summarise their respective experiences in writing, and these summaries are included in the end report. In some branches of the student union the branch leader writes these summaries for all courses using the participating students' notes as material, and in other cases it is the students who took part in the meeting who do this on their own. Some branches of the student union also use a Facebook page or other social media platforms to distribute these summaries to all students. This is an attempt to raise awareness of what happens with the evaluation results and hopefully inspire more students to actually fill out the CEQ. Because of the fact that the branches have routines to compensate for low response rates, and the fact that studies show that even a small number of answers usually reflect the opinions of the entire group, it would be easier and more efficient to downplay discussions about response rates altogether in the CEQ-meetings and instead focus on what can be meaningful input in the development process.

The atmosphere

The meeting atmosphere is almost always described by the various branches of the student union as positive and constructive (Eftring, 2021). However, exceptions and variation do exist. Sometimes it is certain discussion topics that cause the atmosphere to become strained and less constructive. Things might become too personal for the teacher, some things are hard to change and sometimes the students are simply being questioned. Things can come into a deadlock where no progress is made, and no solutions are suggested. If the meetings concerning a specific course do not lead anywhere or repeatedly end in stalemate, the branch leader may raise issues with the programme coordinator outside the meetings or put things forward to the board of the student union to possibly be discussed elsewhere in the organisation. It should be emphasised, though, that even though this happens it is not too common.

Student representatives – acting on behalf of others

We started this chapter by referring to Bovill and Wollmer (2020), who argued for involving students in "meaning-making processes that take place in evaluation as well as involving students in the actions taken as a result" (p.88). In the above we have described such a routine within the Faculty of Engineering. Both teachers (Åkerman, 2020) and students (Eftring, 2021; Eftring and Roxå, 2021) appreciate this routine and the outcome is a measurable overall improvement of courses (Roxå et al., 2022).

But asking students to do this is not without challenges. As stated by scholars (Lizzio and Wilson, 2009; Bols, 2017, 2020), student representation is generally enhanced if: (a) the role student representatives have to take on is clear; (b) the meeting structure is clear and predictable; (c) the student representatives are sufficiently prepared for the task; and, not least, (d) the academic culture and the academics participating are supportive of students' participation.

In the example above the student union recruit and prepare students for these meetings (c), the meetings are not only transparent but also monitored by a programme coordinator (b). As for conditions (a) and (d) one can note that both student representatives and teachers are trained by the student union (Eftring, 2021) and by the faculty (Roxå et al., 2022) respectively to take part in the process. From the description above it is understood that students in our example prepare extra carefully if they may foresee a conversation that might become personal and/or sensitive for the teacher. Thus, it can be concluded that the four conditions (a)–(d) in large part are met. It can be concluded that students are invited to evaluate courses, interpret survey data and discuss potential improvements. In addition, they have a specific space in the end report where they can formulate their own interpretation of the meeting – an opportunity also provided to teachers and programme coordinators. Despite this, the system still displays challenges and problems.

What about representation? Both the students in the example above (Eftring, 2021) and other elected students engaged in developing Higher Education at large (Bols, 2017) see themselves as representing other students. Furthermore, the issue on representation is a heated debate in relation to student evaluations (Roxå et al., 2022), even though studies suggest that relatively low response rates also provide robust data (Borell and Gudmundsson, 2009; Borell, Alveteg and Andersson, 2010; Havtun and Hjelm, 2019). Hence, students who take these meetings seriously and prepare according to existing routines deserve to be taken seriously, even though they might be just two individuals. The mere fact that an academic teacher does not know about these representatives' preparation and training does not provide grounds for questioning their representativeness.

Challenges and recommendations

One of the central challenges for the students in this course evaluation process is to strike the balance between being clear and straightforward with feedback without being confrontational. Although it is reasonable that the students are expected to deliver the feedback in a professional way, it is also a fact that in order to be productive the teacher also has to act professionally. As has been stated above, this is also usually the case. Teachers are trained through professional development courses and students are trained by the student union. Without these measures the challenge would be greater and problematic meetings would become more frequent.

What else can the teachers and faculty do to support the student engagement in this practice? For one, we believe it is important for academic teachers to be aware of the preparations done by students as they go into these meetings. Since the student union oversees the student representation in the evaluation process, many teachers do not seem to know how much work and preparation the students do before a meeting. As has been made clear in this chapter, students do not just show up and start to vent their own opinions about a course. Perhaps it is easier for teachers to handle criticism with this in mind. With that said, we believe that another important improvement would be to provide support for teachers in processing and implementing the issues that are brought up in the evaluation meetings. Currently, the teachers are left to 'fend for themselves' once the meeting is over (Roxå and Bergström, 2013) and it can be understandably difficult to process the aftermath of a difficult meeting. Since the faculty requires teachers to go through this process, the faculty should also provide support that is meaningful for the teachers.

In addition to the above, another challenge faced by the students is related to the recruitment of representatives. The fact that the student union and its branches are responsible for the recruitment is important for ensuring the independence, objectivity and representativeness of the student representation. Just as in any situation where the interests of a group are to be represented, the legitimacy of the representation is unclear if the representatives are chosen by another stakeholder. However, the recruitment of representatives is time consuming and challenging. In this lies a challenge. The student union often is in need of support from the faculty to make the system work. On the other hand, if the faculty support is substantial the legitimacy of the student representatives may be influenced negatively.

As in most matters concerning course evaluations the students working in the system rarely experience the changes they contribute to. Finding students who are prepared to spend even more time on their education, especially if the task can be time consuming and challenging, instead of planning recreational activities is sometimes hard. One way to tackle this problem is to provide 'rewards' for the work put in by the student representatives, something that is already done by most branches. Another way is to improve the transparency and provide more information about what actually occurs within the meetings and how much change has been brought about. This responsibility should ideally be shared between the student organisation and the faculty. The student union has argued for increased feedback and exchange of information between cycles in the course evaluation process, as the student union branches (and by extension the students in general) will not know if their feedback has yielded any changes until the next round of the course has already started (Eftring, 2021). Although data from the CEQ shows improvements over the years (see below), it is difficult for the students who are currently on courses, and those who are participating in the evaluation, to judge whether their feedback and efforts actually make a difference.

Finally, there are other ways in which the faculty could support the student union with their work, without compromising their independence. For example, the faculty could help advertise the meetings and the representative positions. The faculty could also provide economic resources so that the student union can provide better and more attractive rewards for engaging in the course evaluation process. This could allow the student union to reach a wider range of students, and not only those who are especially interested in improving the education.

Discussion

The above is a brief description of a practice that has been in place since 2003 at the Faculty of Engineering. At the heart of this is that students and teachers meet and talk to each other about a course they all have experiences from. The data from the course evaluation are used but it is not the data that set the scene. It is those that are present who do this. One might ask why this was natural; where 2003 was long before the student as partners wave took off in wider Higher Education. The answer is that students and teachers were deemed key stakeholders, they know best what has taken place in a course. Therefore, they should be the ones who try to figure out what can be improved or not. Thus, the practice described is aligned with what Bovill and Wollmer (2020) suggest: students can and ideally should be involved in the meaning-making process, which is at the core of any evaluation (Henderson et al., 2018).

Usual comments around these mandatory meetings concern worries around the amount of time they consume, or worries about poorly prepared and agitated students, or overly defensive teachers. The report that this text builds upon (Eftring, 2021) acknowledges that this can happen but that it is not common. It has also been shown that the CEQ-meetings are also considered valuable by academic teachers (Åkerman, 2020). A contributing factor to these positive experiences is probably the work that is done by the student union and by the individual students who allow themselves to be engaged in this practice. Once the people are in the room, having their CEQ-meeting, the atmosphere is mostly constructive and developmental.

In what way does this example fit into the literature on students as partners? If we use the diagram discussed by Lowe and Bols (2020, p.272; see Figure 10.2) we suggest that the practice described is indeed a partnership as it involves both:

- **Representative partnership**, the student union oversees the recruiting of student representatives and the training and scaffolding these go through, thereby securing independence in relation to the faculty.
- **Cooperative partnership**, since the CEQ-meetings have the character of a joint interpretation of the material, in combination with these students being volunteers and thereby free to act as individuals. A significant detail is that students in these meetings are not recruited by the teacher, they are recruited and organised by the student union.

We know from other studies that LTH courses have developed linearly in quality since 2003 (Roxå et al., 2022). An analysis of the material collected from the CEQ database using up to 300,000 filled-out questionnaires shows that for all scales (Good Teaching, Goals and Standards, Appropriate Assessment, and Generic Skills) the numbers have improved from year to year. We suggest that this long-term development is due to the CEQ-meetings, at least partly. It is also due

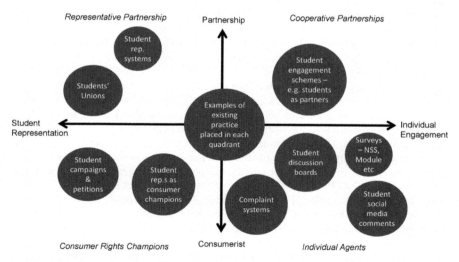

Figure 10.2 Example student engagement practices on paradigm
Lowe and Bols (2020, p.272)

to the holistic approach to academic development (Sutherland, 2018; Troelsen, 2021) that has been pursued for more than two decades, always guided by the principle that the most central stakeholders in critical conversations about teaching and learning drive change. In this work, student voices are crucial.

References

Åkerman, C., 2020. *Utvecklingsmöten inom LTH: kursutvärderings-och dialogmöten samt andra möten*. Lund: Lunds universitet, Lunds Tekniska Högskola, Avdelningen för kvalitetsstöd.

Bols, A., 2020. The changing nature and importance of student representation. In: Lowe, T. and El-Hakim, Y. (eds) *A Handbook for Student Engagement in Higher Education*. Abingdon: Routledge. https://doi.org/10.4324/9780429023033-6

Bols, A., 2017. Enhancing student representation. *Journal of Educational Innovation, Partnership and Change*, 3(1), pp.81–89.

Borell, J. and Gudmundsson, A., 2009. *Vad tycker de som inte svarat på kursvärderingsenkäten?* Paper presented at the Utvecklingskonferensen 09, Lund.

Borell, J., Alveteg, M. and Andersson, K., 2010. *Bortom de lämnade enkätsvaren*. Paper presented at the LTHs 6:e Pedagogiska Inspirationskonferens, Lund, 15 December.

Bovill, C. and Wollmer, C., 2020. Student engagement in evaluation. In: Lowe, T. and El-Hakim, Y. (eds) *A Handbook for Student Engagement in Higher Education*. Abingdon: Routledge. https://doi.org/10.4324/9780429023033-7

Eftring, K., 2021. *Studenternas roll i kursutvärderingsprocessen vid LTH. En kartläggning av studierådsarbetet på A-, E-, F- och W-sektionen inom Teknologkåren på LTH*. Available at: www.lth.se/fileadmin/lth/genombrottet/Eftring2021.studenternas_roll_Kursutva__rdering_LTH.pdf (accessed: 11 December 2021).

Eftring, K. and Roxå, T., 2021. *Students in CEQ-meetings – insights into how students prepare for the core part of the CEQ-process*. Paper presented at the LTHs 11:e Pedagogiska Inspirationskonferens, Lund, 9 December. Available at: www.lth.se/fileadmin/cee/genombrottet/konferens2021/C1_Eftring_Roxa__.pdf (accessed: 1 March 2022).

Havtun, H. and Hjelm, N., 2019. *En undersökning av vad de studenter som inte fyller i kursenkäten tycker om kursen*. Paper presented at the 7 e Utvecklingskonferensen för Sveriges ingenjörsutbildningar, Luleå Tekniska Universitet, 27 November.

Henderson, M., Boud, D., Molloy, E., Dawson, P., Phillips, M., Ryan, T. and Mahoney, P., 2018. *Closing the Assessment Loop*. Available at https://feedbackforlearning.org/framework-of-effective-feedback/definition/ (accessed: 16 May 2021).

Lizzio, A. and Wilson, K., 2009. Student participation in university governance: The role conceptions and sense of efficacy of student representatives on departmental committees. *Studies in Higher Education*, 34(1), pp.69–84. https://doi.org/10.1080/03075070802602000

Lowe, T. and Bols, A., 2020. Higher education institutions and policy makers. In: Lowe, T. and El-Hakim, Y. (eds) *A Handbook for Student Engagement in Higher Education*. Abingdon: Routledge. https://doi.org/10.4324/9780429023033-26Ramsden, P., 2005. *Learning to Teach in Higher Education* (2nd edn). London: RoutledgeFalmer.

Roxå, T. and Bergström, M., 2013. Kursvärderingar i system – akademiska lärares upplevelser och organisationens förmåga till utveckling [Student evaluations as systems –

academic teachers' experiences and the organisation's ability to develop]. *Högre Utbildning* [*Higher Education*], 3(3), pp.225–236.

Roxå, T., Ahmad, A., Barrington, J., Van Maaren, J. and Cassidy, R., 2022. Reconceptualising student ratings of teaching to support quality discourse on student learning: A systems perspective. *Higher Education*. https://doi.org/10.1007/s10734-020-00615-1

Sutherland, K., 2018. Holistic academic development: Is it time to think more broadly about the academic development project? *International Journal for Academic Development*, 23(4), pp.261–273. https://doi.org/10.1080/1360144x.2018.1524571

Troelsen, R., 2021. How to operationalise holistic academic development – The case of a Danish center for teaching and learning. *Hungarian Educational Research Journal*, 11 (3), pp.254–261. https://doi.org/10.1556/063.2021.00069

Warfvinge, P., Löfgreen, J., Andersson, K., Roxå, T. and Åkerman, C., 2022. The rapid transition from campus to online teaching – how are students' perception of learning experiences affected? *European Journal of Engineering Education*. https://doi.org/10.1080/03043797.2021.1942794.

The problem with student engagement during COVID-19

Jim Dickinson

For many years, key actors across UK higher education have proclaimed the importance of student representation and engagement in decision-making. The UK Quality Assurance Agency, for example, says that student engagement through partnership working is "integral" to the culture of UK higher education, and says that it helps to cause the "continuing improvement of higher education and the overall student experience" (QAA, 2022). It can also be argued that a culture of representation and partnership ensures that students feel heard. But perhaps the case for student engagement in decision making within universities is one that tends to be made in times of harmony. What happens when these practices are tested in a time of crisis?

If, for example, we wanted to know whether students in England felt listened to during the first year of the COVID-19 pandemic, the available national evidence is not encouraging. 2021's National Student Survey results for England saw the percentage of students agreeing that it was clear 'how students' feedback on the course has been acted on' fall to an all-time low – 51.9% for full-time students and 45.5% for part-time students – the lowest scoring question on the survey (OfS, 2022). We might have hoped that this revealed a problem with the 'feedback loop' rather than the feedback gathering – but separate national polling carried out by the Office for Students (OfS) (England's regulatory body for higher education) in late November 2020 found that just 48% of students said they had been asked for feedback on the digital teaching and learning they had received since the beginning of the academic year (OfS, 2021a).

It would be easy to raise critical questions about what the evidence is telling us. The NSS asked undergraduate students about their entire experiences rather than just the pandemic year, the OfS polling was carried out before most end-of-module evaluation processes, and in both cases we do not know which aspects of their experience students include and exclude when they think about their 'course'. Nevertheless, in a system that tends to evaluate, enhance, assure and improve on an annual cycle, it would not be odd to assume that during a period where available staff capacity to do anything other than core teaching and learning tasks was heavily restricted, gathering and acting on the nuances of student feedback in real time might not have been the top priority.

DOI: 10.4324/9781003271789-11

The view 'from the top' may be different. In Lowe and Bols's "student engagement utopia", students are able to "feed in their collective perspectives in relation to identification of the issues, analysis of the problem and then development of the solution", and as such students are "engaged in a community of learning and are respected as full equal partners within this community" (2020, p.237). 'Collective' implies 'public' – and students do not appear to believe that discussions (if there were any) were happening.

But the acts of issue identification, problem analysis and solution development imply close working, trust and partnership. In a summary of the evidence presented to a national commission on learning from the pandemic to improve the student experience, Curnock Cook argues that she was "heartened to hear" about what she said felt like a "step-change" in relationships between students' unions and university leadership teams. "SUs have undoubtedly played an enormously positive role", she argues, "and have welcomed more collaborative working with university staff to the benefit of all" (UPP Foundation, 2021).

Contrasted with a range of other issues facing higher education during the pandemic, it feels trivial to ask whether mid-module evaluation during winter lockdown of 2020 was effective, or even really mattered. But at the institutional level, significant student engagement activity was carried out, prioritised, reflected on and labelled as valuable both by student representatives and institutional managers. So what happened?

The author leads a programme of work aimed at improving the efforts of students' union officers (and staff that support them) in carrying out their representative role, with a particular focus on understanding and intervening in policy issues. As this work continued through the pandemic – with the author discussing the pandemic and engagement with university managers on a monthly basis with over 50 higher education providers – reflections on prominent themes in those conversations and the way in which the pandemic intensified or exacerbated underlying issues and tensions provide an opportunity to evaluate the Lowe and Bols utopia in the most difficult of circumstances.

'No detriment' and 'safety net' policy discussions – Spring 2020

The idea that students are able to ask their higher education provider to take into account unexpected events or issues that are beyond their control when considering their performance in assessment is well established (OIA, 2020). It is also accepted that such policies and associated mitigations should give students a fair opportunity to show that they can reach standards, not lower them. Nevertheless, generally such arrangements are designed for individual students with individual sets of circumstances. So what happened when students were collectively advocating for mitigation on an "almost industrial scale" (Kernohan, 2022), to ensure that they did not experience academic detriment from those circumstances?

As students began to pressure their providers – either directly or through their students' union – to implement a version of the 'no detriment' or 'safety net' policies that began to be agreed in the latter half of March 2020, two factors appeared to impact the quality and speed of discussions between managers and student representatives. The first related to the diversity of provision from the provider insofar as it represented an undocumented diversity of purposes of or approaches to assessment, differences in the acceptance of concepts like 'exit velocity' and/or a diversity of external requirements imposed by professional, statutory and regulatory bodies:

> We found that while the Pro Vice Chancellor agreed in principle because of an assumption that students tend to do better in their final year, some schools were very resistant.
>
> One Dean was very concerned that allowing a large number of students to effectively complete later than others was in and of itself a lowering of standards because we expect students to complete on a shared timeline.
>
> We jumped the gun a bit and announced that we'd got a no detriment policy in place, only for various bits of the university to declare that it couldn't apply to them – students were furious.

In these cases fundamental differences in the meaning of 'reaching a standard' were exposed by the pandemic and either made discussions more complex, or more difficult to make progress on. The second factor related to regulatory risk – with some senior figures privately accepting the principle of mass mitigations early on, but expressing concern at the way those mitigations may be viewed particularly in the event of grade inflation:

> They said that the risk of grade inflation was potentially too high, and implied that the reason was that OfS was already 'breathing down their neck', although that was the first we'd heard of it.
>
> Oh they were like, if we offer more support to some students that's one thing, but even if it gave students confidence changing the degree algorithm would be a step too far in OfS's eyes.
>
> What they said was that they'd rather we didn't update students on what we were discussing in case OfS found out, which did make it harder to keep the conversation going with students who were getting more and more impatient.

In these cases either uncertainty in the way in which an approach might have been evaluated by the OfS or uncertainty about the impact an approach might have on a concern previously expressed (either directly or indirectly) by the OfS made discussions more difficult to make progress on.

The design of 'blended learning' approaches – Spring/Summer 2020

As it became clear that there would likely need to be restrictions on the use of space on campus in the new academic year, discussion between students' unions and universities turned to the nature of provision that would be available to students in the Autumn, partly resulting from pressure from the OfS to be clear with students about what was being offered in order that they comply with consumer protection law. Such discussions were difficult in the context of uncertainty about the sorts of restrictions that might prevail, competing pressures to not vary too far from that which had been promised, not putting off students where the perception was there could be significant deferrals, and not overpromising in case of a further lockdown; this meant that again two factors appeared to impact the quality and speed of discussions between managers and student representatives. The first related to the relative confidence that the university had in its recruitment and/or financial position:

> They didn't want to announce anything until someone else had. We'd go to meetings every day where the main topic of discussion was what anyone had heard from anywhere else rather than what might be best for students.
>
> She [Vice Chancellor] was terrified that if we announced what had been agreed in the working group, then international students would cancel. So it kept coming back sounding less and less dramatic.

In these cases the ability of those involved in the engagement exercise to develop or select from solutions perceived to be in the student interest was hampered by the pressure to not demotivate applicants or continuing students from enrolling, and by a related lack of understanding of the way any solution would be perceived when compared against other providers' approaches. The second factor related to the willingness or preparedness of university senior staff to discuss the student experience outside of formally timetabled contact hours and facilities:

> Every meeting was really about how the campus was going to be managed – how many people you could fit in the library or the lecture theatre or the lab. Nobody ever said 'what's this going to be like for students' and we never really scenario-planned even some of the more obvious things that happened.
>
> We actually had a really good meeting where we pointed out how students were going to experience the university if the campus was basically closed where we picked up loads of things I think they'd have missed otherwise, like proactive mental health support because it was obvious they would be lonely.
>
> Haha once Cambridge did that statement and Bolton did that video, they were like well if everyone else can do it we can do it now. It was like a kind of herd immunity.
>
> The level of detail we got into when it came to what students were going to be on campus for, how they would behave, where they would go was amazing. We tried to talk about what life would be like off campus and never really got anywhere.

In these cases the ability of those involved in engagement exercises to identify issues, analyse problems and develop solutions was dependent upon the willingness or preparedness to discuss 'the student experience' rather than just 'what is directly provided by the university'.

(The University of Cambridge statement and University of Bolton video were both issued early in Summer 2020, the former setting out its plans to not hold large group lectures and the latter describing its approach to on-campus social distancing and safety measures.)

Discussions about 'practical redress' – early 2021

By early 2021, both the 'real world' implications of 'in-principle' decisions taken in the summer of 2020, coupled with the dawning reality of the impact of ever-changing restrictions (both in 2020 and those anticipated in 2021), led to discussions surrounding 'practical loss' – where the approach to components of programmes not easily delivered online was under intense scrutiny.

With the OfS (2021b) requiring all providers in England to assess their delivery against promises made from a consumer protection law perspective and notify it of any issues, two factors appeared to impact the quality and speed of discussions between managers and student representatives on resolving 'practical component' concerns. The first related to the relative risk that the provider believed the Office for Students' January edict (OfS, 2021b) to represent:

> We asked about it but we were told that lawyers were doing it and it wasn't for students to feed in on. But most of the casework we were getting was about students saying their placement was off or their labs had been postponed. It made no sense – how can you judge whether promises were kept without student feedback? We were told to feed cases in but they were always like individual issues, not for discussion.
>
> The uni put us on the working group straight away. To be fair they were confident that they'd not overpromised – we probably should have pushed harder in the Summer haha – and that they'd be able to work with us to sort out specific courses through extra provision or postponing and such. That got a lot easier when it was obvious some students would be allowed back on campus.

In these cases it appeared that fear about non-compliance either with consumer protection law or the OfS's regulatory interpretation of it hampered the ability of reps to engage in open discussion with universities about solving problems caused by COVID-19 restrictions. The second related to the extent to which the provider and its management appeared concerned that binding promises had been made about the nature of delivery:

> We were told that it was the learning outcomes that mattered and that as long as the way someone met them was robust then that would be it. But students were saying to us they were worried about not having any actual hands-on experience to talk to people at job interviews.

> They kept coming back to – what did we actually promise, and if it wasn't written down anywhere then basically the attitude was, well pandemic.
>
> We were basically asked to send students to the university – we were told not to get students' hopes up but it felt like a way of keeping students and complaints from us.

In these cases it appeared that students engaging in problem-solving discussions surrounding provision was dependent upon a specific commitment having been made to provide it, and that the range of issues that could be discussed was restricted to where (often conflicting and differing) interpretations of consumer protection law generated a risk. As such consumer protection law and its regulatory interpretation and enforcement by the OfS served to doubly restrict the range of issues permissible to be discussed through engagement – from 'it's only an issue if we think we made a real promise about it' to 'now it's an issue we can't really talk about it because we'd be admitting liability'.

Conclusion

> I honestly think the main reason they stopped us doing no detriment this year and the reason they've stopped us talking about learning loss and what we can do to fix it is because they can't admit that the provision hasn't been up to scratch, because they don't want to pay out fee refunds.

None of the issues, pressures and tensions identified here existed only in the pandemic – although it is easy to see how they might have been intensified or exacerbated by it. We might therefore conclude that identifying what would have helped in this specific situation could have a positive impact on student engagement and the ability of student representatives and university managers to engage in utopian discussions more often and more effectively. In some ways the straightforward conclusion from the above might be that marketisation and market regulation underpinned by consumer protection law actively hindered the ability of student representatives and managers in higher education to engage in constructive, open conversations about the identification of issues, analysis of problems and the development of solutions for students.

But we do have a marketised higher education in England, and consumer protection law does apply for the time being. It also offers protection for students that it is not clear would be retained or enhanced by disapplying consumer protection law. If, as Lowe and Bols note, consumer protection gives students a more powerful position to demand real change and helps to redress power imbalances between themselves and the academics and institution, it would seem strange to suggest that its absence would have helped given the corner universities in England were backed into during the pandemic.

A thematic cause might well be a failure by universities or regulators to appropriately define the boundaries of students' consumer rights and identities.

Elsewhere in this book Bunce, Rathbone and King discuss whether students identifying as consumers might generate problems – but they do so (for example) by associating a 'consumer' mindset with viewing university education as a product being purchased, wanting only to learn things that will help in one's future career, and by assuming that the mere completion of assignments should result in a good grade regardless of the quality of the work produced (Oxford Brookes University, 2022).

No wonder "consumer" mindsets and associated protections are viewed as polar opposites to partnership, to be assessed on a continuum. A different interpretation – where partners make detailed and binding promises to each other and where we differentiate between and integrate that which a university should be responsible for, and that which is generated by a partnership involving student effort, is surely possible (Dickinson, 2013) – and would reflect the reality of a situation where students are (positive) consumers, partners and clients all at the same time. And both government and regulatory interventions principally designed to support both students and providers in delivering against their commitments (and making appropriately ambitious and detailed ones at that) would help. Specifically, if universities that restricted student engagement in the ways described argue that they had little choice but to act as they did during the pandemic given the regulatory, financial and legal issues, then we should identify if anything could have eased those pressures given the way in which they hampered meaningful collective engagement – and identify some of the ways in which regulation and funding could have helped. The following recommendations result from reflecting on the stages of the COVID-19 pandemic's impact on English higher education and student engagement.

No detriment/safety net

- Revisit purpose of assessment across the provider, with specific reference to allowable diversity in approaches. OfS might usefully require this to be done and be regularly revisited as part of its work on defining 'quality'.
- Regularly approach OfS to seek advice on how it might approach judgements involving competing subjective demands on the basis of scenarios and share advice with other providers and share all advice from OfS with student representatives. OfS should in turn create regulatory interventions that require that sharing, generate stability, allow for problem solving and require evidence of student engagement where there are competing tensions and pressures. It should also publish as many examples of its informal advice to providers as it can.

The design of 'blended learning' approaches

- Develop commitment to and structures that support discussion of the 'whole' student experience, from multiple student perspectives (rather than 'students' feeding back on multiple departments/functions) where possible/appropriate. OfS might usefully require this to be done and be regularly revisited as part of its work on defining 'effective student engagement'.

- Operate finances to create significantly deep(er) financial stability and 'wriggle room' in the event of changes. OfS to generate market rules and interventions that commit to reducing sudden changes to the income position of higher education providers both through the control of places and financial cushioning.

Discussions about 'practical redress'

- Develop and implement a commitment to and structures that support the making of clear commitments to students about the breadth and nature of their provision with systems to monitor delivery against those commitments that operate both 'top down' and 'bottom up'.
- OfS to progress previously promised work on consumer protection law with particular reference to the nature of the granularity that should be offered about courses and wider provision, and a requirement for student engagement.

References

Dickinson, J., 2013. A glass of Sangria, my cake and some time to eat it please. Wonkhe. Available at: https://wonkhe.com/blogs/a-glass-of-sangria-my-cake-and-some-time-to-eat-it-please/ (accessed: 5 January 2022).

Kernohan, D., 2022. Can universities safely implement "no detriment" assessment policies? Wonkhe. Available at: https://wonkhe.com/blogs/can-universities-safely-implement-no-detriment-policies/ (accessed: 5 January 2022).

Lowe, T. and Bols, A., 2020. Higher education institutions and policy makers. In: Lowe, T. and El-Hakim, Y. (eds) *A Handbook for Student Engagement in Higher Education.* Abingdon: Routledge. https://doi.org/10.4324/9780429023033-26

Office for Students (OfS), 2022. *National Student Survey – NSS.* Available at: www.officeforstudents.org.uk/advice-and-guidance/student-information-and-data/national-student-survey-nss/ (accessed: 5 January 2022).

Office for Students (OfS), 2021a. *Gravity Assist: Propelling Higher Education towards a Brighter Future.* Available at: www.officeforstudents.org.uk/publications/gravity-assist-propelling-higher-education-towards-a-brighter-future/ (accessed: 5 January 2022).

Office for Students (OfS), 2021b. *Latest Lockdown Should Not Lead to Lost Learning, Says Regulator.* Available at: www.officeforstudents.org.uk/news-blog-and-events/press-and-media/latest-lockdown-should-not-lead-to-lost-learning-says-regulator/ (accessed: 5 January 2022).

Office for the Independent Adjudicator (OIA), 2020. *Requests for Additional Consideration.* Available at: www.oiahe.org.uk/resources-and-publications/good-practice-framework/requests-for-additional-consideration/ (accessed: 5 January 2022).

Oxford Brookes University, 2022. *Student Identities and Inclusion – Student Profiler Quiz.* Available at: https://sites.google.com/brookes.ac.uk/studentidentitiesandinclusion/identities-project/student-profiler-quiz?authuser=0 (accessed: 5 January 2022).

Quality Assurance Agency for Higher Education (QAA), 2022. *Student Engagement.* Available at: www.qaa.ac.uk/quality-code/advice-and-guidance/student-engagement (accessed: 5 January 2022).

UPP Foundation, 2021. *Interim Report: Turbocharging the Future.* Available at: https:// upp-foundation.org/student-futures-commission/news/turbocharging-the-future/ (accessed: 5 January 2022).

Chapter 12

Control, freedom and structure in student–staff partnerships

Jenny Marie and Stuart Sims

Introduction

This chapter focuses on the practice of student–staff partnership, whereby students and staff collaborate in a shared endeavour, taking joint responsibility for the undertaking. They draw on and recognise their different expertise in a process designed to bring benefits not only to all parties participating in the practice but also to others through the outputs. Much has been written about the purpose of student–staff partnership, often arguing that it serves to resist the forces of neoliberalism that are affecting higher education (Dunne and Zandstra, 2011; Mercer-Mapstone et al., 2017) or alternatively that students are an under-utilised resource, who in a neo-liberal system should be drawn upon to maximise efficiency (Gaerdebo and Wiggberg, 2012; Villa et al., 2010). In this chapter we argue for a third philosophical position to lie behind partnership activities: pragmatism. Pragmatists adopt common sense to work for cultural change. As such, pragmatists hold an ideal in mind that they work towards, but they do so taking account of the context in which they are working and what is needed to move from where they are to where they want to be. In working towards cultural change around student–staff partnership, we argue that structures are important. We investigate the role of gatekeepers, being often staff who control access to university-funded partnership schemes, through controlling the finances and the validation that comes from being part of a recognised scheme. This power over who can join student–staff partnership schemes gives those gatekeepers the power over the nature of the practice that occurs, but they also have facilitative power to drive forward institutional change. We then turn our attention to the structures that gatekeepers need to build or ensure already exist to enable effective cultural change. Such structures should serve in part to limit their power in keeping with the value of redistributing power that partnership practice entails (HEA, 2014). Our purpose in this chapter is to aid others in thinking through the structures required for cultural change and to defend the idea of pragmatic idealism in student–staff partnership.

DOI: 10.4324/9781003271789-12

Positionality statement

As authors we feel it is important to clarify our position in relation to partnership practice, as we are far from neutral parties. For many years we acted as the referenced-above gatekeepers to two institutional schemes, respectively for UCL Changemakers at University College London (UCL, UK) and the Student Fellows Scheme at the University of Winchester (UK). As the university leads for these two partnership change-based initiatives, we were responsible for the recruitment, management, training and funding of students to support their engagement with partnership activities. As gatekeepers, this often meant being the third party in a relationship between a staff member and a student as they worked together and strived towards educational developments through partnership. Mediating these relationships can be a key aspect of the gatekeeping role and doing so is never neutral. As employees of the university we had a responsibility to ensure that the reputation of our institutions was upheld but were also subject to significant pressures around how the (quite substantial) budgets of the schemes were spent. We have both since moved on from this particular gatekeeping role (and indeed our previous institutions). In planning this chapter we had numerous discussions which revealed a wealth of shared experiences and challenges, in spite of differences in the schemes themselves and the universities at which they were based. The discussions were themselves unstructured, but led to the conceptualisation of this chapter and its structure. Writing then occurred via a shared online document, with a number of touch-point discussions, which provided further direction to our writing.

Idealism vs pragmatism

The differing philosophies of neo-liberalism and social justice can both underpin student–staff partnership (Dollinger and Mercer-Mapstone, 2019). Neo-liberalism is based on the application of the theory of natural selection to economics and entails the belief that the best way to improve standards is via market pressure. Businesses are thus freed from over-burdensome regulation to fend for survival in a competitive market. Social justice is based on a vision of a more just future, where everyone has just access to resources and opportunities. How justice is determined is open to debate, with popular political discourse often arguing for or pursuing a meritocratic society (Bukodi and Goldthorpe, 2021). However, the term "meritocratic" itself was originally pejorative, arising as part of an argument that those with more capability had no more right to resources and opportunities than anyone else (Young, 1959).

Neo-liberal student–staff partnerships recognise students as a resource for enhancing education, drawing on their experience of the provision and expertise on what matters to students. This recognition of the resource provided by students can lead to financial compensation for their work, which can aid inclusion by enabling participation amongst students who need to work. However, if students are selected on the basis of their engagement or attainment this can exclude the very students whose voices need to be heard (Bovill et al., 2016). The merit of the partnership is likely to be judged by the product arising from the partnership – and power issues would be considered to ensure that the practice is as effective as possible. Social justice student–staff partnerships position students as having a right to a say in their own education. They focus on the way partnership challenges traditional relationships between higher education teachers and students and the mindset of participants. It can be seen as a means of counteracting neo-liberal forces in the academy, by positioning students as collaborators rather than con-sumers. Financial compensation is sometimes seen as making the practice transac-tional, though it could also be seen as a just compensation given that staff are also paid for their time (Mercer-Mapstone et al., 2017). Such partnerships are more likely to focus on the process of the partnership and the outcomes arising from this for all participants.

Some scholars and practitioners of student–staff partnership advocate for scaling up partnership practice to improve inclusivity (Moore-Cherry et al., 2016; Mercer-Mapstone and Bovill, 2020), while others believe that it is such a powerful way of enhancing education that it should be expanded (Mercer-Mapstone et al., 2017; Mercer-Mapstone and Marie, 2019). Nevertheless, there is a fear that the practice is spreading without commitment to social justice and becoming appropriated for neo-liberal ends (Matthews, Dwyer et al., 2018).

The difficulty is perhaps over who owns the idea and practice of partnership and who has the right to use the term. What are the boundaries of partnership? There are two main definitions in use in the literature:

> a collaborative, reciprocal process through which all participants have the opportunity to contribute equally, although not necessarily in the same ways, to curricular or pedagogical conceptualization, decision making, implementa-tion, investigation, or analysis.
>
> (Cook-Sather et al., 2014, pp.6–7)

> partnership is understood as fundamentally about a relationship in which all involved – students, academics, professional services staff, senior managers, students' unions, and so on – are actively engaged in and stand to gain from the process of learning and working together. Partnership is essentially a pro-cess of engagement, not a product. It is a way of doing things, rather than an outcome in itself.
>
> (Healey et al., 2014, p.12)

While it could be argued that the latter definition relates well to the focus of social justice partnership on the relationships and process of engagement, neither explicitly rejects neo-liberalism either in part or totality. These definitions are also those of staff, and staff and student perspectives on this matter do not necessarily match. This argument is implicit in a paper by UCL (UK) geography students:

> Changemaker [partnership] programmes can provide the opportunity for students to develop their employability while also ensuring they are active members of their university, holding themselves as much as the university responsible for their educational experience.
>
> (Thorogood et al., 2018, p.3)

It would be ironic if we were to privilege staff voices and perspectives in defining partnership, particularly whilst as a movement we caution about the importance of not moving students away from a student perspective (Felten and Bauman, 2013). The HEA (2014) identified a number of core values for partnership practice, which included authenticity, inclusivity and challenge. We must therefore learn to be ourselves and work in partnership with others as they are, even if the philosophy underpinning their partnership is different to our own. As such we believe that it is incompatible to exclude those who have other motivations or philosophies than our own, and stay true to the values of partnership. Partnership and social justice are not the same thing. They have strong synergies in calling for the redistribution of power – but what if those that we cede power to want to use it in ways that strengthen neo-liberalism? If we are not prepared to cede our power to them, are we *really* ceding it to other partners we work with more willingly?

Neo-liberalism has become naturalised in Western society. Universities still play a civic role serving their local, national and international communities. Nevertheless, growth and success within them are aided by showing how outcomes align with those upon which universities are judged in this neo-liberal environment. Partnership can occur in pockets working towards radical ends. However, if we want it to grow to support inclusivity and to benefit from the better outcomes of partnership practice (both in terms of outputs and for those participating) we need to be pragmatic. Sleeper (as cited in Maxcy, 2003, p.54) defined pragmatism as "a philosophy rooted in common sense and dedicated to the transformation of culture, to the resolution of conflicts that divide us". As such, we need to keep in mind the cultural transformation we are aiming for (Matthews, Cook-Sather et al., 2018) and use common sense to work towards it.

Without the aim to transform wider culture, pockets of ideal practice risk becoming a form of irrelevant self-indulgence – particularly where the focus is on the benefits to participants rather than people beyond the partnership. The way to mainstream partnership, as part of a pragmatic cultural transformation, is by taking account of the context in which one is working and adding in structures to ensure that the practice is effective and meets its aims.

Those engaged in partnerships often emphasise the importance of respecting context (Healey and Healey, 2018). Prioritising context in this way allows for partnership to avoid some of the pitfalls of other academic development approaches, namely a one-size fits all, technocratic, 'what works?' approach. At the moment, the context is neo-liberal and so recognising where partnership forwards neo-liberal aims can aid its normalisation as a practice. We contend that while neo-liberalism and social justice argue very differently for the distribution of resources, sometimes their agendas align. One example of this is where the redistribution of power from staff to students enables the institution to better meet the goals that determine its financial health. We realise that arguing for partnership in this way reinforces the power of neo-liberalism. However, we believe that the gains partnership makes from this are usually worth the compromise. We also recognise that this may not always be the case: judgement is needed. Where does one make compromises for context and where does one need to make a stand for the ideal? We now turn our attention to gatekeepers and the decisions, such as this, that they make.

The importance of gatekeepers

For the purposes of this chapter, gatekeepers are understood to be anyone who maintains a position of power, authority, control or influence over any staff–student partnership and who is typically not directly involved in that partnership. Gatekeepers by this definition could range from: (1) a senior institutional leader who approves funding for partnership activities, to (2) a quality assurance lead whose regulations oversee the reach of changes feasible from co-designing curricula, to (3) a marketing team who choose whether to promote partnership practice to a wider audience. All gatekeepers have some control over either the nature or the perception of partnership and therefore can heavily impact upon its operation. They also have a vested interest in a particular outcome (or perceived outcome) from partnerships. As such, the extent to which the gatekeeping role can affect partnerships will depend on the nature of that role, where it sits institutionally and the individuals who act as gatekeepers. We will focus here on a common form: individuals who organise and oversee structured student engagement activities.

Student–staff partnership can take place in specific activities or roles (a discussion of the breadth of such roles can be found in Dunne, 2016), which define the boundaries of 'acceptable' behaviour. However, a key area in which student–staff partnership has recently proliferated in the UK is within discrete projects that pair individual or groups of students with staff members (Mercer-Mapstone and Marie, 2019). Such initiatives recruit students with staff to work on issues that arise around learning and teaching. Usually situated within a central academic development team or a students' union, the projects themselves can represent a significant commitment of time and effort from staff and students alike. Students are often provided with training and guidance, and are expected to report on their project work. These projects have a varied scope across different institutions ranging from promoting the use of technology (Harvey, 2017), to the general student experience (El-Hakim et al., 2016) and educational development (Marie et al., 2016). What all of these schemes have in common is prioritising change (Dunne and Zandstra, 2011). The extent to which the partnership is equal within such initiatives hinges on a number of factors. This can include the training provided to staff and students, their own motivation (or incentive) for working in such a way and the nature of the project being undertaken (Lowe et al., 2017).

Gatekeepers play a pivotal role, as they are often the ones who make decisions about the organisation of such schemes. In such a scheme, a gatekeeper is likely to be responsible for some (or all) of the following activities (Mercer-Mapstone and Marie, 2019; Mercer-Mapstone and Bovill, 2020):

- Recruitment of students and staff to participate in the scheme.
- Administration of the scheme, including any payment involved.
- Planning and conducting any evaluation of the scheme.
- Wider institutional reporting.
- Setting expectations of how outcomes and impact from partnerships are reported and disseminated.
- Training of staff and students to support their engagement.

Gatekeepers therefore have a great deal of power and authority. Dwyer (2018) has argued for more organic forms of partnership, which arise from dialogue and negotiation between staff and students leading to shared goals and collaboration. While we do not disagree with this as a goal, in a highly structured and sometimes alienating higher education environment, it can be hard for students and staff to engage in a practice that has no immediate objective or support structures. There are many structural and cultural barriers to engagement and to equal, spontaneous partnership. The role of an effective gatekeeper is to ensure equality of access and inclusivity in partnership practice.

As a cultural environment, universities have their own norms, values and practices. To those unfamiliar with those norms (and even sometimes to those very familiar), universities can be a confusing place. Universities can have arcane rules, and engagement as a process and a principle can become ambiguous. While this ambiguity can affect anyone, students who are from working class backgrounds (Reay et al., 2010), the first in their family to attend (Stephens et al., 2012), from minority ethnic backgrounds (Williams, 2017) and international students are particularly affected (Smith and Khawaja, 2011). Furthermore, this ambiguity is especially pronounced in so-called 'elite' institutions (Reay, 2018). Culture aside, universities are enormous institutions which very often move slowly. That communication can be a barrier to engagement in an environment where you may be one of 40,000 students is hardly surprising. A good gatekeeper should aim for multiple approaches to ensure that students are aware of what opportunities and processes are available to move towards partnership (Mercer-Mapstone et al., 2021). This also means being clear about expectations, responsibilities and rewards. Without a well-organised and structured approach to facilitating engagement, partnerships which are based more in the critical pedagogy tradition risk alienating those who are struggling to adapt to higher education. There is a danger of elitism or selectiveness around engagement which is supposedly more organic, where engagement is more natural to those more accustomed to the norms, values and rules of engagement.

There is a fine line between supporting students to conduct such change work effectively and socialisation into institutional norms and values (Felten and

Bauman, 2013). Decisions and judgements will be made on behalf of the institution to determine who or what is appropriate for inclusion in such activities. This may lead to a degree of performativity as students will need to conform to the expectations set by these gatekeepers and will therefore present themselves and their practice accordingly. While the focus and nature of the practice can be very local (i.e. tied to a specific module), this form of partnership is often part of a wider scheme that operates at the broader institutional or departmental level. If partnership between staff and students is the goal, then its success is too fragile to be left to chance, particularly regarding who the gatekeeper is and what their preferences are. A pragmatic approach to gatekeeping student engagement may need to draw on some of the rationality of neo-liberalism to ensure its effectiveness. However, without being rooted in a meaningful value base, there is a risk it will reinforce aspects which are discriminatory or detrimental to student and staff wellbeing. Greater structures, put in place with the mutual agreement of students from governance to practice, are needed to ensure partnerships are not subject to the individual whims of gatekeepers or institutions who may have changing priorities.

The importance of structures

As well as higher education institutional structures being confusing and difficult to navigate to the uninitiated, the work of any institution is guided and constrained by its structures. For example, staff and students are more likely to undertake activities that are rewarded and recognised, and that they feel capable of undertaking successfully, due to support and/or development activities being available. The relative importance of activities is signalled through strategies and the behaviours of those in charge, and so these also guide engagement. Processes are set up for certain norms and oblique for other scenarios, which tacitly directs people towards some undertakings and away from others. Others in the institution may work towards aims that align or conflict with partnership, thereby creating a sense of acceptance and normality (or resistance and marginalisation) to the practice (Bolman and Deal,2017).

Currently, most higher education institutions have structures that are configured in ways that reinforce the power and authority of staff over students (Bovill et al., 2016). In our experience it is difficult for students to book rooms, edit virtual learning environment sites, order catering, manage a budget and even claim expenses. Students are often listened to through student voice mechanisms but less often do we see examples of partnership in practice, particularly from senior managers. Rarely do students have access to the same development sessions as staff for skills such as managing budgets, teams, projects or time.

Wacquant and Bourdieu (1992) conceptualised the symbolic violence that organisations carry out on individuals in order to ensure that they conform and embody the values of that organisation. The term violence is used as this process is seen as the aggressive imposition of one social groupings' set of values upon another. For example, in professional settings there is an idea that certain forms of dress are more acceptable than others, often with a narrow field of acceptability, otherwise you do not conform and will not succeed within an organisation. Do gatekeepers exist to violently impose the symbolic norms of a university (or a particular social grouping which is seen as the norm in universities) or to challenge it? On the one hand, a key function of a gatekeeper may be to ensure that partnership practice is inclusive. This focus on ensuring equality of access and experience for students when engaging in student–staff partnership should actively remove barriers. However, gatekeepers also usually set expectations, which can be around how, when and where students engage. If these expectations are not fairly and mutually agreed with the students then they are imposing a set of values and norms upon them, to which they may not wish to conform.

VanWynsberghe and Herman (2015) argue that pragmatic approaches to education lead to social change, through changes to habits. They provide the comparison of disrupting the habitual behaviour of disposing of garbage in one go, by presenting people with multiple options (e.g. recycling, compost, landfill). This speaks to the necessity in education for structured and experiential opportunities to challenge established behaviour and stimulate learning and engagement. We argue the process is the same for partnership. It is necessary to support staff and students with structures that facilitate the disruption of their usual, habitual behaviour because we, as learners, all respond to our social conditions.

We believe that partnership practice cannot occur in isolation from wider institutional structures and so an ideal of equal power is a fiction and one that will not change unless these structures are addressed. While there are many laudable attempts to challenge these social norms in revolutionary educational ways this is not scalable in the same way as a values-based pragmatic approach to change. The role of a pragmatic gatekeeper, working for cultural change, must include reflecting upon their role in imposing cultural norms, and moreover include working towards institutional structures that, at the least, do not discourage and hinder partnerships.

Some of the structures we put in place as gatekeepers did not necessarily change the wider structures, but they buffered the partnership from them. We held onto budgets and undertook ordering so that students were not beholden to staff partners. We booked rooms and provided training that the students requested. We created oases within our institutions for partnership practice, but in doing so, we had to demonstrate our worth to the institution and put in place further structures to safeguard our schemes from changing personnel and the whims of senior management. In other words, we could buffer the practice from institutional structures but we could not free it from them. In particular, we had to evaluate the different benefits that arose from the schemes in terms that mattered to the institution (student satisfaction, educational and experiential enhancements, retention). In doing so we became beholden to maximising those benefits by selecting projects that had the greatest potential of impact, teaching students how to make change and undertake effective project work in partnership.

Our pragmatism supported partnership practice in a context that is not conducive to it, but we had to make compromises to the ideal of partnership by exerting our own power over the practice. These are compromises we believe are necessary while the longer-term work of cultural change occurs – but this work must not be forgotten, or pragmatic gatekeepers also risk the self-indulgence of creating oases while perpetuating the status quo.

Conclusion

In this chapter, we have argued that for partnership practice to have meaning, it must be working towards the aim of cultural change, rather than living out an ideal in isolation. We believe that to work towards the ideal goal, one must be aware and adapt to the context in which one is working – using common sense. In other words, we are arguing for a pragmatic approach. This is not to say that there is no place for idealism – the pragmatic idealist puts in place structures to take forward an agenda they believe in, recognising that while this may not be the ideal, pragmatism is needed to move closer to the goal.

Gatekeepers, by their very nature, control a boundary – we argue that by doing so, they can create a safe space for partnership practice. This can allow it to become more normal and thus aid cultural change. However, they can also impose their values and ideals of partnership if they do not carefully reflect and maintain awareness of their biases. As such, gatekeepers both provide freedom for partnership practice and risk limiting freedom from control (Gibbs, 2016). Gatekeepers must be critical, self-reflective and problematise their own position, to get the right balance between pragmatism, whereby they support the existence of a safe space within a hostile context, and idealism. Furthermore, pragmatic idealists, whether they are gatekeepers or other advocates for partnership, must work to change the structures that constrain the practice. Higher education institutions privilege staff and privilege certain demographics systemically; dismantling these systemic advantages is necessary to create the conditions in which a culture of student–staff partnership can flourish.

We therefore offer the following recommendations for student–staff partnership scheme gatekeepers going forward:

1 Be pragmatic to move to the ideal, by considering your context and purpose.
2 Work for institutional cultural change by changing structures and working at different levels.
3 Put in place clear oversight and structures that reinforce the values of partnership, particularly for activities supported by other gatekeepers.
4 Be prepared to work with people whose ideals may be different to your own and to listen and understand each other.
5 Reflect on whether you are supporting partners to make change or socialising them into expected norms and behaviours.

References

Boden, R. and Nedeva, M., 2010. Employing discourse: Universities and graduate 'employability'. *Journal of Education Policy*, 25(1), pp.37–54. https://doi.org/10.1080/02680930903349489

Bolman, L.G. and Deal, T.E., 2017. *Reframing Organizations: Artistry, Choice, and Leadership*. New York: John Wiley and Sons.

Bovill, C., Cook-Sather, A., Felten, P., Millard, L. and Moore-Cherry, N., 2016. Addressing potential challenges in co-creating learning and teaching: Overcoming resistance, navigating institutional norms and ensuring inclusivity in student–staff partnerships. *Higher Education*, 71(2), pp.195–208. *Higher Education*, 71(2), pp.195–208. https://doi.org/10.1007/s10734-015-9896-4

Bukodi, E., and Goldthorpe, J. 2021. *Meritocracy and Populism: Is There a Connection?* UKICE Working Paper 01/2021. https://doi.org/10.31235/osf.io/qgrkf

Cook-Sather, A., Bovill, C. and Felten, P., 2014. *Engaging Students as Partners in Learning and Teaching: A Guide for Faculty*. San Francisco, CA: Jossey-Bass.

Dollinger, M. and Mercer-Mapstone, L., 2019. What's in a name? Unpacking students' roles in higher education through neoliberal and social justice lenses. *Teaching and Learning Inquiry*, 7(2), pp.73–89. https://doi.org/10.20343/teachlearninqu.7.2.5

Dunne, E., 2016. Design thinking: A framework for student engagement? A personal view. *Journal of Educational Innovation, Partnership and Change*, 2(1), pp.1–8.

Dunne, E. and Zandstra, R. 2011. *Students as Change Agents: New Ways of Engaging with Learning and Teaching in Higher Education*. Bristol: Escalate.

Dwyer, A. 2018. Toward the formation of genuine partnership spaces. *International Journal for Students as Partners*, 2(1). https://doi.org/10.15173/ijsap.v2i1.3503

El-Hakim, Y., King, S., Lowe, T. and Sims, S., 2016. Evaluating partnership and impact in the first year of the Winchester Student Fellows Scheme. *The Journal of Educational Innovation, Partnership and Change*, 2(1). https://doi.org/10.21100/jeipc.v2i1.257

Felten, P. and Bauman, H.D.L., 2013. Reframing diversity and student engagement: Lessons from deaf-gain. In Dunne, E. and Owen, D. *(eds) Student Engagement Handbook: Practice in Higher Education*. Bingley: Emerald.

Gaerdebo, J., and Wiggberg, M. 2012. Importance of student participation in future academia. In: Gaerdebo, J. and Wiggberg, M. (eds) *Students, the University's Unspent Resource: Revolutionising Higher Education Using Active Student Participation*. Pedagogical Development Report 12. Uppsala: Uppsala Universitet.

Gibbs, A., 2016. Academic freedom in international higher education: Right or responsibility? *Ethics and Education*, 11(2), pp.175–185. https://doi.org/10.1080/17449642.2016.1181844

Harvey, F., 2017. Using Open Badges to support student engagement and evidence based practice. *The Journal of Educational Innovation, Partnership and Change*, 3(1), pp.234–242. https://doi.org/10.21100/jeipc.v3i1.576

HEA. 2014. *Framework for Partnership in Learning and Teaching in Higher Education*. York: HEA.

Healey, M. and Healey, R., 2018. 'It depends': Exploring the context-dependent nature of students as partners practices and policies. *International Journal for Students as Partners*, 2(1), pp.1–10. https://doi.org/10.15173/ijsap.v2i1.3472

Healey, M., Flint, A. and Harrington, K., 2014. *Engagement through Partnership: Students as Partners in Learning and Teaching in Higher Education*. York: HEA.

Lowe, T., Shaw, C., Sims, S., King, S. and Paddison, A., 2017. The development of contemporary student engagement practices at the University of Winchester and Winchester Student Union, UK. *International Journal for Students as Partners*, 1(1). https://doi.org/10.15173/ijsap.v1i1.3082

Marie, J., Arif, M. and Joshi, T., 2016. UCL ChangeMakers projects: Supporting staff/student partnership on educational enhancement projects. *Student Engagement in Higher Education Journal*, 1(1), pp.393–351.

Matthews, K.E., Cook-Sather, A. and Healey, M., 2018. Connecting learning, teaching, and research through student–staff partnerships: Toward universities as egalitarian learning communities. In: Tong, V., Standen, A. and Sotiriou, M. (ed), *Shaping Higher Education with Students: Ways to Connect Research and Teaching*. London: University College of London Press. https://doi.org/10.2307/j.ctt21c4tcm.7

Matthews, K.E., Dwyer, A., Hine, L. and Turner, J., 2018. Conceptions of students as partners. *Higher Education*, 76(6), pp.957–971. https://doi.org/10.1007/s10734-018-0257-y

Maxcy, S.J., 2003. Pragmatic threads in mixed methods research in the social sciences: The search for multiple modes of inquiry and the end of the philosophy of formalism. In Tashakkori, A. and Teddlie, C. (eds) *Handbook of Mixed Methods in Social and Behavioral Research*. Thousand Oaks, CA: Sage.

Mercer-Mapstone, L. and Bovill, C., 2020. Equity and diversity in institutional approaches to student–staff partnership schemes in higher education. *Studies in Higher Education*, 45(12), pp.2541–2557. https://doi.org/10.1080/03075079.2019.1620721

Mercer-Mapstone, L., and Marie, J., 2019. *Practical Guide: Scaling Up Student–Staff Partnerships in Higher Education*. Edinburgh: Institute for Academic Development, University of Edinburgh.

Mercer-Mapstone, L., Islam, M. and Reid, T., 2021. Are we just engaging 'the usual suspects'? Challenges in and practical strategies for supporting equity and diversity in student–staff partnership initiatives. *Teaching in Higher Education*, 26(2), pp.227–245. https://doi.org/10.1080/13562517.2019.1655396

Mercer-Mapstone, L., Dvorakova, L.S., Matthews, K.E., Abbot, S., Cheng, B., Felten, P., Knorr, K., Marquis, E., Shammas, R. and Swaim, K., 2017. A systematic literature review of students as partners in higher education. *International Journal for Students as Partners*, 1(1). https://doi.org/10.15173/ijsap.v1i1.3119

Moore-Cherry, N., Healey, R., Nicholson, D.T. and Andrews, W., 2016. Inclusive partnership: Enhancing student engagement in geography. *Journal of Geography in Higher Education*, 40(1), pp.84–103. https://doi.org/10.1080/03098265.2015.1066316

Reay, D., 2018. Miseducation: Inequality, education and the working classes. *International Studies in Sociology of Education*, 27(4), pp.453–456. https://doi.org/10.1080/09620214.2018.1531229

Reay, D., Crozier, G. and Clayton, J., 2010. 'Fitting in' or 'standing out': Working-class students in UK higher education. *British Educational Research Journal*, 36(1), pp.107–124. https://doi.org/10.1080/01411920902878925

Smith, R.A. and Khawaja, N.G., 2011. A review of the acculturation experiences of international students. *International Journal of Intercultural Relations*, 35(6), pp.699–713. https://doi.org/10.1016/j.ijintrel.2011.08.004

Stephens, N.M., Fryberg, S.A., Markus, H.R., Johnson, C.S. and Covarrubias, R., 2012. Unseen disadvantage: How American universities' focus on independence undermines the academic performance of first-generation college students. *Journal of Personality and Social Psychology*, 102(6), p.1178. https://doi.org/10.1037/a0027143

Thorogood, J., Azuma, F., Collins, C., Plyushteva, A. and Marie, J., 2018. Changemakers and change agents: Encouraging students as researchers through Changemaker's programmes. *Journal of Geography in Higher Education*, 42(4), pp.540–556. https://doi.org/10.1080/03098265.2018.1460804

VanWynsberghe, R. and Herman, A.C., 2015. Education for social change and pragmatist theory: Five features of educative environments designed for social change. *International Journal of Lifelong Education*, 34(3), pp.268–283. https://doi.org/10.1080/02601370.2014.988189

Villa, R.A., Thousand, J.S. and Nevin, A.I. (eds), 2010. *Collaborating with Students in Instruction and Decision Making: The Untapped Resource*. Thousand Oaks, CA: Corwin Press.

Wacquant, L.J. and Bourdieu, P., 1992. *An Invitation to Reflexive Sociology*. Cambridge: Polity.

Williams, S., 2017. *Beyond Access towards Success for First-Generation College Students of Underrepresented Ethnic Backgrounds: The Role of College Adjustment and Perceived Stressors on Academic Achievement during the First Year*. DePaul University College of Science and Health Theses and Dissertations. 207. https://via.library.depaul.edu/csh_etd/207

Young, M.D., 1959. *The Rise of the Meritocracy, 1870–2033: The New Elite of Our Social Revolution*. New York: Random House.

Chapter 13

To what extent can we really make students partners in neoliberal universities?

Tanya Lubicz-Nawrocka

Introduction

With the dramatic rise of student engagement since the 1980s when the term was conceptualised, ambiguity about the term has also arisen since it is currently used in countless numbers of ways (Lowe and El Hakim, 2020). Now the terms student–staff partnership and curriculum co-creation – as approaches to learning and teaching that promote high levels of student engagement – have similarly gained popularity in the last 10–15 years (Mercer-Mapstone et al., 2017; Bovill and Woolmer, 2019). Along with the enthusiasm for this way of working in collaboration, ambiguity has now similarly arisen in this area with a proliferation of terms for and practices involving partnership and co-creation (Dunne, 2016; Cook-Sather et al., 2018).

There are often similar and overlapping aims, processes, and outcomes involved in partnership and co-creation based on the nature of relationships developed between students and staff. Partnership is often seen as an 'umbrella term' for highly collaborative, curricular and extra-curricular projects that enhance the student experience (Cook-Sather et al., 2018). Sometimes partnership implies a level of equality in decision-making that can sometimes conflict with the reality of academic structures and constraints (Bovill, 2020a). I have focused on using the term curriculum co-creation in my work, which I have come to define as a values-based, creative process in which staff and students work together to share and negotiate decision-making about aspects of curricula, often leading to mutual benefits for learners and teachers (Lubicz-Nawrocka, 2020). This is a relational way of working underpinned by shared responsibility, reciprocity in learning from each other, mutual respect, care, trust, and empathy.

When the editor of this book proposed the question 'How much can we really make students partners in a neoliberal higher education?', I was immediately drawn in. In part, I wanted to reflect more fully on student–staff partnerships in higher education by going beyond my previous research into the benefits and challenges of curriculum co-creation to explore the latter with respect to neoliberal agendas in higher education. I was also intrigued by the word 'make', leading me to dwell on its many facets with respect to partnership. 'To make' is a verb with

DOI: 10.4324/9781003271789-13

many definitions: to force someone to do something, to perform an action, to earn, to produce something, to cause something or someone to be or become, to succeed in, to arrive at or reach successfully (Cambridge Dictionary, 2022). In this chapter, I draw on some of these different angles with respect to recent literature and findings from my doctoral thesis to explore various facets of partnership and co-creation in neoliberal universities.

To make, as in to produce opportunities for partnership with students

Due to staff having expertise, responsibilities, and power concerning curriculum planning and quality assurance, educators are often in a stronger position than students to produce opportunities to work in partnership to co-create aspects of curricula (Lubicz-Nawrocka, 2020). The ethos of partnership and the shared values that serve as a foundation for curriculum co-creation tend to produce opportunities for vibrant learning communities to come together to enhance learning and teaching in higher education. The relational dimension of this work can foster the conditions for student and staff development (Bovill, 2020a). An element of creating and producing during the curriculum co-creation experience has been described as follows:

> There's a symbiosis between us and things that are in the ether now that weren't there before... creating learning materials, creating learning experiences, this idea of the whole being more than the sum of its parts: it's a dialogue between the lecturer and the students, so the learning can be an emergent property of the expertise of the lecturer and the lived experience of the student.
>
> (Staff Participant in Lubicz-Nawrocka, 2020, p.142)

Although engaging in partnership work will not be possible or appropriate for every course, it is also important to produce opportunities so that students and staff can experience the benefits (Lubicz-Nawrocka and Bovill, 2021).

The pandemic has been an extremely challenging period in many ways for those in higher education, but this destabilising time has also created new opportunities for partnership while staff and students have navigated new digital, blended, and hybrid ways of working (Lubicz-Nawrocka and Owen, 2022). For example, some staff and student partners built on the foundations of their previous in-person collaborations that positioned them well to be resilient and creative while adapting to lockdown and changing lived experiences (Ntem et al., 2020; Riddell et al., 2021). Although student partners can help increase institutional capacity, partnership and co-creation cannot be implemented in a tokenistic way or badged as a way to shift staff workloads onto students (Lubicz-Nawrocka, 2020). For example, curriculum co-creation is "not a part [of learning and teaching] that you can just whip out and say, 'Hey, you can do a bit of co-creation!'. It's quite serious and quite difficult" (Lubicz-Nawrocka, 2020, p.203).

Therefore, we need to be extremely careful that we do not produce opportunities for partnership and co-creation for the wrong reasons. Freire (1972), Fielding (1999), and Peters and Mathias (2018) highlight the clear ontological and political distinctions between what could be viewed as instrumental motives that drive collaboration as compared to liberatory motives to advance collegiality and social responsibility. The connections between Freire's work and wider students-as-partners work have been acknowledged elsewhere (Bovill et al., 2009; Peters and Mathias, 2018). Dialogue is key to Freire's work in uniting reflection and action to promote critical analysis and help individuals to perceive possibilities for change (Crotty, 1998). Crotty (1998, p. 153) explains Freire's view:

> The teacher is no longer merely the one who teaches, for the teacher is also taught in dialogue with the students. And the students, while being taught, also teach. In this way, teacher and students become jointly responsible for a process in which all of them grow.

Neoliberal institutions' focus on efficiency, productivity, and growth of the economy (Troiani and Dutson, 2021) can contrast sharply with Freire's conception of dialogical education and partnerships between teachers and students that are motivated by personal growth and social justice (Freire, 1972). Although students and staff are bringing different forms of knowledge and experience, their dialogue, respect, and reciprocity help unite them to work towards shared aims while both students and staff become at once learners and teachers. Developing these positive relationships between students and educators is a process that takes time but is often key to enhancing what we do in higher education (Bovill, 2020b).

To make, as in to force students (or not)

Can we force students to be our partners? Many excellent examples of partnerships include students and staff who self-select to work actively on projects that benefit the wider student experience (Mercer-Mapstone et al., 2017), as well as highly engaged students working with educators in projects to evaluate aspects of the curriculum and co-create enhancements before courses for future students (Bovill and Woolmer, 2019). In these examples, students and educators are far from being forced to engage in partnership work, as evidenced by the energy, enthusiasm, and passion they bring to the collaborations that they actively choose to be a part of (Cook-Sather et al., 2014; Mercer-Mapstone et al., 2017).

Whole-class co-creation in the curriculum – as a course or module is taking place – often aims to foster more inclusive opportunities across a cohort to engage wider numbers of students in this learning opportunity (Bovill and Woolmer, 2019). These examples are increasingly seen to promote inclusion, accessibility, and engagement in active learning and shared decision-making that can take place within smaller cohorts and, increasingly, at scale with larger cohorts, both in person and online (Blau and Shamir-Inbal, 2018; Bovill, 2020b; Lubicz-Nawrocka and Owen, 2022). In these examples, staff are often choosing to adopt a relational pedagogy that is dialogic (Bovill, 2020a), and they can require some aspects of co-creation as part of a course, but this engagement is built on shared values and aims.

Students could choose not to engage in whole-class co-creation and, in the spirit of partnership, this is a legitimate option that can and should be discussed. As one educator has described, the benefits and challenges involved should be clear: "If you're going to be involved in this, here's what you need to do. If you don't want to do that, then there needs to be dialogue about why" (Staff Participant in Lubicz-Nawrocka, 2020, p.118). Therefore, rather than feeling forced, student and staff co-creators often view this experience as an opportunity to negotiate an outcome that enhances the learning and teaching experience (Lubicz-Nawrocka, 2019b).

The popularity of student engagement and partnerships may be, in part, due to the tangible benefits for student learning as seen 'on the ground' in courses where students engage more actively in learning and teaching, and also in part due to a strong push from the top from the Quality Assurance Agency, the Office for Students, and funding councils in the UK context (Lowe and El Hakim, 2020). With this popularity, some have critiqued that student engagement has lost its focus on benefitting student learning as neoliberal higher education institutions have embedded the term into discourse, structures, and policy (Macfarlane and Tomlinson, 2017). In this way, student engagement "has been referred to as the product of a marketised, neoliberal system which seeks to appropriate the student voice" (Lowe and El Hakim, 2020, p. 16). We also need to be wary that some neoliberal institutions may try to appropriate partnership and co-creation. These institutions should not force co-creation on individuals – thus contradicting its liberatory aims of fostering agency and social justice. Instead, universities should support those who do wish to engage in partnership, but they will also need to be prepared for what giving students agency means in practice. Furthermore, both staff and students will need to be supported to navigate these new ways of working by sharing decision-making power.

To make, as in to perform an action of partnership working

Both staff and students can find working in partnership to co-create curricula extremely rewarding and fulfilling forms of learning and teaching (Cook-Sather et al., 2014; Lowe and El Hakim, 2020; Lubicz-Nawrocka, 2020). For example, when students and staff become partners, there are many positive outcomes for their development in relation to their engagement, communication, relationships, motivation, and confidence in particular (Mercer-Mapstone et al., 2017; Matthews et al., 2018). This experience is often found to be transformational for students and, potentially, for staff and institutions (Cook-Sather et al., 2014; Matthews et al., 2018; Lubicz-Nawrocka and Bovill, 2021). For example, a student co-creator has reflected: "It really makes you feel proud of what you have done and it makes you see what you can achieve within the university when you get given the opportunity" (Student Participant in Lubicz-Nawrocka, 2020, p.181).

While there are many benefits of co-creating curricula, we also need to recognise the challenges of performing the action of partnership working within neoliberal universities. It is important to note that different types of challenges can arise from different types of co-creation projects depending on the number of participants, the nature and timing of their co-creation work, the nature of the university environment, and many other variables (Lubicz-Nawrocka, 2020). Healey and Healey (2018) also describe the many different manifestations of partnership where, often, 'it depends' based on each context. Despite these differences, there are some cross-cutting structural and procedural challenges for curriculum co-creation in neoliberal universities which I discuss briefly in this section.

Academic structures, processes, and cultures can present challenges for partnerships. For example, the way teaching is organised within universities can make implementing curriculum co-creation difficult, since bureaucratic functions such as which faculty takes responsibility for which examination board, the timing of Boards of Studies' course planning and approval processes, and the constraints of timetabling can all hinder more innovative and interdisciplinary approaches to teaching and learning (Lubicz-Nawrocka, 2020). Rather than engaging in partnerships, lecturers tend to re-use presentation slides and recorded lectures since "Universities reward that model. If you do something outwith that, timetabling and workload for instance can be a problem" (Staff Participant in Lubicz-Nawrocka, 2020, p.199). Neoliberal workload allocation models – focused on efficiency and measurement – are a challenge. Academics' high workloads across teaching, research, and other university contributions all reduce their time available to work in partnership with students. For instance, many educators "haven't really got a lot of space to be thinking outside the box... [so] you're just going to fall back on what you always do" (Staff Participant in Lubicz-Nawrocka, 2020, p.199).

Both educators and students describe how developing partnerships takes time, including building relationships and navigating new ways of working and communicating (Healey and Healey, 2018; Matthews et al., 2018; Bovill, 2020a; El Hakim et al., 2020). How we relate to students and communicate has a strong influence on our working relationships with students, which can influence what students perceive as quality teaching (Lubicz-Nawrocka and Bunting, 2019; MacKay et al., 2019). However, sometimes staff workloads, stress, and pressures in neoliberal institutions can lead to unintended brusqueness that can make students feel that staff are being rude or de-prioritising teaching. Whether intended or not, rudeness or incivility in the eyes of the recipient has been found in psychological research to lead to declines in individuals' engagement, collaboration, creativity, and ability to meet their potential (Riskin et al., 2015; Porath and Erez, 2017).

Nurturing students' active engagement, collaboration, creativity, and ability to meet their potential are of course key aspects of curriculum co-creation (Lubicz-

Nawrocka, 2019a). Others such as Troiani and Dutson (2021) have argued that we need to reclaim how neoliberal universities have used our material, human, and intellectual resources and instead rethink how we act as socially and ethically responsible members of our academic community. Staff co-creators work flexibly to do so while listening to students, for example:

> It is very much a course that has adapted to what they [students] have wanted to do and what we have collectively agreed might be useful… A lot of the course design was leaving enough leeway that an external [examiner] wouldn't question why things were in the course guide, but you had flexibility to change things.
>
> (Staff Participant in Lubicz-Nawrocka, 2020, p.198)

Furthermore, other staff co-creators shift their mindset and look for how to mitigate challenges:

> You take a risk, but actually we have lots of structures within the University which are there to mitigate that risk… [With an exam board, for example] you can see it as a safety net so that's how I started looking at it.
>
> (Staff Participant in Lubicz-Nawrocka, 2020, p.210)

Those working in partnership and co-creating curricula appear to be overcoming structural and procedural challenges to do so (Peters and Mathias, 2018; Lubicz-Nawrocka, 2019b).

To make, as in to cause to be or become partners

To be or become partners can also require students and staff to overcome cultural or personal vulnerabilities while embedding partnerships that can contrast sharply with institutional norms and cultures (Bovill et al., 2016; Lubicz-Nawrocka, 2020). For instance, curriculum co-creation can challenge the status quo with respect to 'traditional' university cultures including their ethos, academic hierarchies, and pedagogies (Lubicz-Nawrocka, 2017; Peters and Mathias, 2018). Some educators, though, recognise these constraints in neoliberal institutions but actively work to overcome challenges to enact curriculum co-creation, which can be a way of seeing "how we take the constraints that we have to live with and work against them to create those communities of trust and genuine learning" (Staff Participant in Lubicz-Nawrocka, 2020, p.198).

Another educator also described the potential for co-creators who overcome challenges:

> It is a powerful way in which we can reengage and rethink the University rather than complaining about it… [However] we have a lot of resistance because people have always done things in certain ways and it is much easier

to be didactic and not have to engage in that type of [partnership-based] learning and teaching… Certainly we have a whole system of support which is… patronising students.

(Staff Participant in Lubicz-Nawrocka, 2020, p.190)

By contrast, curriculum co-creation gives students agency. In so doing, this can expose some personal vulnerabilities for staff who share decision-making power with students and try more innovative teaching practices; similarly, students can feel vulnerable when developing the confidence to engage in these different ways of more active learning in partnership with staff (Lubicz-Nawrocka, 2020). For example, one student co-creator reflected: "I think the purpose of the module wasn't to have students feel comfortable… It is about engaging, not being afraid of saying what you have to say, trusting other people, respecting other people" (Student Participant in Lubicz-Nawrocka, 2020, p.216).

In overcoming vulnerabilities and embracing new forms of agency, curriculum co-creation and partnership working can also have a positive influence on individuals' identities. For instance, a "partnership identity seemed to provide a space where partners could move away from distinctions between group identities of 'us' and 'them' to a shared space of 'we' as partners" (Mercer-Mapstone et al., 2018, p.21). Similarly, in line with Freire's work (1972), "co-creating the curriculum can contribute to students' development when they embrace responsibility as confident contributors who enter a Third Space in-between traditional student and staff roles and identities as both learners and teachers" (Lubicz-Nawrocka, 2019b, p.41).

This is powerful for staff and students as they disrupt previous ways of working since "Co-creation is challenging and there is bound to be some resistance to changing accepted ways of learning and teaching, but transformation is by its very nature disruptive" (Lubicz-Nawrocka and Bovill, 2021, p. 15). Indeed, some staff and students actively choose to become partners since they are motived to challenge neoliberal or consumerist attitudes in higher education (Peters and Mathias, 2018; Lubicz-Nawrocka, 2020).

To make, as in to reach a successful sense of partnership

There are notable challenges for curriculum co-creation since some elements of partnership are at odds with how neoliberal universities are structured and work. With the urge to develop an efficient higher education system that produces graduates who will benefit the economy, universities have often focused on measurable positive outcomes in relation to students' experiences, outcomes, and employability (Troiani and Dutson, 2021). Aspects of curriculum co-creation such as students' intangible experiences, journeys, and transformations through their engagement with staff and peers can be difficult to capture and measure. In the UK, end-of-course evaluations, National Student Survey[1] results, and data on students' destinations following the completion of their degree programmes tend to be used to measure positive outcomes of higher education experiences. However, student voice as captured only through measurable surveys and data can position students as customers rather than as partners.

El Hakim et al. (2020, p.28) have cautioned that "The 'customer' rhetoric increases the likelihood of creating an environment where it is harder for students to work closely with staff to enhance their learning experiences". Some educators in my research also saw this rhetoric as problematic and hindering curriculum co-creation, for example:

> We have taken on this language of neo-liberalism without actually challenging it in many ways... Just because you said, it doesn't mean we have to do anything and just because you didn't say it doesn't mean we shouldn't do something.
>
> (Staff Participant in Lubicz-Nawrocka, 2020, p.195)

Similarly, Bovill and Woolmer (2020) describe how 'you said, we did' outcomes of evaluations in neoliberal institutions contrast sharply with student engagement and partnerships in conducting evaluations of learning and teaching that can provide staff with new insights. They described how "Involving students in the meaning-making processes that take place in evaluation, as well as involving students in the actions we take as a result, is particularly important" since otherwise staff perspectives and motivations can dominate decision-making in neoliberal universities (Bovill and Woolmer, 2020, p.88).

How do we know if we have reached a successful sense of partnership working? In an ideal world, we could involve students as partners who help us evaluate a wide range of aspects of learning and teaching – including our partnerships and curriculum co-creation opportunities – to understand what success looks like. Partnership and co-creation are often recognised as context-specific, dialogic processes of developing the ways in which students and staff share responsibility (Bovill, 2020b; Healey and Healey, 2018), so we may not always feel that we have successfully reached partnership since we may be focused on the continual process of development and enhancement. However, this recognition of ongoing, sustained partnership work is a form of success in itself cited by students and staff who differentiate between process and outcome (Cook-Sather et al., 2021).

Student and staff authors also reflect on other hallmarks of effective partnerships, including: shared ownership, decision-making, and mutual benefits; recognising and attending to the unique needs of partners; pushing the boundaries of individuals' comfort zones by challenging norms and asking new questions; and promoting adaptability and responsiveness, particularly in response to the COVID-19 pandemic (Cook-Sather et al., 2021, p. 222). Many of these themes have been discussed above in relation to the development of student and staff partners as they reap benefits while overcoming challenges presented by neoliberal institutions. In this way, partnership and co-creation have been seen to advance transformation for individuals (Mercer-Mapstone et al., 2018; Lubicz-Nawrocka and Bovill, 2021) which can also promote civic engagement and innovation that may lead to institutional, local community, and national change (Lubicz-Nawrocka, 2019b; El Hakim et al., 2020).

Recommendations for practice

It is important that we do not use partnership and curriculum co-creation as buzzwords so that we avoid neoliberal institutions co-opting the terms and so that we mitigate their tokenistic use in higher education discourse. Instead, we need to recognise the complexities of these terms and return to their original aims. We need to be clear about why and how we can produce opportunities for partnership with students, starting small and building confidence for everyone involved. Rather than forcing individuals – either students or staff – to engage in partnership, institutions should create spaces to foster co-creation including flexible and inclusive physical spaces as well as digital learning spaces that advance collaboration. It is also important to make space in our busy lives and commitments to allow us to engage in meaningful conversations about learning and teaching. To do this, we can make time and foster wellbeing by simplifying academic approval and quality processes and also by hiring appropriate numbers of staff so that workloads are manageable.

By creating these spaces for curriculum co-creation and sharing our learning and teaching practices more broadly with our students, we can start to change academic cultures and hierarchies to empower students and staff to work as partners. We also need to recognise the complexities of relationship-based and dialogic pedagogies that change based on each community of learners and educators involved. These relationships take time to build, and they are difficult to measure and quantify in terms of reaching a sense of successful partnership. However, by re-emphasising the ways in which partnership and co-creation foster engagement with learning and teaching, both students and educators can work collaboratively to navigate any obstacles or risks that may arise.

Concluding thoughts

Returning to the title of this chapter, we can ask to what extent can we really make students partners in neoliberal universities? We can offer opportunities for students and staff to become partners, but we want to make sure they can choose to do so in ways that foster agency and meaningful learning experiences for all involved.

In this chapter, I have explored the ways in which we can produce space for partnership when working towards liberatory aims, what the action of partnership can look and feel like, why we may face challenges when becoming partners, and how we can reach a sense of successful partnership. I have attempted to expose and reflect on some of the challenges for partners working in neoliberal institutions since it is important for those who may want to start engaging in partnership and co-creation to anticipate and work to overcome obstacles. However, I have also explored the benefits of partnership and curriculum co-creation which have been seen to drive change by using relational pedagogy to promote innovation within neoliberal institutions. With innovation comes risk, but risk can also give us new opportunities to learn, rethink how we work, and pursue what it is that we find most valuable about higher education.

Note

1 The National Student Survey is a UK-wide, official survey administered to final-year undergraduate students to help understand student satisfaction with their degree programme.

References

Blau, I. and Shamir-Inbal, T., 2018. Digital technologies for promoting 'student voice' and co-creating learning experience in an academic course. *Instructional Science*, 46(2), pp.315–336. https://doi.org/10.1007/s11251-017-9436-y

Bovill, C., 2020a. *Co-Creating Learning and Teaching: Towards Relational Pedagogy in Higher Education*. St Albans: Critical Publishing.

Bovill, C., 2020b. Co-creation in learning and teaching: The case for a whole-class approach in higher education. *Higher Education*, 79, pp.1023–1037. https://doi.org/10.1007/s10734-019-00453-w

Bovill, C. and Woolmer, C., 2020. Student engagement in evaluation: Expanding perspectives and ownership. In: Lowe, T. and El-Hakim, Y. (eds) *A Handbook for Student Engagement in Higher Education*. Abingdon: Routledge.

Bovill, C. and Woolmer, C., 2019. How conceptualisations of curriculum in higher education influence student–staff co-creation in and of the curriculum. *Higher Education*, 78, pp.407–422. https://doi.org/10.1007/s10734-018-0349-8

Bovill, C., Cook-Sather, A., Felten, P., Millard, L. and Moore-Cherry, N., 2016. Addressing potential challenges in co-creating learning and teaching: Overcoming resistance, navigating institutional norms and ensuring inclusivity in student–staff partnerships. *Higher Education*, 71(2), pp.195–208. https://doi.org/10.1007/s10734-015-9896-4

Bovill, C., Morss, K. and Bulley, C., 2009. Should students participate in curriculum design? Discussion arising from a first year curriculum design project and a literature review. *Pedagogical Research in Maximising Education*, 3(2), pp.17–25.

Cambridge Dictionary, 2022. 'Make'. Available at: https://dictionary.cambridge.org/dictionary/english/make (accessed: 16 June 2022).

Cook-Sather, A., Slates, S., Allen, M., Baskaran, R., Crombie, P., Derounian, J.G., Dianati, S., Dudson, M., Grayson, D., Haroon, M.A., Fraser, C., Jardine, H., Millmore, A., Milton, E., Mori, Y., Morgan, A., Pereira, J.V.-B., Salman, M., Scharff, L., Storey, J., Sum, K. and Tisdell, C.C., 2021. The many manifestations of successful partnership. *International Journal for Students as Partners*, 5(2), pp.221–232. https://doi.org/10.15173/ijsap.v5i2.4911

Cook-Sather, A., Matthews, K.E., Ntem, A. and Leathwick, S., 2018. What we talk about when we talk about students as partners. *International Journal for Students as Partners*, 2(2), pp.1–9. https://doi.org/10.15173/ijsap.v2i2.3790

Cook-Sather, A., Bovill, C. and Felten, P., 2014. *Engaging Students as Partners in Learning and Teaching: A Guide for Faculty*. San Francisco, CA: Jossey-Bass.

Crotty, M., 1998. *The Foundations of Social Research: Meaning and Perspective in the Research Process*. Thousand Oaks, CA: Sage.

Dunne, L., 2016. Preface. *Journal of Educational Innovation, Partnership and Change*, 2 (1). https://doi.org/10.21100/jeipc.v2i1.317

El Hakim, Y., Kandiko Howson, C. and Freeman, R., 2020. Creating relationships between students, staff and universities for student engagement in educational developments. In: Lowe, T. and El-Hakim, Y. (eds) *A Handbook for Student Engagement in Higher Education*. Abingdon: Routledge. https://doi.org/10.4324/9780429023033–3

Fielding, M., 1999. Radical collegiality: Affirming teaching as an inclusive professional practice. *The Australian Educational Researcher*, 26(2), pp.1–34. https://doi.org/10.1007/BF03219692

Freire, P., 1972. *Pedagogy of the Oppressed*. Harmondsworth: Penguin Books.

Healey, M. and Healey, R., 2018. 'It depends': Exploring the context-dependent nature of students as partners practices and policies. *International Journal for Students as Partners*, 2(1), pp.1–10. https://doi.org/10.15173/ijsap.v2i1.3472

Lowe, T. and El Hakim, Y., 2020. An introduction to student engagement in higher education. In: Lowe, T. and El-Hakim, Y. (eds) *A Handbook for Student Engagement in Higher Education*. Abingdon: Routledge.

Lubicz-Nawrocka, T., 2020. *An Exploration of How Curriculum Co-Creation Advances Student and Staff Aims for Scottish Higher Education*. Unpublished doctoral thesis, University of Edinburgh. http://dx.doi.org/10.7488/era/496

Lubicz-Nawrocka, T., 2019a. Creativity and collaboration: An exploration of empathy, inclusion, and resilience in co-creation of the curriculum. *Student Engagement in Higher Education Journal*, 2(3), pp.199–213.

Lubicz-Nawrocka, T., 2019b. "More than just a student": How co-creation of the curriculum fosters Third Spaces in ways of working, identity, and impact. *International Journal for Students as Partners*, 3(1), pp.34–49. https://doi.org/10.15173/ijsap.v3i1.3727

Lubicz-Nawrocka, T., 2017. Co-creation of the curriculum: Challenging the status quo to embed partnership. *Journal of Educational Innovation, Partnership and Change*, 3(2). https://doi.org/10.21100/jeipc.v3i2.529

Lubicz-Nawrocka, T. and Bovill, C., 2021. Do students experience transformation through co-creating curriculum in higher education? *Teaching in Higher Education*. https://doi.org/10.1080/13562517.2021.1928060

Lubicz-Nawrocka, T. and Bunting, K., 2019. Student perceptions of teaching excellence: An analysis of student-led teaching award nomination data. *Teaching in Higher Education*, 24(1), pp.63–80. https://doi.org/10.1080/13562517.2018.1461620

Lubicz-Nawrocka, T. and Owen, J., 2022. Curriculum co-creation in a postdigital world: Advancing networked learning and engagement. *Postdigital Science and Education*. https://doi.org/10.1007/s42438-022-00304-5

Macfarlane, B. and Tomlinson, M., 2017. Critiques of student engagement. *Higher Education Policy*, 30(1), pp.5–21. https://doi.org/10.1057/s41307-016-0027-3

MacKay, J.R.D., Hughes, K., Marzetti, H., Lent, N. and Rhind, S., 2019. Using National Student Survey (NSS) qualitative data and social identity theory to explore students' experiences of assessment and feedback. *Higher Education Pedagogies*, 4(1), pp.315–330. https://doi.org/10.1080/23752696.2019.1601500

Matthews, K.E., Cook-Sather, A. and Healey, M., 2018. Connecting learning, teaching, and research through student–staff partnerships: Toward universities as egalitarian learning communities. In: Tong, V.C.H., Standen, A. and Sotiriou, M. (ed) *Shaping Higher Education with Students*. London: UCL Press.

Mercer-Mapstone, L.D., Marquis, E. and McConnell, C., 2018. The 'partnership identity' in higher education: Moving from 'us' and 'them' to 'we' in student–staff partnership. *Student Engagement in Higher Education Journal*, 2(1), pp.12–29. https://sehej.raise-network.com/raise/article/view/Mercer-Mapstone

Mercer-Mapstone, L.D., Dvorakova, S.L., Matthews, K.E., Abbot, S., Cheng, B., Felten, P., Knorr, K., Marquis, E., Shammas, R., Swaim, K., 2017. A systematic literature review of students as partners in higher education. *International Journal for Students as Partners*, 1(1). https://doi.org/10.15173/ijsap.v1i1.3119

Ntem, A., Nguyen, E., Raferty, C., Kwan, C. and Benlahcene, A., 2020. Students as partners in crisis? Student co-editors' perspectives on COVID-19, values, and the shift to virtual spaces. *International Journal for Students as Partners*, 4(3), pp.1–8. https://doi.org/10.15173/ijsap.v4i2.4432

Peters, J. and Mathias, L., 2018. Enacting student partnership as though we really mean it: Some Freirean principles for a pedagogy of partnership. *International Journal for Students as Partners*, 2(2), pp.53–70. https://doi.org/10.15173/ijsap.v2i2.3509

Porath, C. and Erez, A., 2017. Does rudeness really matter? The effects of rudeness on task performance and helpfulness. *Academy of Management Journal*, 50(5). https://doi.org/10.5465/amj.2007.20159919

Riddell, J., Gadoury-Sansfaçon, G.-P. and Stoddard, S., 2021. Building institutional capacities for students as partners in the design of COVID classrooms. *International Journal for Students as Partners*, 5(2), pp.111–122. https://doi.org/10.15173/ijsap.v5i2.4603

Riskin, A., Erez, A., Foulk T.A., Kugelman, A., Gover, A., Shoris, I., Riskin, K.S. and Bamberger, P.A., 2015. The impact of rudeness on medical team performance: A randomized trial. *Pediatrics*, 136(3), pp.487–495. https://doi.org/10.1542/peds.2015-1385

Troiani, I. and Dutson, C., 2021. The neoliberal university as a space to learn/think/work in higher education. *Architecture and Culture*, 9(1), pp.5–23. https://doi.org/10.1080/20507828.2021.1898836

Critical challenges to support Generation Z learners

Mollie Dollinger

Universities around the world have already educated millions of Generation Z learners. But with birth years ranging from 1996 to 2012, there will be many more of this cohort to educate in the years ahead. The Pew Research Center (2020) predicts that Generation Z learners are on track to be the best-educated generation yet, with estimates that over half will participate in some form of higher education. Frequently nicknamed the world's first 'digital natives' or the 'zoom generation', Generation Z learners have often grown up with technology in a remarkably different way than the generations before them. Studies have also begun to draw conclusions on the preferences of Generation Z learners. These include a proclivity for media-rich learning environments and their preference for educational approaches that embed a career focus, perhaps relating to their more practical and financially conscious tendencies than the generations before them (Mosca, Curtis and Savoth, 2019; Seemiller and Grace, 2017).

While generational studies and their subsequent findings can be problematic if taken as gospel, they can provide insight into a specific cohort's shared life experiences. Major events, such as 9/11 for example, have been shown to impact everyone regardless of age (Costanza et al., 2017). However, it is possible that the timing of the event, or when the event took place in a person's life, can have particular meaning or impact. To illustrate, some researchers often refer to the Generation Z cohort as having grown up during key social justice movements such as Black Lives Matter and School Strike for Climate, as well as an increase in public mass shootings, and the growth of social media as key markers in their formative years (Miller and Mills, 2019; Seemiller and Grace, 2017). Of course, the COVID-19 pandemic has also impacted many Generation Z learners at a particularly formative time in their lives, not only affecting the way they study, but their social lives, work opportunities, and beliefs about healthcare and science, to name a few (Ang et al., 2021; Jayathilake et al., 2021; Marshall and Wolanskyj-Spinner, 2020).

In this chapter, I will briefly touch upon some of the key topics that relate to how universities can support Generation Z learners. These insights are often taken from literature that focuses on a specific country or context, so I urge the reader to consider these findings within their own specific context and in regard to their

DOI: 10.4324/9781003271789-14

targeted student cohort. The topics I will cover include Generation Z's technological exposure, the emergence of new online platforms that allow for user content creation, the potential impact on tuition fees of Generation Z learners, and the rise of what some have coined the 'we-centric' culture (Mohr and Mohr, 2017).

Technological exposure

A frequently cited point of difference in the Generation Z cohort is how they were exposed to technology from a young age (Prenksy, 2001). However, while some simplistically may assume this means incoming students are better or more comfortable with technology, scholars have noted the situation is likely far more complicated (Bennett, Maton and Kervin, 2008). Imagine growing up with social media, where classmates know you not only as a person in their school, but as your online identity (or, potentially, lack thereof). Depending on the specific personality and preferences of the person, some may thrive in this environment, and use online platforms to connect with their peers on topics that are unrelated to school (i.e., social causes, fashion trends, sport) while others may find the added extra social layer of their daily life tiring and stressful. Some studies have in fact linked social media use among young people to correlate with depression, anxiety, and psychological distress (Keles, McCrae and Grealish, 2020).

The implications of this fraught relationship with technology are important for educators and university professional staff. Students for instance may be more aware of their online footprint and prefer to engage in online activities anonymously (Pulevska-Ivanovska et al., 2017). Rather than assume all Generation Z learners are always online, there may be some students in this cohort who carefully choose when and how they engage online. In a study of Generation Z workers in India, Chillakuri (2020) found that participants often stressed the importance of work–life balance and the need to sometimes unplug from technology. Though again this may relate more to the change in everyone's environment, regardless of age, such as the constant 24/7 news cycle, than a specific generational cohort preference.

Different generations or cohorts of students, depending on a range of factors including age and environment, also exhibit different preferences for which online platform to use. For example, one study found that Millennials (those born between 1982 and the mid-90s) are more likely to use Facebook, while Generation Z participants preferred Instagram and Snapchat (Curtis et al., 2019). Bennett, Maton and Kervin caution for educators to remember that "while technology is embedded in their lives, young people's use and skills are not uniform" (2008, p.783. It is therefore also critical for teachers and university support staff to continually consider the diversity of ways in which students may choose to engage and consider the varying levels of technology mastery which may be present in target student cohorts.

Content co-creators

Since the start of the 21st century there has been growing attention on how technological advances and the internet could support a democratisation of media. Benkler in 2008 wrote that the internet could transform the consumption of media from a passive act to one where people could engage in ongoing dialogue and the co-creation of content. And indeed, his predictions proved correct, with examples ranging from networked e-commerce sites such as eBay to a plethora of user-generated content now accessible on blogs and other social media sites.

The proliferation of content creation has also begun to have a profound impact on the way education is delivered and supported. For example, in the higher education space, there are growing case studies of staff integrating student-created content (i.e., blogs or videos) to provide peer-to-peer advice on learning or the student experience (Dollinger and Lodge, 2020a; Tekinarslan, 2008). Platforms have also begun to emerge that foster student content creation towards learning resources, which can become a part of the formal curriculum. For example, in Australia a platform known as RiPPLE (Recommendation in Personalised Peer Learning Environments) allows for students to create learning resources for their peers, as well as link to a recommender system that suggests content based on students' missed questions on quizzes or exams (McDonald et al., 2021). However, an evaluation of the platform has found that while many students are comfortable using peer-created resources to learn, only a select few may choose to author resources for others (McDonald et al., 2021). This may be related just to authoring curriculum although, as other findings show, more than 50% of Generation Z learners regularly create content on social media platforms (Fong et al., 2019).

The emergence of student content co-creation has so far also been lacking problematisation of the phenomenon. Students who create content may not have the professional training to be aware of the responsibility that may need to accompany media creation. For example, Parker (2013) reflects on a project where high school seniors in California produced a video documentary on Latino immigration. She found that while students were engaged in the project, the project also highlighted the ethical tensions between the student filmmakers and the subjects in the film. Parker recommends that teachers who wish to support student media creation should also consider how students are supported to develop meta-awareness in their projects and reflection on how their media creation decisions can have an impact on others.

Student-generated content is likely going to continue to grow in prominence throughout the educational landscape. Even simple examples of students providing peer-to-peer advice or support can have significant impact. At Charles Sturt University in Australia students who had previously taken subjects created short 3–5 minute audio podcasts for current students to listen to pre-class that helped summarise key learning goals and alleviate pre-class anxiety (Lee, McLoughlin and Chan, 2008). Models such as these can be applied to a broad range of higher education experiences including orientation, study support programmes, and student leadership and employability.

Tuition fees for Generation Z learners

As the global university sector is increasingly being shaped by neoliberal ideologies, many have reflected on what the rising tuition fees will mean for the next generation of students. The Organisation for Economic Co-Operative Development (OECD) (2019) reports that while two-thirds of member countries have moderate to low tertiary tuition fees, the other remaining third of member countries, including the UK, United States, Chile, Canada, Japan and Australia, have average fees ranging from 3,000–5,000 USD per year for national students and often twice that fee for international students. Analysis of the difference of tuition fees further reveals that "the level of tuition fees charged by institutions rarely reflects labour-market opportunities" indicating that in more than half of OECD countries, "public institutions charge similar tuition fees regardless of the level of education", showing a mismatch between tuition fees and subsequent potential earnings or salary advantage (OECD, 2019).

Goldrick-Rab and Steinbaum (2020) reflect on the issue of student debt, writing that students, when left with few financial options, often make decisions that are 'sub-optimal' including taking out loans with high interest rates. The issue only further compounds if the student does not complete their degree, leaving the student in debt and without the potential financial stability of a career that may have occurred after graduation, had they completed. In the United States, student loan debt is now the second-largest source of household debt, with over a third of US adults under 30 with an outstanding student loan (Hedlund, 2021). Unsurprisingly, the current system has sparked a rise in student activism, often in the form of student protests, in several of the most impacted countries, including the United States, United Kingdom, Chile, Canada and South Africa (Cole and Heinecke, 2020; Della Porta and Portos, 2020).

It is unclear what direction tuition fees will take in the coming years and how those changes may affect Generation Z learners. The growth of online courses may translate into lower fees for students, even for those not studying online, as tuition fees are driven down to stay competitive. Alternatively, if government funding for universities continues to decrease, universities may be left with little choice but to increase tuition to cover the costs, much of which is likely to be shouldered by international students, should they choose to enrol. However, what is clear is that universities will need to continue to consider what their value is to potential students and how they justify the costs of a tertiary degree (Dollinger and Lodge, 2020b; Tomlinson, 2021).

Rise of the we-centric culture

Years ago, many sought to stigmatise the Millennial generation as 'me-centric' and self-absorbed (Holt, Marques and Way, 2012). While research has since debunked many of the generational studies that came to this conclusion (Rudolph et al., 2020), there is rise again of a broad sweeping urge to classify our latest Generation

Z learners. Known as 'we-centric' culture the argument is that Generation Z learners are particularly passionate about social justice issues (Mohr and Mohr, 2017). Scholars suggest that by witnessing global campaigns and activism at a young age, including Black Lives Matters, #MeToo and climate change rallies, young people today are more conscious of social justice and global inequalities (Seemiller and Grace, 2017). Research from Sweden suggests that young people's growing activism in social justice may instead be heightened due to social media and online participation, which allows for young people to connect, share and learn about issues more accessibly (Kim, Russo and Amnå, 2017). Studies of future nurses in the United States have also found Generation Z participants displayed greater hope, optimism and resilience than their Millennial counterparts (Cartwright-Stroupe and Shinners, 2021) and suggest that these events have empowered them towards social justice causes.

As Reinikainen, Kari and Luoma-aho (2020) have pointed out, young people's growing awareness of political activism has consequences beyond social issues and campaigns, to also impact their consumer behaviour. Many brands for example have adjusted their advertising to capitalise on what they perceive as a growing social advocacy in young people. For example, brands such as Nike and Adidas linked their advertising campaigns to Black Lives Matter, for instance with Nike asking consumers "for once, don't do it" (Jones, 2020). Interestingly, survey results from Finland and the UK show that young people also have more trust in organisations that listened to users and engaged in dialogue with them via social media (Reinikainen, Kari and Luoma-aho, 2020). In multicultural societies, such as Australia, reports have also found that young people are increasingly concerned about racism and combating structural inequalities (Wyn, Khan and Dadvand, 2018).

Young people's passion for social justice comes at a time when higher education is becoming an increasingly diverse space. Growth in traditionally underrepresented student cohorts has been seen across the world, including students with a disability, neurodiverse students, students from low socioeconomic backgrounds, and students with carer responsibilities (Chowdry et al., 2013; Michalski, Cunningham and Henry, 2017). The diversity that comes from widening participation in university systems should be leveraged to further consider how the student experience can be more inclusive and accessible. Scholars such as Alison Cook-Sather (2018) have argued that by engaging in authentic partnership with students who identify as members of equity-seeking groups, staff can learn how to better support students as well affirm students' contributions and value to the university community.

University staff may also want to consider how they can support students' passion for activism within the curriculum. In Melbourne, Australia several secondary schools have featured Student Action Teams (SATs) that support a group of students to identify an issue of concern in their community and then investigate it and provide solutions and/or recommendations (Holdsworth, 2010). Mayes and Holdsworth (2020) argue that initiatives such as SATs support students and communities "...to envision the world in which they/we want to live, and gain the knowledge and skills required to change circumstances and re/create that world" (p.6).

Conclusion and recommendations

In this chapter I have attempted to highlight some of the key educational shifts occurring with Generation Z learners. However, the changes impacting our world, whether it be technological advances or a greater awareness of social inequalities, are not only changing Generation Z learners. For example, we all are witnessing the change of how we share or create content and how global inequalities continue to persist. Yet as Black and Walsh (2021) discuss, young people are disproportionally affected by many of the current societal innovations and challenges, as many of these changes can increase the volatility of global markets and subsequently impact employment options or pathways. A good example of this is how technological advances have proliferated the freelance workforce, also known as the 'gig economy' (Black and Walsh, 2021).

University staff, whether in academic or professional roles, are no doubt used to the changing nature of student cohorts and environments. The university space has already undergone significant changes in the past few decades, including the increasing shift to online learning and the greater focus on employability and graduate capabilities. In such a constantly evolving environment it is continually pertinent for staff to take time to reflect on their practices. While generational studies are best taken as broad indications of a cohort's preferences, rather than rigorous studies that proclaim a single behaviour or truth, they can be helpful to prompt reflection and consider one's current approaches. As discussed in this chapter, some of those reflections for supporting Generation Z learners can – and should – include considering their relationship with technology, their potential preference for creating content, and their passion for social justice causes. But these considerations should only be the beginning of an ongoing process for staff to consider how best to support inclusive student success at their institutions.

References

Ang, W.H.D., Shorey, S., Lopez, V., Chew, H.S.J. and Lau, Y., 2021. Generation Z undergraduate students' resilience during the COVID-19 pandemic: A qualitative study. *Current Psychology*. https://doi.org/10.1007/s12144-021-01830-4

Benkler, Y., 2008. *The Wealth of Networks*. New Haven, CT: Yale University Press.

Bennett, S., Maton, K. and Kervin, L., 2008. The 'digital natives' debate: A critical review of the evidence. *British Journal of Educational Technology*, 39(5), pp.775–786. https://doi.org/10.1111/j.1467-8535.2007.00793.x

Black, R. and Walsh, L., 2015. Educating the risky citizen: Young people, vulnerability and schooling. In te Riele, K., and Gorur, R. (eds) *Interrogating Conceptions of "Vulnerable Youth" in Theory, Policy and Practice*. Boston, MA: Brill. https://doi.org/10.1007/978-94-6300-121-2_12

Cartwright-Stroupe, L.M. and Shinners, J., 2021. Moving forward together: What hope, efficacy, optimism, and resilience tell us about Generation Z. *The Journal of Continuing Education in Nursing*, 52(4), pp.160–162. https://doi.org/10.3928/00220124-20210315-02

Chillakuri, B., 2020. Understanding Generation Z expectations for effective onboarding. *Journal of Organizational Change Management.* https://doi.org/10.1108/jocm-02-2020-0058

Chowdry, H., Crawford, C., Dearden, L., Goodman, A. and Vignoles, A., 2013. Widening participation in higher education: Analysis using linked administrative data. *Journal of the Royal Statistical Society: Series A (Statistics in Society)*, 176(2), pp.431–457. https://doi.org/10.1111/j.1467-985X.2012.01043.x

Cole, R.M. and Heinecke, W.F., 2020. Higher education after neoliberalism: Student activism as a guiding light. *Policy Futures in Education*, 18(1), pp.90–116. https://doi.org/10.1177/1478210318767459

Cook-Sather, A., 2018. Listening to equity-seeking perspectives: How students' experiences of pedagogical partnership can inform wider discussions of student success. *Higher Education Research and Development*, 37(5), pp.923–936. https://doi.org/10.1080/07294360.2018.1457629

Costanza, D.P., Darrow, J.B., Yost, A.B. and Severt, J.B., 2017. A review of analytical methods used to study generational differences: Strengths and limitations. *Work, Aging and Retirement*, 3(2), pp.149–165. https://doi.org/10.1093/workar/wax002

Curtis, B.L., Ashford, R.D., Magnuson, K.I. and Ryan-Pettes, S.R., 2019. Comparison of smartphone ownership, social media use, and willingness to use digital interventions between Generation Z and millennials in the treatment of substance use: Cross-sectional questionnaire study. *Journal of Medical Internet Research*, 21(4), p.e13050. https://doi.org/10.2196/13050

Della Porta, D. and Portos, M., 2020. Social movements in times of inequalities: Struggling against austerity in Europe. *Structural Change and Economic Dynamics*, 53, pp.116–126. https://doi.org/10.1016/j.strueco.2020.01.011

Dollinger, M. and Lodge, J., 2020a. Student-staff co-creation in higher education: An evidence-informed model to support future design and implementation. *Journal of Higher Education Policy and Management*, 42(5), pp.532–546. https://doi.org/10.1080/1360080X.2019.1663681

Dollinger, M. and Lodge, J., 2020b. Understanding value in the student experience through student–staff partnerships. *Higher Education Research and Development*, 39(5), pp.940–952. https://doi.org/10.1080/07294360.2019.1695751

Fong, J., Lope, N., Lucchi, M., McDermott, P. and Trench, B., 2019. An insider's guide to Generation Z and higher education. *University Professional and Continuing Education Association.* https://upcea.edu/wp-content/uploads/2019/04/Generation-Z-eBook-Version-4.pdf

Furman, E., Singh, A.K., Darko, N.A. and Wilson, C.L., 2018. Activism, intersectionality, and community psychology: The way in which Black Lives Matter Toronto helps us examine white supremacy in Canada's LGBTQ community. *Community Psychology in Global Perspective*, 4(2), pp.34–54. https://doi/org/10.1285/i24212113v4i2p34

Goldrick-Rab, S. and Steinbaum, M., 2020. What is the problem with student debt? *Journal of Policy Analysis and Management*, 39(2), pp.534–540. https://doi.org/10.1002/pam.22208

Hedlund, A., 2021. What can be done to address rising student debt? The Center for Growth and Opportunity. Available at: www.thecgo.org/research/what-can-be-done-to-address-rising-student-debt/ (accessed: 15 December 2021).

Holdsworth, R., 2010. Students leading in investigating and enacting values in school communities. In: Lovat, T., Toomey, R. and Clement, N. (ed), *International Research Handbook on Values Education and Student Wellbeing*. Dordrecht: Springer. https://doi.org/10.1007/978-90-481-8675-4_48

Holt, S., Marques, J. and Way, D., 2012. Bracing for the millennial workforce: Looking for ways to inspire Generation Y. *Journal of Leadership, Accountability and Ethics*, 9(6), pp.81–93.

Jayathilake, H.D., Daud, D., Eaw, H.C. and Annuar, N., 2021. Employee development and retention of Generation-Z employees in the post-COVID-19 workplace: A conceptual framework. *Benchmarking: An International Journal*, 28(7), pp.2343–2364. https://doi.org/10.1108/BIJ-06-2020-0311

Jones, C., 2020. Brands may support Black Lives Matter, but advertising still needs to decolonise. Available at: https://theconversation.com/brands-may-support-black-lives-matter-but-advertising-still-needs-to-decolonise-133394 (accessed: 29 August 2021).

Keles, B., McCrae, N. and Grealish, A., 2020. A systematic review: The influence of social media on depression, anxiety and psychological distress in adolescents. *International Journal of Adolescence and Youth*, 25(1), pp.79–93. https://doi.org/10.1080/02673843.2019.1590851

Kim, Y., Russo, S. and Amnå, E., 2017. The longitudinal relation between online and offline political participation among youth at two different developmental stages. *New Media and Society*, 19(6), pp.899–917. https://doi.org/10.1177/1461444815624181

Lee, M.J., McLoughlin, C. and Chan, A., 2008. Talk the talk: Learner-generated podcasts as catalysts for knowledge creation. *British Journal of Educational Technology*, 39(3), pp.501–521. https://doi.org/10.1111/j.1467-8535.2007.00746.x

Marshall, A.L. and Wolanskyj-Spinner, A., 2020. COVID-19: Challenges and opportunities for educators and Generation Z learners. *Mayo Clinic Proceedings*, 95(6), pp.1135–1137. https://doi.org/10.1016/j.mayocp.2020.04.015

Mayes, E. and Holdsworth, R., 2020. Learning from contemporary student activism: Towards a curriculum of fervent concern and critical hope. *Curriculum Perspectives*, 40 (1), pp.99–103. https://doi.org/10.1007/s41297-019-00094-0

McDonald, A., McGowan, H., Dollinger, M., Naylor, R. and Khosravi, H., 2021. Repositioning students as co-creators of curriculum for online learning resources. *Australasian Journal of Educational Technology*. https://doi.org/10.14742/ajet.6735

Michalski, J.H., Cunningham, T. and Henry, J., 2017. The diversity challenge for higher education in Canada: The prospects and challenges of increased access and student success. *Humboldt Journal of Social Relations*, 39, pp.66–89. www.jstor.org/stable/90007872

Miller, A.C. and Mills, B., 2019. 'If they don't care, I don't care': Millennial and Generation Z students and the impact of faculty caring. *Journal of the Scholarship of Teaching and Learning*, 19(4), pp.78–89. https://doi.org/10.14434/josotl.v19i4.24167

Mohr, K.A. and Mohr, E.S., 2017. Understanding Generation Z students to promote a contemporary learning environment. *Journal on Empowering Teaching Excellence*, 1(1), p.9. https://doi.org/10.15142/T3M05T

Mosca, J.B., Curtis, K.P. and Savoth, P.G., 2019. New approaches to learning for Generation Z. *The Journal of Business Diversity*, 19(3), pp.66–74. https://doi.org/10.33423/jbd.v19i3.2214

OECD (Organisation for Economic Co-Operative Development), 2019. *Education at a Glance 2019: OECD Indicators. Indicator C5. How Much Do Tertiary Students Pay and*

What Public Support Do They Receive? Available at: www.oecd-ilibrary.org/sites/9721a 904-en/index.html?itemId=/content/component/9721a904-en (accessed: 15 December 2021).

Parker, J.K., 2013. Critical literacy and the ethical responsibilities of student media production. *Journal of Adolescent and Adult Literacy*, 56(8), pp.668–676. https://doi.org/ 10.1002/JAAL.194

Pew Research Center, 2020. *On the Cusp of Adulthood and Facing an Uncertain Future: What We Know about Z So Far.* Available at: www.pewresearch.org/social-trends/2020/ 05/14/on-the-cusp-of-adulthood-and-facing-an-uncertain-future-what-we-know-about-gen-z-so-far-2/ (accessed: 28 August 2021).

Prenksy, M., 2001. Digital natives, digital immigrants. *On the Horizon*, 9(5), pp.1–6. https:// doi.org/10.1108/10748120110424816

Pulevska-Ivanovska, L., Postolov, K., Janeska-Iliev, A. and Magdinceva Sopova, M., 2017. Establishing balance between professional and private life of Generation Z. *Research in Physical Education, Sport and Health*, 6(1), pp.3–10.

Reinikainh en, H., Kari, J.T. and Luoma-Aho, V., 2020. Generation Z and organizational listening on social media. *Media and Communication*, 8(2), pp.185–196. https://doi. org/10.17645/mac.v8i2.2772

Rudolph, C.W., Rauvola, R.S., Costanza, D.P. and Zacher, H., 2020. Generations and generational differences: Debunking myths in organizational science and practice and paving new paths forward. *Journal of Business and Psychology*. https://doi.org/10. 1007/s10869-020-09715-2

Seemiller, C. and Grace, M., 2017. Generation Z: Educating and engaging the next generation of students. *About Campus*, 22(3), pp.21–26. https://doi.org/10.1002/abc.21293

Tekinarslan, E., 2008. Blogs: A qualitative investigation into an instructor and undergraduate students' experiences. *Australasian Journal of Educational Technology*, 24(4). https://doi.org/10.14742/ajet.1200

Tomlinson, M., 2021. Missing values: Engaging the value of higher education and implications for future measurements. *Oxford Review of Education*. https://doi.org/10. 1080/03054985.2021.1908247

Wyn, J., Khan, R. and Dadvand, B., 2018. Multicultural youth Australia census status report 2017/18. Youth Research Centre in University of Melbourne. Available at: http://hdl.voced.edu.au/10707/494349 (accessed: 16 May 2021).

Chapter 15

Student–instructor partnerships for curricular justice

Sophia Abbot

Higher education has the potential to promote radical social change by empowering students from all backgrounds to learn, develop, and be successful. Frequently, however, universities are over reliant on curriculum that reifies current inequitable social hierarchies and explicitly or implicitly marginalizes women, students of color, disabled students, and other equity-seeking groups (Connell, 1992; Peters, 2015). For example, for many postcolonial nations, curriculum that continues to focus on European topics and scholars maintains educational systems as "colonialist outposts" (McKaiser, 2016 in Heleta, 2016) even after independence. Students and instructors have described the way students attending university experienced western knowledge "first downplaying then supplanting their own culturally inflected understanding" (Naidoo et al., 2020, p.969). One student co-researcher explained that language, "becomes like a barrier because sometimes you cannot express yourself enough" (Naidoo et al., 2020, p.972).

This injustice is not accidental. Educational systems—especially those in post-colonial nations—have been and remain built with the express purpose of disseminating western ways of knowing (Heleta, 2016). At the most extreme end, spreading education was the named method for pursuing imperialist agendas. For instance, in Puerto Rico, the United States (US) introduced industrial school models focused on "habituating [Black and Indigenous] students in 'proper behavior'" in order to assimilate Puerto Rican students "into the culture and history of 'Western Civilization'" (Sullivan, 2007, p.161). Doing so erased Puerto Rican culture and language, and accomplished what Tuck and Gaztambide-Fernández (2013) have called 'white futurity'—the idea that through the perpetuation of white western histories, language, and culture, settlers can ignore the fact that their existence comes at the price of continued occupation.

Even within dominant western nations, students outside of the dominant classes are prevented from learning their own histories and may feel discouraged from continuing their post-secondary degree or from pursuing post-graduate studies (Naidoo et al., 2020). As Indigenous student Yahlnaaw reflected on a higher eductable ation conference on teaching and learning: "the dominance of colonial knowledges and pedagogical practices left me feeling I had little room to share my knowledge" (2019, p.7). This can create a vicious cycle in which few equity-seeking students progress to graduate school and even fewer attain faculty and research positions from

DOI: 10.4324/9781003271789-15

which they could participate in new academic knowledge creation (Ysseldyk et al., 2019).

Students and scholars internationally have worked to call attention to and disrupt this phenomenon of hegemonic western curriculum, such as through decolonization efforts in Canada (Gaudry and Lorenz, 2019), South Africa (Naidoo et al., 2020), and Aotearoa New Zealand (McBreen, 2019), among other places; and Black Lives Matter efforts on campuses in the US (White, 2016). In addition to critiquing the white imperialist and settler ways of knowing which dominate educational spaces, these movements have called attention to histories of exclusion at universities and the continued inequity in access that students face in attending and succeeding in higher education.

Drawing on data comparing the demographics of current students in higher education to those of instructors in higher education, this chapter argues that *students as partners* is a necessary frame for enacting curricular justice in higher education. As Cook-Sather (2018) has argued, student success is contingent on social integration—and partnership provides opportunities not only for meaningful social integration, but also agentic integration. Connecting work on partnership to research in curriculum theory, this chapter suggests partnership can affect change in the curriculum to enhance equity for all.

The current landscape in higher education

Participation in higher education is more diverse today than it has ever been, and yet colleges and universities still frequently fail to reflect broader social demographics. In the US, we have seen a promising trend of student diversification but have not seen this shift to the same extent among instructors on university campuses. Table 15.1 shows the total number of full-time instructors and students in US institutions in 2015 and in 2020 by race or ethnicity.

In many cases, the numbers appear hopeful. Outside of American Indian and Alaska Native instructors, the number of full-time faculty and instructional staff of color grew in every category. For students, growth was less constant; analysts have attributed that to overall economic growth which is generally associated with more direct entrance into the labor market post-high school (Alexander, 2021; Nadworny, 2019). Additionally, the 2020 data were collected during the global COVID-19 pandemic, so enrollment declines may be associated with that context (Conley and Massa, 2022). Nonetheless, the number of Hispanic, Asian, and multiracial students grew over the five-year period.

However, viewing the data in another form reveals a different story for students and instructors (see Table 15.2).

The table above shows the 2020 faculty and student data as percentages disaggregated by race of the total number of instructional faculty and enrolled students, respectively. When viewing these numbers as percentages of a whole, the disproportionate numbers of faculty across racial-ethnic groups compared to students is immediately clear. White faculty and instructional staff are overrepresented as compared to white students in the US, while Black and Hispanic faculty and instructional staff are underrepresented. This disparity is even more visible when viewed as ratios (see Table 15.3).

Table 15.1 US aggregate full-time faculty and instructional staff and aggregate students by race / ethnicity

	White	Black	Hispanic	Asian	Pacific Islander	American Indian / Alaska Native	Two or more races	Race / Ethnicity Unknown	Non-resident
2015 Faculty	575,752	44,106	35,811	76,298	1,158	3,530	6,469	22,359	41,626
2020 Faculty	563,609	47,477	44,340	90,438	1,215	3,266	9,578	26,655	50,019
2015 Student	87,604,052	21,917,744	27,935,970	9,987,146	460,206	1,220,492	5,487,694	7,860,520	6,890,624
2020 Students	77,331,450	19,207,630	30,990,300	10,744,858	399,074	994,682	6,280,890	6,598,146	5,979,260

(National Center for Education Statistics, 2020a, 2020b)

Table 15.2 Percentages of US faculty and students by race / ethnicity, 2020

	White	Black	Hispanic	Asian	Pacific Islander	American Indian / Alaska Native	Two or more races	Race / Ethnicity Unknown	Non-resident
2020 Faculty	67.37%	5.68%	5.30%	10.81%	0.15%	0.39%	1.14%	3.19%	5.98%
2020 Students	48.78%	12.12%	19.55%	6.78%	0.25%	0.63%	3.96%	4.16%	3.77%

(National Center for Education Statistics, 2020a, 2020b)

Table 15.3 Ratio of US students to faculty by race / ethnicity, 2020

	White	Black	Hispanic	Asian	Pacific Islander	American Indian / Alaska Native	Two or more races	Race / Ethnicity Unknown	Non-resident
Faculty	1	1	1	1	1	1	1	1	1
Students	137.2	404.6	698.9	118.8	328.5	304.6	655.8	247.5	119.5

(National Center for Education Statistics, 2020a, 2020b)

There are over three times as many Black students per Black instructor compared to the ratio of white students per white instructor. There are over five times as many Hispanic students per Hispanic instructor compared to the ratio of white students to white instructors. Indigenous students from the Americas and Pacific Islands similarly have fewer instructors who share their identities, as is the case for multiracial students. Only Asian and International students have better representational odds than white students. Put another way, most students of color have far fewer instructors and potential mentors who look like them.

There are curricular implications for this relative homogeneity among university instructors. As the *Why Is My Curriculum White* movement in the United Kingdom (UK) indicates, the preponderance of white scholars reinforces a white-dominated curriculum (Peters, 2015). In his summary and analysis of this UK movement, Michael Peters explored the example of philosophy as a space that has been "resistant to taking race seriously" (2015, p.644) and suggested that the intersection between racist thinking and dominant thinkers in philosophy (Nietzsche and Hegel are offered as two examples) has continued to prevent the discipline from making critical and anti-racist progress. Our current ways of knowing and even our critiques of those current ways are dominated by 'Western Cartesian' points of view (Leibowitz, 2017), which privilege a belief in objective truth, knowable through quantifying human experiences, and resulting in generalizable knowledge. Curriculum scholar Michael Apple has connected curriculum more broadly to matters of knowledge creation and power, writing that "education and power are terms of an indissoluble couplet" (2000, p.44). Fewer instructors of color means that the multiplicity of ways of knowing in the academy are diminished. And when dominant viewpoints make up the majority of higher education instructors, the potential for curricular transformation is much more limited.

Students as partners: describing a movement

Simultaneous to growing movements calling for the diversification of curriculum, pedagogy, and populations in higher education has been the growth of a field of practice variously called 'students as partners', student–faculty partnership, or student–staff partnership (Abbot and Shirley, 2020). For a number of scholars in the field, there are explicitly critical goals of partnership stemming from critical pedagogy (e.g. Abbot, 2017; Peters and Mathias, 2018). Within the last three years in particular, the field has exploded with work examining partnership's potential to advance equity and justice in higher education—and for good reason. A 2017 meta-analysis found much research in the field reported partnership had positive impacts on students' confidence and self-efficacy, engagement, metacognitive awareness about their learning, and sense of belonging on campus (Mercer-Mapstone et al., 2017). Scholars since have published on partnership's potential to advance gender equity (Acai, Mercer-Mapstone, and Guitman, 2019), epistemic justice (de Bie et al., 2019), equity in particular disciplinary fields (Narayanan and

Abbot, 2020), and equity for students more broadly (Cook-Sather, 2018; O'Shea, 2018). Scholars have also explored the complexities of engaging in partnership for minoritized faculty (Guitman and Marquis, 2020; Marquis et al., 2020).

Partnership itself is a process with varying goals. Healey, Flint, and Harrington's (2016) Engagement Through Partnership model is made up of four spheres in which partnership may occur: learning, teaching, and assessment; curriculum design and pedagogic consultancy; subject-based research and inquiry; and scholarship of teaching and learning. The second sphere points explicitly to curricular transformation, though each has implications for the construction of knowledge and therefore the shaping of curriculum.

Examples of partnership specifically in curricular design are promising. For example, in the US, Alison Cook-Sather, Crystal Des-Ogugua, and Melanie Bahti (2018) described their process of co-creating a course called 'Advocating Diversity in Higher Education' in response to the student protests for racial justice in 2015–16 which occurred nationally across US college campuses. Through the interviewing of minoritized students on their campus, and the development of these student interviews into required course reading, the authors were able to "bring them into being/presence in the classroom" (p.379). This process not only legitimized perspectives and ways of knowing that Cook-Sather was unable to offer as a white cisgender woman, but it also transformed the course. The authors further suggested that institutional efforts towards inclusion "must consider the degree to which the experience of intersecting identities on campus is mediated and informed by the social value inscribed in the student's identity outside the walls of the institution" (Cook-Sather, Des-Ogugua, and Bahti, 2018, p.384). In other words, as Apple (2000) suggested, education and power are an 'indissoluble couplet'.

In another example of curricular co-creation, scholars in South Africa explored ways of bringing rural students' perspectives into the curriculum. Following student protests calling for decolonizing South African higher education, three universities embarked on co-research with rural students who studied their own lives and communities and interviewed university leaders and instructors. Their collective work revealed that students traditionally have had to adapt to the curriculum rather than the other way around; the student researchers demanded that curriculum development "foster epistemic reciprocity" and be co-created with students (Naidoo et al., 2020, p.974). This would help ensure students' rural knowledge, which is mostly absent among the faculty, has a place in the curriculum. The authors suggested that transforming curriculum in this way would lead to African universities rather than simply universities in Africa.

Cognitive, epistemic, and curricular justice

Definitions of student–faculty partnership overlap in significant ways with the idea of 'cognitive justice' (Leibowitz, 2017). Leibowitz (2017) described cognitive justice as a theoretical solution to current modes of thinking about knowledge (re) production and teaching. She expanded on Van der Velden's unpublished definition to define cognitive justice as a "principle for the equal treatment of all forms of knowledge", specifying that "the equality of knowers forms the basis of dialogue between knowledges, and that what is required for democracy is a dialogue amongst knowers and their knowledges" (Leibowitz, 2017, pp.100–1). Leibowitz saw cognitive justice as a tool for more inclusive and just curriculum development. Similar themes are clear in Cook-Sather, Bovill, and Felten's (2014) definition of partnership as a collaborative process in which "all participants have the opportunity to contribute equally, though not necessarily in the same ways, to curricular or pedagogical conceptualization" (p.7). Central to both concepts is the belief in the equality of participants' contributions. From this assumption of equality, multiple perspectives may be weighed in the construction of knowledge and curriculum—diversifying the potential output.

Additionally, several scholars who write about and work in student–faculty partnership have embraced the theory of 'epistemic justice' (Fricker, 2007) as a way of understanding the transformative benefits of these relationships for students. For example, de Bie et al. (2019) suggested that partnership helped students feel more "ownership" over their experiences and recognize their contributions have value. They also described the ways students learned "insider knowledge" (de Bie et al., 2019, p.40) about higher education through these partnerships, which supported their engagement in the creation of knowledge. The most significant element of their findings centered on Fricker's (2007) idea of "epistemic confidence" which they described as a way to prevent the "erosion of knowledge" (p.45) which occurs when individuals resist creating knowledge out of the belief that they are not knowers. Instead, de Bie et al. (2019) argue, pedagogical partnerships between students and instructors can create epistemic justice in which students are affirmed in "their own capacity as knowers" (p.40).

All three of these theories—cognitive, epistemic, and curricular justice—are united in the belief that knowledge can come from anyone and should be equally considered. Student–faculty partnerships offer a method through which this can occur.

Conclusion

What do students gain from such partnerships? In their systematic review of partnership literature, Mercer-Mapstone et al. (2017) found the most commonly reported benefit for students overall was increased engagement in and ownership of learning, followed by increased confidence or self-efficacy. Given how essential epistemic confidence is for students' recognition of themselves as knowers, these findings are significant. More specifically for equity-seeking students, Cook-Sather (2019) has suggested that partnership offers them the opportunity to "mobilize their own cultural identities" in order to transform the university, allows them to recommend pedagogical and curricular approaches that would better support them as learners, and makes space for them to reinforce pedagogical and curricular practices that are already inclusive, but which instructors may not have recognized in that capacity.

The demographic disparities in higher educational teaching and partnership will not resolve themselves within the next few years. In the meantime, a generation of students will find insufficient representation of themselves in their instructors and may therefore feel excluded from further participation in higher education and the construction of knowledge. Even upon attaining equal participation, students and scholars will need to confront dominant viewpoints in curriculum that restrict non-hegemonic ways of knowing. Students, then, are essential to transforming our curriculum as they come already with perspectives and knowledges that are missing from our institutions. Student–faculty partnerships offer a framework of practice for enacting curricular justice.

References

Abbot, S., 2017. Book review of *Teaching to Transgress: Education as the Practice of Freedom*. *International Journal for Students as Partners*, 1(2). doi:10.15173/ijsap.v1i2.3230.

Abbot, S. and Shirley, C., 2020. Engaging students as partners in learning and teaching: A retrospective. Center for Engaged Learning, 4 November. Available at: www.centerforenga gedlearning.org/engaging-students-as-partners-in-learning-and-teaching-a-retrospective/ (accessed: 8 May 2021).

Acai, A., Mercer-Mapstone, L. and Guitman, R., 2019. Mind the (gender) gap: Engaging students as partners to promote gender equity in higher education. *Teaching in Higher Education*. doi:10.1080/13562517.2019.1696296.

Alexander, B., 2021. American higher education enrollment declined in spring 2021, continuing a multi-year trend. Bryan Alexander, 3 May. Available at: https://bryanalexander.org/ enrollment/american-higher-education-enrollment-decline-in-spring-2021-continuing-a-multi-year-trend/ (accessed: 5 May 2021).

Apple, M.W., 2000. *Official Knowledge: Democratic Education in a Conservative Age* (2nd edn). Abingdon: Routledge.

Conley, B. and Massa, R., 2022. The great interruption. Inside Higher Ed, 28 February. Available at: www.insidehighered.com/admissions/views/2022/02/28/enrollment-cha nges-colleges-are-feeling-are-much-more-covid-19 (accessed: 3 April 2022).

Connell, R.W., 1992. Citizenship, social justice and curriculum. *International Studies in Sociology of Education*, 2(2), pp.133–146. doi:10.1080/0962021920020202.

Cook-Sather, A., 2019. *Increasing Inclusivity through Pedagogical Partnerships between Students and Faculty*. Available at: www.aacu.org/diversitydemocracy/2019/winter/ cook-sather (accessed: 17 September 2020).

Cook-Sather, A., 2018. Listening to equity-seeking perspectives: How students' experiences of pedagogical partnership can inform wider discussions of student success. *Higher Education Research and Development*, 37(5), pp.923–936. doi:10.1080/07294360.2018.1457629.

Cook-Sather, A., Des-Ogugua, C. and Bahti, M., 2018. Articulating identities and analyzing belonging: A multistep intervention that affirms and informs a diversity of students. *Teaching in Higher Education*, 23(3), pp.374–389. doi:10.1080/13562517.2017.1391201.

Cook-Sather, A., Bovill, C. and Felten, P., 2014. *Engaging Students as Partners in Learning and Teaching: A Guide for Faculty*. San Francisco, CA: Jossey-Bass.

de Bie, A., Marquis, E., Cook-Sather, A., and Luqueño, L.P., 2019. Valuing knowledge(s) and cultivating confidence: Contributions of student–faculty pedagogical partnerships to epistemic justice. In: Hoffman, J., Blessinger, P. and Makhanya, M. (eds) *Innovations in Higher Education Teaching and Learning*. Bingley: Emerald Publishing. doi:10.1108/S2055-364120190000016004.

Fricker, M., 2007. *Epistemic Injustice: Power and the Ethics of Knowing*. Oxford: Oxford University Press.

Gaudry, A. and Lorenz, D.E., 2019. Decolonization for the masses? Grappling with indigenous content requirements in the changing post-secondary environment. In: Smith, L. T., Tuck, E. and Yang, K.W. (eds) *Indigenous and Decolonizing Studies in Education: Mapping the Long View* (Indigenous and Decolonizing Studies in Education). New York: Routledge. https://doi.org/10.4324/9780429505010-11

Guitman, R. and Marquis, E., 2020. A radical practice? In: Mercer-Mapstone, L. and Abbot, S. (eds) *The Power of Partnership: Students, Staff, and Faculty Revolutionizing Higher Education*. Elon, NC: Elon University Center for Engaged Learning. https://doi.org/10.36284/celelon.oa2

Healey, M., Flint, A. and Harrington, K., 2016. Students as partners: Reflections on a conceptual model. *Teaching and Learning Inquiry*, 4(2), pp.8–20. doi:10.20343/teachlearninqu.4.2.3.

Heleta, S., 2016. Decolonisation of higher education: Dismantling epistemic violence and Eurocentrism in South Africa. *Transformation in Higher Education*, 1(1), p.8.

Leibowitz, B., 2017. Cognitive justice and the higher education curriculum. *Journal of Education*, 68, pp.93–112.

Marquis, E., Guitman, R., Nguyen, E., and Woolmer, C., 2020. "It's a little complicated for me": Faculty social location and experiences of pedagogical partnership. *Higher Education Research and Development*. doi:10.1080/07294360.2020.1806789.

McBreen, K., 2019. E kore au e ngaro, he kākano i ruia mai i Rangiātea (I will never be lost, i am a seed sown from Raniātea): Te wānanga o raukawa as an example of educating for indigenous futures. In: Smith, L.T., Tuck, E. and Yang, K.W. (eds) *Indigenous and Decolonizing Studies in Education: Mapping the Long View* (Indigenous and Decolonizing Studies in Education). New York: Routledge. https://doi.org/10.4324/9780429505010-12

Mercer-Mapstone, L., Dvorakova, S.L., Matthews, K.E., Abbot, S., Cheng, B., Felten, P., Knoor, K., Marquis, E., Shammas, R. and Swaim, K., 2017. A systematic literature review of students as partners in higher education. *International Journal for Students as Partners*, 1(1). doi:10.15173/ijsap.v1i1.3119.

Nadworny, E., 2019. Fewer students are going to college: Here's why that matters. Available at: www.npr.org/2019/12/16/787909495/fewer-students-are-going-to-college-heres-why-that-matters (accessed: 5 May 2021).

Naidoo, K., Trahar, S., Lucas, L., Muhuro, P. and Wisker, G., 2020. "You have to change, the curriculum stays the same": Decoloniality and curricular justice in South African higher education. *Compare: A Journal of Comparative and International Education*, 50 (7), pp.961–977. doi:10.1080/03057925.2020.1765740.

Narayanan, D. and Abbot, S., 2020. Increasing the participation of underrepresented minorities in STEM classes through student–instructor partnerships. In: Mercer-Mapstone, L. and Abbot, S. (eds) *The Power of Partnership: Students, Staff, and Faculty Revolutionizing Higher Education*. Elon, NC: Elon University Center for Engaged Learning. https://doi.org/10.36284/celelon.oa2

National Center for Education Statistics, 2020a. *Digest of Education Statistics, 2019*. Available at: https://nces.ed.gov/programs/digest/d19/tables/dt19_315.20.asp?current= yes (accessed: 4 May 2021).

National Center for Education Statistics, 2020b. *Summary Tables*. Available at: https://nces.ed. gov/ipeds/SummaryTables/report/270?templateId=2700&years=2019,2018,2017,2016, 2015,2014,2013,2012,2011,2010&expand_by=0&tt=aggregate&instType=1 (accessed: 4 May 2021).

O'Shea, S., 2018. Equity and students as partners: The importance of inclusive relationships. *International Journal for Students as Partners*, 2(2), pp.16–20. doi:10.15173/ ijsap.v2i2.3628.

Peters, J. and Mathias, L., 2018. Enacting student partnership as though we really mean it: Some Freirean principles for a pedagogy of partnership. *International Journal for Students as Partners*, 2(2), pp.53–70. doi:10.15173/ijsap.v2i2.3509.

Peters, M.A., 2015. Why is my curriculum white? *Educational Philosophy and Theory*, 47 (7), pp.641–646. doi:10.1080/00131857.2015.1037227.

Sullivan, S., 2007. White ignorance and colonial oppression: Or, why i know so little about Puerto Rico. In: Sullivan, S. and Tuana, N. (eds) *Race and Epistemologies of Ignorance*. New York: State University of New York Press.

Tuck, E. and Gaztambide-Fernández, R.A., 2013. Curriculum, replacement, and settler futurity. *Journal of Curriculum Theorizing*, 29(1), p.18. https://journal.jctonline.org/ index.php/jct/article/view/411.

White, K., 2016. Black lives on campuses matter: The rise of the new black student movement. *Soundings*, 63, pp.86–97. https://doi.org/10.3898/136266216819377002

Yahlnaaw, 2019. T'aats'iigang—Stuffing a jar full. *International Journal for Students as Partners*, 3(2), pp.6–10. doi:10.15173/ijsap.v3i2.4081.

Ysseldyk, R., Greenaway, K.H., Hassinger, E., Zutrauen, S., Lintz, J., Bhatia, M.P., Frye, M., Starkenburg, E. and Tai, V., 2019. A leak in the academic pipeline: Identity and health among postdoctoral women. *Frontiers in Psychology*, 10, p.1297. doi:10.3389/ fpsyg.2019.01297.

Chapter 16

Embracing student agentic engagement and enacting equity in higher education through co-creating learning and teaching

Alison Cook-Sather and Jia Yi Loh

Introduction

In the final portfolio that Jia Yi Loh created to document their work through the undergraduate educational studies minor at Bryn Mawr College (USA), they wrote:

> Co-creation with students involves the intentional move to creating structures and mechanisms through which both the teacher/facilitator and students/participants have significant stake in creating the substance of the course as well as the evaluation criteria of the course. It disrupts the reductive teacher–student power hierarchy by granting agency and power to both sides to shape the classroom experience while also being cognisant of the different functional roles that each person inhabits.

This definition is based on lived experience: Loh, second author of this chapter and recently graduated student, and Alison Cook-Sather, first author and academic staff member at Bryn Mawr College (USA), engaged in multiple forms of co-creation during the 2020–21 academic year. The two of us use the term 'co-creation' to signal what Cook-Sather, Bovill, and Felten (2014) have also called pedagogical partnership: "a collaborative, reciprocal process through which all participants have the opportunity to contribute equally, although not necessarily in the same ways, to curricular or pedagogical conceptualization, decision making, implementation, investigation, or analysis" (pp.6–7). Loh's definition names key elements of co-creation as those are explored in the scholarship on such work, including shared power and shared responsibility as well as equal but different contributions based on role.

The agency Loh notes as key to co-creation inspired us to focus in this chapter not on traditional, teacher-initiated and teacher-guided forms of behavioural, affective, and cognitive engagement but rather on the proactive, collaborative, student-initiated contributions to learning that Reeve and colleagues term agentic engagement (Reeve, 2013; Reeve and Shin, 2020; Reeve and Tseng, 2011). Agentic engagement fostered through co-creation can expand notions and

DOI: 10.4324/9781003271789-16

practices of engagement to encompass student empowerment and equity both within and beyond classrooms (Cook-Sather et al., 2021). As Marcovici (2021) writes:

> The agency that I cultivated through my partnership [with a staff member]... granted me ownership over my own educational experiences... [and]... led me to develop a sustainable way of pursuing greater educational equity, not only for students I was advocating for in my partnership, but at the college more broadly.

Like Marcovici, we link that potential of individual student agentic engagement to enacting and supporting the pursuit of equity in higher education through co-creation.

In this chapter, we review approaches to, potential benefits of, and barriers to student–staff co-creation of learning and teaching for equity as reported in the literature. We then reflect on our own co-creation experience that spanned two courses and student-led strikes for racial justice, highlighting the ways in which these co-creation experiences fostered agentic engagement for students. We conclude with reflections on why co-creation is impactful for student engagement and for staff–student relationships, particularly during times of disruption, and how it is particularly well suited to striving for equity. Finally, we offer recommendations for future practice.

Approaches to co-creating learning and teaching focused on equity

The co-creation approach "contrasts distinctly with the idea of teaching delivery" because knowledge is developed through student–student and student–teacher interaction (Bovill, 2020, p.18). Co-creation of teaching and learning takes many forms, and a growing body of literature maps that range and diversity (Bovill, 2017; Healey, Flint and Harrington, 2016; Matthews et al., 2018). While a full review of that literature is beyond the scope of this chapter, we review selected co-creation approaches that foster agentic engagement and equity.

Co-creation of curricular and pedagogical approaches with student partners not enrolled

When student partners not enrolled in a course (class/module/unit of study) engage with staff in co-creation for equity, they draw proactively on their lived experiences and identities outside of the standard teacher–student power dynamic to foster more egalitarian and equitable learning communities (Cook-Sather, 2020a; Cook-Sather et al., in press; Cook-Sather et al., 2019). Such partnerships might focus on building faculty confidence in revising curricular and pedagogical approaches that are "not inclusive enough... to create a successful learning environment" (Brunson, 2018, p.2) or on developing and enacting anti-racist pedagogies (Wilson and Cook-Sather, 2022) and trauma-informed, anti-racist pedagogical approaches for remote and hybrid contexts at the intersection of the global pandemic and movements for racial justice (Ameyaa et al., 2021). Such student–staff co-creation efforts foster students' agentic engagement by, as one self-identified Black, first generation, international student wrote, inviting them

> to join in the conversation and express myself in multiple ways ranging from how my perspectives… could help the [staff] cohort I worked with create courses that take steps ahead in addressing racism in higher education… and ensure equitable and livable atmosphere for students of several backgrounds in and out of the classroom.
>
> (Ameyaa et al., 2021)

Whole-of-course co-creation with enrolled students

Whole-of-course co-creation includes co-creation of curriculum and forms of engagement. "Creating spaces for student engagement through co-creating curriculum", argue Bergmark and Westman (2016, p.28), embraces "students' abilities and willingness to contribute, collaborate, and take action in their education" (p.30). Negotiated curriculum within a Sustainability Education classroom was found to improve both agentic engagement and student learning (Thomas and Reynolds, 2020). Whole-of-course co-creation "may be inherently more inclusive of students" (Bovill, 2020, p. 1023), particularly when it strives to create forums "for marginal voices to be heard and respected" (Cook-Sather, Des-Ogugua and Bahti, 2018, p.375; Wilson and Cook-Sather, 2022). For instance, one student explained that a co-created assignment she experienced "made me feel that my voice and experience are important to understanding and advocating diversity in higher education" and "it gave me the space to actually reflect and process all the tools and methods that allowed me to feel like I was a part of the inclusive yet dynamically growing community" (Cook-Sather, Des-Ogugua and Bahti, 2018, p.383).

Co-creation of course and programme-level assessment with students who are and are not enrolled

Course-level co-creation of assessment by instructors and enrolled students afford students greater agency in their own learning and in support of their peers' learning (Deeley and Bovill, 2017) and can "empower and improve perceptions of the classroom, toward the end of fostering a more equitable learning environment for all students" (Chase, 2020, p.11). Co-creating assessment criteria and approaches with enrolled students requires designing opportunities for students "to exercise more power, choice and freedom in their learning" (Deeley and Brown, 2014, p.3; Monsen et al., 2017). A student partner who experienced a co-creation approach to assessment not only came "to understand the important distinction between being educated and actively learning" (Deeley and Brown, 2014, p.3), she also felt "able to direct my own interests and demonstrate taking responsibility for my learning" (Deeley and Brown, 2014, p.9). Co-creating assessment processes at the programme level "provides opportunities for greater equity and inclusion in our processes, stronger evidence for the validity of our interpretations and is likely to result in more impetus for changing our systems of learning and development" (Curtis and Anderson, 2021b, p.12; Curtis and Anderson, 2021a; Jankowski, 2017).

Whole-of-programme co-creation

The student-led co-creation with staff of interdisciplinary courses through The Centre for Environment and Development Studies at Uppsala University in Sweden (Barrineau and Anderson, 2018) offers an example of whole-of-programme co-creation at the institutional level. Many pedagogical partnership programmes are also co-created by staff and students, such as at Davidson College (USA), "to promote equity and inclusivity within Davidson STEM disciplines" (Hossain, 2021, p. 1; see also Hernandez Brito, 2021), and at Victoria University of Wellington in Aotearoa/New Zealand, where the Ako in Action programme enacts the principle of 'akoranga', understood as a "collective responsibility for learning" (Leota and Sutherland, 2020, p.93). When students and staff work in partnership to conceptualise, develop, and launch whole programmes, whether cross-disciplinary and curriculum based or cross-institutional and partnership based, students develop a sense of agentic engagement and work toward equity. As student Ali Leota describes, he not only co-founded and co-facilitated Ako in Action, he took responsibility "to foster **whai mātauranga** [intellectual curiosity] by creating a resource to be left behind for the next Ako in Action cohort" (Leota and Sutherland, 2020, p.98)—a manifestation of agentic engagement and commitment to equity similar to Marcovici (2021) developing "a sustainable way of pursuing greater educational equity" both for the students she was advocating for in her partnership and "at the college more broadly" (p.3).

The potential benefits of co-creating learning and teaching focused on equity

A rapidly expanding body of literature reports on the potential of co-creation to: improve disciplinary learning (students) and learning about teaching (teachers); deepen engagement as students and as teachers; promote gains in confidence as learners or teachers; support a shift toward more shared responsibility for learning and teaching; enhance curricular materials and teaching approaches; build stronger learning relationships that promote empathy and trust; and foster a sense of belonging to a learning community within the university (Cook-Sather et al., 2014; Healey et al., 2016; Kaur and Mohammad, 2019; Matthews et al., 2019; Mercer-Mapstone et al., 2017).

Here we focus on two particular benefits related to agentic engagement and equity: fostering in individual students in partnership a sense of belonging to a learning community within the university, and redressing for all students in partnership, especially those underrepresented in and underserved by the institutions they attend, the epistemic, affective, and ontological harms of higher education (de Bie et al., 2021).

Foster a sense of belonging to a learning community within the university

Co-creation can foster belonging for students (and staff), particularly those who have traditionally been marginalised in higher education (Cook-Sather, 2020b; Cook-Sather and Felten, 2017). It can make underrepresented students who at first feel "out of the loop, uninvolved, small, superfluous" come to "feel like an integral part of the school and its processes" (Perez-Putnam, 2016, p.1). Having the opportunity to "practice understanding and equity" through co-creation at their college or university, international students can start to feel they "belong in this new place" (Colón García, 2017, pp.1, 5). These individual experiences of belonging can lead to agency and action; according to Perez-Putnam (2016), the co-creation work felt "important and [as though it] would have a lasting impact" (p.1), and according to Colón García (2017), the partnership experiences "made me feel a sense of belonging that was founded in the acceptance and celebration of my identity and what it could contribute to the transformation of our classroom culture" (p.4). Black female students who had participated in pedagogical partnership programmes at Berea, Bryn Mawr, and Haverford Colleges (USA) reported experiencing themselves: being perceived as "valued and recognized for the work they contribute"; feeling "involved as an equal member of the community"; and engaging "as a leader and change agent" (Cook-Sather and Seay, 2021, pp.9, 10).

Since sense of belonging is fundamental to students' engagement, persistence, and success (Ahn and Davis, 2020; Asher and Weeks, 2014; Gopalan and Brady, 2019), the experiences these and many other students describe of belonging and agency offer strong support for the potential of co-creation to promote equity.

Redressing epistemic, affective, and ontological harms of higher education

Working toward epistemic justice, co-creation approaches affirm students as knowers; recognise students' knowledge gained from diverse backgrounds and experiences; and support the development and sharing of students' knowledge, which can, in turn, facilitate broader change (de Bie et al., 2019, 2021). Working toward affective justice, pedagogical partnership can redress some of the emotional effects of oppression (e.g., increased sense of confidence, empowerment, belonging, joy and energy; creation of counter-spaces that mitigate affective harms); provide relief from some forms of emotional labour in the academy; and support the development of new forms of affective relations between students and faculty (e.g., empathy, 'politicised compassion'; de Bie et al., 2021; Gibson and Cook-Sather,

2020). Finally, pedagogical partnership rehumanises through respecting the dignity and worth of students, especially those from equity-seeking groups; creates social conditions and relationships through which students can develop—and have affirmed—their sense of self and agency and explore possibilities for who they can be; and supports the development and enactment of different worldviews that counter dominant academic and neoliberal ontologies (de Bie et al., 2021).

As former student partner, now doctoral candidate, Leslie Patricia Luqueño writes, "As I have transitioned out of my undergraduate institution and into an elite graduate school, I have increasingly seen and experienced first-hand the confidence-building and harm-redressing potential of pedagogical partnership". Luqueño (2021) explains that pedagogical partnerships "make space for students by privileging their educational expertise as they advise their faculty partners on inclusive and equitable classroom instruction", and they "have contributed to developing my own politics and shaped what I value in mentorships, pedagogy, and research".

The barriers to co-creating learning and teaching

Recognised barriers to student–staff co-creation include resistance against disrupting traditional power dynamics; time; unequal demand for both vulnerability and emotional labour; curricular or other structural constraints; inclusivity; and resources and support (Bovill, Cook-Sather, and Felten, 2011; Bovill et al., 2016; Cook-Sather and Matthews, 2021). Here we focus on navigating power dynamics and the need for progressive scaffolding to support co-creation.

Who takes on what responsibility should be an ongoing conversation in co-creation because taking on new roles challenges old habits structured and reinforced by established power dynamics (Delpish et al., 2010). The navigation of power dynamics is central to all co-creation work, and it can create conflict both internal (within individuals) and interpersonal (among students and between students and the teacher), which can be both challenging and generative (Godbold et al., 2021). As student partner Mariah R. Madigan explains regarding when power is shared:

> I fully committed to my project with the belief that I was a researcher with the power to learn something and to say something. This was real agency. I became responsible for my coursework in a way that I had never experienced before.
>
> (Cates, Madigan, and Reitenauer, 2018, p. 41)

Because co-creation work runs counter to the typical power dynamic in the classroom, it requires students to do the dual work of dismantling previously engrained practices (that may still be enforced in other classrooms and courses) while feeling assured and equipped to take on ownership and partnership in a novel learning process. It is thus insufficient merely to provide opportunities and structures within which students can co-create the learning and teaching process. Part of the changing role of the educator is to create spaces and processes within which students are equipped with co-creation skills, are made cognisant of the reasoning behind co-creation and the expectations of the course, and are allowed sufficient room to doubt, question, stumble, and troubleshoot with confidence—or, as Madigan describes above, fully embrace their own agency.

An example of our own co-creation experience that spanned two courses and student-led strikes for racial justice

The two of us engaged in three of the forms of co-creation we discuss above, one of which overlapped with student-led strikes for racial justice and the other two of which were informed by those strikes.

Cook-Sather engaged in whole-of-course co-creation with enrolled students when Loh was a student in Community Learning Collaborative (CLC) that Cook-Sather co-taught in the Fall 2020 term. This is the introductory or gateway course to the Education Program at Bryn Mawr and Haverford Colleges, and it aims to explore relationship, facilitation, and change, with decolonising approaches where possible, as core elements of education work. The course provides detailed guidelines for activities, assignments, and assessments, and each student charts their own path through the course in ways that contribute to the paths of all enrolled students. In the latter part of the Fall 2020 semester, student leaders at Haverford and Bryn Mawr Colleges launched strikes for racial justice, after which enrolled students in CLC had the option of focusing their work on the student-led strikes, which were enacting in reality the conceptual framework upon which the course had been focused.

As a student enrolled in the course, Loh chose to refocus on actively creating spaces outside of the classroom that facilitated learning across and beyond traditional power structures within higher education. The series of teach-ins that they and other student leaders organised brought individuals with relevant and necessary lived *and* learned experience—regardless of professional and academic qualification—to assume positions of trusted authority in community-constructed learning spaces. Loh also refocused their final portfolio, which allows self-determination of how the required course components are met by the individual enrolled student. Loh chose to focus on the ways in which they implemented the theoretical aspects of the course in concrete spaces other than the course itself throughout the semester, bringing to bear the need to broaden what is recognised as learning and class contribution, to what students gain the facility to implement through the course.

In the Spring 2021 term, Cook-Sather invited Loh to co-facilitate Advocating for Diversity in Higher Education, which Loh had completed the previous year. One of the electives for students pursuing the minor in educational studies that can be used as the culminating course, where the curriculum aims to make space for students to bring their lived experience into dialogue with theory in order to consider how to advocate for diversity, equity, and justice in higher education contexts. Cook-Sather had co-created this course with an undergraduate student in 2015 (Cook-Sather, Des-Ogugua and Bahti, 2018), and each year since then she or a colleague has co-redesigned and co-facilitated the course with an undergraduate student with the goal of enacting and supporting anti-racist pedagogies (Cook-Sather, 2022; Wilson and Cook-Sather, 2022).

The two of us co- and re-designed curriculum and co-created assessment approaches and criteria for the course to engage with and recognise student experiences throughout hybridised semesters, as a result of COVID-19, and the student-led strikes on Bryn Mawr and Haverford's campuses. We created distinct spaces for both content learning and process-based learning to enable students to meaningfully and manageably engage in the level and type of agentic engagement into which they were being invited. This process was one of constant dialogue and negotiation, both between us as the facilitators of the course and with student participants as a large group and individually. By actively providing avenues for feedback and decision-making on both sides, we endeavoured to make the course continually responsive and dynamic in addressing student needs.

Self-assessment was a key facet of the course, and we scaffolded the process of developing opportunities for meaningful self-assessment throughout the semester. We revisited the intentional approach to assessments as qualitative rather than quantitative evaluations of each individual student's engagement and depth of development throughout the course between ourselves in weekly planning meetings and with the students through written and verbal feedback. We provided both in-class and out-of-class opportunities for self-assessment, framed differently throughout the semester so as to progressively build the skill of self-reflection and to combat tendencies of students to undervalue their own work and contributions.

The arc that joins courses such as CLC and Advocating for Diversity is an arc of accepting co-creation as an intentional and foundational force within the teaching, learning, and planning process rather than being forced to accept necessary 'concessions' as a product of circumstance. Co-creation is the active choice in response to the constancy and inescapability of change and tumult, and it provides structures that develop agentic engagement within the individual students in order to create courses, programmes, and institutions that better reflect and address those students' desires and needs. This co-creation took place not only in *how* the class functioned, but also in what the class studied. The multivocal products that were created by enrolled students in Advocating for Diversity, for instance, became a core set of texts from which the class community actively learned. This process allowed us to bring to bear the need for multiple identifiable voices as sources of knowledge and documentations of learning, as well as further embedded the practice of agentic engagement within the fabric of the class. The enrolled students were co-creators not only of the class community and how it was assessed, but also of the very knowledge that they were learning through it.

This arc is also marked by the needs of students at various points in order for them to most fruitfully engage in co-creation. The level of scaffolding we offered as facilitators shifted in response to students' willingness to be active co-creators.

We recommend a more structured beginning invitation to learning the process of co-creation in an earlier course such as CLC, whereas later courses within the same programme, such as Advocating for Diversity, may require students to be actively developing agency and exercising it at the same time. The expanding circles of co-creation Loh experienced—from enrolled student to course co-facilitator—embodies the move from agentic engagement within a course to enacting equity in higher education through co-creation.

Takeaways and recommendations for practice

The impetus behind student–staff co-creation approaches has always been the fostering of more democratic—and, increasingly, equitable and just—modes of engagement. When both damaging and productive disruptions—such as the global pandemic and the movement for racial justice, respectively—challenge established norms in higher education, co-creation can offer structures and processes for supporting meaningful, inclusive, equitable, and empowering learning (Cook-Sather and Bala, 2022). The disruption caused by the pandemic both "made visible realities [students] were always already contending with" (Labridy-Stofle, 2020, p.3) and created new inequities (Fain, 2020). As it intersected with the growing movement for racial justice, it "prompted a clarion call for more effective strategies that will result in more equitable outcomes for underrepresented populations" (Clayton, 2021).

Given the potential for co-creation to move us toward more equitable practices, in part through developing in students a sense of agentic engagement that, as Marcovici (2021) describes, can help students "develop a sustainable way of pursuing greater educational equity", we offer the following recommendations, based on findings reported in the literature and our own co-creation experiences:

- Develop—and foster in staff the development of—'partnership attitudes', including epistemic confidence in students and open-mindedness to students' knowledge and contributions accompanied by the intention to work with students as partners (Cook-Sather and Kaur, 2022).
- Consider ways that the forms of co-creation efforts we discuss here—design and redesign of curricular and pedagogical approaches with student partners not enrolled in courses; whole-of-course co-creation with enrolled students; course- and programme-level co-creation of assessment approaches with enrolled and not-enrolled students; and whole-of-programme co-creation—as well as other forms can be resituated within a "more specifically equity- and justice-focused frame" (de Bie et al., 2021, p.106).
- Scaffold co-creation efforts, as we recommend in relation to our work: perhaps start with a more structured beginning invitation to co-creation and shift or slowly remove scaffolding as students actively develop and exercise agency.
- Take small steps, co-creating the classroom environment, a single assignment, or an activity, rather than taking on an entire course or programme (unless you feel inspired and prepared to take on larger co-creation efforts!).

- Consult the growing body of resources that offer both conceptual frameworks and step-by-step, practical guides for engaging in this work (Cook-Sather, Bovill and Felten, 2014; Cook-Sather et al., 2019; de Bie et al., 2021).
- Actively seek feedback and student responses to activities and assignments aimed at co-creation and fostering agentic engagement of students, and address the results of such feedback with the students.

In times of disruption, co-creation is still impactful for student agentic engagement, perhaps more so. It creates educational environments in which students can continually and reliably demand that courses, programmes, and educators be responsive to the impact of the changing situation on student wellbeing and needs. It centres and establishes practices and processes that create genuine relationships and avenues for communication between educators and students that reduce the power gap, which are most at risk during times of disruption.

References

Ahn, M.Y. and Davis, H.H., 2020. Students' sense of belonging and their socio-economic status in higher education: A quantitative approach. *Teaching in Higher Education*. https://doi.org/10.1080/13562517.2020.1778664.

Ameyaa, R.A., Cook-Sather, A., Ramo, K. and Tohfa, H., 2021. Undergraduate students partnering with faculty to develop trauma-informed, anti-racist pedagogical approaches: Intersecting experiences of three student partners. *Journal of Innovation, Partnership and Change*, 7(1). https://journals.studentengagement.org.uk/index.php/studentchangeagents/article/view/1020.

Asher, S.R. and Weeks, M.S., 2014. Loneliness and belongingness in the college years. In: Coplan, R.J. and Bowker, J.C. (eds) *The Handbook of Solitude: Psychological Perspectives on Social Isolation, Social Withdrawal, and Being Alone*. New York: John Wiley & Sons. https://doi.org/10.1002/9781118427378.ch16

Barrineau, S. and Anderson, L., 2018. Learning "betwixt and between": Opportunities and challenges for student-driven partnership. *International Journal for Students as Partners*, 2(1). https://doi.org/10.15173/ijsap.v2i1.3224

Bergmark, U. and Westman, S., 2016. Co-creating curriculum in higher education: Promoting democratic values and a multidimensional view on learning. *International Journal for Academic Development*, 21(1), pp.28–40.

Bovill, C., 2020. Co-creation in learning and teaching: The case for a whole-class approach in higher education. *Higher Education*, 79, pp.1023–1037. https://doi.org/10.1007/s10734-019-00453-w

Bovill, C., 2017. A framework to explore roles within student–staff partnerships in higher education: Which students are partners, when, and in what ways? *International Journal for Students as Partners*, 1(1). https://doi.org/10.15173/ijsap.v1i1.3062

Bovill, C., Cook-Sather, A., Felten, P., Millard, L. and Moore-Cherry, N., 2016. Addressing potential challenges in co-creating learning and teaching: Overcoming resistance, navigating institutional norms and ensuring inclusivity in student–staff partnerships. *Higher Education*, 71(2), pp.195–208. https://doi.org/10.1007/s10734-015-9896-4

Bovill, C., Cook-Sather, A. and Felten, P., 2011. Students as co-creators of teaching approaches, course design and curricula: Implications for academic developers. *International Journal for Academic Development*, 16(2), pp.133–145.

Brunson, M. 2018. The formation and power of trust: How it was created and enacted through collaboration. *Teaching and Learning Together in Higher Education*, 23. https://repository.brynmawr.edu/tlthe/vol1/iss23/2

Cates, R., Madigan, M. and Reitenauer, V., 2018. 'Locations of possibility': Critical perspectives on partnership. *International Journal for Students as Partners*, 2(1). https://doi.org/10.15173/ijsap.v2i1.3341

Chase, M.K., 2020. Student voice in STEM classroom assessment practice: A pilot intervention. *Journal of Research and Practice in Assessment*, 15(2). www.rpajournal.com/student-voice-in-stem-classroom-assessment-practice-a-pilot-intervention/

Clayton, T.B., 2021. Refocusing on diversity, equity, and inclusion during the pandemic and beyond: Lessons from a community of practice. *Higher Education Today*. www.higheredtoday.org/2021/01/13/refocusing-diversity-equity-inclusion-pandemic-beyond-lessons-community-practice/

Colón García, A., 2017. Building a sense of belonging through pedagogical partnership. *Teaching and Learning Together in Higher Education*, 22. http://repository.brynmawr.edu/tlthe/vol1/iss22/2

Cook-Sather, A., 2022. *Co-Creating Equitable Teaching and Learning: Structuring Student Voice into Higher Education*. Boston, MA: Harvard Education Press.

Cook-Sather, A., 2020a. Student engagement through classroom-focused pedagogical partnership: A model and outcomes from the United States. In: Lowe, T. and El Hakim, Y. (eds) *Global Perspectives of Student Engagement in Higher Education: Models for Change*. London: Routledge. https://doi.org/10.4324/9780429023033-9

Cook-Sather, A., 2020b. Respecting voices: How the co-creation of teaching and learning can support academic staff, underrepresented students, and equitable practices. *Higher Education*, 79(5), pp.885–901. https://rdcu.be/bQfu5

Cook-Sather, A. and Bala, N., 2022. When distance deepens connections: How intercollegiate partnership programs support empathetic, engaged, and equitable teaching approaches. *Student Engagement in Higher Education Journal*, 4, p.2.

Cook-Sather, A. and Felten, P., 2017. Where student engagement meets faculty development: How student–faculty pedagogical partnership fosters a sense of belonging. *Student Engagement in Higher Education Journal* 1(2), pp.3–11. https://journals.gre.ac.uk/index.php/raise/article/view/cook

Cook-Sather, A. and Kaur, A., 2022. Embracing epistemic confidence, open-mindedness, and co-creation: An exploration of how the psychological constructs of attitudes and intentions can inform staff contributions to successful student–staff partnership. *Journal of Educational Innovation, Partnership and Change*, 8, p.2.

Cook-Sather, A. and Matthews, K.E., 2021. Engaging with students as pedagogical consultants, curriculum co-designers, and knowledge co-creators. In Hunt, L. and Chalmers, D. (eds), *University Teaching in Focus: A Learning-Centred Approach* (2nd edn). Abingdon: Routledge.

Cook-Sather, A. and Seay, K., 2021. "I was involved as an equal member of the community": How pedagogical partnership can foster a sense of belonging in black, female students. *Cambridge Journal of Education*. www.tandfonline.com/eprint/QXRZDMGSM3YQPZFNGDPQ/full?target=10.1080/0305764X.2021.1926926

Cook-Sather, A., Ho, L., Kaur, A. and Tamim, T., in press. *Translating Pedagogical Partnership in/to Academic Staff Development in the Global South.*

Cook-Sather, A., Allard, S., Marcovici, E. and Reynolds, B., 2021. Fostering agentic engagement: Working toward empowerment and equity through pedagogical partnership. *International Journal for the Scholarship of Teaching and Learning*, 15(2). doi:10.20429/ijsotl.2021.150203.

Cook-Sather, A., Bahti, M. and Ntem, A., 2019. *Pedagogical Partnerships: A How-to Guide for Faculty, Students, and Academic Developers in Higher Education.* Elon, NC: Elon University Center for Engaged Teaching.

Cook-Sather, A., Krishna Prasad, S., Marquis, E. and Ntem, A., 2019. Mobilizing a culture shift on campus: Underrepresented students as educational developers. *New Directions for Teaching and Learning*, 159, pp.21–30. https://onlinelibrary.wiley.com/toc/15360768/2019/2019/159

Cook-Sather, A, Des-Ogugua, C. and Bahti, M., 2018. Articulating identities and analyzing belonging: A multistep intervention that affirms and informs a diversity of students. *Teaching in Higher Education*, 23(3), pp.374–389. https://doi.org/10.1080/13562517.2017.1391201

Cook-Sather, A., Bovill, C. and Felten, P., 2014. *Engaging Students as Partners in Learning and Teaching: A Guide for Faculty.* San Francisco, CA: Jossey-Bass.

Curtis, N.A. and Anderson, R.D., 2021a. Moving toward student-faculty partnership in systems-level assessment: A qualitative analysis. *International Journal for Students as Partners*, 5(1), pp.57–75. https://doi.org/10.15173/ijsap.v5i1.4204

Curtis, N.A. and Anderson, R., 2021b. *A Framework for Developing Student–Faculty Partnerships in Program-Level Student Learning Outcomes Assessment* (Occasional Paper No. 53). Urbana, IL: University of Illinois and Indiana University, National Institute for Learning Outcomes Assessment (NILOA). www.learningoutcomesassessment.org/wp-content/uploads/2021/05/OccPaper53_Partnership.pdf

de Bie, A., Marquis, E., Cook-Sather, A. and Luqueño, L.P., 2021. *Promoting Equity and Justice through Pedagogical Partnership.* Sterling, VA: Stylus Publishers.

de Bie, A., Marquis, E., Cook-Sather, A. and Luqueño, L.P., 2019. Valuing knowledge(s) and cultivating confidence: Contributions of student–faculty pedagogical partnerships to epistemic justice. In: Hoffman, J., Blessinger, P. and Makhanya, M. (eds) *Strategies for Fostering Inclusive Classrooms in Higher Education: International Perspectives on Equity and Inclusion* (Innovations in Higher Education Teaching and Learning, Vol. 16). Bingley: Emerald Publishing Limited. https://doi.org/10.1108/S2055-364120190000016004

Deeley, S.J. and Bovill, C., 2017. Staff–student partnership in assessment: Enhancing assessment literacy through democratic practices. *Assessment and Evaluation in Higher Education*, 42(3), pp.463–477. https://doi.org/10.1080/02602938.2015.1126551

Deeley, S.J. and Brown, R.A., 2014. Learning through partnership in assessment. *Teaching and Learning Together in Higher Education*, 1(13). http://repository.brynmawr.edu/tlthe/vol1/iss13/3

Delpish, A., Holmes, A, Knight-McKenna, M., Mihans, R., Darby, A., King, K. and Felten, P., 2010. Equalizing voices: Student-faculty partnership in course design. In: Werder, C. and Otis, M.M. (ed), *Engaging Student Voices in the Study of Teaching and Learning.* Sterling, VA: Stylus.

Fain, P., 2020. Higher education and work amid crisis. Inside Higher Ed. www.insidehighered.com/news/2020/06/17/pandemic-has-worsened-equity-gaps-higher-education-and-work

Gibson, S. and Cook-Sather, A., 2020. Politicised compassion and pedagogical partnership: A discourse and practice for social justice in the inclusive academy. *International Journal for Students as Partners*, 4(1). https://mulpress.mcmaster.ca/ijsap/article/view/3996

Godbold, N., Hung, T.Y. and Matthews, K.E., 2021. Exploring the role of conflict in co-creation of curriculum through engaging students as partners in the classroom. *Higher Education Research and Development*. doi:10.1080/07294360.2021.1887095.

Gopalan, M. and Brady, S.T., 2019. College students' sense of belonging: A national perspective. *Educational Researcher*. https://doi.org/10.3102/0013189X19897622

Healey, M., Flint, A. and Harrington, K., 2016. Students as partners: Reflections on a conceptual model. *Teaching and Learning Inquiry*, 4(2). http://tlijournal.com/tli/index.php/TLI/article/view/105/97

Hernandez Brito, C., 2021. Creating more inclusive learning environments at Davidson College. *Teaching and Learning Together in Higher Education*, 33. https://repository.brynmawr.edu/tlthe/vol1/iss33/3/

Hossain, S., 2021. Embracing the risk and responsibility of starting a pedagogical partnership program focused on fostering inclusivity and respect in science. *Teaching and Learning Together in Higher Education*, 33. https://repository.brynmawr.edu/tlthe/vol1/iss33/2/

Jankowski, N., 2017. *Mixing it all together: Recipes for inclusion.* Keynote for the Assessment Network of New York conference, New York.

Kaur, A. and Mohammad, N., 2019. Investigating students' experiences of students as partners (SaP) for basic need fulfilment: A self-determination theory perspective. *Journal of University Teaching and Learning Practice*, 17(1). https://ro.uow.edu.au/jutlp/vol17/iss1/8

Labridy-Stofle, C., 2020. Uprooted rhizomes: Collaborating in times of troubling transitions. *Teaching and Learning Together in Higher Education*, 30. https://repository.brynmawr.edu/tlthe/vol1/iss30/4

Leota, A. and Sutherland, K., 2020. With your basket of knowledge and my basket of knowledge, the people will prosper: Learning and leading in a student–staff partnership program. In Cook-Sather, A. and Wilson, C. (eds) *Building Courage, Confidence, and Capacity in Learning and Teaching through Student-Faculty Partnership: Stories from across Contexts and Arenas of Practice.* Lanham, MD: Lexington Books.

Luqueño, L.P., 2021. Learning to honor my own epistemology: The long-term effects of student–faculty partnerships. Available at: www.centerforengagedlearning.org/learning-to-honor-my-own-epistemology-the-long-term-effects-of-student-faculty-partnerships (accessed: 16 May 2021).

Marcovici, E., 2021. Taking ownership of my learning and pushing for change. *Teaching and Learning Together in Higher Education*, 34. https://repository.brynmawr.edu/tlthe/vol1/iss34/3

Matthews, K.E., Mercer-Mapstone, L., Dvorakova, S.L., Acai, A., Cook-Sather, A., Felten, P., Healey, M., Healey, R.L. and Marquis, E., 2019. Enhancing outcomes and reducing inhibitors to the engagement of students and staff in learning and teaching partnerships: Implications for academic development. *International Journal for Academic Development*, 24(3), pp.246–259. https://doi.org/10.1080/1360144x.2018.1545233

Matthews, K.E., Cook-Sather, A., Acai, A., Dvorakova, S.L., Felten, P., Marquis, E. and Mercer-Mapstone, L., 2018. Toward theories of partnership praxis: An analysis of interpretive framing in literature on students as partners in university teaching and learning. *Higher Education Research and Development*. doi:10.1080/07294360.2018.1530199.

Mercer-Mapstone, L., Dvorakova, S.L., Matthews, K.E., Abbot, S., Cheng, B., Felten, P., Knorr, K., Marquis, E., Shammas, R. and Swaim, K., 2017. A systematic literature review of students as partners in higher education. *International Journal for Students as Partners*, 1(1), pp.1–23. https://doi.org/10.15173/ijsap.v1i1.3119

Monsen, S., Cook, S. and Hannant, L., 2017. Students as partners in negotiated assessment in a teacher education course. *Teaching and Learning Together in Higher Education*, 21. https://repository.brynmawr.edu/tlthe/vol1/iss21/2

Perez-Putnam, M., 2016. Belonging and brave space as hope for personal and institutional inclusion. *Teaching and Learning Together in Higher Education*, 18. http://repository.brynmawr.edu/tlthe/vol1/iss18/2

Reeve, J., 2013. How students create motivationally supportive learning environments for themselves: The concept of agentic engagement. *Journal of Educational Psychology*, 105(3), pp.579–595. https://doi.org/10.1037/a0032690

Reeve, J. and Shin, S.H., 2020. How teachers can support students' agentic engagement. *Theory into Practice*, 59(2), pp.150–161. doi:10.1080/00405841.2019.1702451.

Reeve, J. and Tseng, C.-M., 2011. Agency as a fourth aspect of students' engagement during learning activities. *Contemporary Educational Psychology*, 36(4), pp.257–267. doi:10.1016/j.cedpsych.2011.05.002.

Thomas, B. and Reynolds, W., 2020. *Applying student-faculty partnership lessons in a negotiated course redesign*. Conference of the Professional and Organizational Development Network, Fort Myers, FL, 13 November. www.fgcu.edu/lucascenter/blog/pod-conference-2020

Wilson, C. and Cook-Sather, A., 2022. Rippling the patterns of power: Enacting anti-racist pedagogy with students as co-teachers. In: Neuhaus, J. (ed) *Picture a Professor: Intersectional Teaching Strategies for Interrupting Bias about Faculty and Increasing Student Learning*. Morgantown, WV: West Virginia University Press.

Chapter 17

Defining, delivering and evaluating student engagement in a professional service in higher education

A case study of a student engagement team in an academic library

Madalene George

Introduction

When, in 2015, the University of Worcester (UK) Library Services developed the role of Student Engagement Coordinator, the concept of a dedicated and named student engagement team was still relatively unusual in UK higher education (HE) libraries (Pittaway, 2016a, p.249). Student engagement theory and practice had been a part of HE discourse for decades and was a growing phenomenon in the HE landscape, but much of this more visible work seemed to be taking place in lecture theatres, seminar rooms and students' unions, rather than professional services settings (Bryson and Hand, 2007; Cook-Sather, Bovill and Felten, 2014; El Hakim et al., 2020).

As Appleton (2020) demonstrates, work to engage with students and engage students with services is widespread in HE libraries, yet the role of academic libraries and other professional services is rarely featured in the wider student engagement discourse. Professional services, including libraries, are an integral aspect of the fabric of HE and of the overall student experience. As Carey (2013) argues, "An engagement culture needs to happen inside, as well as outside, the classroom. In this way, it extends beyond design and into the living curriculum to become a distinguishing feature of the learning and assessment strategy" (p.259). Professional services can learn a great deal from classroom-based student engagement theories and activity, whilst using their own unique insight to support institution-wide student engagement. Moreover, they can be a valuable addition to the conversation and, by developing and sharing their own examples of good practice, can contribute to a body of research which takes a holistic view of student engagement and the wider student experience.

However, developing a student engagement strategy outside of the classroom is challenging. Student engagement is a notoriously tricky concept to pin down (Trowler, 2010; Gibbs, 2016; El Hakim, Kandiko Howson and Freeman, 2020)

DOI: 10.4324/9781003271789-17

and this is no less true in a library environment (Appleton, 2020, p.189). For professional services, the difficulty of defining, delivering, and evaluating meaningful student engagement practice is compounded by a relative distance from conventional teaching spaces and the *ad hoc* nature of interactions with students. Whilst HE libraries and other professional services often contribute to students' teaching and learning experience, they are rarely afforded the opportunity to develop the more meaningful relationships that come from a longer-term learner–teacher partnership. Moreover, interactions with students may take place exclusively online or they may be quick, transactional experiences. In these instances, it can be easy to begin to frame students as consumers, rather than partners in the collective HE experience (Temple et al., 2016, p.40).

This chapter considers some of these barriers to engaging students with professional services. It explores different definitions of student engagement and the impacts these can have on the delivery of inclusive and meaningful engagement activities. It looks at some of the perils of relying on transactional or isolationist approaches to delivering engagement, and the challenges that professional services face to demonstrating the impact of engagement activities. It does, however, also offer some reassurance that, with an innovative approach, it is possible for professional services teams to foster partnerships between staff and students and embed meaningful student engagement into service design.

Defining student engagement

Some of the most exciting and innovative examples of global student engagement activity include inspiring case studies of the evaluation and co-creation of modules, courses, or curricula, or staff-student partnerships which seek to enact meaningful changes to academic processes. However, these can be difficult to translate from the classroom to other areas of the student experience. In many ways, this discord amplifies the perception that professional services, including libraries, student support, careers and others, exist in a liminal space in student engagement discourse. Professional services teams are student-facing, they support students' learning and help to define the student experience but, with little to no scheduled contact time and a cohort that encompasses the entire student body, what does it mean for students to be engaged with these services?

To define quality student engagement with professional services, it is important to consider interpretations of the term which are unhelpful or, at least, incomplete. In an academic library, for example, the concept of student engagement might be understood through the transactional lens that is so often applied to professional services. This perspective considers an engaged student to be one who visits the library often, borrows plenty of books and accesses library support (Pittaway, 2016a, p.250). This definition of engagement might use easily measured metrics, such as footfall or book borrowing, combined with satisfaction scores measured by the National Student Survey to ascertain whether services are in demand and meeting students' needs. Like other data analytics used in HE, these metrics have their place in service design, but gathering and studying them cannot, in itself, be defined as student engagement (Lowe, 2018). For professional services departments, already more exposed to a transactional staff–student relationship, this approach further confines students to the role of consumer and frames staff expertise in the context of customer satisfaction. A passive, metric-driven definition of engagement also incentivises the pursuit of quick wins in exchange for increased access statistics or enhanced student satisfaction scores, rather than meaningful partnership or dialogue (Temple et al., 2016, p.40).

Perhaps most importantly, a focus on transactions, interactions and aggregated student satisfaction also ignores the complex and often highly individual ways in which students access and engage with professional services (Pittaway, 2016a, pp.250–251). Chapter 4 argues that there is no one student experience of HE, and this can equally be said of students' experience of the academic library and other professional services. Students' needs and experiences have, of course, always varied, but this diversity became increasingly apparent during the COVID-19 pandemic and the shift to remote learning and teaching (Matizirofa et al., 2021, pp.372–373). A student with no quiet place to work may visit the library building more frequently than one who has adequate access to a suitable study space at home; equally, a student in need of additional support may contact enquiry services more readily than one who prefers to look for the answer on the library website. These students will be represented differently by usage metrics, but one is not necessarily more or less engaged than the others (Pittaway, 2016a, pp.249–250).

An alternative definition of engagement, often used by professional services, focuses on students' participation in extracurricular activity, including their involvement in volunteer roles, or attendance at optional engagement sessions, such as focus groups (Gourlay, 2015, pp.402–403). Many academic libraries, including at the University of Worcester (UK), promote highly visible, voluntary engagement opportunities which support library services or the wider community. These activities are frequently used to demonstrate 'good' levels of student engagement and, more often than not, have a measurably positive impact on both students and the service (Walton, 2010, pp.117–119; Pittaway, 2016a, pp.250–251). Yet, whilst these are, without doubt, valuable examples of good practice, they still offer an imperfect and incomplete definition of meaningful and inclusive engagement.

Professional services must remember that not all students want to, or can, engage with extracurricular activity (Strudwick et al., 2017 pp.83–84) and that these opportunities are only truly accessible to a small number of students, often from groups who are already well-represented in service design. Many students may recognise the value of involving themselves in additional or extracurricular activity but the competing demands on their time, such as academic workload, caring responsibilities or paid employment, may mean that they do not prioritise voluntary activities over their studies (Gibbs, 2016, p.2) or miss out on valuable opportunities altogether (Strudwick et al., 2017, pp.83–84). As Gourlay (2015) argues, if services only "focus on activity which is communicative, recordable, public, observable" they risk ignoring or even isolating those whose engagement is "quiet, private, non-verbal and non-observable" (pp.404–405). To deliver an inclusive offer, professional services must recognise the diversity of students' experiences and motivations and seek alternative ways to build on this definition of student engagement.

At Worcester, student engagement is defined by the aim "to engage with students as partners and agents for change who are actively involved in evaluating, developing and delivering our library service" (Pittaway, 2016a, p.249). This embeds engagement at the core of library service practice, resulting in three essential strands of work: communication, collaboration and co-creation. Or, as Donaldson (2020) so neatly summarises, "Ask [students to] work with [students] and be inspired by [students] to facilitate positive engagement for all" (p.47). This approach demonstrates that libraries and other professional services are not bound by usage metrics, satisfaction scores and volunteering opportunities to engage with students. Rather, services can embrace a complex and comprehensive definition of student engagement which puts students at the centre of service development (Appleton, 2020, p.208).

Delivering student engagement

At the most fundamental level, student engagement activities at Worcester seek to create meaningful dialogue between students and the library service. This means communicating core messages to create a welcoming, collaborative space and proactively challenge the library anxiety that students so often experience (Mellon, 1986; Larsen et al., 2019). But it also means giving students ownership of their library by amplifying the role of student voice in service design. Consultation and dialogue with students are an integral part of student engagement practice and, at Worcester, it has become standard practice to engage with students any time the library service wants to change something or introduce something new.

Implementing this level of consultation outside of the classroom is challenging. Like most professional services, libraries rarely have scheduled contact with students and often rely on methods such as surveying to gather student opinion. But survey fatigue is a well-documented phenomenon in HE (Porter, Whitcomb and Weitzer, 2004) and asking for feedback at the wrong point in a student's library journey may prove disruptive and counterproductive. Recruiting students to provide richer feedback, for example at focus groups, is equally challenging, as professional services cannot generally contact class or cohort lists without the support of academic colleagues. Understandably, students also struggle to see the immediate benefits of engaging in activities which are not visibly related to their course or assessment. In these instances, it is easy to rely on participation from students who are already interested and engaged in library services to inform service design. However, in doing so, libraries fall into the trap of simply responding to the loudest, or easiest to reach, voices.

To ensure an inclusive approach to engagement that responds to a diverse range of student experiences, it is important to consider alternative methods of facilitating communication and understanding students' needs. At Worcester, this has resulted in a user experience (UX)-led approach, which focuses on "human-centred" and ethnography-driven research (Potter, 2016). This approach uses techniques such as customer journey or cognitive mapping and informal interviews to understand the student experience (Ramsden, 2016).

At its best, UX research identifies large-scale trends, whilst also valuing the rich data provided by individual learner journeys (Priestner and Borg, 2016). But, like any consultation method, UX is only as representative as practitioners allow it to be. When designing UX-led engagement activities, it is vital to include measures to capture the experiences of students who, for whatever reason, do not engage proactively with consultation. This might include using observational activities to better understand students' lived experience (Ramsden, 2016) or moving outside of the library space to gather feedback from students who do not use the building. Creating targeted but flexible engagement opportunities can help encourage a more diverse range of students to contribute. Moreover, collaboration with other services, such as Disability and Dyslexia Services, the Students' Union, societies and staff or student networks, can be an invaluable tool to reach students who may be underrepresented in, or disadvantaged by, existing service design.

Consultation with students is an integral component of engagement activities but, if employed in isolation, the process can begin to appear performative and intensify the feeling that students are consumers of the services we provide, rather than partners in their academic experience (Lea, 2016; El Hakim, Kandiko Howson and Freeman, 2020). Students can easily become disheartened by engaging with consultation that produces few benefits for themselves or their peers, does not enact meaningful change, or that removes students from the conversation before defining or developing outcomes (Carey, 2013, p.257). As a result, partnership work has become a defining feature of successful student engagement practice (Healey, Flint and Harrington, 2014; Cook-Sather, Bovill and Felten, 2014).

Staff–student partnerships in library or professional services settings can be a powerful tool in supporting students to develop their academic and professional skills and experience. Nevertheless, it can be challenging to demonstrate the value of partnership with professional services if students cannot envisage how their involvement might enrich their CV or equip them with the experience they require for graduate life. Enhancing employability prospects and the potential to enact change and improve the academic environment for themselves and others are both important motivators in a student's decision to engage with partnership work (Rowland, 2020, pp.129–131). However, it can be complicated to fulfil these aims in a professional services environment. In academic libraries, for example, a students' library experience is often entangled with other professional and academic services (Pittaway, 2016a, p.256), making it difficult to act in isolation to affect the type of highly visible changes that come as a result of, say, curriculum co-design.

However, libraries and other professional services can deliver meaningful partnerships outside of traditional teaching spaces if they embrace their distinct role in the HE environment and adopt an innovative approach to collaboration. The Higher Education Authority described student engagement partnerships as a "relationship in which all involved – students, academics, professional services staff, senior managers, students' unions, and so on – are actively engaged in and stand to gain from the process of learning and working together" (Healey, Flint and Harrington, 2014, p.12). This could mean thinking beyond the immediate service delivery to devise tangible opportunities for students. At Worcester, for example, student volunteers are included on recruitment panels for all student-facing library staff. This initiative offers students invaluable experience of professional recruitment processes and enables them to feel empowered in the future development of the service (Pittaway, 2016b, p.40). Professional work placements in areas such as health and wellbeing, business, communications, and education are also designed to equip students with vital employability skills and communicate the diversity of services delivered within contemporary libraries. In these instances, libraries can even benefit from their distance from the power imbalances of the classroom (Matthews et al., 2018, p.963) and the perceived risks related to conventional student–teacher dialogues (Carey, 2013, pp.255–256); students become the experts in the room and are empowered to recognise the value of putting their learnt skills into practice to enhance professional services.

For professional services teams, collaboration with colleagues from across the institution can also help to overcome barriers to delivering effective student partnerships or student-led change. Like many other institutions, University of Worcester runs a *Students as Academic Partners* scheme that enables institution-wide collaboration between staff and paid student partners (University of Worcester Library Services, 2021). Professional services teams often overlook these schemes, but they can provide invaluable opportunities to develop engagement projects and deliver meaningful change. At Worcester, for example, a partnership project undertaken by Library Services, academic colleagues and students to review representation in Resource Lists has empowered student participants to take an active role in content creation and devise student-led training sessions for both professional services and academic staff.

Seeking collaborations with staff outside of professional services also offers an opportunity to connect with the wider university community and presents a fresh perspective on the student experience. Working with students and colleagues who are engaged in academic research can help professional services develop their research practice and acquire skills that can be used in future engagement projects. Moreover, close partnership working allows professional services staff to share innovative practice from within their teams, establish themselves as valuable professional colleagues (Pittaway, 2018, p.16) and advocate for student engagement strategies across the institution.

Evaluating the impact of student engagement

To advocate for student engagement in professional services departments and across institutions, it is vital to evaluate and communicate the impact of this work.

Like academic colleagues, professional services teams often have many roles and responsibilities competing for limited resources. Meaningful student engagement is time-consuming, and it can be difficult for colleagues to understand the need for targeted work in this area if they cannot see the value for students or the service.

A multi-layered, innovation- and partnership-focused student engagement approach, of the type adopted at Worcester, presents many additional challenges to measuring and communicating impact. The variety of initiatives generates a daunting quantity of messy qualitative and quantitative data. This makes it difficult to connect individual projects and communicate the wider impacts of engagement activities. Moreover, the distance between the library and individual students makes it more challenging to assess the longer-term impacts of engagement projects. Professional services are rarely able to see evidence of engagement in students' assignments and cannot easily check back in with students at the end of a module or throughout their studies to assess the impact of any service changes they have made.

To combat this, professional services must take a proactive approach to embedding impact into design and delivery of student engagement activities. At Worcester, this has resulted in a standardised planning process for all engagement activity, including the introduction of pre- and post-project forms which monitor:

- The overall aim and expected outcomes of the project.
- How short-term impacts are assessed and communicated.
- How longer-term impacts are assessed and communicated.

It is also vital to remember the wider impacts of targeted student engagement activities, rather than focusing solely on the impact that engagement-led service developments have on subsequent student experiences. University of Worcester Library Services have taken measures to capture the impact that engagement projects have on individual students taking part, as well as the shared value of high-quality engagement activities to colleagues and to the service. This approach informs a simple framework which is used for individual projects and to review the cumulative impact of engagement activity.

This framework allows the service to measure and communicate:

- **The impact on the students taking part in engagement activities**: this is measured through post-engagement surveys, which ask students to reflect on their experience and evaluate the personal impact of their involvement in engagement activities, including whether they learnt anything, gained any new skills or felt more valued because of their engagement.
- **The impact on the service**: this evaluates the changes that have been made to the service in response to student feedback, new initiatives that have been introduced or the tangible gains made from student-generated content, or partnership with students and colleagues.

- **The impact on the wider student body or university community**: this considers the big picture of student engagement activities and uses national and internal survey results, school or subject-level feedback and targeted evaluation activities to assess the impact of focused student engagement activities.

This framework makes it possible to measure the complex impacts of diverse projects and to bring together a more complete understanding of impact at the end of the academic year. By considering the impact that engagement activities have on individual students, the service and the wider university community, the library team can communicate the impact of the student engagement role and advocate for the value of student engagement activities across the institution.

Conclusion

This chapter seeks to address some of the challenges of defining and delivering student engagement in professional services settings. It demonstrates how hard it can be to engage students in a meaningful way outside of the classroom and the barriers to measuring and communicating the impact of student engagement across institutions. However, it also shows that, whilst engaging students in an academic library is different to working in conventional teaching spaces, professional services teams can address some of the challenges posed by their relative distance from students and the *ad hoc* nature of student interactions by focusing on innovation and partnership. By adopting distinct ways of defining and delivering student engagement and collaborating with colleagues, professional services – including libraries – can be pioneers of creative engagement practice and use their unique perspectives on the university environment to develop services that support and engage diverse student communities.

References

Appleton, L., 2020. Academic libraries and student engagement: A literature review. *New Review of Academic Librarianship*, 26(2–4), pp.189–213. doi:10.1080/13614533.2020.1784762.

Bryson, C. and Hand, L., 2007. The role of engagement in inspiring teaching and learning. *Innovations in Education and Teaching International*, 44(4), pp.349–362. doi:10.1080/14703290701602748.

Carey, P., 2013. Student as co-producer in a marketised higher education system: A case study of students' experience of participation in curriculum design. *Innovations in Education and Teaching International*, 50(3), pp.250–260. doi:10.1080/14703297.2013.796714.

Cook-Sather, A., Bovill, C. and Felten, P., 2014. *Engaging Students as Partners in Learning and Teaching: A Guide for Faculty*. San Francisco, CA: Jossey-Bass.

Donaldson, G., 2020. "I am part of the university": Why universities offering non-traditional students extracurricular activities leads to higher levels of student engagement: A mature student's perspective. In: Lowe, T. and El-Hakim, Y. (eds) *A Handbook for Student Engagement in Higher Education*. Abingdon: Routledge. doi:10.4324/9780429023033.

El Hakim, Y., Kandiko Howson, C. and Freeman, R., 2020. Creating relationships between students, staff and universities for student engagement in educational developments. In: Lowe, T. and El-Hakim, Y. (eds) *A Handbook for Student Engagement in Higher Education*. Abingdon: Routledge. doi:10.4324/9780429023033.

Gibbs, G., 2016. Idea number 42: Student engagement is a slippery concept – 53 powerful ideas all teachers should know about. Available at: www.seda.ac.uk/resour ces/files/publications_199_42%20'Student%20engagement'%20is%20a%20slippery% 20consept.pdf (accessed 10 August 2021).

Gourlay, L., 2015. "Student engagement" and the tyranny of participation. *Teaching in Higher Education*, 20(4), pp.402–411. doi:10.1080/13562517.2015.1020784.

Healey, M., Flint, A. and Harrington, K., 2014. Engagement through partnership: Students as partners in learning and teaching in higher education. Available at: https://s3. eu-west-2.amazonaws.com/assets.creode.advancehe-document-manager/documents/ hea/private/resources/engagement_through_partnership_1568036621.pdf (accessed: 21 August 2021).

Larsen, D. *et al.* 2019. From cubicles to community: Reducing library anxiety through critically reimagined social spaces. *New Review of Academic Librarianship*, 25(2–4), pp.408–423. doi:10.1080/13614533.2019.1615966.

Lea, J., 2016. Turning down the volume control on student voice in order to enhance student engagement. *Student Engagement in Higher Education Journal*, 1(1), pp.1–4.

Lowe, T., 2018. Data analytics –a critique of the appropriation of a new measure of 'student engagement'. *Student Engagement in Higher Education Journal*, 2(1), pp.2–6.

Matizirofa, L. *et al.* 2021. Maintaining student engagement: The digital shift during the coronavirus pandemic – a case of the library at the University of Pretoria. *New Review of Academic Librarianship*, 27(3), pp.364–379. doi:10.1080/13614533.2021.1976234.

Matthews, K. *et al.* 2018. Concepts of students as partners, *Higher Education*, 76, pp.957–971. doi:10.1007/s10734-018-0257-y.

Mellon, C., 1986. Library anxiety: A grounded theory and its development. *College and Research Libraries*, 47(2), pp.160–165. doi:10.5860/crl_47_02_160.

Pittaway, S., 2018. "Not just the help": Library Services as professional colleagues. *ALISS Quarterly*, 13(3), pp.13–16.

Pittaway, S., 2016a. Engaging students, shaping services: The changing face of student engagement at The Hive. *Insights*, 29(3), pp.249–257. doi:10.1629/uksg.315.

Pittaway, S., 2016b. Students as partners in recruitment. *SCONUL Focus*, 65, pp.40–43.

Porter, S.R., Whitcomb, M.E. and Weitzer, W.H., 2004. Multiple surveys of students and survey fatigue. *New Directions for Institutional Research*, 121, pp.63–73. doi:10.1002/ ir.101.

Potter, N., 2016. What is UX and how can it help your organisation? UX in libraries resource list. Available at: www.ned-potter.com/ux-in-libraries-resource-list (accessed: 21 August 2021).

Priestner, A. and Borg, M., 2016. Uncovering complexity and detail: The UX proposition. In Priestner, A. and Borg, M. (eds) *User Experience in Libraries: Applying Ethnography and Human-Centred Design*. Abingdon: Routledge. https://doi.org/10.4324/ 9781315548609

Ramsden, B., 2016. Using ethnographic methods to study library use. In Priestner, A. and Borg, M. (eds) *User Experience in Libraries: Applying Ethnography and Human-Centred Design*. Abingdon: Routledge.

Rowland, S., 2020. A students-as-partners approach to developing a work-integrated learning program for science. In: Lowe, T. and El-Hakim, Y. (eds) *A Handbook for Student Engagement in Higher Education*. Abingdon: Routledge. doi:10.4324/9780429023033.

Sims, S., King, S., Lowe, T. and El-Hakim, Y., 2016. Evaluating partnership and impact in the first year of the Student Fellows Scheme. *Journal of Educational Innovation, Partnership and Change*, 2(1). doi:10.21100/jeipc.v2i1.257.

Strudwick, K., Jameson, J., Gordon, J., Brookfield, K. and McKane, C., 2017. 'Understanding the gap' to participate or not? Evaluating student engagement and active participation. *Student Engagement in Higher Education Journal*, 1(2), pp.81–87.

Temple, P.A. *et al.*, 2016. Managing the student experience in English higher education: Differing responses to market pressures. *London Review of Education*, 14(1), pp.33–46. doi:10.18546/lre.14.1.05.

Trowler, V., 2010. *Student Engagement Literature Review*. Available at: www.heacademy. ac.uk/system/files/StudentEngagementLiteratureReview_1.pdf (Accessed: 10 August 2021).

University of Worcester Library Services, 2021. *Projects and Publications*. Available at: https:// library.worc.ac.uk/projects-and-publications (accessed: 17 July 2022).

Walton, G., 2010. University libraries and student engagement. *New Review of Academic Librarianship*, 16(2), pp.117–120. doi:10.1080/13614533.2010.514762.

University estates

From spaces to places of student engagement

Zachery Spire

Introduction

In this chapter I explore the relationship between university estates and student engagement. To do so, I position student engagement with and in university estates along three dimensions: material, social and personal. I examine some of what has been said about the impact of the university estate for students, staff and the wider public. This chapter was proposed and written in a time of crisis (2020–2021) when a global pandemic (COVID-19) influenced the material, social and personal spaces of universities across the globe and the future need of the campus estate began to be questioned. COVID-19 has induced a critical return for reflection on the influence of the material university (Whyte, 2019b) for teaching, learning, research and the ideas and ideals of *being* a university (Barnett, 2007).

University estates

University estates have become a key topic in contemporary higher education studies. Scholars have found ample room and range to pour over the forms, functions and stated purpose of the material environment of universities. Some of the lenses being utilized draw from: architectural history (Muthesius, 2000; Whyte, 2006, 2018, 2019a, 2019b), education (Barnett, 2011; Temple and Barnett, 2007; Temple, 2008; Temple, 2007) and the built environment (Boys, 2018; Marmot, 2002; Goodyear, Ellis, Marmot, 2018; Rymarzak and Marmot, 2020). For scholars like Muthesius (2000) and Whyte (2006, 2019b), the material environment reflects a physical engineering with design intention to influence the social and personal practices of students (and staff/wider public) with and in a university.

Similarly, Temple (2008) explores the relationship of learning space design and use. He highlights how a lack of empirical findings and data leaves substantive gaps in our understanding of the relationships of the physical design of learning spaces to the production of teaching, learning and research in and across universities. Taking a more philosophical turn, Barnett (2011) and Barnett and Jackson (2019) highlight the ecology of material space for social and personal learning

DOI: 10.4324/9781003271789-18

with and in universities. As Temple (2008) proposes, use of university spaces by students, staff, guests and visitors transforms *space* to *place*.

Beyond the philosophy of space and place, university buildings act as a driver to access, participation, recruitment and retention of staff and students. An institution risks over-recruiting when it recruits several hundred more students a year, year on year, with no appreciable change in the built environment in which to accommodate (student residences), teach and research (lecture theatres, classrooms, libraries). Tensions arising between the number of students and staff requiring accommodations (i.e. teaching, learning, research, housing) and processes like transportation, timetabling, auxiliary services, student and staff support services (i.e. psychology services, academic advising, food service, study spaces, technology hubs). The ecology of how a university estate enshrines a plan, or lack thereof, and perpetuates an idea that master planning is both possible and a necessary requisite of contemporary university estate practice is a perennial and perpetual question for both student and staff engagement.

In parallel to scholarship on university estates and the influence on students' and staff members' engagement, the Higher Education Design Quality Forum (HEDQF) (2019a, 2019b, 2021) and the Association of University Directors of Estates (AUDE) focus on the influence and importance of the university estate for the operations of universities, and, the relations of students and staff to their respective institutions. The HEDQF has a longstanding interest in the forms and functions of university estates for teaching, learning and research (2019a, 2019b, 2021). As Temple (2008) notes, several authors (Blimling, 2015; Astin, 1984, 1993) allude to and argue about the influence of university estates on students, staff and the wider public; little evidence has been generated on the relations between university estates, student and staff engagement. What has been broadly defined as student and staff engagement focuses on allocation of time, energy and financial resources into educationally purposive activities (Astin, 1984, 1993; Coates, 2006; Pace, 1980). In the context of the United Kingdom, Trowler (2010) completed a literature review on student experience and student engagement, noting that literature in this area for the United States (Astin, Pace, ibid.) was largely framed as access, participation, recruitment and retention. Again, alluding to but offering little empirical evidence to support claims about the relations and relationship of the university built environment for student engagement with and in the university. A dearth of publicly available data and the narrow nature of study into the university estate have left substantial gaps in evidence upon which to base university estate decisions for student engagement (Spire, 2022).

Student engagement as a lens for university estates

Student engagement for this chapter is defined as the intentional investment of time, energy, financial and other relevant resources for educationally purposive activities with and in universities (Trowler, 2010). This investment is defined by the material, social and personal spaces, place and placemaking (Holton, 2019) students and staff engage in while teaching, learning and researching with and in their institution.

Material environments

The university estate is, first and foremost, material. From the primitive halls of medieval Oxford and Cambridge to the contemporary modular buildings of universities across the globe, university estates are foremost material. In his work on the architectural history of university estates in England, Stefan Muthesius (2000) outlines how various categories and generations of universities draw from and adapt exigent models of university estates. For example, the English universities established across the 1960s/70s are positioned as *experimental,* in using existing architectural conventions from Oxbridge and Redbrick universities to 'engineer' material environments that would (it was hoped) influence and develop social relations amongst students and staff across the university. The aim of greenspace in and across many 'plateglass' universities (Beloff, 1970) was to test whether, and how, the built environment of campus model universities influenced peer–peer and peer–staff relations.

Similarly, Whyte (2019a, 2019b; Burke and Whyte, 2021) highlights how the architectural history of university estates across England and the wider United Kingdom (UK) has been emergent and complexifying for generations. Highlighting Oxbridge and using a number of universities across London as case studies of architectural history in universities, Whyte (2020) highlights how the material environment both reflected and defined the forms, functions and stated purpose of university estate learning and residential environments for students and staff. Whyte (2020) notes that, for much of the history of British universities, the university estate was a patchwork of materials, aimed at supporting the ways and means of teaching, learning and research in institutions that were dominated by aristocratic men and not necessarily aimed to serve larger quantities of students. As such, university estates acted to represent a walled-off approach, concentrating on a style of teaching and learning (later research) that reifies and prioritises how and what it defines as 'quality' of engagement over the 'quantity' of students and staff who could engage (read, access and participate) in university and by extension university estate spaces.

Much of the underlying argument assumes that the built environment directly informs relationship development in and across university faculties. Pathways, open space and informal working spaces were defined and designed to 'drive cooperation and collaboration' across universities (Beloff, 1970). In my anecdotal experience, these types of spaces are found from the garden squares of Bloomsbury (Central London, England) to the South Downs of Winchester, from the shoreline of Brighton Beach just south of the University of Brighton out to the quadrangles of Oxbridge colleges and north where Northumbria and Newcastle highlight the winding path of the rivers that slowly snake through the towns and cities of England. The idea that the material shapes student engagement has spark, however, an absence of empirical evidence persists. Lacking empirical evidence leaves a gap in our understanding of whether, and how, the material informs the social and personal. And, deriving the influence and meaning of spaces to students' engagement is largely left to anecdotal evidence of for whatever and however students (and others) use space.

Social environments

Does the material environment of universities influence their social environment? Contrasting the material as vital to the social engagement of students with and in institutions, Danvers and Gagnon (2014) instead argue student engagement is a *mirage*. Rather than a useful framework to explore the dimensions and relations between students, staff, universities and the wider public, student engagement is framed as a token buzzword. This token buzzword is positioned as shielding universities from taking responsibility for the influence(s) of shifting policy, planning and practice and disproportionately placing the burden of teaching, learning and research outcomes on to students. In short, a university education is whatever a university student makes of it. What this article may prompt in readers, such as myself, is to reflect and be reflexive about the immense gravity of numerous social dimension(s) of universities on the relations of students and staff to their institution(s). And the limitations of defining student engagement too broadly, too narrowly or without adequate study to substantiate claims about engagement with and in universities. Here, by deploying the term university, in relation to student engagement, the physical/material environment is posited as framing the very social relations that define teaching, learning, research and the social *being* of a university (Barnett, 2007).

The material dimensions of universities frame and influence the social dimensions and relations that define *being* a university. Social dimensions include intrapersonal and interpersonal relations in and between groups (student, staff and the wider public). The university estate as a defined set of material spaces designs, enshrines and conserves a material preset for the human social activity (social space) of university education (policy, planning and practice). The relations and dimensions of material and social space define the being of a university. This would materialize in university policies, planning, mission statements, vision statements, strategies and other documents that set out the aims, objectives and agreements students and staff agree to when they join a university and agree to uphold during and after their participation with and in a university. We see the relationship of university material spaces and the transformation/transcendence of space to place in the ongoing and active work to create and sustain university policies, planning, missions and vision statements (Marginson, 2011, 2020; Marginson and Xu, 2021).

While student engagement may be a buzzword to some like Danvers and Gagnon (2014), it is a useful lens to explore the range and nuance of dimensions and relations a university sets out to students, staff and the wider public.

Highlighting the range and nuance of the material environments of universities and their cascading influence on the social relations that disproportionately influence and define being a university amplifies rather than obfuscates university and student relations and responsibilities. The material and social also influence what individuals make of these relations, and dimensions are also a vital component of how university estate space becomes *place* (Temple, 2008).

Personal environments

University estates set the material conditions, frame social relations and support students' individual university engagement. Astin (1984, 1993) notes that students' engagement is a personal investment of time, energy, attention, financial and other relevant resource supporting academically purposeful activity. The estates of universities scaffold the investments students make across a range of individual resources that, for many, define practice and engagement in and with a university.

As this chapter demonstrates, scholars are continuously debating a range of material and social dimensions and relations for *what, how, where* and *why* that define spaces and places with and in universities. Nested within these deep and ongoing debates is a subordinate debate about what an individual derives from accessing and participating in and with the physical, social and personal environments of a university. The debate often highlights the *value* of accessing and participating in a university, especially along the dimensions of teaching, learning and research (Office for Students, 2021). For example, in England, departments have been constructed to study the quality of teaching, learning and research with and in universities (Office for Students, Quality Assurance Agency, Research England). Because not all universities are alike, because they do not all have a monoculture (which would likely suppress the very nature and essence of what defines being a university), it is difficult to argue that students, staff and the wider public will derive specific outcome(s) from accessing, participating and otherwise matriculating through universities. Instead, most discussions focus on the principles and values of a university-educated individual for self and society (Marginson, 2011, 2020).

A university is material, it is social and it is personal. The university estate is a resource invested in by its members, students, staff and the wider public alike. This material resource shared by students, staff (and other publics) for university-related activities reflects on the interlocking, interrelated and relations of the material to the social and the personal derived therein. Activities like teaching, learning, research, formal and informal conversations, or, as Boys (2018) notes, an assemblage of peoples, ideas, converging and diverging in spaces and places are what we signify as a university. The university estate sets the scene/space(s) students, staff (and the wider public) use to co-create and co-construct being an individual, part of a society, and contribute to an ongoing project of universities to develop, share and refine what knowledge is, how knowledge operates at an individual and social level, a type of hub where knowledge is researched, taught and learned, and why knowledge (teaching, learning and research) is helpful in the life of an individual. What an individual derives being in a university is irreducible to a pre-determined/pre-set set of outcomes.

The material of university estates underpins the experiences and engagement of students and staff. Students and staff engage in and with the built environment of universities' estates, whether materially, digitally or otherwise, the material underpins the material, social and personal praxis of university education. This has been a vital aspect of universities throughout history and into the present. Here, the university estate as a set of material spaces provides a 'space' for students and staff to draw from a range of opportunities (teaching, learning, research, student clubs, student representation, athletics). Still, even during a period of intense focus on the influence of a global pandemic (COVID-19), the rise of so-called university digital spaces, interest in post-digital university education and placemaking in all its forms (material, social and personal), the material of universities persists as a driving factor for university work. Considering the material, social and personal dimensions of student engagement and university estates, what can be gleaned from exigent literature and research that both highlights and challenges student engagement with and in the material, social and personal spaces and places of universities?

Universities, student engagement and relationships

A university is a complex web of leadership and relationships. A university is an open, ongoing, emergent and complex project of human social activity. The material environment – in this case, university spaces – frames the human social activity that defines the forms, functions and stated purpose of a university to and for students, staff and the wider public. Here, there are three key types of relationships that university estates support: peer-to-peer, student and staff, and university to surrounding town or city.

Peer relationships

As Kennan (2014), for The Higher Education Academy, notes, a critical dimension of student engagement and experience in and with a university are peer-to-peer relationships. The social networking effect of being materially present within a university estate is still a robust driver of interactions with and in student peer groups (Coates, 2006). Recent work on student experience and student engagement during the COVID-19 global pandemic highlights how the absence of access to the university estate and material peer-to-peer interactions has influenced students' attitudes, perceptions and experiences of, in and with a university (Chiu and Wong, 2021). Across these scholars, university estates anchor peer-to-peer relations and relationships.

While peer relationships frequently develop in formal university spaces, it is the informal university spaces like students' unions, university accommodations, local shops and open and green spaces in and around university estates that also feature in the development of peer relationships. Student life is not confined to formal spaces with and in a university. Rather, the formal spaces of university estates anchor and give way to the more estuarial formal–informal living and learning spaces that students cultivate their intra- and interpersonal relations with themselves and their peers (McCrone, 2019). Both formal and informal material spaces frame the daily routines, rhythms and rituals (Lefebvre and Nicholson-Smith, 1991) of students in and across the university.

Student–staff relations

Another vital set of relationships underpinned by the university estate and its material spaces are staff–student relationships. Staff and student relationships are vital to the formal and informal activities of teaching, learning and research that define what being a university is and how universities contribute to the individual and cultural fabric of societies.

Historically, the formal academic space of universities defines student–staff relations. From lecture theatres to classrooms, labs to breakout rooms, libraries to cafes, students relate to staff (academic and non-academic) in relation to the material environment, social markers and attitudes and perceptions students bring into their environment and how they apply these in the present and presence of university staff. In contemporary studies of university estate space (Boys, 2018; Carnell, 2017; Goodyear, Ellis and Marmot, 2018), the power geometry (Massey, 2005) no longer follows traditional ideas and ideals. In a time of intense neoliberalism in and around university education, students are positioned as customers/consumers who are paying and expect a return on their investment. Through this lens, universities and higher education more generally are a 'service' industrialized through a lens of university (providers) and student (customers/consumers). This is an explicitly economized and functionalist approach which, rather than empowering students, appears to be obfuscating and delegating responsibilities for students' access, participation, retention and learning outcomes to students themselves, as Danvers and Gagnon (2014) speculate. As such, students have a right and universities have a responsibility to provide means and ways for students to influence the policies, plans and practices of the academic and non-academic staff who provide academic and non-academic 'services'. However, I am sceptical that it is all neoliberalism, all 'their' rights and responsibilities. I believe staff and student relations are continuously shaped by power, authority and the work of student and staff together. This materializes in the social and the relations, communication and coordination between students, academic and non-academic staff alike.

Across these lenses and arguments surrounding student–staff relations, what endures is this idea that student–staff relationships are vital, and that the material spaces of university estates are consequential to the relations and work, purposeful investment of relevant resources (Trowler, 2010) by students and staff in educationally purposeful activities. While intentions and perceptions and attitudes towards these relationships may vary, the fundamental work of teaching, learning and research that underpins these relationships endures and extends beyond the university.

University estates, engagement, towns and cities

The relationships of students, staff and the university ultimately rest with and in towns and cities across the globe. From university cities to studies on *town and gown*, the university estate anchors the daily routines, rituals and rhythms (Lefebvre and Nicholson-Smith, 1991) of students and staff to and from their institution. Even in digital space, the material manifestation of university spaces is transcended and transformed through the daily practices of students and staff. While university digital spaces may be a key driver of moving away from estates-based university education, digital space is non-democratic. Access to technology (personal electronics, internet) is not equitably distributed across local, regional, national and international contexts. As such, university digital space is still vulnerable to exigent power relations and concentrations of resources that allow some students to 'stay home' even when they have moved away to attend university.

University estates act as anchors for towns and cities. Town and city policies and planning have caught on to the impacts and influence university estates and the related activities of staff and students have on towns and cities. We are finding more and more evidence that university cities are confronting issues related to housing, transportation and provision of private and public services. Goddard and Vallance (2013) reflect on how universities are being positioned as "key urban (and suburban) institutions with significant local direct and indirect impacts on employment, the built environment, business, innovation, and wider society" (p.1). The authors suggest that, far from being ivory towers and inward looking, universities are powerful agents whose actions have a cascading influence on the towns and cities within which they are nested. Even in times of sharp change, university estates act as an anchor for institutional activity and its residual influence on the ecology of resources in and around the university. The university estate anchors staff and student engagement in and with the university, the surrounding town/city/region, and national and international contexts. So, what does the university estate mean for student engagement?

University estates: still part of a student engagement story?

The university estate does influence student engagement. This is measurable in the daily movement of students to, through and away from university estates. As evidenced by a study Caird et al. (2015), student and staff travel and use of university estate facilities is the largest influencer on facilities' energy, water, heating and space use. From *home* to *university* and back again is part of a ritual underpinning many students' engagement in and with their university. Even so, recently a sharp shift to digitizing higher education provision has had a cascading influence on the forms, functions and stated purpose of university estates. And if digitizing higher education provision accelerates, what are the consequences for students (individually, socially) and universities (financially, physically and ideologically)? Is *being* a university inextricably tied to an estate? Are our universities understood as knowledge hubs in materiality, as an idea and ideal, in name, as evidenced by time/place activities? Does it matter that there is a range and nuance to universities, and this includes their material, social and by extension individual environment(s)? It would appear the answers are more opaque, largely based on perceptions and attitudes towards quality of teaching, learning, research and a holistic understanding/lens on universities globally.

Will distance make hearts grow fonder? Is the flexible teaching-learning-researching a permanent shift or a temporary adaptation? It is difficult to know what 'sticks' when researchers are in the midst of an ongoing global pandemic. At best, speculation that the university estate is dated, in need of 'letting go of' a bygone era when students treated going to university as participating in a specific set of built environments, learning environments and university estates runs counter to the crushing demand for returning to learning, and the university estate we observe now as the COVID-19 pandemic enters an endemic phase.

Perhaps the university of the future will be a hybrid, part material and part digital. The hologram professoriate and 'meta' university are no longer abstract imaginaries. Instead, there are real actors in the private sector working to unpack whether, and how, the university estate as a bounded set of material living-learning environments requires a deep reset. Perhaps, to reduce the impacts of students and staff on the environment, a more balanced approach to providing 'places' to teach and research are needed. Across Europe, Scandinavia, Canada, Australia and the United Kingdom the university estate is under review. A global pandemic has highlighted the tensions created by university built environments and estates planning. From student halls of residence to lecture theatres, longstanding traditions of using particular venues in particular manners with a professoriate still sharing expertise and knowledge is facing pushback from numerous sides whose interests of compete (directly and indirectly) for financial, material, social and personal resource.

While these questions are beyond the purview of this chapter, they are not ahistorical, apolitical or asocial. Does the university estate influence student engagement? On the surface, the obvious response is 'yes'. Students create routines, rhythms and rituals around the built environments of university estates (Lefebvre, 1991). The learning environment, both material and digital, is underpinned by the resources and operations of universities. The university estate is the infrastructure for organizing and facilitating student engagement with peers, staff and the wider surrounding community. Likewise, the pull of the university estate has a tractor-beam-like effect on students who perceive a university, perhaps first, as a material space where they (and others) create a sense of place, a belonging to a particular set of spaces.

Knowing there is the university estate and being unable to access it 'as normal' has highlighted the social nature of the university. Lost in so much of the debate and discourse surrounding the university estate now is the powerful attraction university estates hold for students who see their 'experience' and 'engagement' as frustrated. Not in halls, not visiting campus lecture halls and breakout rooms, computer labs and coffee shops, the absence of being 'in' a university has highlighted the critical value of the estate for students' sense of engagement in and with their university education. Perception and attitude towards how students can participate is driving questions about the value and importance of the university estate. University estates persist as a hot topic. The impacts of a global pandemic (COVID-19) have been local, regional, national and international. Higher education student mobility ground to a halt for much of 2020 and into 2021. Undergraduate and postgraduate students have shifted some, if not all, of their courses from 'in-person' to 'online' learning environments.

Academic chatter has focused on the substitution effects of moving from material university learning environments to digital learning environments. This has had a number of consequences for staff and student engagement. As Diana Laurillard of the UCL Institute of Education (2017, 2018) notes, the result has been an increase in staff time to prepare, facilitate and follow up with students in digital learning environments. A pivot to digital learning environments was not more efficient, less time consuming and without measurable (and immeasurable) costs. Even so, the university estate continues to define student engagement with and in universities.

Conclusion

This chapter focused on the university estate as a driver of student engagement. Here, university estates are discussed along three key dimensions: material, social and personal. These key dimensions help shape the relationships between students and staff teaching, learning, researching and participating in the wider university environment. Moreover, the university estate is positioned as a key anchor for staff and student engagement by providing spaces where students and staff engage in a range of university-based activities (teaching, learning, research, clubs, athletics, volunteering) through which student engagement is defined as the range of opportunities students pick up whilst enrolled on their university course.

Recently, in light of the COVID-19 global pandemic, and, a surge in the use of university digital spaces, scholars are debating if the material space of universities will recede and be replaced with more technology-driven spaces in the near to medium term. While technology is a great augment to reality, technology does not (yet) replace the material environment for students and staff. Students and staff continue to highlight how 'different', 'costly' and 'inequitable' digital spaces can be for students and staff. As such, the material environments of universities, and their ability to be a resource of space to co-create and co-construct 'place', will continue to feature in the forms, functions and purpose of universities for students, staff and the wider publics of our societies.

References

Association of University Directors of Estates, 2021. *Higher Education Estates Management Report 2021.* Available at: www.aude.ac.uk/news-and-blogs/emr-report/ (accessed: 10 December 2021).

Association of University Directors of Estates, 2020. *Higher Education Estates Management Report 2020.* Available at: www.aude.ac.uk/news/publications/ (accessed: 16 May 2021).

Astin, A.W., 1993. *What Matters in College? Four Critical Years Revisited.* San Francisco, CA: Jossey-Bass.

Astin, A.W., 1984. Student involvement: A developmental theory for higher education. *Journal of College Student Development,* 25, pp.297–308.

Barnett, R., 2007. *A Will to Learn: Being a Student in an age of Uncertainty.* London: McGraw-Hill Education.

Barnett, R., 2011. The coming of the ecological university. *Oxford Review of Education,* 37 (4), pp.439–455.

Barnett, R. and Jackson, N., 2019. *Ecologies for Learning and Practice: Emerging Ideas, Sightings, and Possibilities.* Abingdon: Routledge.

Beloff, M., 1970. *The Plateglass Universities.* Teaneck, NJ: Fairleigh Dickinson University Press.

Blimling, G.S., 2015. *Student Learning in College Residence Halls: What Works, What Doesn't, and Why.* New York: John Wiley & Sons.

Boys, J., 2022. Exploring inequalities in the social, spatial and material practices of teaching and learning in pandemic times. *Postdigital Science and Education,* 4, pp.13–32. https://doi.org/10.1007/s42438-021-00267-z

Boys, J., 2018. Cripping spaces? On dis/abling phenomenology in architecture. *Log,* 42, pp.55–66. https://doi.org/10.1177/1206331220941285

Burke, C. and Whyte, W. 2021. The spaces and places of schooling: Historical perspectives. *Oxford Review of Education,* 47(5), pp.549–555. https://doi.org/10.1080/03054985.2021.1973984

Caird, S., Lane, A., Swithenby, E., Roy, R. and Potter, S., 2015. Design of higher education teaching models and carbon impacts. *International Journal of Sustainability in Higher Education,* 16(1), pp.96–111. https://doi.org/10.1108/IJSHE-06-2013-0065

Carnell, B., 2017. Connecting physical university spaces with research-based education strategy. Available at: https://discovery.ucl.ac.uk/id/eprint/1561146. (accessed: 10 December 2021).

Chiu, Y.L.T. and Wong, B., 2021. *The Ideal Student: Deconstructing Expectations in Higher Education.* London: McGraw-Hill Education.

Coates, H., 2006. *Student Engagement in Campus-Based and Online Education: University Connections.* New York: Taylor and Francis.

Danvers, E. and Gagnon, J., 2014. 'Is 'student engagement' just a mirage? The case for student activism. *Student Engagement and Experience Journal,* 3(2). https://doi.org/10.7190/seej.v3i2.89

DiSalvo, B., Yip, J., Bonsignore, E. and DiSalvo, C., 2017. *Participatory Design for Learning: Perspectives from Practice and Research.* Abingdon: Routledge.

Goddard, J. and Vallance, P., 2013. *The University and the City.* Abingdon: Routledge.

Goodyear, P., Ellis, R.A. and Marmot, A., 2018. Learning spaces research: Framing actionable knowledge. In Ellis, R.A. and Goodyear, P. (eds) *Spaces of Teaching and Learning.* Singapore: Springer. https://doi.org/10.1007/978-981-10-7155-3_12

Guy, S. and Shove, E., 2014. *The Sociology of Energy, Buildings and the Environment: Constructing Knowledge, Designing Practice.* Abingdon: Routledge.

Higher Education Design Quality Forum, 2019a. *Learning Space Compass Framework.* Available at: www.hedqf.org/wp-content/uploads/2020/10/HEDQF_A4-Framework_ExecutiveSummary.pdf (accessed: 1 January 2022).

Higher Education Design Quality Forum, 2019b. *The Future of Learning Environments.* Available at: www.hedqf.org/wp-content/uploads/2020/10/HEDQF_A4-Rationale_ExecSummary-1.pdf (accessed: 1 January 2022).

Higher Education Design Quality Forum, 2021. Sustainable campuses: Student views on climate change impacts and the design of the university estate. Available at: www.hedqf.org/wp-content/uploads/2021/03/HEDQF-Sustainable-Campuses_2021_short.pdf (accessed: 13 October 2021).

Higher Education Statistics Agency, 2021. *Who's Studying in HE?* Available at: www.hesa.ac.uk/data-and-analysis/students/whos-in-he#numbers (accessed: 1 January 2022).

Holton, M., 2019. Debating the geographies of contemporary higher education students: diversity, resilience, resistance? *Children's Geographies*, 17(1), pp.13–16.

Kennan, C., 2014. Mapping student-led peer learning in the UK. Available at: https://s3.eu-west-2.amazonaws.com/assets.creode.advancehe-document-manager/documents/hea/private/resources/peer_led_learning_keenan_nov_14-final_1568037253.pdf (accessed: 3 January 2023).

Laurillard, D., 2018. Teaching as a design science: Teachers building, testing and sharing pedagogic ideas. In: Voogt, J., Knezek, G., Christensen, R. and Lai, K.W. (eds) *Springer International Handbooks of Education. Handbook of Information Technology in Primary and Secondary Education.* New York: Springer.

Laurillard, D. and Kennedy, E., 2017. The potential of MOOCs for learning at scale in the Global South. Centre for Global Higher Education (Working Paper Series, 31). Available at: www.researchcghe.org/perch/resources/publications/wp31.pdf (accessed: 6 January 2021).

Lefebvre, H., 1991. *The Production of Space.* New York: Wiley.

Lefebvre, H. and Nicholson-Smith, D., 1991. *The Production of Space* (Vol. 142). Blackwell: Oxford.

Little, B., Locke, W., Scesa, A. and Williams, R., 2009. *Report to HEFCE on Student Engagement.* Centre for Higher Education Research and Information, The Open University. Available at: www.sparqs.ac.uk/ch/E4%20Report%20to%20HEFCE%20on%20student%20engagement.pdf (accessed: 6 January 2021).

Locke, W. 2021. 'Futurology' and higher education in the post-COVID-19 environment. *International Higher Education*, 105, pp.7–9. https://ejournals.bc.edu/index.php/ihe/article/view/14369

Marginson, S., 2020. Public and common goods. *Changing Higher Education for a Changing World.* https://doi.org/10.5040/9781350108448.0029

Marginson, S., 2011. Higher education and public good. *Higher Education Quarterly*, 65 (4), pp.411–433. https://doi.org/10.1111/j.1468-2273.2011.00496.x

Marginson, S. and Xu, X., 2021. Moving beyond centre-periphery science: Towards an ecology of knowledge. Centre for Global Higher Education (Working Paper Series, 63). Available at: www.researchcghe.org/perch/resources/publications/working-paper-63. pdf (accessed: 6 January 2021).

Marmot, A., 2002. Architectural determinism: Does design change behaviour? *The British Journal of General Practice*, 52(476), p.252.

Massey, D.B., 2005. *For Space*. London: Sage.

McCrone, L., 2021. *Transitional Space in Active Learning: Perspectives from an Undergraduate STEM Education Context*. Available at: https://spiral.imperial.ac.uk/handle/ 10044/1/93793 (accessed: 2 February 2022).

McCrone, L., 2019. Luke McCrone. Available at: https://blogs.imperial.ac.uk/educa tion-research/category/luke-mccrone/ (accessed: 2 February 2022).

Muthesius, S., 2000. *The Postwar University: Utopianist Campus and College*. New Haven, CT: Yale University Press.

Office for Students, 2021. Place matters: Inequality, employment and the role of higher education. Available at: www.officeforstudents.org.uk/media/e450160f-7c5e-48d9-93c6-b9425531747e/insight-briefing-place-and-deprivation-2021.pdf (accessed: 11 November 2021).

Pace, C.R., 1980. Measuring the quality of student effort. *Current Issues in Higher Education*, 2, pp.10–16.

Rymarzak, M. and Marmot, A., 2020. Higher education estate data accountability: The contrasting experience of UK and Poland. *Higher Education Policy*, 33(1), pp.179–194. https://doi.org/10.1057/s41307–41018–0109–0105

Spire, Z., 2022. University estates and postdigital higher education: Space, place, and being a university. *Postdigital Science and Education*. https://doi.org/10.1007/ s42438-022-00314-3

Temple, P., 2014. *The Physical University: Contours of Space and Place in Higher Education*. Abingdon: Routledge.

Temple, P., 2008. Learning spaces in higher education: An under-researched topic. *London Review of Education*, 6(3), pp.229–241.

Temple, P., 2007. *Learning Spaces for the 21st Century: A Review of the Literature*. York: Higher Education Academy.

Temple, P. and Barnett, R., 2007. Higher education space: Future directions. *Planning for Higher Education*, 36(1), pp.5–15.

Trowler, V., 2010. Student engagement literature review. *The Higher Education Academy*, 11(1), pp.1–15.

Whyte, W., 2020. Learning from Redbrick: Utopianism and the architectural legacy of the civic universities. In: Taylor, M., and Pellew, J. (eds) *Utopian Universities: A Global History of the New Campuses of the 1960s*. London: Bloomsbury.

Whyte, W. 2019a. Private benefit, public finance? Student funding in late-twentieth-century Britain. In: Goldman, L. (ed) *Welfare and Social Policy in Britain Since 1870: Essays in Honour of Jose Harris*. Oxford: Oxford University Press. https://doi.org/10.1093/ oso/9780198833048.003.0004

Whyte, W.H., 2019b. *Somewhere to Live: Why British Students Study Away from Home, and Why It Matters*. Oxford: Higher Education Policy Institute.

Whyte, W., 2018. Architecture and experience: Regimes of materiality in the nineteenth century. In: Gillin, E. (ed) *Experiencing Architecture in the Nineteenth Century: Buildings and Society in the Modern Age*. London: Bloomsbury Visual. https://doi.org/10.5040/9781350045972.0008

Whyte, W., 2006. How do buildings mean? Some issues of interpretation in the history of architecture. *History and Theory*, 45, pp.153–177. https://doi.org/10.1111/j.1468-2303.2006.00355.x

Chapter 19

Learning analytics in higher education

The ethics, the future, the students

Zoheir Beig

Although this paper will predominantly focus on some of the more problematic aspects of learning analytics, it would first be prudent to establish what we mean when we use this term. One particularly succinct definition posits learning analytics as "the measurement, collection, analysis, and reporting of data about learners and their contexts, for the purposes of understanding and optimizing learning and the environments in which it occurs" (Siemens, 2013, p.1382). They are mainly a behavioural measurement, collating such quantifiable data as the number of times a student has logged into their virtual learning environment or whether they have downloaded a paper in advance of next week's class. They can be very useful, especially when it comes to monitoring the engagement (or lack thereof) of students, which extrapolates to wider issues around student success and even whether a student is keeping within the rules of their International Student Visa. Theoretically each student can be assigned a number, an engagement rating, based on their learning analytics 'score'; however, what this score stands for is another question entirely.

The use of such measurements is not solely the preserve of universities. Log-in to Microsoft 365 and you can find what Microsoft calls your organisation's Productivity Score. Comprised of a series of metrics, ranging from content collaboration to teamwork (e.g. 70% of people in your company are contributing to shared workspaces), the Productivity Score purports to reflect the performance of a specific organisation by assessing, according to the Microsoft 365 website, "people and technology experience measures". The language of performance analysis may not always be so impersonal, but the Microsoft example shows how widespread such metrics are, embedded within everyday systems and technologies. Though the concept of learning analytics is not new, their use in such largely invisible ways is increasingly common within higher education.

It helps to define what we mean when we talk about learning analytics in this higher education context, given its myriad uses. In 2017 Ferguson and Clow went further than Siemens by setting out four propositions of learning analytics. These were:

A: Learning analytics improve learning outcomes
B: Learning analytics improve learning support and teaching, including retention, completion and progression

DOI: 10.4324/9781003271789-19

C: Learning analytics are taken up and used widely, including deployment at scale

D: Learning analytics are used in an ethical way

(Ferguson and Clow, 2017, p.58)

Although these propositions are well intentioned, with their focus on ethics and scale, the propositions of A and B in particular highlight the problematic tendency of learning analytics to side-line wider pedagogical discourses on the idea of learning. The criticisms of a focus on the metrics of behavioural indicators of learning (i.e. attendance, grades) to the detriment of the "sensory, embodied, practical and situated" (Wintrup, 2017, p.95) elements that learning can also embody leads to a proposed implication "that there is an emphasis on a snapshot of performance as a means of determining student learning rather than seeing learning for what it is, a developmental process leading to an (ongoing) outcome" (Lodge et al., 2017, p.388). This also ties into the wider role that student engagement plays in the discussion of learning analytics, recalling Astin's definition of student engagement being "the amount of physical and psychological energy that the student devotes to the academic experience" (1984, p.518); energy that is, 20 years on, arguably measurable at even more levels, now including digital behavioural indicators beyond physical attendance prior.

Such arguments, that learning analytics are a mere fraction of a larger whole, echo those around the issue of reducing the assessment of teaching to data sets or, as it has often been referred to, 'teaching to the test'. In a critical overview of such schemes, Jerry Z. Muller cites the example of the American Government's initiative 'No Child Left Behind'. NCLB sought to improve the education of disadvantaged students by measuring the grades students were awarded in a few select areas of study against set high standards. Such focus on the tangible outcome of learning led teachers to focus attention on the subject areas that mattered (in this case Maths and English), to the detriment of the areas which were not being measured. Other more chilling implications of this scheme included a study of schools in Texas and Florida which "showed that average achievement levels were increased by reclassifying weaker students as disabled, thus removing them from the assessment pool" (Muller, 2018, p.93). Although the focus in this paper is on learning analytics within higher education, this example suggests it remains a problematic area at all levels of education worthy of critical reflection.

As the use of automated, digital systems has become more widespread within higher education, so has the availability of sources for data collection and the attendant rise in learning analytics. Examples of such "proxy methods of learning" (Gasevic et al., 2015, p.66) include: library data on lending, attendance monitoring, discussion forum posts and the use of virtual learning environments (VLEs) such as Moodle and Canvas. However, although all of this wealth of data is now available to university management and administrators, is there any benefit to its widespread collation unless we know why it is being collected? Or, as Fincham et al. put it: "simple count metrics count for little if we know not what they measure" (2019, p.502). Such so-called simple data can actually have an inverse negative effect if employed without any semblance of context. For example, on the subject of VLEs, "The assignment may be open, but is the student really reading it?" (Kruse and Pongsajapan, 2012, p.3). Reliance on a measure such as this could lead teaching staff to assume that the class is wholly engaged with the reading whereas more detailed inquiry may reveal that, although the majority of students opened the document, not all understood the academic text.

To use a famous, extremely hubristic, historical precedent, such surface-level use of data recalls what is known as McNamara's Fallacy, named after the Vietnam War-era US Secretary of Defence Robert McNamara. McNamara "over-relied on crude quantifications such as total numbers of casualties to determine progress in the war. These crude measures did not adequately capture the complexity of the war, and ineffective strategies were employed thus" (Lodge et al., 2017). The inherent lesson here is in not taking any of the data collected at face value, or certainly not relying on one set of figures without relating them to a corresponding wider picture. To apply to higher education, the learning analytics scores and dashboards often will not capture the complexity of individual students' experiences and their engagement.

Indeed, the data collected on students need not fall into such binary categories. A more nuanced approach was outlined by Lodge et al. (2017) who sought to outline how the interpretation of data within higher education can develop over time, rather than staying static. Their chart, shown in Figure 19.1, also utilised audit trails such as attendance monitoring (the aforementioned 'passive methods'),

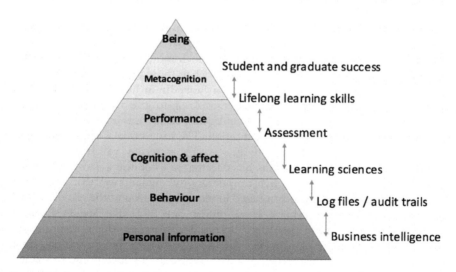

Figure 19.1 Representation of a linear translation process for big data interpretation
Adapted from Lodge et al. (2017, p.395)

before developing into areas that support a more developmental process such as learning sciences feeding into the idea of cognition and affect and the practice of assessment becoming an aspect of data collection in itself.

Regardless of what form the data collection takes, a number of critical studies into the practice have raised several issues, which institutions should be mindful of when putting together a plan for gathering and communication. One risk is to approach learning analytics from an overly reductionist perspective – i.e. the problem that "learning analytics researchers come not from the starting point of how do we partner with our students, but rather, how do we help them?" (Dollinger and Lodge, 2019, p.225). Providing students with agency – such as the example of the University of Edinburgh's (UK) Learning Analytics Report Card,[1] which allows students to choose what data is included and how any report is presented – may prove more beneficial than taking a prescriptive top-down approach. The prospect of students taking control of their own engagement in this way was developed by Ochoa and Friend Wise, who outlined three ways in which students can be helped to accept learning analytics in this manner:

1   Involve students in the creation of analytic tools meant to serve them;
2   Develop analytics that are contextualized, explainable and configurable;
3   Empower students' agency in using analytic tools as part of their larger process of learning.

(Ochoa and Friend Wise, 2020)

These are statements that reiterate the strength of learning analytics when they are used in collaborative, contextual ways and not as holistic blocks of information with no overriding purpose or cohesion.

Another risk is that of data control. "Many universities are increasingly using external systems from a range of different suppliers, and the complexities of movement of data around those systems are much more of a headache than they were in the past" (McKie, 2020); data leaks such as those experienced by Yahoo in August 2013 (3 billion accounts affected) or LinkedIn in June 2021 (700 million users affected) coupled with the stricter controls of, to give a European example, GDPR (the General Data Protection Regulation), ensure this is an area that needs to be carefully considered by each institution. The issue of data control and privacy links directly to one of the core aspects of this debate, which is the ethical dimension. Should data on students be collected, just because it can be? This is a discussion now commonplace when considering the digital traces that individuals leave, as evidenced by the concern raised in recent years around the use of data by such firms as Apple and Facebook. It was only in early 2021 that Apple responded to pressure by introducing the App Tracking Transparency which, according to Apple's website "requires apps to get the user's permission before tracking their data across apps or websites owned by other companies for advertising, or sharing their data with data brokers".

A striking example of the use of learning analytics within institutions that exemplifies the threat of data use overstepping an ethical boundary is that from

Arizona State University (USA). Matt Pittinsky, co-founder of Blackboard, started an academic research project whose raw material was the anonymous logs made by swipes from Arizona State ID cards. Pittinsky's thesis rested on the idea that, as the cards recorded nearly every potential transaction, from buying food to accessing the library, these swipes could create patterns. For example, "say two students swipe within 5 or 10 seconds of each other at different times of day in different contexts. Are they more likely to be friends? And can you predict attrition by pinpointing changes in how a student uses a campus? Say someone goes to Starbucks at 2pm every day before 2:15pm class. Then stops" (Parry, 2012, p.8). Worryingly, for anyone tracking the potential invasive effect of learning analytics, Pittinsky goes on to say:

> If that happens three weeks in a row... and we're not seeing log-ins into Blackboard, and maybe you've made a request at the registrar to have your transcript sent somewhere, there ought to be an adviser with a really big red flashing light saying, reach out to this student.
>
> (Parry, 2012)

Slade and Prinsloo encapsulated the ethical concerns of learning analytics into the following three "broad, often overlapping categories":

1 The location and interpretation of data
2 Informed consent, privacy and the de-identification of data
3 The management, classification and storage of data

(Slade and Prinsloo, 2013, p.1511)

The above areas should ideally be the foundation for any implementation of a learning analytics strategy. De-identification in particular is a key aspect in the ethical argument around learning analytics. A mass of data can point to wider trends within an institution but the finer the detail the more possible it may be to identify individuals within the information set. As the 'Code for Practice for Learning Analytics' attests, "Institutions should take steps to ensure that trends, norms, categorisation or any labelling of students do not bias staff, student or institutional perceptions and behaviours towards them, reinforce discriminatory attitudes or increase social power differentials" (Jisc, 2018).

For example, the University of the Arts London (UK) examines attainment rates as divided by the following ethnic categories: Asian – Black – Mixed – White – Other. The purpose of this exercise, as part of the institution's Access and Participation Plan,[2] is to examine the difference between the proportion of white and black students getting a 1st or 2:1. The intention here, with its emphasis on addressing inequality, is important. However, this usage of learning analytics brings with it its own inherent complexities:

> The notion that the persistent gap in attainment, despite equal entry qualifications, between white and BAME students is somehow to be reduced

through the use of analytics, is to forget that structural forms of oppression, implicit bias, and inequalities exist… and will only be altered by radically different cultures and policies within HE.

(Wintrup, 2017, p.98)

In all of this, it is key to remember that students and their engagement should exist at the heart of learning analytics. As Oblinger states, "rather than allowing students to fall through the cracks or become 'just a number', colleges and universities can – through analytics – see and act upon individual students' needs" (Oblinger, 2012, p.12). As examples throughout this study have shown, just as learning should be seen as a combination of both fixed, measurable aspects and fluid, intangible concepts, so "It is crucial to see student identity as a combination of permanent and dynamic attributes… the ethical implications of this are that learning analytics provides a snapshot view of a learner at a particular time and context" (Slade and Prinsloo, 2013, p.1520).

It seems apparent, from the widespread use of electronic interfaces that collate data and the myriad checks within higher education that rely on the collection of student data – the UK National Student Survey,[3] University League Tables,[4] the Research Education Framework[5] – that learning analytics are not going away and may even come to be seen as an inevitability (if they are not already) by both institutions and students. As Macfadyen et al. note,

> In a world of larger and larger data sets, increasing populations of increasingly diverse learners, constrained education budgets and greater focus on quality and accountability, some argue that using analytics to optimize learning environments is no longer an option but an imperative.
>
> (2014, p.17)

Given this, universities – modern, often multi-disciplinary institutions – need to remember that data cannot tell the full picture by itself, both for the institution as a whole but also within individual programmes.

> Learning analytics must, and can, account for the fluid nature of technology use within a course offering rather than assume that the trace data of different offerings of the same course can be aggregated to create a single joint predictive model for academic success and retention.
>
> (Gasevic et al., 2016)

In other words, one size does not fit all.

Instead of being hidden in the background of a student's journey, with numbers gathered in an invisible way akin to a Microsoft 365 algorithm, learning analytics and their use should be discussed with students in conjunction with other, more pastoral approaches. As Lowe suggests, "creating a summary of possible factors which influence performance analysis and a score for all students at HE is not the answer over practice, personal interaction and engaging each other on a personal basis, through representation, conversation and partnership" (2018, p.4). Learning analytics alone are not the answer, otherwise metrics will be considered as "the blunt instruments used by managers who seek to control activities they do not fully understand" (Collini, 2018, p.37) and not as tools integral to a well-rounded and supportive student journey.

Therefore, it seems vital that the numbers behind learning analytics are placed within a broader student engagement narrative. Building on Kuh's definition of student engagement as "the time and effort students devote to activities that are empirically linked to desired outcomes of college **and** what institutions do to induce students to participate in these activities" (2009, p.683), it would seem that one way universities and college could use data is to help shape these activities. For example, if a module sees a lower than average number of downloads for the set texts and the attainment scores within that cohort dip, it could be that the curriculum needs to be reconsidered. This is not to say that pedagogical concerns should be led by student opinion, but given that student engagement is – from a UK perspective at least – now at the heart of regulatory oversight, this is just one way in which learning analytics can be harnessed to paint a useful picture.

From the examples cited, it appears that the majority of successful occasions of learning analytics use have been when focus has been brought to what the numbers tell us about students' engagement and not how the institution can improve its standing. The former should in theory lead to the latter, so it is a surprise that there are still so many instances of learning analytics and their use being detached from helping to support the optimisation of learning environments. Viberg et al. (2018) used the four propositions outlined by Ferguson and Clow at the beginning of this paper to assess the evidence that learning analytics can improve learning practice, based on 252 relevant research papers. Their findings suggested that, of the 252, the following percentages showed evidence that:

A: Learning analytics improve learning outcomes – 9%;
B: Learning analytics improve learning support and teaching, including retention, completion and progression – 35%;
C: Learning analytics are taken up and used widely, including deployment at scale – 6%;
D: Learning analytics are used in an ethical way – 18%.

(Viberg et al., 2018, p.102)

Based on this analysis, "the potential of learning analytics to improve learning outcomes is significantly higher than its current evidence" (Viberg et al., 2018, p.103); far more attention seemingly needs to be paid to what a student's engagement 'score' means, what is being measured and what is missing, and how this reflects on their overall learning experience. As Melanie Booth wrote in her 2012 essay:

Even though learning analytics offers powerful tools and practices to improve the work of learning and assessment, well-considered principles and propositions for learning assessment should inform its careful adoption and use. Otherwise, learning analytics risks becoming a reductionist approach for measuring a bunch of 'stuff' that ultimately does not matter. In my world, learning matters.

(2012, p.52).

Notes

1 Available at: www.de.ed.ac.uk/project/learning-analytics-report-card
2 Available at: www.officeforstudents.org.uk/advice-and-guidance/the-register/search-for-access-and-participation-plans/#/AccessPlans/accessplans/10007162
3 www.thestudentsurvey.com/
4 www.thecompleteuniversityguide.co.uk/
5 www.ref.ac.uk/

References

Astin, A.W., 1984. Student involvement: A development theory for higher education. *Journal of College Student Development*, 40, pp.518–529. www.researchgate.net/publication/220017441_Student_Involvement_A_Development_Theory_for_Higher_Education.

Booth, M., 2012. Learning analytics: The new black. *EDUCAUSE Review*, 47(4). https://er.educause.edu/articles/2012/7/learning-analytics-the-new-black

Collini, S., 2018. Kept alive for thirty days. *London Review of Books*, 40(21), pp.35–38. www.lrb.co.uk/the-paper/v40/n21/stefan-collini/kept-alive-for-thirty-days

Dollinger, M. and Lodge, J., 2019. What learning analytics can learn from students as partners. *Educational Media International*, 56(3), pp.218–232. https://doi.org/10.1080/09523987.2019.1669883

Ferguson, R. and Clow, D., 2017. Where is the evidence? A call to action for learning analytics. In: *LAK '17 Proceedings of the Seventh International Learning Analytics and Knowledge Conference* (ACM International Conference Proceeding Series). New York: ACM. https://doi.org/10.1145/3027385.3027396

Fincham, E., Whitelock-Wainwright, A., Kovanovic, V., Joksimovic, S., van Staalduinen, J-P., Gasevic, D., 2019. Counting clicks is not enough: Validating a theorized model of engagement in learning analytics. In: *LAK '19 Proceedings of the Ninth International Learning Analytics and Knowledge Conference* (ACM International Conference Proceeding Series). New York: ACM. https://doi.org/10.1145/3303772.3303775.

Gasevic, D., Gasevic, D. and Rogers, T., 2016. Learning analytics should not promote one size fits all: The effects of instructional conditions in predicting academic success. *The Internet and Higher Education*. https://doi.org/10.1016/j.iheduc.2015.10.002

Gasevic, D., Dawson, S. and Siemens, G., 2015. Let's not forget: Learning analytics are about learning. *TechTrends*, 59(1), pp.64–71. https://doi.org/10.1007/s11528-014-0822-x

Jisc, 2018. *Code of Practice for Learning Analytics*. Available at: www.jisc.ac.uk/guides/code-of-practice-for-learning-analytics (accessed: 16 May 2021).

Kruse, A. and Pongsajapan, R., 2012. Student-centered learning analytics. CNDLS Thought Papers. Available at: https://cndls.georgetown.edu/m/documents/thoughtpaper-krusepongsajapan.pdf (accessed: 16 May 2021).

Kuh, G.D., 2009. What student affairs professionals need to know about student engagement. *Journal of College Student Development*, 50(6), pp.683–706. doi:10.1353/csd.0.0099.

Lodge, J.M., Alhadad, S.S.J., Lewis, M.J. and Gasevic, D., 2017. Inferring learning from big data: The importance of a transdisciplinary and multidimensional approach. *Technology, Knowledge and Learning*, 22(3), 385–400. https://doi.org/10.1007/s10758-017-9330-3

Lowe, T., 2018. Data analytics – A critique of the appropriation of a new measure of 'student engagement'. *Student Engagement in Higher Education Journal*, 2(1), pp.2–6. https://cris.winchester.ac.uk/ws/portalfiles/portal/338318/12071207_Lowe_DataAnalyticsApp ropriation_withstatement.pdf

Macfadyen, L.P., Dawson, S., Pardo, A. and Gasevic, D., 2014. Embracing big data in complex educational systems: The learning analytics imperative and the policy challenge. *Research & Practice in Assessment*, 9, pp.17–28. www.rpajournal.com/dev/wp-content/uploads/2014/10/A2.pdf

McKie, A., 2020. Do edtech apps keep student data safe? *Times Higher Education*, 14 January. Available at: www.timeshighereducation.com/news/do-edtech-apps-keep-student-data-safe (accessed: 16 May 2021).

Muller, J.Z., 2018. *The Tyranny of Metrics*. Princeton, NJ: Princeton University.

Oblinger, D.G., 2012. Let's talk… analytics. *EDUCAUSE Review*, 47(4), pp.10–13. https://er.educause.edu/articles/2012/7/lets-talk–analytics

Ochoa, X. and Friend Wise, A., 2020. Supporting the shift to digital with student-centred learning analytics. *Educational Technology Research and Development*, 69, pp.357–361. https://doi.org/10.1007/s11423-020-09882-2

Parry, M., 2012. Big data on campus. *The New York Times*, 18 July. Available at: www.nytimes.com/2012/07/22/education/edlife/colleges-awakening-to-the-opportunities-of-data-mining.html (accessed: 16 May 2021).

Siemens, G., 2013. Learning analytics: The emergence of a discipline. *American Behavioral Scientist*, 57(10), pp.1380–1400. https://doi.org/10.1177/0002764213498851

Slade, S. and Prinsloo, P., 2013. Learning analytics: Ethical issues and dilemmas. *American Behavioral Scientist*, 57(10), pp.1510–1529. https://doi.org/10.1177/0002764213479366

Viberg, O., Hatakka, M., Balter, O. and Mavroudi, A., 2018. The current landscape of learning analytics in higher education. *Computers in Human Behaviour*, 89, pp.98–110. doi:10.1016/j.chb.2018.07.027

Wintrup, J., 2017. Higher education's panopticon? Learning analytics, ethics and student engagement. *Higher Education Policy*, 30(1), pp.87–103. https://doi.org/10.1057/s41307-016-0030-8

Placing sport at the heart of the university community

A critical reflection on sports club membership and what it means for student engagement from a Bourdieusian perspective

Maria Moxey, Keith Parry and Hazel Brown

Introduction

Literature on university sport in the UK is scarce and its value is often overlooked (McKenna and Dunstan-Lewis, 2004; Harris and Clayton, 2008). Within student engagement discourse, much of the focus is on learning and teaching and engagement in the curriculum (Bryson, 2014; Cook-Sather, Bovill, and Felten, 2014), student engagement in the development of education (Healey, Flint, and Harrington, 2014), and the wider student experience (NUS, 2012). There is also a wealth of literature pointing towards the importance of students becoming socially integrated into the campus community for enhancing transition, belonging, and overall success (Kramer and Gardner, 2007; Hunter et al., 2009; Van Herpen et al., 2020). While the value of extracurricular activities in contributing towards student success is increasingly being recognised (Stuart et al., 2011; Dickinson, Griffiths, and Bredice, 2021), the role of university sport is often missing from this discourse. For many students, becoming a member of a sports club is central to the student experience and becomes a dominant aspect of their life at university. With time and financial pressures ever-increasing, students and higher education institutions (HEIs) alike are struggling to prioritise sport (Northumbria University, 2018). Therefore, this chapter will look critically at the value of being a member of a sports club, positioning it at the centre of the student experience.

The social, psychological and physical benefits of being involved in sport at university are commonly accepted (Quinton and Brunton, 2018; Brunton and Mayne, 2020), and this tends to justify investment in facilities, staffing, transport, kit, and equipment, among others. However, the impact and value of sport are often left unquestioned. While there are many positives that come with being involved in sport at university, membership is also closely linked with lad culture and associated behaviours such as alcohol consumption, overcommitment to sport at the sacrifice of studies, and peer pressure (Clayton and Humberstone, 2006; Harris and Clayton, 2008). This chapter reflects on the role of extracurricular

DOI: 10.4324/9781003271789-20

sport at university from a sociological perspective, and through considering some of the social practices that take place, looks critically at what it means to be a member of a university sports club. Applying Bourdieu's theoretical concepts allows for a deeper exploration into how many of the taken-for-granted practices that occur are indeed an important part of what makes being a member of a university sports club so significant.

Some cautionary thoughts

While it is commonly believed that sport is positive, provides opportunity for inclusion, and leads to individual and community development, others argue that sport as an institution is exclusionary since it is by nature elitist and competitive, and segregates individuals based on traditional binary ideas of gender (Anderson and White, 2017). Therefore, it is important to be critical of the notion that sport is inherently pure and good (Coakley, 2014). The purpose of this chapter is to look critically at university sports club culture, and to provide a deeper understanding of the meaning behind social practices in order to provoke thought around the impact that these engrained practices have on students' identities and feelings of belonging.

Theorising university sport: a Bourdieusian perspective

The work of educational theorist and anthropologist Bourdieu has been widely applied to higher education as well as the discipline of sport and sociology. Bourdieu asserts that individuals from different backgrounds have varying degrees of capital: economic (power and money), cultural (encompassing knowledge, behaviour, manners, and cultural goods), social (friends, family, acquaintances, and colleagues), and symbolic (reputation and prestige which is contextual) (Bourdieu, 1984). Habitus refers to the way in which individuals embody the social norms, rules, and behaviours of a particular group which become second nature (Bourdieu, 1984). The concept of the field considers society as being made up of subsections in which individuals share common interests and are governed by tacit social rules, and actors within a field are vying for power (Bourdieu 1984). Doxa is the unquestioned attachment to, and respect for, the cultural norms of the field.

Individuals from different backgrounds have varying degrees of symbolic, cultural, and social capital. While educational institutions can exacerbate these inequalities (DiMaggio, 1979), arguably HEIs can provide opportunity for social mobility as a space in which individuals can learn and accrue capital (Curtis, 2015). For example, universities offer opportunities intended to help students accrue cultural and social capital such as volunteering; however, this may not be accessible for students from widening participation backgrounds who do not have the time or financial resources to volunteer, due to limited economic capital (Stevenson and Clegg, 2011). Bourdieu's conceptual tools have also been applied to sport subcultures to make sense of the process by which individuals become immersed within a group and therefore embody the behaviours, values, and characteristics of the group, which are illustrated through various means of consumption (see Beal, 1995; Wacquant, 1995; Wheaton, 2000). Bourdieu's theoretical tools have been used to critically explore higher education as well as sport subcultures in relation to capital building, habitus, and identity, and are therefore particularly useful when considering the role of membership within sports clubs at university.

University sports clubs: a subculture

A subculture is defined as a subgroup who share beliefs, values, and natural habits, making them distinguishable from wider society, and which often become a dominant aspect of one's identity (Donnelly, 1981; Green, 2001; Muggleton, 2002; Atkinson and Young, 2008). University sports clubs are made up of unique traditions, and membership often becomes a dominant part of one's identity at university since it is closely intertwined with the university lifestyle. Therefore, this chapter is positioning university sport as a subculture, and hopes to provoke thoughts and raise questions through reflecting, critiquing, and challenging the role of sports clubs at university.

Upon reflecting on the role of sports clubs in creating a sense of belonging at university, it is useful to draw on the growing body of literature exploring this in North America. Early literature such as Tinto's interactionalist model and theory of student departure (Tinto, 1975, 1993), as well as Astin's theory of student involvement (Astin, 1975, 1984, 1985), demonstrate that extracurricular activities such as sport are important for socialisation into university life, and successful transition is likely to lead to retention. More recent research has demonstrated the importance of university sports clubs in creating a sense of belonging due to the opportunity to build community, as well as an attachment to the institution, and therefore assisting with retention as well as other university outcomes (see Miller, 2011; Warner and Dixon, 2011; McElveen and Ibele, 2019; Lifschutz, 2019; Lower-Hoppe et al., 2020). Nevertheless, applying this body of literature to the UK is problematic since the culture of university sport is very different. University sport in the United States of America fosters talent through to professional level, whereas in the UK elite athletes tend to be harvested from a young age through clubs, and therefore there are distinctions in the ways in which university sport is funded, structured, and valued (Harris and Clayton, 2008). With market-driven forces increasing pressure on UK institutions to deliver a better university experience, as well as ensure social mobility and employability (Milburn-Shaw and Walker, 2017), the growing indication of the significance that university sport involvement can have on belonging, retention, and student success cannot be ignored, and therefore needs further attention in the UK.

University sport in the UK

HEIs in the UK offer varied sporting opportunities ranging from recreational physical activity and intramural sport, to competitive varsity-level sport (McKenna and Dunstan-Lewis, 2004; Harris and Clayton, 2008). Sport in UK universities is primarily non-elite and organised as inter-university competition by British University and College Sport (BUCS, UK). Circa 170 institutions across the UK are affiliated to BUCS and therefore invest substantial amounts of funding and resources to facilitate the running and organisation of BUCS. Many institutions even timetable Wednesday afternoons free from teaching sessions to encourage sport participation (NUS, 2017). While university sport is as an optional extra-curricular activity intended to enhance the student experience outside of studies (Clayton and Humberstone, 2006), this degree of investment and commitment to facilitating sport demonstrates that while sporting identities may vary across institutions, sport is clearly a highly valued and core aspect of university life.

Although benefits are recognised, limited time and space are hugely challenging for timetabling teaching sessions, and institutions are finding it increasingly difficult to protect Wednesday afternoons for sport (NUS, 2017). This is coupled with a growth in recreational-based participation schemes aimed at increasing physical activity on campus (Quinton and Brunton, 2018), and funding cuts that are making BUCS teams difficult to prioritise (Northumbria University, 2018). Nevertheless, while recreational alternatives are intended to be inclusive for all students, a limited number of students choose to participate (Quinton and Brunton, 2018). This demonstrates that while university sport in the UK is steeped in history and tradition, it is undergoing contestation and change, highlighting the need to critically reflect on the impact and value of university sports clubs.

The typical student engagement journey with sport starts with signing up to desired teams at Fresher's Fair, attending trials, and being invited to club socials. Early interactions offer new students the opportunity to integrate with students from higher year groups and can be a means of becoming integrated into the wider university community as it provides the opportunity for new students to learn social norms, language, and traditions, and thus accrue the symbolic capital necessary to demonstrate belonging to the university community. For many students, BUCS competition is the highest sporting ability they will reach and there is a lot of pride and esteem associated with being selected to represent one's university as a BUCS player. To become fully integrated into sports clubs there are various means of demonstrating commitment beyond paying membership fees. It is due to an innate need to belong that members will engage with the club norms to become integrated (Donnelly and Young, 1988). There is a fine line to be considered, though, between integration and indoctrination, and it is therefore important to look critically at the social practices that are engrained within the habitus of university sports clubs.

It is commonplace in sport to conform to what is termed the sport ethic. This involves striving for excellence, sacrificing one's own needs for the team, accepting risk of injury and playing through pain (Hughes and Coakley, 1992; Coakley, 2015). Conforming to the sport ethic can involve uncritically accepting its norms and therefore individuals may exceed reasonable limits to prove their commitment to their athletic status and/or team, also termed over-conformity (Coker-Cranney et al., 2017). In the university sport subculture, examples of ways in which new members are expected to demonstrate their commitment include engaging with the drinking culture, adhering to 'fresher challenges' imposed on them through indoctrination practices, and prioritising commitment to the club over studies, for example due to social pressure to miss lectures to attend a match (Clayton and Humberstone, 2006; Harris and Clayton, 2008).

Integration vs indoctrination

Initiations have been defined as "any activities expected of someone joining or participating in a group that humiliates, degrades, abuses or endangers them, regardless of a person's willingness to participate" (Hoover and Pollard, 1999, p.8). Research across the USA and UK points to a strong relationship between sport, alcohol consumption, and initiation or hazing rituals at university (Donnelly and Young, 1988; Harris and Clayton, 2008; Clayton, 2013; Groves et al., 2012; Thompson et al., 2018). Despite being banned across institutions, hazing and initiation practices are supposedly an important part of the socialisation into many university sports clubs. This often involves new members undergoing degrading and humiliating behaviours imposed on them by members from higher years, as a means of establishing hierarchy and demonstrating a willingness to abide by the norms of the team, and are viewed by members as a rite of passage (Waldron et al., 2011; Anderson et al., 2012). Arguably, such behaviours are symbolic and serve to preserve club culture, and in particular the hierarchical nature. Also, drinking practices are said to bring about friendships as alcohol facilitates release of inhibitions and provides opportunity to express oneself, share feelings, and develop tight bonds beyond those formed when playing sport (McDonald and Sylvester, 2014). Members who can consume alcohol in high amounts are often held in high regard, and thus alcohol consumption is a key means of capital building, and such social practices can bring about enduring capital (McDonald and Sylvester, 2014).

This issue can be theorised in terms of Bourdieu's conceptualisation of doxa which is the unquestioned attachment to, and respect for, the cultural norms of the field (Bourdieu, 1977, 1990), in this case, university sports clubs. When a logic of practice is embedded within the institutional structure and individuals who associate with the field, this leads to unquestioned adherence. As it is embedded within the university sport culture that new members must undergo these social practices to become authentic members of their respective sports clubs, members unquestioningly oblige (Hughes and Coakley, 1992). This obligation is emphasised as these acts are encouraged by older more established members who are deemed to hold more symbolic capital, and therefore are a means of gaining respect from older members and accruing cultural and symbolic capital.

A report by Universities UK sheds light on this issue drawing attention to the risks involved with initiations which has led to fatal accidents and calls for action to put an end to such behaviours (Haigh and de Pury, 2019). What is more, many individual students do not believe that initiations are positive, however the influence of groupthink helps to preserve the narrative that they are beneficial for team cohesion (Lafferty et al., 2017). Indeed, research suggests that appropriate teambuilding activities, such as meals out, positive behaviour contracts and team oaths may be more effective for developing team cohesion than initiation or hazing activities (Van Raalte et al., 2007; Lafferty et al., 2017). However, despite being banned by students' unions and universities, initiations are embedded within sport culture and need redressing (Groves et al., 2012). It is important to note that initiations and drinking culture are not social practices in every sports club and there are progressive student-led practices going on within clubs that resist this.

Signifying belonging

Branding is often intended to tie clubs together and cultivates feelings of belonging and pride, which can in turn lead to pride in being a member of the institution as a whole and enhance feelings of institutional attachment. The use of team colours (kit or apparel), chants, and mascots to ritualistically unify group members and demonstrate belonging and distinctiveness is a longstanding tradition. This is particularly the case among North American universities where the mascot is highly regarded and embodies a set of values and principles deemed important to the collective group (Chidester, 2012). As members become more familiar with the culture and practice embedded within the field or subculture, they begin to adopt traits, language, and behaviours to demonstrate affiliation.

As with many subcultures, dress is a significant way of demonstrating membership and collective identity (Wheaton and Beal, 2003). In the case of university sports clubs, leisurewear such as team hoodies and playing kit have symbolic meaning attached and cultivate pride in representing one's team, the university sport subculture, and the wider university. According to Bourdieu (1984) dress is an indicator of possessing capital. Habitus predisposes members of a social group to dress and behave a certain way as dress is a symbol of cultural location of the group to which one belongs (Entwisle, 2000; Warde, 2006). Wearing team kit around campus signifies membership to one's team while simultaneously separating them from non-sports members of the wider university, providing a sense of distinction (Holt and Sparkes, 2001).

Another social practice that serves as a marker of identity to the university sport subculture is through themed fancy dress at post-match socials on Wednesday evenings. Fancy-dress provides a sense of anonymity enabling and facilitating group mentality whereby eccentric, negative, risk-taking, and in some cases criminal behaviour associated with sports teams may be more likely when members feel they are disguised and anonymous (Jackson and Sundaram, 2015; Chaney and Goulding, 2016). While dress can be a marker of collective identity, it simultaneously acts as a means of demonstrating distinction from others (Bourdieu, 1984). Thus, from wearing branded kit around campus to fancy dress at the Wednesday night social, individuals signify membership which can bring about feelings of esteem, pride, and insider status. While insider status brings about benefits associated with inclusivity and feelings of belonging, it also means that outsiders of the university sports subculture, or those who wish to be involved in sport but do not buy in to the accompanying socials practices, may feel excluded.

The social hierarchy: becoming an authentic member

Subcultural groups create internal hierarchies based on acquisition of insider knowledge (Thornton, 1995). The internal structure of university sports clubs consists of committee roles including president, captain, treasurer, and social secretary, among others, who are voted in democratically on an annual basis. While such roles entail differing types of symbolic capital and may be respected in different ways, social secretary roles will often have just as much power and authority in a club as a sport-related role such as captain, which highlights the significance of social practices to the university sport culture. As members progress through their university journeys, they may embody club habitus and in doing so accrue capital, climb the social hierarchy, and become more established members within their respective clubs.

Voluntary opportunities at university such as sports team committee roles is a key means for developing social capital in order to foster social mobility (Bathmaker, 2014). Sports club members develop confidence and other transferable skills such as time management, leadership and employability, especially as a result of being a committee member on a team (Allen et al., 2013; Moxey and Simpkin, 2021). This means club committee roles which bring about social capital can also be exchangeable for institutionalised cultural capital, enhancing students' future employability prospects (Tchibozo, 2007). Sport participation, particularly in voluntary and leadership roles, helps students to accrue such forms of capital and is viewed as a strength by employers (Tchibozo, 2007; Allen et al., 2013). Students accrue cultural and social capital which can be converted into economic capital through improved employability. Sports club members seemingly develop an attachment to fellow sportspeople, their institution, and local area, which can influence decisions to search for employment in the local area, demonstrating the lasting impact of university sport. Feeling a valued member within one's sports club can bring about feelings of mattering, which Strayhorn (2019) identifies is necessary for a sense of belonging to the wider university.

The university sport lifestyle

For many, being part of a university sports club is synonymous with the university lifestyle. Members train multiple times per week, compete, socialise, and often live together. Sports club members' weekly routine is centred around their sports club which means they spend significant amounts of time with their teammates and form meaningful and tightknit bonds. The connections formed among sports clubs are often compared to a family-like bond. Indeed, some students suggest that their sports club are like a replacement family away from home. The routine nature of the university sport lifestyle and emotional support gained through club membership is beneficial for students' wellbeing and progression through their university journey.

Sports team/club culture is replicated year on year. Members in higher years often take newer members 'under their wing' and play an informal mentor role, comparable to formal practices emerging in universities such as peer mentoring schemes (Keenan, 2014). However, this mentoring has happened organically in sports clubs as a longstanding tradition, and while hugely beneficial for social support and transition into university life, could be considered as part of the indoctrination process. As members progress through their student journey as a member of a sports club their social network expands. This is one of the main motivators for joining a sports club at university (Quinton and Brunton, 2018) and the value, impact, and lasting effect of this support network developed must not be underestimated.

While the social support from a sports club can be very beneficial, commitment to one's university sports club can sometimes be a distraction or to the detriment of one's studies, for example if there is pressure to attend training and matches despite exam stress (Holt and Sparkes, 2001; Clayton and Humberstone, 2006). Prioritising sports club commitments such as training, matches, or even socials over studies can be a means of capital building and proving one's loyalty to the club. Conversely, the weekly routine can help students to structure their study time around their sporting commitments which can be beneficial, as well as providing a welcome stress relief from studies (Brunton and Mayne, 2020). Moreover, the support network that students develop through their sports clubs can be invaluable for supporting students through the stress of studies as well as living away from home and all the uncertainties that come with it.

Teammates providing a strong level of support in terms of mental wellbeing as well as supporting each other to complete their degrees indicates the understated value sports clubs play at university. Mental health of students is a global concern and university counselling services in the UK have reported increased referrals and challenges with being able to meet demands (Macaskill, 2012). It has been suggested that widening participation in education has contributed to this as the changing demographic of students may have increased financial pressures, or less family support for example (Macaskill, 2012). Furthermore, due to funding cuts students are now taught in larger groups, and more teaching takes place online (even before COVID-19 enforced lockdowns), which can make it more difficult to make friends and develop a sense of belonging (Macaskill, 2012). COVID-19-enforced lockdowns led to the expansion of online learning, and challenges relating to students' mental wellbeing have been exacerbated by the COVID-19 pandemic due to isolation making it harder to feel a sense of belonging with peers (Savage et al., 2020; Cox and Brewster, 2020). Therefore, sports team membership can substitute this lack of belonging in the classroom, through facilitating social interactions and enhancing feelings of connectedness. The support network students develop through involvement in university sport helps them feel well connected and supported, which helps to prevent dropout, providing an outlet and support where other aspects of university may be distressing.

One of the most common motivations for joining a university sports club is to expand one's social network and build friendships (Quinton and Brunton, 2018); however, students do not necessarily anticipate the strength and impact these deep-seated social connections will have on their student journey and beyond (Moxey et al., 2022). Teammates provide a support network which help many students to develop, thrive, and succeed during their time at university.

Considerations for the future: a slowly changing culture

It is clear that there are many social practices that make up the culture of university sport which can bring about a meaningful sense of belonging. The deep-seated connections and support network formed among sports club members have a profound impact on students' decisions to stay on at university. The development of family-like bonds leads to students supporting each other in various capacities such as sport, studies, and personal life. Therefore, the role that sport plays in preventing dropout and fostering a sense of belonging needs further consideration. Furthermore, the altruistic behaviours that sports club members engage with such as volunteering, community work and fundraising also needs further consideration and should be celebrated by staff and students (Moxey et al., 2022).

While there are many positives to be considered, negative aspects such as the drinking culture, initiation ceremonies, and overcommitment to sporting and social activities are engrained within the university sport lifestyle, and training and raising awareness of the potential harm that such practices can bring about is needed to help create a culture change. Examples of emerging practice in the sector include the NUS Alcohol Impact programme and Challenging Hazing and Negative Group Events in Sport (CHANGES) (Haigh and de Pury, 2019). Alcohol Impact is a programme designed by the NUS to create responsible drinking as a social norm. Through using the online toolkit, institutions can implement a broad array of activities and events to promote students to consume alcohol responsibly. CHANGES is an intervention that has emerged out of research conducted by Lafferty et al. (2017) who explored initiations among student sports teams in the UK. In partnership with BUCS, the intervention is delivered in the form of a workshop that aims to promote positive teambuilding and challenges attitudes and behaviours surrounding initiation ceremonies. Through engaging with film clips and tasks, participants learn about the impact of initiations and the physical, psychological, and societal risks associated with them (Haigh and de Pury, 2019). More training and initiatives such as these should be conducted in order to inform as many students as possible about the potential harm that such practices can bring about.

Equipping students early on, for example through training at school or college prior to attending university, with the skills and empowerment to say no, rather than feeling they need to earn respect through over-conformity, may go some way to begin a culture shift. Currently, student-led clubs attempt to keep initiation practices a secret which tends to result in punishment or sanctions if caught by staff. However, if being caught or reported triggered training around the risks associated with initiations, and with simple and anonymous reporting processes in place, student sports club members may see more value in reporting instances where they witness or experience coercive practices taking place. Initiatives such as this are taking place in some institutions.

While there is no 'quick fix' to these issues and any culture change will take time, students have proven themselves to be impactful activists for change for many campaigns, so by raising awareness of the risks attached to overconforming to the university sports subculture, this could be next on the agenda. A consideration for the future is involving students and influential members of the university community in creating policies and practices that reduce lad culture, excessive alcohol consumption, and pressure to overconform. Getting buy-in from students themselves, and students and staff working together in partnership, will be more impactful in creating a culture change. What is more, the COVID-19 pandemic has provided a break in the engrained traditions for many clubs, which could provide the perfect opportunity for staff and students to work together to make a positive change.

Concluding thoughts

For many students, their sports club is central to university life. Through the weekly routine of training, competing, and socialising, traditions and social practices are replicated year on year and are maintained and preserved over time. This can be hugely positive in terms of the support network created, which can help to reduce dropout, enhance the student experience, as well positively influence graduate outcomes. Conversely, some of the social practices that accompany university sports clubs such as the drinking culture and social pressure to overconform can be exclusionary and high risk. It is possible that the disruption of the COVID-19 pandemic to university life has provided a break in the cycle, which could therefore be an opportunity for staff members and clubs to work in partnership to reinvent new norms and traditions and remove the problematic and exclusionary ones.

While social practices that make up the university sports subculture are significant and foster a deep and meaningful sense of belonging for some, they serve to exclude others. University sports club membership can be beneficial to the student experience, providing students with the opportunity to accrue capital and develop skills necessary for bettering their future. However, questions should be raised about the accessibility of sports clubs, and whether the traditions which are engrained in the habitus of clubs that make membership so unique and memorable are beneficial for all. Indeed, work needs to be done to improve the inclusivity and accessibility of university sport to ensure all students can reap the benefits.

References

Allen, K.B.S., Cole, D., Shibli, S. and Wilson, J., 2013. *The Impact of Engagement in Sport on Graduate Employability*. Sheffield: Sheffield Hallam University Sport Industry Research Centre.

Anderson, E. and White, A., 2017. *A Sport, Theory and Social Problems: A Critical Introduction*. Abingdon: Routledge.

Anderson, E., McCormack, M. and Lee, H., 2012. Male team sport hazing initiations in a culture of decreasing homohysteria. *Journal of Adolescent Research*, 27(4), pp.427–444. https://doi.org/10.1177/0743558411412957

Astin, A.W., 1985. *Achieving Educational Excellence: A Critical Assessment of Priorities and Practices in Higher Education*. San Francisco, CA: Jossey-Bass.

Astin, A.W., 1984. Student involvement: A developmental theory for higher education. *Journal of College Student Personnel*, 25(4), pp.297–308.

Astin, A.W., 1975. *Preventing Students from Dropping Out*. San Francisco, CA: Jossey-Bass.

Atkinson, M. and Young, K., 2008. *Tribal Play: Subcultural Journeys through Sport*. London: Emerald.

Bathmaker, A., 2014. Higher education, social class, and the mobilisation of capitals: Recognising and playing the game. *British Journal of Sociology of Education*, 34(5–6), pp.723–743. https://doi.org/10.1080/01425692.2013.816041

Beal, B., 1995. Disqualifying the official: An exploration of social resistance through the subculture of skateboarding. *Sociology of Sport journal*, 12(3), pp.252–267. https://doi.org/10.1123/ssj.12.3.252

Bourdieu, P., 1990. *The Logic of Practice*. R. Nice (trans, ed). Stanford, CA: Stanford University Press.

Bourdieu, P., 1984. *Distinction: A Social Critique of the Judgement of Taste*. Cambridge: Harvard University Press.

Bourdieu, P., 1977. *Outline of a Theory of Practice*. Cambridge: Cambridge University Press.

Brunton, J. and Mayne, V., 2020. *The Value of University Sport and Physical Activity: British Universities and Colleges Sport (BUCS) Position Statement and Evidence*. London: British University and College Sport.

Bryson, C., 2014. *Understanding and Developing Student Engagement*. Abingdon: Routledge.

Chaney, D. and Goulding, C., 2016. Dress, transformation, and conformity in the heavy rock subculture. *Journal of Business Research*, 69(1), pp.155–165. https://doi.org/10.1016/j.jbusres.2015.07.029

Chidester, P., 2012. Farewell to the chief: Fan identification and the sports mascot as postmodern image. In: Earnheardt P.A.C. and Haridakis, B.H. (ed) *Sports Fans, Identity, and Socialization: Exploring the Fandemonium*. Lanham, MD: Lexington.

Clayton, B., 2013. Initiate: Constructing the 'reality' of male team sport initiation rituals. *International Review for the Sociology of Sport*, 48(2), pp.204–219. https://doi.org/10.1177/1012690211432659

Clayton, B. and Humberstone, B., 2006. Men's talk: A (pro)feminist analysis of male university football players' discourse. *International Review for the Sociology of Sport*, 41(3–4), pp.295–231. https://doi.org/10.1177%2F1012690207078380

Coakley, J., 2015. Drug use and deviant overconformity: A sociological approach. In: Hoberman, J., Waddington, I. and Moller, V. (ed) *The Routledge Handbook of Drugs and Sport*. London: Routledge. https://doi.org/10.4324/9780203795347-31

Coakley, J., 2014. Assessing the sociology of sport: On cultural sensibilities and the great sport myth international. *Review for the Sociology of Sport*, 50(4–5), pp.402–406. https://doi.org/10.1177/1012690214538864

Coker-Cranney, A., Watson, J.B.M. and Voelker, C.J., 2017. How far is too far? Understanding identity and overconformity in collegiate wrestlers. *Qualitative Research in Sport, Exercise and Health*, 10(1), pp.92–116. https://doi.org/10.1080/2159676X.2017.1372798

Cook-Sather, A., Bovill, C. and Felten, P. 2014. *Engaging Students as Partners in Learning and Teaching: A Guide for Faculty*. San Francisco, CA: John Wiley & Sons.

Cox, A. and Brewster, L. 2020. Library support for student mental health and well-being in the UK: Before and during the COVID-19 pandemic. *Journal of Academic Librarianship*, 46(6), pp.2–10. https://doi.org/10.1016/j.acalib.2020.102256

Curtis, M., 2015. *Student Identities in New Spaces of Higher Education*. PhD thesis, University of Brighton.

Dickinson, J., Griffiths, T.L. and Bredice, A. 2021. "It's just another thing to think about": Encouraging students' engagement in extracurricular activities. *Journal of Further and Higher Education*, 45(6), pp.744–757.

DiMaggio, P., 1979. Review essay: On Pierre Bourdieu. *American Journal of Sociology*, 84(6), pp.1460–1474. https://doi.org/10.1086/226948

Donnelly, P., 1981. Toward a definition of sport subcultures. In: Hart, M. and Birrell, S. (ed) *Sport in the Sociocultural Process*. Dubuque, IA: William C. Brown.

Donnelly, P. and Young, K., 1988. The construction and confirmation of identity in sport subcultures. *Sociology of Sport Journal*, 5(3), pp.223–240. https://doi.org/10.1123/ssj.5.3.223

Entwisle, J., 2000. Fashion and the fleshy body: Dress as embodied practice. *Fashion Theory*, 4(3), pp.323–347. https://doi.org/10.2752/136270400778995471

Green, B., 2001. Leveraging subculture and identity to promote sport events. *Sport Management Review*, 4(1), pp.1–19. https://doi.org/10.1016/S1441-3523(01)70067-70068

Groves, M., Griggs, G. and Leflay, K., 2012. Hazing and initiation ceremonies in university sport: Setting the scene for further research in the United Kingdom. *Sport in Society*, 15(1), pp.117–131. https://doi.org/10.1080/03031853.2011.625287

Haigh, K. and de Pury, J., 2019. *Initiations at UK Universities*. London: Universities UK.

Harris, J. and Clayton, B., 2008. Tales from the pitch: Some observations on the gendered dynamics of English collegiate soccer. *Journal for the Study of Sports and Athletes in Education*, 2(2), pp.239–262. https://doi.org/10.1179/ssa.2008.2.2.239

Healey, M., Flint, A. and Harrington, K. 2014. *Engagement through Partnership: Students as Partners in Learning and Teaching in Higher Education*. York: Higher Education Academy.

Holt, N. and Sparkes, A., 2001. An ethnographic study of cohesiveness in a college soccer team over a season. *The Sport Psychologist*, 15(3), pp.237–259. https://doi.org/10.1123/tsp.15.3.237

Hoover, N. and Pollard, N., 1999. *Initiation Rites and Athletics: A National Survey of NCAA Sports Teams*. New York: Alfred University and Reidman Insurance Co.

Hughes, R. and Coakley, J., 1992. Positive deviance among athletes: The implications of overconformity to the sport ethic. *Sociology of Sport Journal*, 8(4), pp.307–325. https://doi.org/10.1123/ssj.8.4.307

Hunter, M., Tobolowsky, B., Gardner, J., Evenbeck, S., Pattengale, J., Schaller, M. and Schreiner. L., 2009. *Helping Sophomores Succeed: Understanding and Improving the Second Year Experience*. New York: John Wiley & Sons.

Jackson, C. and Sundaram, V., 2015. *Is 'Lad Culture' a Problem in Higher Education? Exploring the Perspectives of Staff Working in UK Universities*. Final report, Society for Research into Higher Education. Available at: www.srhe.ac.uk/downloads/Jackson SundaramLadCulture.pdf (accessed: 16 May 2021).

Keenan, 2014. *Mapping Student-Led Peer Learning in the UK*. London: The Higher Education Academy.

Kramer, G. and Gardner, J., 2007. *Fostering Student Success in the Campus Community*. San Francisco, CA: Jossey-Bass.

Lafferty, M.E., Wakefield, C. and Brown, H., 2017. "We do it for the team": Student-athletes' initiation practices and their impact on group cohesion. *International Journal of Sport and Exercise Psychology*, 15(4), pp.438–446. https://doi.org/10.1080/1612197X.2015.1121507

Lifschutz, L., 2019. Examining what variables lead to improved outcomes for club sports participants. *Recreational Sports Journal*, 43(2), pp.117–125. https://doi.org/10.1177/1558866119889903

Lower-Hoppe, L.M., Beattie, M.A., Wray, D.E., Bailey, R.L., Newman, T.J. and Farrell, A., 2020. The relationships between sport club activities and university and member attachment. *Recreational Sports Journal*, 44(1), pp.5–14. https://doi.org/10.1177/1558866120904037

Macaskill, A., 2012. The mental health of university students in the United Kingdom. *British Journal of Guidance and Counselling*, 41(4), pp.426–441. https://doi.org/10.1080/03069885.2012.743110

McDonald, B. and Sylvester, K., 2014. Learning to get drunk: The importance of drinking in Japanese university sports clubs. *International Review for the Sociology of Sport*, 49(3–4), pp.331–345. https://doi.org/10.1177/1012690213506584

McElveen, M. and Ibele, K., 2019. Retention and academic success of first-year student-athletes and intramural sports participants. *Recreational Sports Journal*, 43(1), pp.5–11. https://doi.org/10.1177/1558866119840466

McKenna, J. and Dunstan-Lewis, M., 2004. An action research approach to supporting elite student-athletes in higher education. *European Physical Education Review*, 10(2), pp.179–198. https://doi.org/10.1177/1356336X04044070

Milburn-Shaw, H. and Walker, D., 2017. The politics of student engagement. *Politics*, 37(1), pp.52–66. https://doi.org/10.1177/0263395715626157

Miller, J., 2011. Impact of a university recreation center on social belonging and student retention. *Recreational Sports Journal*, 35(2), pp.117–129. https://doi.org/10.1123/rsj.35.2.117

Moxey, M. and Simpkin, E., 2021. Harnessing the potential of extracurricular opportunities to enhance graduate employability in higher education. *Journal of Learning Development in Higher Education*, 21. https://doi.org/10.47408/jldhe.vi21.631

Moxey, M., Brown, H. and Parry, K. 2022. University sports clubs: Culture, belonging and adapting to change during COVID-19. *Journal of Educational Innovation, Partnership and Change*, 8(1), pp.1–16.

Muggleton, D., 2002. *Inside Subculture: The Postmodern Meaning of Style*. Oxford: Berg.

Northumbria University, 2018. Northumbria University axes elite sports teams amid cuts. Available from: www.bbc.com/news/uk-england-tyne-44778994 (accessed: 4 June 2018).

NUS, 2012. *A Manifesto for Partnership*. London: National Union of Students. Available at: www.nusconnect.org.uk/resources/a-manifesto-for-partnership (accessed: 23 August 2015).

NUS, 2017. *Keep Wednesday Afternoons Free: SUs Making the Case.* Available at: www. nusconnect.org.uk/articles/keep-wednesday-afternoons-free-sus-making-the-case (accessed: 8 June 2018).

Quinton, T.S. and Brunton, J.A., 2018. The identification of salient beliefs concerning university students' decisions to participate in sport. *Recreational Sports Journal*, 42(1), pp.48–63. https://doi.org/10.1123/rsj.2016-0037

Savage, M.J., James, R., Magistro, D., Donaldson, J., Healy, L.C., Nevill, M. and Hennis, P.J., 2020. Mental health and movement behaviour during the COVID-19 pandemic in UK university students: Prospective cohort study. *Mental Health and Physical Activity*, 19, 1–6. https://doi.org/10.1016/j.mhpa.2020.100357

Stevenson, J. and Clegg, S. 2011. Possible selves: Students orientating themselves towards the future through extracurricular activity. *British Educational Research Journal*, 37(2), pp.231–246. https://doi.org/10.1080/01411920903540672

Strayhorn, T., 2019. *College Students' Sense of Belonging* (2nd edn). New York: Routledge.

Stuart, M., Lido, C., Morgan, J., Solomon, L. and May, S. 2011. The impact of engagement with extracurricular activities on the student experience and graduate outcomes for widening participation populations. *Active Learning in Higher Education*, 12(3), pp.203–215. doi:10.1177/1469787411415081.

Tchibozo, G. 2007. Extra-curricular activity and the transition from higher education to work: A survey of graduates in the United Kingdom. *Higher Education Quarterly*, 61 (1), pp.37–56. https://doi.org/10.1111/j.1468-2273.2006.00337.x

Thompson, J., Johnstone, J. and Banks, C., 2018. An examination of initiation rituals in a UK sporting institution and the impact on group development. *European Sport Management Quarterly*, 18(5), pp.544–562. https://doi.org/10.1080/16184742.2018.1439984

Thornton, S., 1995. *Club Culture: Music, Media and Subcultural Capital.* Cambridge: Blackwell.

Tinto, V., 1993. *Leaving College: Rethinking the Causes and Cures of Student Attrition.* Chicago: University of Chicago Press.

Tinto, V., 1975. Dropouts for higher education: A theoretical synthesis of recent research. *Review of Educational Research*, 45(1), pp.89–125. https://doi.org/10.3102/00346543045001089

Van Herpen, S., Meeuwisse, M., Hofman, A. and Severiens, S. 2020. A head start in higher education: The effect of a transition intervention on interaction, sense of belonging, and academic performance. *Studies in Higher Education*, 45(4), pp.862–877. https://doi.org/10.1080/03075079.2019.1572088

Van Raalte, J.L., Cornelius, A.E., Linder, D.E. and Brewer, B.W., 2007. The relationship between hazing and team cohesion. *Journal of Sport Behavior*, 30(4), p.491.

Wacquant, L., 1995. Pugs at work: Bodily capital and bodily labour among professional boxers. *Body and Society*, 1(1), pp.65–93. https://doi.org/10.1177/1357034X95001001005

Waldron, J., Lynn, Q. and Krane, V., 2011. Duct tape, icy hot and paddles: Narratives of initiation onto US male sport teams. *Sport, Education and Society*, 16(1), pp.111–125. https://doi.org/10.1080/13573322.2011.531965

Warde, A., 2006. Cultural capital and the place of sport. *Cultural Trends*, 15(2–3), pp.107–122. https://doi.org/10.1080/09548960600712827

Warner, S. and Dixon, M., 2011. Understanding sense of community from the athlete's perspective. *Journal of Sport Management*, 25(3), pp.257–271. https://doi.org/10.1123/jsm.25.3.257

Wheaton, B., 2000. 'Just do it': Consumption, commitment, and identity in the windsurfing subculture. *Sociology of Sport Journal*, 17(3), pp.254–274. https://doi.org/10.1123/ssj.17.3.254

Wheaton, B. and Beal, B., 2003. 'Keeping it real': Subcultural media and the discourses of authenticity in alternative sport. *International Review for the Sociology of Sport*, 38(2), pp.155–117. https://doi.org/10.1177/1012690203038002002

Towards inclusive student partnership

Challenges and opportunities for student engagement in the Australian context

Kate Walsh and Alison Jaquet

In Australia, the language of student engagement and partnership is now prevalent in institutional strategic visions, reflecting the view of students as 'key stakeholders' in their education. However, across the sector, there is variation in the understanding of and approaches to student partnership, student governance and student representation. Within a diversity of settings there is an emerging body of research and practice to inform a growing understanding of what authentic student engagement looks like in Australian higher education. In this chapter we will discuss recent developments in student engagement in the sector and key drivers for these developments. We set the context, highlight key challenges to inclusive practice and discuss emerging trends that may signal the future of diverse student engagement and partnership in an increasingly disrupted higher education landscape.

Student engagement in Australia

As a concept 'student engagement' is contextual and relational, and multiple frameworks have influenced practice in Australia (see Coates, 2008; Kahu, 2013; Kahu and Nelson, 2018; Lizzo and Wilson, 2009; Trowler, 2010). Trowler (2013, p.92) offers an influential definition, highlighting the perceived benefits of engagement to both students and institutions:

> Student engagement is the investment of time, effort and other relevant resources by both students and their institutions intended to optimise the student experience and enhance the learning outcomes and development of students, and the performance and reputation of the institution.

A key theme in the literature is the need for diverse engagement approaches that reflect institutional contexts (Lowe and El Hakim, 2020; Kahu, 2013; Trowler, 2010). Like engagement, student partnership (or student–staff partnership or students as partners) has been described in multiple ways, and is conceptualised as "a primary path towards" (Bovill and Felten, 2016, p.1) and "process of" engagement (Healey, Flint and Harrington, 2014, p.7). At its core, engaging

DOI: 10.4324/9781003271789-21

students in partnership is a deeply collaborative and relational process built around principles of respect, reciprocity and shared responsibility, that acknowledges that differing contributions and expertise are equally valued (Cook-Sather, Bovill and Felten, 2014). Broad definitions of partnership recognise multiple stakeholders, inclusive of professional and academic staff, student unions and university management (Healey, Flint and Harrington, 2014, p.12). This is a double-edged proposition where partnership offers a way to rethink power dynamics between staff and students as beneficial for all. However, mitigating the challenges and tensions that accompany power imbalances between students and staff when working in partnership are similarly well documented (Bovill and Felten, 2016; Healey, Flint and Harrington 2014; Matthews et al., 2019). Influenced by student as partners (SaP) pioneers in the UK and US, student partnership has gained traction in Australia, albeit largely focused on partnership in learning and teaching (Matthews, 2017; Matthews et al., 2018; Mercer-Mapstone 2020; Peseta et al., 2020) with some emerging analysis of partnership in governance and decision-making (Cornelius-Bell, 2021; Louth, Walsh and Goodwin-Smith, 2019; Naylor et al., 2021; Varnham, 2020; Varnham et al., 2018). This chapter will focus on student partnership and engagement practices that involve student representation, decision-making and governance.

At the time of writing, Australia has 188 higher education providers, including 42 universities (TEQSA, 2021) operating across varied geographical and socio-economic contexts. Reforms in higher education policy in Australia over the past 30 years have driven the broadening of student engagement practice across the sector. In part, this reflects the massification of higher education and the need and/or perceived imperative to respond to an increasingly diverse student population (Ho Mok and Neubauer, 2016; Maloshonok and Shcheglova, 2021). From the late twentieth century, higher education shifted from an exclusive opportunity for the most privileged, to education more accessible to the wider population (Gale and Tranter, 2011; Macintyre, Brett and Croucher, 2017). This was achieved through a series of government-led policies and reforms including a period of free education in the 1970s, to interest-free student loans in the late-1980s (Higher Education Contribution Scheme), the expansion into a demand-driven system from 2012–2018, and enhanced funding to support the participation of students from low-SES backgrounds (Gale and Tranter, 2011). In this period, the marketisation of higher education and the shift in costs of higher education to students has repositioned students as consumers – whether by institutions, the sector or, indeed, by themselves (Dollinger and Mercer-Mapstone, 2019; Gravett, Kinchin and Winstone, 2020; Manathunga and Bottrell, 2019). As many have argued, this is a limiting approach (Matthews et al., 2019; Peters and Mathias, 2018; Wijaya Mulya, 2019) where the marketised environment impacts how education is valued (Woodall, Hiller and Resnick, 2014) and has direct consequences for how student voices are incorporated and valued within institutions and the wider sector.

Within this environment, Australia's Tertiary Educational Quality and Standards Agency (TEQSA), the national quality assurance and regulatory agency, advocates and regulates, where appropriate, student involvement in governance and decision-making practices within institutions. TEQSA's Higher Education Standards Framework outlines minimum requirements for the provision of higher education, including that "students have opportunities to participate in the deliberative and decision-making processes of the higher education provider" and "the opportunity to participate in academic governance" (Commonwealth of Australia, 2021, Clauses 6.1.4 and 6.3.3). Indeed, TEQSA has established its own Student Expert Advisory Group to advise on the engagement of students in its activities (TEQSA, 2021), although the rationale is not well-defined beyond gaining the 'advice' or opinions of students (see TEQSA Advisory Group ToRs). This is in contrast to the UK's Quality Assurance Agency (QAA), which provides guidance notes articulating what "meaningful participation of students in quality assurance and enhancement processes" looks like (QAA, 2018). Thus, in the Australian context, student engagement is not defined at the national level in a way that is systematically inclusive or incentivised to enhance meaningful participation of students in decision-making (Naylor et al., 2021; Varnham et al., 2018).

The growth of student engagement in Australia has been greatly influenced by international approaches at a national level, particularly Student Partnerships in Quality Scotland (sparqs), the National Student Engagement Program (NSTEP) in Ireland and The Student Engagement Partnership (TSEP) in England. Informed by the approaches of these bodies, Student Voice Australia (SVA) was established in 2018, by ten tertiary education institutions. This project, led by Sally Varnham at the University of Technology Sydney (AUS), followed from sector-wide collaboration to facilitate the growth of student partnership in tertiary institutions (Varnham, 2020). This ongoing work has created a body of knowledge and resources, including good practice guidelines, a practitioner network and an annual symposium to enhance practice around student representation in Australia (SVA, 2023). Evaluation of the pilot phase indicated that over 95% of participants surveyed supported further development of SVA's national presence; and 90% of institutions and national bodies/agencies surveyed agreed that investment to strengthen student partnership in governance and decision-making was important (Louth, Walsh and Goodwin-Smith, 2019). In 2021, SVA has grown to 16 partner institutions and includes the Technical and Further Education (TAFE) sector. SVA funding is based on a subscription model, where members contribute funding to sustain the network, which contrasts to equivalent bodies in Scotland and Ireland, where both sector agencies and government contribute funding and support. Without secure ongoing funding, networks such as Student Voice Australia remain vulnerable, at least if they are to maintain the current level of output and outreach.

Student partnership in practice

The role of elected student bodies (inclusive of student associations, unions, guilds, councils) in governance and decision making has changed in recent decades (Cornelius-Bell, 2021; Rochford, 2014; Varnham et al., 2018). Once the primary student voices on campus, there has been a shift away from student bodies as the central voice of authority regarding student matters. The introduction of voluntary student unionism (VSU) by the Howard Government in 2007 reduced resources and funding, and thus significantly diminished student organisations' capacity for democratic student representation (DEEWR, 2008). The introduction of the student services and amenities fee (SSAF) legislation in 2011 re-established the ability of universities to charge students a capped fee towards a prescribed set of student support services and amenities. SSAF funding, in addition to providing a conditional funding stream to student bodies, has led to growth in university-administered services focused on the broader student experience, and thus student engagement activities have taken on a new (and more regulated) dimension (Rochford, 2014). Services such as student advocacy, clubs and societies and student representation (such as student representative councils) have tended to remain with students' unions. However, universities have also established their own additional student engagement mechanisms to inform improvements to the student experience (Dollinger and Vanderlelie, 2019; Milburn and Jones, 2019; Shaw et al., 2017). The current focus on the student experience is also driven by recently introduced performance-based funding measures aimed at retaining students and maintaining satisfaction (Wellings et al., 2019). Despite the importance of individual student experiences, there is a risk that the power to influence or drive substantive change within an institution is limited if students are less able to advocate as a collective (Lowe and Bols, 2020).

The political imperatives and affiliations of student organisations, historically at odds with university management, are increasingly sidelined or subsumed by the 'neoliberal university', limiting authentic partnering opportunities (Matthews et al., 2018; Rochford, 2014; Zepke, 2015). As Healey et al. (2014) have noted (p.10), there is a compromise inherent in partnership that can undermine traditional roles that may be detrimental to traditional student unions – and, we might add, to institutions also. When there is authentic engagement between student bodies and universities, genuine partnerships remain possible. Indeed, some student associations in Australia have formed Student Partnership Agreements (SPAs) with their institutions to formalise these relationships (for example this has occurred at the Australian National University, The University of Western Australia and Curtin University). Despite these successes, it is unlikely that SPAs will have a large uptake, due to scepticism by student bodies around whether partnership represents the best interests of independent student bodies. Moreover, it is not uncommon for management to lose interest in negotiations with the student body where compromise would negatively impact on the desired institutional direction (for example, see Cornelius-Bell and Bell, 2020; Moore, 2019). The extent to which authentic partnership is achieved will always be contingent upon the institution's appetite for power-sharing. Yet, students' unions still have recognised authority as the democratically elected student body on campus and their role as advocates, sometimes in opposition to institutions, is an important element of their authenticity. Most, if not all, hold *ex officio* positions on the most senior governance bodies within their institution. Whilst there is still power in student bodies, they face serious challenges to their relevance and effectiveness as advocates for the broad student experience (Cornelius-Bell, 2021; Flint and Goddard, 2020; Healey et al., 2014; Peters and Mathias, 2018).

Unlike the UK, it is less common for Australian course-level student academic representatives to be managed via the student organisation, particularly post-VSU, although some notable examples exist at Flinders University Student Association and the University of Western Australia Guild (FUSA, n.d.; Pelican Magazine, 2018). Increasingly, universities are establishing their own centrally organised student representative structures, alongside (or sometimes in lieu of) an independent student association (Dollinger and Vanderlelie, 2019; University of the Sunshine Coast (AUS), 2021; The University of Queensland (AUS), n.d.). The extent to which the resident student association is involved in these structures is not always clear. Any lack of connection and continuity to wider representative structures can impact a student organisation's knowledge and understanding of broader student-related issues, in turn limiting their ability to speak authoritatively on behalf of a growing diversity of student constituents.

The ability of student representatives, on boards, committees and other groups, to effectively influence decisions within an institution is often dictated by the protocols, practices and cultural norms in place within the institution itself (see: Flint and Goddard, 2020; Lizzo and Wilson, 2009; Naylor et al., 2021). Whilst the contribution of student representatives is often welcomed and encouraged, there are a number of challenges that impact students' influence on agendas, discussions and decision making. These include confidentiality issues and short timelines that prevent wider consultation and, at times, impact understanding of the issues, decisions and governance processes (Naylor et al., 2021). While these barriers may limit meaningful participation, training student representatives to understand their responsibilities and their right to question helps mitigate this risk. The SVA project was premised in large part on building these training opportunities and capacities across the member organisations. Yet the onus cannot be just on training student representatives. Success will be limited until staff are included in training to work collaboratively to mitigate bureaucratic challenges and power imbalances (Varnham, 2020).

From diversity to inclusion

A serious challenge to student engagement in Australian higher education is the effective engagement of an increasingly diverse student population. Student bodies and student representatives are under pressure to represent 'all students' to demonstrate their legitimacy. However, voter turnout for student association elections is low, and many students in representative roles are appointed without a transparent democratic process. Although, conversely, direct appointment has been used as a strategy to encourage representation of traditionally marginalised groups (Alhadad et al., 2021). Furthermore, student representatives not routinely networked into their representative cohort may find it difficult to make these connections themselves with limited time, resources and experience organising. Mercer-Mapstone, Islam and Reid (2021) point out that institutions risk only engaging 'the usual suspects' in partnership initiatives if they do not design and resource student engagement activities to include and support diverse voices. This includes creating safe spaces where students who have been traditionally under-represented feel empowered and able to fully engage (Marquis et al., 2018; Mercer-Mapstone, Islam and Reid, 2021). As Gibson and Cook-Sather (2020, p.27) argue: "A more critical and nuanced understanding of students' stories and analyses of their lived experiences is necessary, whether connected to matters of gender, race, disability, sexuality and/or social class alongside an understanding of the affective domain in their learning". In particular, in the Australian context, a key gap exists in terms of how we embed the knowledges and perspectives of Aboriginal and Torres Strait Islander students.

In Australia, the inclusion of First Nations peoples' knowledges, perspectives and voices in spaces of higher education is slow and large gaps remain in the student engagement space. There are calls for a range of strategies to enhance engagement and inclusion of Aboriginal and Torres Strait Islander people in higher education, including: improvements to staff and student representation (Behrendt et al., 2012; Oliver et al., 2013; Universities Australia, 2011); culturally inclusive curricula and pedagogies (Barney and Williams, 2021; Behrendt et al., 2012; Carter et al., 2018; Fredericks et al., 2017); explicit recognition of the strengths of Indigenous learners (Fredericks et al., 2017; Hollinsworth et al., 2021) and staff development to enhance cultural safety (Hollinsworth et al., 2021; Rochecouste et al., 2014). It is not difficult to argue that the values inherent in student partnership, including collaboration, mutual respect, power-sharing, reciprocity and capacity building, align well with these strategies. Researchers in both higher and secondary education have employed yarning circles as "culturally appropriate, ethical and strengths-based" (Eady and Keen, 2021, p.15) approaches to amplify Aboriginal and Torres Strait Islander student voices in discussions of their learning (Barney and Williams, 2021; Donovan, 2015). Additionally, Walsh et al. (2019), writing in the schools context, argue for the transformative potential of student voice initiatives for Indigenous students to enhance learner engagement. In Canadian and UK higher education contexts, SaP practitioners have demonstrated how reciprocal partnership and flexible inclusive strategies enhance intercultural understanding and inclusion of traditionally marginalised students and knowledges inside and outside the curriculum (Islam, Burnett and Collins, 2021; Yeung et al., 2020). However, Australian and Aoteora/New Zealand researchers caution that the findings of student voice initiatives should be interpreted carefully, in recognition of the wider impacts of colonial legacies that problematise the notion of empowerment for First Nations peoples beyond these defined contexts (Charteris and Smardon, 2019; Walsh and Black, 2021).

Reconciliation movements also offer a broader societal opportunity to include Indigenous student voices. Under the guidance of Reconciliation Australia, organisations across Australia, inclusive of universities, are increasingly developing Reconciliation Action Plans (RAP). As co-designed instruments, RAPs aim to monitor and support practical actions to drive meaningful change. Most Australian universities have developed a RAP (although not all are current) and while they offer demonstrably good actions, they are primarily focused on recruitment, retention and employment pathways for First Nations students, and are mostly silent on student voice. Indigenous voices in RAPs regarding governance are mostly limited to staff and external stakeholders. The University of Southern Queensland (AUS) is one exception, offering a clear commitment to engage the student voice: "Indigenous Student Association to be actively supported and encouraged to play an active role in providing input into institutional decision-making" (2019, p.16). First Nations student voices are also heard via national bodies for undergraduates (the Union of Aboriginal and Torres Strait Islander Students[1]) and postgraduate (National Aboriginal and Torres Strait Islander Postgraduate Association[2]) students. Both UATSIS and NATSIPA sit on TEQSA's Student Advisory Group. Like similar student organisations, they experience challenges with appropriate resourcing, recruitment, succession and support. As Australia matures its partnership work, inclusion of Indigenous voices requires a nuanced and considered approach in order to avoid reproducing marginalisation, and needs to be shaped by practitioners in recognition of the diversity of Indigenous identities (Hollinsworth et al., 2021) in local, regional and national contexts.

Conclusion

There have been varied responses across the sector to embedding student engagement, and these differ based on institutional context, culture and maturity. However, the expansion of the Student Voice Australia[3] network signals that a growing number of institutions are willing to work with their students to determine a way forward. A key challenge is to sustain partnership when students are experiencing new levels of complexity and disruption in their daily lives. In this context, there is an urgent need to recognise student contributions via tangible means to acknowledge their vital service to our higher education institutions and the broader community, and this should include the protection, evolution and centrality of elected student bodies. This may require new forms of student organisation to emerge that amplify a diversity of voices, experiences and needs. This is especially important to ensure First Nations voices, perspectives and ways of doing and being are appropriately and safely included. This commitment needs to be at a 'whole of university' level.

Authentic student engagement cannot be achieved via the well-established paths of tick box student consultation, nor should the change be borne through the time and labour of students alone. Staff need access to training, resources and time to deepen their understanding and experience of authentic student partnership practice. Having a national network, such that Student Voice Australia provides, allows for cross-institutional collaboration and the sharing of experiences, which is vital to the maturation of the work. However, this requires ongoing investment from institutions and the sector more broadly, which means re-prioritising resources and funding within a tight fiscal environment. Any such commitment should be accompanied by continuous research, evaluation and systems innovation to test, measure and enhance the mutual benefits and utility of partnering with students.

University leaders also need to allow space for students in decision-making forums and work harder to find areas of commonality and opportunities for students to lead in these spaces. This requires leaders to challenge entrenched power dynamics in their institutions in order to create and foster space for student voices. And this needs to be done repeatedly and systematically until it becomes a key part of the culture of governance and decision-making at the institution. Building trust is essential for genuine partnership, particularly when it may have been eroded by competing agendas. The ongoing challenge for institutions is navigating present disruptions while sustaining partnership practices that are inclusive, authentic and drive meaningful student-centred change. With disruption comes opportunity, and with opportunity comes creative potential for more inclusive embedding of diverse student voices in the governing of higher education institutions in Australia.

Notes

1 Union of Aboriginal and Torres Strait Islander Students, www.education.gov.au/ higher-education-reviews-and-consultations/resources/union-aboriginal-and-torres-strait-islander-students
2 National Aboriginal and Torres Strait Islander Postgraduate Association, https://natsipa. edu.au/
3 Student Voice Australia, https://studentvoiceaustralia.com/

References

Alhadad, S.S., Vasco, D., Williams, J.C., Dizon, P., Kapnias, R.L., Khan, S.B., Payne, H., Simpson, B.C. and Warren, C.D., 2021. Learning, unlearning, and relearning together: Unmasking power in a students as partners program using collaborative autoethnography. *Student Success*, 12(2), pp.38–50. doi:10.5204/ssj.1934.

Barney, K. and Williams, H., 2021. A stepping stone that just pushed me further into wanting to go to university: Student perspectives on 'what works' for effective outreach strategies for indigenous students. *Student Success*, 12(2), pp.8–17. doi:10.5204/ssj.1913.

Behrendt, L.Y., Larkin, S., Griew, R. and Kelly, P., 2012. *Review of Higher Education Access and Outcomes for Aboriginal and Torres Strait Islander People* (Behrendt Review). Canberra: Department of Industry, Innovation, Science, Research and Tertiary Education.

Bovill, C. and Felten, P., 2016. Cultivating student–staff partnerships through research and practice. *International Journal for Academic Development*, 21(1), pp.1–3. doi:10.1080/1360144x.2016.1124965.

Bradley, D., Noonan, P., Nugent, H. and Scales, B. 2008, *Review of Australian Higher Education: Final Report* (Bradley Review). Canberra: DEEWR.

Carter, J., Hollinsworth, D., Raciti, M. and Gilbey, K., 2018. Academic 'place-making': Fostering attachment, belonging and identity for Indigenous students in Australian universities. *Teaching in Higher Education*, 23(2), pp.243–260. doi:10.1080/13562517.2017.1379485.

Charteris, J. and Smardon, D., 2019. The politics of student voice: Unravelling the multiple discourses articulated in schools. *Cambridge Journal of Education*, 49(1), pp.93–110. doi:10.1080/0305764x.2018.1444144.

Coates, H., 2008. *Attracting, Engaging and Retaining: New Conversations about Learning* (Australasian Student Engagement Report). Camberwell: Australian Council for Educational Research.

Commonwealth of Australia, 2021. *Higher Education Standards Framework*. Available at: www.teqsa.gov.au/higher-education-standards-framework-2021 (accessed: 10 June 2022).

Cook-Sather, A., Bovill, C. and Felten, P., 2014. *Engaging Students as Partners in Learning and Teaching: A Guide for Faculty*. New York: John Wiley & Sons.

Cornelius-Bell, A., 2021. University governance, radicalism and the market economy: Where student power gave way to economics and educative possibility to the corporate university. *International Journal of Social Sciences and Educational Studies*, 8(2), pp.125–136. doi:10.31235/osf.io/dbw7u.

Cornelius-Bell, A. and Bell, P.A., 2020. Partnership as student power: Democracy and governance in a neoliberal university. *Radical Teacher*, 118, pp.21–30. doi:10.5195/rt.2020.738.

Department of Education, Employment and Workplace Relations (DEEWR), 2008. *The Impact of VSU on Services, Amenities and Representation for Australian University Students*. Discussion Paper. Available at: https://apo.org.au/node/4022 (accessed: 3 January 2023).

Dollinger, M. and Mercer-Mapstone, L., 2019. What's in a name? Unpacking students' roles in higher education through neoliberal and social justice lenses. *Teaching & Learning Inquiry*, 7(2), pp.73–89. https://doi.org/10.20343/teachlearninqu.7.2.5

Dollinger, M. and Vanderlelie, J., 2019. Developing and enacting student governance and leadership training in higher education. *Student Success*, 10(2), pp.59–64. doi:10.5204/ssj.v10i2.1309.

Donovan, M.J., 2015. Aboriginal student stories, the missing voice to guide us towards change. *The Australian Educational Researcher*, 42(5), pp.613–625. doi:10.1007/s13384-13015-0182-0183.

Eady, M.J. and Keen, J., 2021. Employability readiness for Aboriginal and Torres Strait Islander students: Yarning Circles as a methodological approach to illuminate student voice. *Journal of Teaching and Learning for Graduate Employability*, 12(2), pp.1–18. doi:10.21153/jtlge2021vol12no2art962.

Flint, A. and Goddard, H., 2020. Power, partnership, and representation. In: Mercer-Mapstone, L. and Abbot, S. (eds) *The Power of Partnership: Students, Staff, and Faculty Revolutionizing Higher Education*. Elon, NC: Elon University Center for Engaged Learning. https://doi.org/10.36284/celelon.oa2

Fredericks, B., Kinnear, S., Daniels, C., Croft-Warcon, P. and Mann, J., 2017. Perspectives on enabling education for Indigenous students at three comprehensive universities in regional Australian. In: Frawley, J., Larkin, S. and Smith J.A. (ed), *Indigenous Pathways, Transitions and Participation in Higher Education*. Singapore: Springer.

FUSA (Flinders University Student Association), n.d. Student representation opportunities. Available at: https://fusa.edu.au/student-representation-opportunities/ (accessed: 16 May 2021).

Gale, T. and Tranter, D., 2011. Social justice in Australian higher education policy: An historical and conceptual account of student participation. *Critical Studies in Education*, 52(1), pp.29–46. https://doi.org/10.1080/17508487.2011.536511

Gibson, S. and Cook-Sather, A., 2020. Politicised compassion and pedagogical partnership: A discourse and practice for social justice in the inclusive academy. *International Journal for Students as Partners*, 4(1), pp.16–33. doi:10.15173/ijsap.v4i1.3996.

Gravett, K., Kinchin, I.M. and Winstone, N.E., 2020. 'More than customers': Conceptions of students as partners held by students, staff, and institutional leaders. *Studies in Higher Education*, 45(12), pp.2574–2587. doi:10.1080/03075079.2019.1623769.

Healey, M., Flint, A. and Harrington, K., 2014. Engagement through partnership: Students as partners in learning and teaching in higher education. *Higher Education Academy*. Available at: www.heacademy.ac.uk/system/files/resources/engagement_through_partnership.pdf (accessed: 16 May 2021).

Ho Mok, K. and Neubauer, D., 2016. Higher education governance in crisis: A critical reflection on the massification of higher education, graduate employment and social mobility. *Journal of Education and Work*, 29(1), pp.1–12. doi:10.1080/13639080.2015.1049023.

Hollinsworth, D., Raciti, M. and Carter, J., 2021. Indigenous students' identities in Australian higher education: Found, denied, and reinforced. *Race Ethnicity and Education*, 24(1), pp.112–131. doi:10.1080/13613324.2020.1753681.

Islam, M., Burnett, T.L. and Collins, S.L., 2021. Trilateral partnership: An institution and students' union collaborative partnership project to support underrepresented student groups. *International Journal for Students as Partners*, 5(1), pp.76–85. doi:10.15173/ijsap.v5i1.4455.

Kahu, E.R., 2013. Framing student engagement in higher education. *Studies in Higher Education*, 38(5), pp.758–773. doi:10.1080/03075079.2011.598505.

Kahu, E.R. and Nelson, K., 2018. Student engagement in the educational interface: Understanding the mechanisms of student success. *Higher Education Research and Development*, 37(1), pp.58–71. doi:10.1080/07294360.2017.1344197.

Lizzo, A. and Wilson, K., 2009. Student participation in university governance: The role conceptions and sense of efficacy of student representatives on departmental committees. *Studies in Higher Education*, 34(1), pp.69–84. doi:10.1080/03075070802602000.

Louth, J., Walsh, K. and Goodwin-Smith, I. 2019. *Making Sure that Students Aren't Just a Tick Box: Evaluating the Student Voice Australia Pilot*. Adelaide: University of South Australia.

Lowe, T. and Bols, A., 2020. Higher education institutions and policy makers: The future of student engagement. In: Lowe, T. and El Hakim, Y. (eds) *A Handbook for Student Engagement in Higher Education*. Abingdon: Routledge. doi:10.4324/9780429023033-26.

Lowe, T. and El Hakim, Y. 2020. An introduction to student engagement in higher education. In: Lowe, T. and El Hakim, Y. (eds) *A Handbook for Student Engagement in Higher Education*. Abingdon: Routledge. doi:10.4324/9780429023033-2.

Macfarlane, B. and Tomlinson, M., 2017. Critiques of student engagement. *Higher Education Policy*, 30(1), pp.5–21. doi:10.1057/s41307–41016–0027–0023.

Macintyre, S., Brett, A. and Croucher, G., 2017. *No End of a Lesson: Australia's Unified National System of Higher Education.* Melbourne: Melbourne University Publishing.

Maloshonok, N. and Shcheglova, I., 2021. From "customer" to "partner": Approaches to conceptualization of student-university relationships. In Padró, F.F., Kek, M. and Huijser, H. (eds) *Student Support Services: University Development and Administration.* Singapore: Springer. doi:10.1007/978-981-13-3364-4_4–1.

Manathunga, C. and Bottrell, D., 2019. Prising open the cracks in neoliberal universities. In Manathunga, C. and Bottrell, D. (eds) *Resisting Neoliberalism in Higher Education* (Vol. 2). London: Palgrave. doi:10.1007/978-973-319-95834-7_1.

Marquis, E., Jayaratnam, A., Mishra, A., and Rybkina, K., 2018. "I feel like some students are better connected": Students' perspectives on applying for extracurricular partnership opportunities. *International Journal for Students as Partners*, 2(1), pp.64–81. doi:10.15173/ijsap.v2i1.3300.

Matthews, K.E., 2017. Five propositions for genuine students as partners practice. *International Journal for Students as Partners*, 1(2). doi:10.15173/ijsap.v1i2.3315.

Matthews, K.E., Dwyer, A., Russell, S. and Enright, E., 2019. It is a complicated thing: Leaders' conceptions of students as partners in the neoliberal university, *Studies in Higher Education*, 44(12), pp.2197–2207. doi:10.1080/03075079.2018.1482268.

Matthews, K.E., Dwyer, A., Hine, L. and Turner, J., 2018. Conceptions of students as partners. *Higher Education*, 76(6), pp.957–971. doi:10.1007/s10734–10018–0257-y.

Mercer-Mapstone, L., 2020. The student–staff partnership movement: Striving for inclusion as we push sectorial change. *International Journal for Academic Development*, 25 (2), pp.121–133. doi:10.1080/1360144x.2019.1631171.

Mercer-Mapstone, L., Islam, M. and Reid, T., 2021. Are we just engaging 'the usual suspects'? Challenges in and practical strategies for supporting equity and diversity in student–staff partnership initiatives. *Teaching in Higher Education*, 26(2), pp.227–245. doi:10.1080/13562517.2019.1655396.

Mercer-Mapstone, L., Dvorakova, S.L., Matthews, K.E., Abbot, S., Cheng, B., Felten, P., Knorr, K., Marquis, E., Shammas, R. and Swaim, K., 2017. A systematic literature review of students as partners in higher education. *International Journal for Students as Partners*, 1(1), pp.1–23. doi:10.15173/ijsap.v1i1.3119.

Milburn, L. and Jones, D., 2019. The Deakin 'Students helping students' and 'students as partners' collection: A contemporary take on the classic cut. A practice report. *Student Success*, 10(2), pp.65–70. doi:10.5204/ssj.v10i2.1311.

Moore, T., 2019. UQ students loudly vote 'No' to private degree program. *Brisbane Times*, 29 May. Available at: www.brisbanetimes.com.au/national/queensland/uq-students-loudly-vote-no-to-racist-private-degree-program-20190529-p51sjo.html (accessed: 24 June 2021).

Naylor, R., Dollinger, M., Mahat, M. and Khawaja, M., 2021. Students as customers versus as active agents: Conceptualising the student role in governance and quality assurance. *Higher Education Research and Development*, 40(5), pp.1026–1039. doi:10.1080/07294360.2020.1792850.

Oliver, R., Rochecouste, J., Bennell, D., Anderson, R., Cooper, I., Forrest, S. and Exell, M., 2013. Understanding Australian Aboriginal tertiary student needs. *International Journal of Higher Education*, 2(4), pp.52–64. doi:10.5430/ijhe.v2n4p52.

Pelican Magazine, 2018. Guild experiments with new Class Rep System. *Pelican Magazine*, 9 March. Available at: https://pelicanmagazine.com.au/2018/03/09/guild-experiments-new-class-rep-system/ (accessed: 24 June 2021).

Peseta, T., Pizzica, J., Beathe, A., Jose, C., Lynch, R., Manthos, M., Nguyen, K. and Raza, H., 2020. A partnership mindset: Students as partners for and beyond the university. In: Mercer-Mapstone, L. and Abbot, S. (eds) *The Power of Student–Staff Partnerships: Revolutionizing Higher Education*. Elon, NC: Center for Engaged Learning Press. doi:10.36284/celelon.oa2.

Peters, J. and Mathias, L., 2018. Enacting student partnership as though we really mean it: Some Freirean principles for pedagogy of partnership. *International Journal for Students as Partners*, 2(2), pp.53–70. doi:10.15173/ijsap.v2i2.3509.

Quality Assurance Agency for Higher Education (QAA), 2018. *UK Quality Code – Advice and Guidance Student Engagement*. Available at: www.qaa.ac.uk/quality-code/advice-and-guidance/student-engagement (accessed: 24 June 2021).

Rochecouste, J., Oliver, R. and Bennell, D., 2014. Is there cultural safety in Australian universities? *International Journal of Higher Education*, 3, pp.153–166. doi:10.5430/ijhe.v3n2p153.

Rochford, F., 2014. Bringing them into the tent – student association and the neutered academy. *Studies in Higher Education*, 39(3), pp.485–499. doi:10.1080/03075079.2014.896184.

Shaw, N., Rueckert, C., Smith, J., Tredinnick, J. and Lee, M., 2017. Students as partners in the real world – A whole-institution approach. *International Journal for Students as Partners*, 1(1), pp.1–8. doi:10.15173/ijsap.v1i1.3079.

Student Voice Australia (SVA), 2023. *Student Voice Australia: Our Work*. Available at: https://studentvoiceaustralasia.com/ (accessed 4 January 2023).

TEQSA, 2021. *National Register*. Available at: www.teqsa.gov.au/national-register (accessed: 9 September 2021).

Trowler, V., 2013. Leadership practices for student engagement in challenging conditions. *Perspectives: Policy and Practice in Higher Education*, 17(3), pp.91–95. doi:10.1080/13603108.2013.789455.

Trowler, V., 2010. Student engagement literature review. *The Higher Education Academy*, 11(1), pp.1–15.

Tudge, A. (Minister for Education and Youth), 2021. *Protecting Freedom of Speech at Australian Universities* (Media Release). Parliament House, Canberra, 16 March.

Universities Australia, 2011. National best practice framework for Indigenous cultural competency in Australian universities. Available at: www.universitiesaustralia.edu.au/wp-content/uploads/2019/06/National-Best-Practice-Framework-for-Indigenous-Cultural-Competency-in-Australian-Universities.pdf (accessed: 9 September 2021).

The University of Queensland, n.d. *UQ Student Representation*. Available at: https://employability.uq.edu.au/student-staff-partnerships-student-representation (accessed: 24 June 2021).

University of Southern Queensland, 2019. *Innovate Reconciliation Action Plan (RAP) 2019–2021*. Available at: www.usq.edu.au/rap (accessed: 24 June 2021).

University of the Sunshine Coast, 2021. *USC Student Senate*. Available at: www.usc.edu.au/current-students/students-as-partners/volunteer/usc-student-senate (accessed: 12 September 2021).

Varnham, S., 2020. Creating a national framework for student partnership in university decision-making and governance (National Senior Teaching Fellowship Report). Available at: https://ltr.edu.au/resources/FS16-0272_Varnham_Report_2020.pdf (accessed: 11 September 2021).

Varnham, S., Olliffe, B., Waite, K., and Cahill, A., 2018. *Student Engagement in University Decision-Making and Governance: Towards a More Systemically Inclusive Student Voice:*

2015–2016 Final Report. Canberra: Learning and Teaching Support, Australian Government Department of Education and Training.

Walsh, L. and Black, R., 2021. The problem of empowerment: The social ecologies of Indigenous youth leadership. *Pedagogy, Culture and Society.* doi:10.1080/14681366.2021.1891451.

Walsh, L., Black, R., Zyngier, D. and Fernandes, V., 2019. Harnessing student voice and leadership: A study of one Australian Indigenous leadership program. *Pedagogy, Culture and Society*, 27(3), pp.383–401. doi:10.1080/14681366.2018.1502205.

Wellings, P., Black, R., Craven, G., Freshwater, D. and Harding, S., 2019. *Performance-based funding for the Commonwealth Grants Scheme.* Canberra: Commonwealth of Australia. Available at: https://apo.org.au/sites/default/files/resource-files/2019-08/apo-nid252261.pdf (accessed: 16 May 2021).

Wijaya Mulya, T., 2019. Contesting the neoliberalisation of higher education through student–faculty partnership. *International Journal for Academic Development*, 24(1), pp.86–90. doi:10.1080/1360144x.2018.1520110.

Woodall, T., Hiller, A. and Resnick, S., 2014. Making sense of higher education: Students as consumers and the value of the university experience. *Studies in Higher Education*, 39(1), pp.48–67. doi:10.1080/03075079.2011.648373.

Yeung, S., Ge, Y., Shanbhag, D., Liu, A., Downey, B., Hill, K., Martin-Hill, D., Amster, E., McKnight, C. and Wahi, G. 2020. A collective education mentorship model (CEMM): Responding to the TRC calls to action in undergraduate Indigenous health teaching. *International Journal for Students as Partners*, 4(1), pp.138–147. doi:10.15173/ijsap.v4i1.3878.

Zepke, N., 2017. *Student Engagement in Neoliberal Times: Theories and Practices for Learning and Teaching in Higher Education.* Cham: Springer. doi:10.1007/s10734–10018–0325–0323.

Zepke, N., 2015. What future for student engagement in neo-liberal times? *Higher Education*, 69(4), pp.693–704. doi:10.1007/s10734–10014–9797-y.

Chapter 22

Recognising the hidden impact of extra-curricular activity on student engagement and success

Eddie Corr

Introduction

Student engagement is an all-encompassing term which despite instigating a large volume of research has not reached a consensus on definition in the higher education community. Research in the area displays a strong focus on what happens in the classroom in terms of pedagogy (Buckley, 2014; QAA, 2012), student–staff partnership (Neary, 2010; Cook-Sather, Bovill and Felten, 2014; van der Velden, 2012) and student success (Kuh et al., 2011; Tinto, 2012). Alongside this dominant focus there is also research into how outside agents can influence student engagement: particularly the areas of well-being and belonging (Mann, 2001; Humphrey and Lowe, 2017); life-wide learning (Barnett, 2011); and extra-curricular activity (Tchibozo, 2007; Stuart et al., 2009). With such a variety of associations a clear definition has proven elusive, dependent on the context of research or practice and potentially open to dominance by some areas over others.

It is important to challenge and provoke in this area of focus in higher education, as often the focus of student engagement research is on the academic-related elements with extra-curricular activity on the fringes of the conversation due to being outside institutions' direct locus of control (Pickford, 2016). In progressing the narrative of student engagement, there is a need to better understand what it is like to be a student today, to better research the inter-connected student experience across course, institution and social circles (Tight, 2019). This chapter will demonstrate how extra-curricular activity should be considered a key component of student personal development and the wider student engagement picture, which is deserving of increased recognition and development in advancing the concepts of student engagement and success.

Extra-curricular activity and student engagement

The definition of extra-curricular activity is broad and varied, very much depending on what context it is being addressed within. This is perhaps no surprise as extra-curricular activity encompasses areas as diverse as employment; volunteering; student involvement in clubs or societies; student involvement in student voice

DOI: 10.4324/9781003271789-22

activities/roles; and well-being or personal development activities. In the literature, there is a consensus that extra-curricular activity, as opposed to co-curricular activity, is something that occurs outside of the classroom (Kuh 1995; Stuart et al., 2009; Thompson et al., 2013). Tensions exist when it comes to the main benefits extra-curricular activities can have within student engagement. One body of literature would stress the link between extra-curricular activities and academic development, and ultimately enhanced employability. This literature very much puts successful extra-curricular activity as something that primarily serves employability (Nemanick and Clark, 2002; Stuart et al., 2009; Tchibozo, 2007; Tomlinson, 2017; Macfarlane and Tomlinson, 2017).

But this view of extra-curricular activities is subject to critique. An emerging body of research espouses their more holistic nature. Building on the concept of life-wide learning, these activities, which are not part of the formal degree classification, serve to enhance areas such as integration and belonging. This places extra-curricular activity as an important driver of student engagement by serving the 'wider student experience' (Thompson et al., 2013). It is this tension around the relevance of the role extra-curricular activities play in furthering student engagement that poses problems and merits debate. **After all, why should we care about what happens outside the lecture hall?**

We start at the beginning of the student journey: integration and belonging. Of particular interest is the role extra-curricular involvement plays within student engagement during the first semester, when new students first arrive at university. The theories of Astin (1984) and Tinto (1993) have informed much writing in this area with focus on phases such as transition and integration dominating. Beginning college is a major transition in a student's life. In many cases, a student is stretching their ties with family, friends and the surroundings they have become comfortable in. Many researchers liken this phase to a new beginning or even a 'culture shock' (Mann, 2001). Therefore, many involvement opportunities happen in the first few weeks of the semester, as different parts of the institution attempt to reach students in the hope of aiding integration.

Extra-curricular activities by their very nature revolve around groups of students interacting with their peers and can thus be viewed as core to building a sense of belonging. Involvement in peer representative bodies such as students' unions, or social support mechanisms such as sports teams, clubs and/or societies, also emerge strongly in recent research as key determinants of belonging and student success (Thomas, 2002; Zepke, 2015). Many of these opportunities are extra-curricular by nature and deserve credit for the role they play in promoting a sense of belonging, evidenced as a key component of transition and integration (Burdett and Crossman, 2010).

Next, let us consider student success. Research in this area of student success is principally focused on analysing and measuring the impact student engagement initiatives have on pedagogical practice within the classroom setting (Zepke, 2014). Student success is something often measured by retention, completion rates, and the level of grade received (Macfarlane and Tomlinson, 2017). Indeed, engagement and pedagogical practice are intertwined to the point of being described as the 'mainstream view' (Zepke, 2015). However, if we accept that every student has a unique background, unique strengths and a unique path to college and a career then every student has a multitude of influences when it comes to their own perception of success, both within the lecture hall and beyond in wider activities beyond the curriculum.

Extra-curricular activity occurs outside the lecture hall, often among students from different courses and faculties, and typically without the direct influence or involvement of university teaching staff. Therefore, extra-curricular activity operates in a 'blind spot' when it comes to student engagement: most student success research centres around classroom experiences and is often conducted by the academics involved. Extra-curricular activity, by its very nature, is happening outside the classroom – beyond their gaze.

We have established that early and ongoing student engagement is a good thing, and we recognise the importance of student success (Braxton, 2008), which inevitably leads to a desire to measure these things. Surveys are a long-standing instrument used in measuring levels of student engagement. However, whether it is a national student engagement survey or the more local form of module feedback survey, many of them limit their focus to measuring satisfaction of classroom-based indicators of engagement, limiting their oversight (Dunne and Owen, 2013; Kahu, 2013). There is a similar trend when it comes to the field of learning analytics. Definitions have varied over the years, but there is a general understanding that learning analytics is the process through which data about students' learning behaviour and experience is gathered and analysed to improve understanding and affect positive retention and pedagogical outcomes (SOLAR, 2011; National Forum, 2019b; Tsai et al., 2018). As a result, teaching and learning are the main drivers in this area, with what happens outside of this a secondary concern.

Higher education is traditionally portrayed as transformative, with students encouraged to develop their sense of agency and construct a learning experience for themselves beyond that which is laid out in their course plan (Klemenčič, 2015). Transformative events, by their nature, often take place beyond the classroom, in activities shared with peers from across the institution with many taking place off-campus itself. However, there is a familiar problem here due to extra-curricular activities operating in the 'blind spot' of focus. Student engagement measurement surveys mostly focus on defined learning outcomes and general satisfaction with areas common to most students. Extra-curricular activity, outside the gaze of the lecture hall, generally does not have identified learning outcomes that can be easily measured. **How can you measure what you cannot see?**

The hidden impact of extra-curricular activity

For us to explore the hidden impact of extra-curricular activity let us look for a minute at the college experiences of two hypothetical students: Jon and Jan. At first glance (see Figure 22.1), who do you think is the better-engaged student?

Jon

Jan

- High Grade Average
- Uses VLE regularly
- No progression issues
- Daily Library usage

- Poor Grade Average
- Low VLE usage
- Repeat examinations
- Infrequent Library usage

Figure 22.1 Hidden extra-curricular activity

The one more likely to be successful? Whose data here might be about to trigger a call from student services? When we look at everything that is going on academically, and everything inside the classroom, we can see clear differences between them. Jon is scoring excellently on their assessments, progressing well and engaging with their learning tools. Jan on the other hand has struggled with their grades, had to repeat exams frequently and has poor engagement with their learning tools. But what if we were to include their extra-curricular engagement – would that change our perception of success?

When we recognise the extra-curricular, we can see that there is a lot more going on with Jan than we first thought (see Figure 22.2). They are heavily

Jon

Jan

- High Grade Average
- Uses VLE regularly
- No progression issues
- Daily Library usage

- Poor Grade Average
- Low VLE usage
- Repeat examinations
- Infrequent Library usage

- Elected Student Representative
- Student Textline Volunteer
- Mental Health Soc. President
- Accessibility issue impacts study

Figure 22.2 Visible extra-curricular activity

involved in extra-curricular activities, spending an average of 30 hours a week actively engaging with them. Interacting with peers, advocating on their behalf, affecting the mental health discussion on campus and developing countless soft skills. If you were to ask Jan if they were engaged in their university experience and confident of a successful outcome, they would answer a resounding yes. Jon on the other hand does not engage in any extra-curricular activities. This is down to a focus on their academic work and a result of being a time-strapped commuter student. While they are doing exceptionally academically, they feel disconnected from their institution and do not really feel that they belong. This in turn is creating an anxiety that Jon worries will impact negatively on their final assessments. If you asked Jon if they were engaged with their university experience and confident of a successful outcome, they might give an unexpected reply.

While this example is simplistic and plays with our assumptions and bias, it serves to illustrate the point that there is value in what we cannot see and what is difficult to measure. Analytics and causal engagement observations may lead you to believe that a student is disengaged and at risk of dropping out when the complete opposite might be true. Student success is individual to each student and can change over time. Which brings us back to the earlier question: **Why care about what happens outside the lecture hall?** We care because what happens outside the lecture hall impacts the experience of the students sitting in it. Put simply, extra-curricular activity impacts student success. That is why catering for the extra-curricular as part of student engagement and student success is so important.

Recommendations

The clearly defined link between engagement and curriculum activity has been established, with extra-curricular activity shown to be operating on the fringes. Engagement programmes and measurement tools are primarily viewing student engagement through an academic lens measuring indicators such as retention and completion (Kuh, 2001); the complementary nature of extra-curricular activities is something that is not actively championed. It is time to change this and better integrate extra-curricular activities into our student engagement practice at both institutional and personal levels.

I. Consider 'student success' as something fluid and unique to each student

Similar to 'student engagement', we should always question what is implied when using the term 'student success'. The established view of student success as intrinsic to employability (Poole and Zahn, 1993) or completion (Kelly and Schneider, 2012) focuses on its academic nature. This narrow focus of what constitutes a successful college experience leaves it difficult for the impact of outside classroom influences to be measured and appreciated. There are signs, however, that this view is widening and there is opportunity here for extra-curricular activity to step forward in prominence. In Ireland right now there is a national movement underway to build sectoral consensus as to what constitutes student success in different contexts and at different stages. One of the core tenets of the 'Embedding Student Success: A Guiding Framework', recently launched by the National Forum for Teaching and Learning, is that "success is too highly nuanced and individualised to be concisely defined. It can, nonetheless, be understood and facilitated" (National Forum, 2021). This recognition is important as it recognises that student success is more than access, progression and completion rates and lives as much in the corridors of an institution as it does in the classroom or in the curriculum (National Forum, 2019a). In taking this approach individual institutions need to consider how the national understanding of student success is to be interpreted in their own context, identifying good practice, and highlighting areas of further development.

This approach to student success opens the door for extra-curricular activity on many levels. In being encouraged to critically reflect on how student engagement and student success work within our institution we have an opportunity to consider the extra-curricular; to examine how students navigate through university and interpret their success in different ways. Considering student success as something fluid and ever-changing allows us the opportunity to explore the role of extra-curricular activity when considering success within our own student engagement practice.

2. Evaluate the impact of extra-curricular activity on student engagement

Once we start to consider student success as something fluid and acknowledge the role extra-curricular activities can play in achieving it, we will naturally want to quantify this. For the impact of extra-curricular activities to be measured and appreciated their metrics will need to be captured. There are options for how this could be introduced. We know that surveys are an established mechanism for measuring levels of student engagement – these could be broadened to incorporate questions related to outside classroom activity. However, the over reliance on surveys in measuring student engagement is seen as a limitation (Kahu, 2013) and criticised as measuring levels of student satisfaction rather than engagement (Dunne and Owen, 2013), so caution would be advised in using this method. Alternatively, there could be independent research and evaluation projects carried out that would provide a snapshot in time of extra-curricular activity at institutional and even national levels. This took place recently in Ireland in relation to digital learning through the Irish National Digital Experience (INDEx) Survey (National Forum, 2019c). This project established an evidence base of practice across the country which helped to inform decision-making and support development practices, establishing that such an approach to extra-curricular activity is feasible.

Another area that could be explored is that of data analytics. We currently collect vast amounts of data concerning the student experience (Shacklock, 2016).

The chief issue would be that learning analytics has a clear focus on capturing and analysing data about the academic experience – grades, attendance and virtual learning environment metrics. What about students like Jan, who is heavily engaged in extra-curricular activity but not captured in this data (Lowe, 2018)? Many of these activities are currently measured in some form, whether it is manual attendance forms, reflective journals or online activity metrics. Like how our definition of student success should be fluid, we need to discuss how our learning analytics models could be more holistic in bringing together engagement metrics to support student success.

3. Consider the extra-curricular

Astin's Theory of Student Involvement (1984) states that students learn from their participation in both the academic and social aspects of the collegiate experience, which makes it curious that extra-curricular activity has operated mainly on the fringes of the discourse on student engagement compared to academic endeavours. How can this beneficial relationship between student engagement, the curriculum and extra-curricular activity be strengthened? Inspiration can come from projects which have looked to blur the line between what is considered co-curricular and extra-curricular. The Play and Creativity Festival at the University of Winchester (UK) outlined that the success of student engagement is that it remains flexible (Lowe and James, 2019). In providing a platform for staff and students to share creative and playful methods of teaching, the Festival showcased over 65 sessions of activities that would usually stay within their classrooms and not be shared with the wider university community. A key part of projects such as this, and the parallel they draw with many extra-curricular activities on campus, is that students are very much in the driving seat. They engage with each other and fuse their learning from within the classroom with wider learning that comes through the nature of whatever activity they are involved in. Students are not passive agents to the educational process; instead, students become active agents of their own and their peers' learning (Felten et al., 2019).

Extra-curricular activity has the power to bring students from across the university together to work on a project with a common goal in a way that no classroom-bound activity can. This is something that deserves to be considered as a driver of student engagement and success alongside anything that happens in the classroom. At institutional level this can be achieved through introducing credit-bearing programmes rewarding extra-curricular activities or recognising the role these activities play in developing graduate attributes. On a more personal level, as higher education professionals we often input on student engagement initiatives in our own institution. While doing so, we can understandably be focused on what is directly in front of us: teaching and learning, quality assurance, peer mentoring or student partnership for example. What we need to do is check-in with ourselves every now and again and ask: is there relevant extra-curricular activity happening here that deserves attention or recognition? This small change in awareness should lead to extra-curricular practice being considered and valued when projects and policies are being developed.

Conclusion

If student engagement discourse continues to prioritise pedagogical activities over extra-curricular ones, and the analytical systems that we put in place to measure student engagement do the same, then extra-curricular engagement will continue to remain unrecognised and unappreciated by many. This chapter has illustrated how the role that extra-curricular activity plays in the student experience is personal and often unseen. Three recommendations have been outlined that can amplify the role of extra-curricular activity within student engagement and student success practice on both institutional and personal scales. Used as a prompt, any one of these three recommendations can help those working in higher education to broaden their focus. This provides a good starting point for discussion and further research.

For extra-curricular activity to be widely accepted as a valued component of student engagement there will need to be some expansion of the student engagement narrative to shine a light on extra-curricular activity and the effects it can have in furthering student engagement. What are the benefits of extra-curricular activity, for students and our institutions? What are the risks of not recognising these activities? How can we measure what we cannot see? What we need to do is remember the extra-curricular when we discuss, enhance and further student engagement within our own practice. As higher education practitioners you are challenged to use these recommendations when considering student engagement and success to support extra-curricular activity, recognise its benefits and champion its development. Looking forward, it is time for extra-curricular activity to emerge from the student engagement blind spot and to prove its place as a key driver for student engagement and a vitally important element of an improved student experience.

References

Astin, A.W., 1984. Student involvement: A developmental theory for higher education. *Journal of College Student Personnel*, 25(4), pp.297–308.

Atherton, M., Shah, M., Vazquez, J., Griffiths, Z., Jackson, B. and Burgess, C., 2017. Using learning analytics to assess student engagement and academic outcomes in open access enabling programmes. *Open Learning: The Journal of Open, Distance and e-Learning*, 32 (2), pp.119–136. https://doi.org/10.1080/02680513.2017.1309646

Barnett, R., 2011. Lifewide education: A new and transformative concept for higher education? In: Jackson, N. (ed) *Learning for a Complex World: A Lifewide Concept of Learning, Personal Development and Education*. AuthorHouse.

Braxton, J.M., 2008. Toward a theory of faculty professional choices in teaching that foster college student success. In: Smart, J.C. (ed) *Higher Education: Handbook of Theory and Research*. Dordrecht: Springer. https://doi.org/10.1007/978-1-4020-6959-8_6

Buckley, A., 2014. How radical is student engagement? (And what is it for?). *Student Engagement and Experience Journal*, 3(2), pp.1–23. https://doi.org/10.7190/seej. v3i2.95

Burdett, J. and Crossman, J., 2010. Checking the pulse. *Journal of International Education in Business*, 3(1/2), pp.53–67. https://doi.org/10.1108/18363261011106885

Cook-Sather, A., Bovill, C. and Felten, P., 2014. *Engaging Students as Partners in Learning and Teaching: A Guide for Faculty*. New York: John Wiley & Sons.

Dunne, E. and Owen, D. (eds), 2013. *Student Engagement Handbook: Practice in Higher Education*. Bingley: Emerald Group Publishing.

Felten, P., Abbot, S., Kirkwood, J., Long, A., Lubicz-Nawrocka, T., Mercer-Mapstone, L. and Verwoord, R., 2019. Reimagining the place of students in academic development. *International Journal for Academic Development*, 24(2), pp.192–203.

Government of Ireland, 2011. *National Strategy for Higher Education 2030*. Available at: https://hea.ie/assets/uploads/2017/06/National-Strategy-for-Higher-Educa tion-2030.pdf (accessed: 9 May 2020).

Humphrey, O. and Lowe, T., 2017. Exploring how a 'Sense of Belonging' is facilitated at different stages of the student journey in Higher Education. *Journal of Educational Innovation, Partnership and Change*, 3(1), pp.172–188. https://journals.studentengagement. org.uk/index.php/studentchangeagents/issue/view/54Kahu, E.R., 2013. Framing student engagement in higher education. *Studies in Higher Education*, 38(5), pp.758–773. https://doi.org/10.1080/03075079.2011.598505

Kelly, P., Fair, N. and Evans, C., 2017. The engaged student ideal in UK higher education policy. *Higher Education Policy*, 30(1), pp.105–122. http://dx.doi.org/10.1057/ s41307-016-0033-5

Kelly, A.P., and Schneider, M., 2012. *Getting to Graduation: The Completion Agenda in Higher Education*. Baltimore, MD: Johns Hopkins University Press.

Klemenčič, M., 2015. What is student agency? An ontological exploration in the context of research on student engagement. In: Klemenčič, M., Bergan, S. and Primožič, R. (eds) *Student Engagement in Europe: Society, Higher Education and Student Governance*. Strasbourg: Council of Europe Publishing.

Kuh, G.D., 2001. *The National Survey of Student Engagement: Conceptual Framework and Overview of Psychometric Properties*. Bloomington, IN: University Centre for Postsecondary Research.

Kuh, G.D, 1995. The other curriculum: Out-of-class experiences associated with student learning and personal development. *The Journal of Higher Education*, 66(2), pp.123–155. https://doi.org/10.2307/2943909

Kuh, G.D., Kinzie, J., Schuh, J.H. and Whitt, E.J., 2011. *Student Success in College: Creating Conditions that Matter*. Oxford: John Wiley & Sons. Lowe, T., 2018. Data analytics – A critique of the appropriation of a new measure of 'student engagement'. *Student Engagement in Higher Education Journal*, 2(1), pp.2–6.

Lowe, T. and Bols, A., 2020. Higher education institutions and policy makers: The future of student engagement. In: Lowe, T. and El-Hakim, Y. (eds) *A Handbook for Student Engagement in Higher Education*. Abingdon: Routledge. https://doi.org/10.4324/ 9780429023033-26

Lowe, C. and James, A., 2019. Play and creativity as extra-curricular festivities: A case study following the Winchester Play and Creativity Festival. *Student Engagement in Higher Education Journal*, 2(3), pp.172–180. https://sehej.raise-network.com/raise/article/ view/862

Mann, S.J., 2001. Alternative perspectives on the student experience: Alienation and engagement. *Studies in Higher Education*, 26(1), pp.7–19. https://doi.org/10.1080/03075070020030689

Macfarlane, B. and Tomlinson, M., 2017. Critiques of student engagement. *Higher Education Policy*, 30(1), pp.5–21. http://dx.doi.org/10.1057/s4130701600273

Neary, M., 2010. Student as producer: A pedagogy for the avant-garde? *Learning Exchange*, 1(1). https://eprints.lincoln.ac.uk/id/eprint/4186/1/15-72-1-pb-1.pdf

National Forum for the Enhancement of Teaching and Learning in Higher Education (National Forum), 2021. *Seven Cs for Embedding Student Success: A Toolkit for Higher Education Institutions.* Available at: https://studentsuccess.teachingandlearning.ie/ (accessed: 29 December 2021).

National Forum for the Enhancement of Teaching and Learning in Higher Education (National Forum), 2019a. *Understanding and Enabling Student Success in Irish Higher Education.* Available at: www.teachingandlearning.ie/publication/understanding-and-enabling-student-success-in-irish-higher-education/ (accessed: 9 March 2020).

National Forum for the Enhancement of Teaching and Learning in Higher Education (National Forum), 2019b. *Developing Learning Analytics Policies to Support Student Success.* Available at: www.teachingandlearning.ie/publication/developing-learning-analytics-policies-to-support-student-success/ (accessed: 21 December 2021).

National Forum for the Enhancement of Teaching and Learning in Higher Education (National Forum), 2019c. *INDEx Survey.* Available at: www.teachingandlearning.ie/index/ (accessed: 21 December 2021).

National Student Engagement Programme (NStEP), 2019. *Strategy 2019–2021.* Available at: https://nstepsite.files.wordpress.com/2019/11/nstep-strategy-2019-2021-online.pdf (accessed: 9 May 2020).

Nemanick, Jr, R.C. and Clark, E.M., 2002. The differential effects of extracurricular activities on attributions in resume evaluation. *International Journal of Selection and Assessment*, 10(3), pp.206–217. https://doi.org/10.1111/1468-2389.00210

Pickford, R., 2016. Student Engagement: Body, Mind and Heart – A Proposal for an Embedded Multi-Dimensional Student Engagement Framework. *Journal of Perspectives in Applied Academic Practice*, 4(2), pp.25–32. https://doi.org/10.14297/jpaap.v4i2.198

Poole, V.A. and Zahn, D.K., 1993. Define and teach employability skills to guarantee student success. *The Clearing House*, 67(1), pp.55–59. https://doi.org/10.1080/00098655.1993.9956019

Quality Assurance Agency for Higher Education (QAA), 2012. *UK Quality Code for Higher Education – Part B: Assuring and Enhancing Academic Quality – Chapter B5: Student Engagement.* Available at: www.qaa.ac.uk/quality-code/UK-Quality-Code-for-Higher-Education-2013-18 (accessed: 9 May 2020).

Shacklock, X., 2016. *From Bricks to Clicks – The Potential of Data and Analytics in Higher Education* (Project Report). London: Higher Education Commission.

Society for Learning Analytics Research (SOLAR), 2011. *What is Learning Analytics?* Available at: www.solaresearch.org/about/what-is-learning-analytics/ (accessed: 1 September 2021).

Stuart, M., Lido, C., Morgan, J. and May, S., 2009. *Student Diversity, Extra-Curricular Activities and Perceptions of Graduate Outcomes* (Project Report). York: Higher Education Academy.

Tchibozo, G., 2007. Extra-curricular activity and the transition from higher education to work: A survey of graduates in the United Kingdom. *Higher Education Quarterly*, 61(1), pp.37–56. http://dx.doi.org/10.1111/j.1468-2273.2006.00337.x

Thompson, L.J., Clark, G., Walker, M. and Whyatt, J.D., 2013. "It's just like an extra string to your bow": Exploring higher education students' perceptions and experiences of extracurricular activity and employability. *Active Learning in Higher Education*, 14 (2), pp.135–147. http://dx.doi.org/10.1177/1469787413481129

Tight, M., 2019. Student retention and engagement in higher education. *Journal of Further and Higher Education*, 44(5), pp.689–704. https://doi.org/10.1080/0309877X.2019.1576860

Tinto, V., 2012. Enhancing student success: Taking the classroom success seriously. *Student Success*, 3(1), p.1. http://dx.doi.org/10.5204/intjfyhe.v3i1.119

Tinto, V., 1993. *Leaving College: Rethinking the Causes and Cures of Student Attrition* (2nd edn). Chicago, IL: University of Chicago Press.

Thomas, L., 2002. Student retention in higher education: The role of institutional habitus. *Journal of Education Policy*, 17(4), pp.423–442. https://doi.org/10.1080/02680930210140257

Tomlinson, M., 2017. Student engagement: Towards a critical policy sociology. *Higher Education Policy*, 30(1), pp.35–52. http://dx.doi.org/10.1057/s41307-016-0035-3

Tsai, Y.-S., Gašević, D., Whitelock-Wainwright, A., Muñoz-Merino, P.J., Moreno-Marcos, P. M., Fernández, A.R., Kloos, C.D., Scheffel, M., Jivet, I., Drachsler, H., Tammets, K., Calleja, A.R. and Kollom, K., 2018. *SHEILA: Supporting Higher Education to Intergrate Learning Analytics Research Report*. Available at: https://sheilaproject.eu/wp-content/up loads/2018/11/SHEILA-research-report.pdf (accessed: 1 September 2021).

van der Velden, G., 2012. Institutional level student engagement and organisational cultures. *Higher Education Quarterly*, 66(3), pp.227–247. https://doi.org/10.1111/j.1468-2273.2012.00521.x

Zepke, N., 2015. Student engagement research: Thinking beyond the mainstream. *Higher Education Research & Development*, 34(6), pp.1311–1323. http://dx.doi.org/10.1080/07294360.2015.1024635

Zepke, N., 2014. Student engagement research in higher education: Questioning an academic orthodoxy. *Teaching in Higher Education*, 19(6), pp.697–708. http://dx.doi.org/10.1080/13562517.2014.901956

Widening the aperture on college students' sense of belonging

A critical ecological perspective

Terrell L. Strayhorn

> It's like everything was telling me... I belong here. I matter to *this school* [emphasis added]. Admissions kept my parents informed because it's like they knew that would be important to me. They asked for preferred pronouns during enrollment confirmation, like they knew I would need that. Every action caused a reaction... me realizing, I belong here.
>
> (JB, 2nd year, communications major)

College students' sense of belonging is a key to educational success for *all* students in higher education. Everybody wants to belong and it is a basic human need that takes on heightened importance at certain times, in certain places, and under certain conditions where individuals feel vulnerable or prone to alienation, isolation, invisibility, marginalization, or judgment (Strayhorn, 2019). Although decades of empirical research has consistently suggested that sense of belonging matters in college (e.g., Freeman et al., 2007; Strayhorn, 2020b), the role belonging plays in shaping college students' experiences, the meaning they make of critical moments, and whether and how the university can foster conditions that nurture or enable students' sense of belonging varies greatly across diverse groups.

Diversity is a hallmark of higher education in democratic countries like the United States (US), which is primarily reflected in the variety of institutions and students. Consider, for instance, that over 4,300 colleges and universities comprise the US sector, including more than 2,000 two-year community colleges, 600 comprehensive colleges, 260 research universities, and 103 historically Black colleges and universities (HBCUs); HBCUs represent just 3% of the enterprise but enroll over 300,000 students annually. Women outnumber men on most college campuses, over one-third of all students are first in their family to attend college (hereafter, 'first-generation'), and with ethnoracial minorities (Brady et al., 2020), these groups represent the 'new majority' of today's college students in the US.

The weight of empirical evidence, to date, focuses almost exclusively on traditional-age, undergraduate students who enter higher education immediately after high school graduation (Cole and Kinzie, 2021; Hoffman et al., 2002). Obscured in existing scholarship are the experiences of the new majority, which also includes low-income, immigrant (George Mwangi, 2016), parenting students, and youth

DOI: 10.4324/9781003271789-23

in/from foster care (Johnson, 2021). For example, there are approximately 21 million students enrolled in US postsecondary education, including 3.8% parenting students; 10–20% gay, lesbian, bisexual, transgender (GLBT) students, and women who outnumber men by a margin of nearly 3 to 1 (Rankin, 2006; US Department of Education, 2020). The weight of empirical evidence demonstrates that key factors and conditions like engagement (Kuh, 2003), involvement (Astin, 1997), and belonging (Strayhorn, 2019; Walton and Cohen, 2011) matter for student success based on traditional samples, but much more information is needed to assess and understand the role that sense of belonging plays on those in the new majority who have been *marginalized* or 'pushed to the margins' of campus life, the sidelines of scholarship, and the periphery of policy and programmatic focus.

In this chapter, the author 'widens the aperture' on college students' sense of belonging by presenting a *critical ecological perspective* on Strayhorn's (2019) model that takes into account environmental, institutional, and broader societal factors. Using anecdotes and data from his various belonging studies over the past decade, he casts much-needed attention to students living on the margins of the 'campus bubble' in a way that calls educators to radically inclusive, equitable practices that expand the bubble for all.

Problem statement

Student success is a major indicator of institutional effectiveness in higher education. Consider the fact that the US Department of Education monitors postsecondary institutions' eligibility for federal aid through Title III and Title IV based on a range of factors including default rates, fiscal stability, and four-year graduation rates. The *US News and World Report* ranks colleges and universities annually, placing the greatest weight on measures of students' academic progress including first-year retention and four- and six-year graduation rates. Despite the emphasis placed on student success metrics in national ranking and regional accreditation standards, still today only about 50% of all college students complete their degree within six years of initial college entry. Rates are generally low(-est) among new majority populations, including historically underrepresented and minoritized groups such as ethnoracial minorities, first-generation, low-income, and non-traditional aged students, averaging 30% (US Department of Education, 2020).

One factor that has shown to be a key to educational success is sense of belonging (Strayhorn, 2019) or, generally, the nature and quality of students' positive relationships with others on campus. Though definitions vary, belonging is typically defined as "students' perceived social support on campus, a feeling or sensation of connectedness, the experience of mattering or feeling cared about, accepted, respected, valued by, and important to the group or others on campus" (Strayhorn, 2012, p.3). It also refers to a shared faith or belief that an individual's needs (i.e., basic, academic, and emotional) will be met or satisfied *by the group*, as part of their commitment to be together. Sense of belonging encompasses authentic feelings of acceptance, inclusion, mattering, visibility, and value.

A strong, and growing, corpus of studies has shown that belonging is consistently linked with positive outcomes. For instance, research indicates that high levels of belonging lead to purposeful life (Guo and Cheng, 2016), good grades (Anderman and Freeman, 2004), and academic success (Strayhorn, 2021) even among Black students at HBCUs, largely based on individual- or person-level processes such as peer-to-peer support. But more information is needed to understand how institutional and broader societal forces condition, cultivate, conspire, or compromise *sense of belonging* for new majority students in higher education. This is the gap addressed by the present chapter.

Sense of belonging: a critical socioecological view

Sense of belonging is a basic human need that affects human behaviors (Maslow, 1954), though not experienced equitably by all groups. Sense of belonging is part of a larger set of human desires and yearnings that crave satisfaction, each associated with positive outcomes in relevant domains. For example, sense of belonging is consistently correlated with greater college satisfaction, educationally purposeful engagement, and improved academic, work, and health practices among ethnoracial minority students (Carales and Nora, 2020; Ostrove and Long, 2007; Strayhorn, 2020a, 2020b).

A preponderance of evidence suggests that college students' sense of belonging ascends in importance at certain times, under certain conditions, and in certain spaces where individuals holding marginalized or *minoritized* [1] identities are prone to feeling anxious, stereotyped, or vulnerable for alienation, isolation, or judgment (Bui, 2002; Strayhorn, 2021). For instance, JB, the sophomore featured in the chapter's opening vignette, explained via interview that his first year in college was rife with challenges, self-doubt, and setbacks. He spent considerable time worrying about making friends, being accepted just as he is, and adjusting to college life. Anxiety and fear gave rise to confidence and competence over time, especially as he met new people, joined clubs, and gained a sense of pride for being celebrated by campus media and friends as a male cheerleader. But, as JB's story reveals, *student* sense of belonging is often shaped by broader socioecological currents— namely, a constellation of *structural*, organizational, and *societal* forces—that can instigate, inspire or inhibit perceptions of campus climate and social supports, to name a few. For instance, imagine if JB attended an institution that did not offer clubs and organizations related to his interests, one that failed to feature students like him in campus communications (e.g., website, newspaper), or one that lacked resources to sustain a cheerleading program. It is unlikely that JB would develop a sense of belonging in such contexts. Figure 23.1 presents a graphical summary of the revised critical socioecological model.

There are other ways that *individual* sense of belonging contends with prevailing *institutional* conditions, campus cultures, and broader societal forces. Indeed,

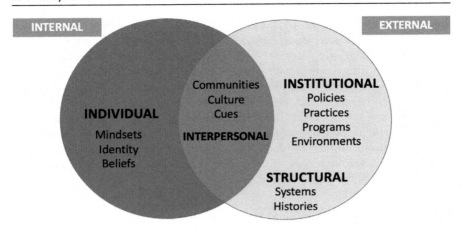

Figure 23.1 Modified sense of belonging critical socioecological model

individual or *material* insecurities intertwine with the larger institutional and structural forces that conspire to constrict or construct identity, membership, and community as consequences of individual effort (i.e., failure), organizational dysfunction, or structural disadvantage. For instance, without a critical socioecological frame in mind, educators would wrongly conclude that JB's *belonging uncertainty* at the start of college is an indicator of academic unreadiness, rather than a common feeling among entering students and an opportunity for the institution to take strategic steps to *affirm* his belonging through parental outreach, student engagement, early alerts, and community-building experiences vis-à-vis clubs, organizations, and university-sanctioned teams like cheerleading. A critical view on belonging that accounts for organizational responsibilities helps avoid the risk of pathologizing students, placing priority on changing institutional structures and provisions, not just students, as I have said elsewhere (Strayhorn, 2019).

A critical socioecological perspective on sense of belonging highlights the ways in which individual and group distinctions (e.g., at-risk, undecided) are established through institutional and broader discourses, including dominant narratives about who and what constitutes 'college material', 'academically prepared', and 'underrepresented minorities' (URMs), to name a few. A critical perspective intentionally challenges dominant ideologies like meritocracy, race neutrality, and respectability of differently positioned groups or subjects. For example, in the full interview, JB and other students like him explained that there were times when they felt ignored, invisible, or overlooked by faculty and staff who did not "see them as college material", to quote a few. Such judgments shaped the advice and support they received—"it's like they didn't think I could do it so it wasn't worth really helping me or going out of their way... which made me feel stupid like I guess I shouldn't be here" (JB). So it is not just the interpersonal interaction that diminished JB's sense of belonging, but he reveals in his own words how dominant images powerfully shaped college student personnel's beliefs, which, in turn, influenced their policies, practices, and work with students like JB. Prevailing beliefs in society and the broader institutional environment condition *perspectives* and *practices* of personnel at the organizational level, which, in turn, influence *what they do* with students at the individual, person-to-person level. Indeed, the intertwining of multi-level factors across a critical socioecological perspective avoids inadvertently homogenizing the college experience, erasing or ignoring the impact of inequality that structures students' lives, and downplaying the social nightmares that threaten *some* students' educational dreams. Figure 23.2 presents a graphical analysis.

Students who lack the basic, material, and cultural resources to assure safety and security, achieve community, and connectedness often get rendered as morally inept, cognitively delayed, socially awkward, or 'alien', to quote insights from my studies over the last decade. Such students become public symbols of failure, disengagement, or misconduct, not part of the campus bubble negatively impacted (intentionally or unintentionally) by larger institutional and structural currents. This clearly demonstrates the limits of constructing sense of belonging as a mere function of individual behaviors, choices, or mindsets, rather than a multilevel social phenomenon (Strayhorn, 2019). For instance, without adequate structural diversity (i.e., sheer numbers of diverse people) on campus, some students of color will struggle to "find their crew [village]" or "build a squad", as some study participants say, among same-race or ethnoracial peers (Strayhorn, 2020a). Traditional models blame the student for being anti-social, close-minded, or 'failing to *find* a sense of belonging', whereas a critical socioecological view directs attention to the institutional and structural problems that act as barriers to meaningful cross-racial interactions, as well as engagement with fellow peers and campus personnel. For instance, in my interview study with Black medical school students, I found that these students struggled to 'see themselves' as bona fide members of the department and profession *not because* they were academically underprepared or lacked interpersonal skills, but because there were too few faculty of color to serve as advisors and role models. It is also true that exposure to racialized stereotypes negatively impacted their perception of the school's climate.

There are other examples. An insecure labor market, high levels of unemployment, homelessness, hunger, anxiety, threats to physical safety and security, hostile housing markets (buying or renting) all constitute structural conditions for students' sense of belonging/alienation, especially as changing structures make familial support more or less secure. When we focus or define the *campus bubble* based on typical conceptions of 'family' per se, we assume that basic needs are met, safety is set, and students are supported by families to move away, enroll, and return as needed. We miss, however, how some new majority students, like former foster youth, may have limited or tenuous relationships with biological parents or siblings making it difficult to determine *if* they are first-generation, low-income, 'legacy' (i.e., alumni-related), or connected to others on campus. It's also important to note that some may experience homelessness or financial insecurity

Self-actualization
creativity
innovation,
self-authorship, morality,
spontaneity, integrity

Esteem:
respect, confidence,
achievement

Love and Belongingness:
care, support, mattering, community

Safety and Security: physical, emotional,
financial, spiritual, food, housing

Physiological Needs: air, water, food, shelter, sleep, sex

INDIVIDUAL	INSTITUTIONAL	STRUCTURAL
Learning Partners(hip) Pathways & Roadmaps Critical Consciousness Ethics	Learning Communities Promoting Experimentation Taking Risks Organizational Agility	Acknowledging Cultural Norms Admitting Barriers Mitigating Risks Avoiding Linearity Assumption
Role-modeling Practice Verbal Persuasion	Communicating Positivity Nurturing Sense of Pride Providing Collective Identity	Acknowledging Shame Avoiding Systematic Defense Respectability Politics
Mattering -Attention -Dependence -Importance -Ego-extension	Prioritizing Community Celebrating Connectedness Framing Unity Rewarding Engagement Praising Difference	Acknowledging Histories Admitting Racist Origins Imagining Inclusive Futures Mapping Fixed Terrains
Personal Space Mental Health/Self-Care Work for Pay Meditation/Prayer Purposeful Living	Prioritizing Safety & Security Setting Security Standards Codes of Conduct Sanctions for Violations NEW: Cybersecurity & Zoom	Acknowledging Threat Histories Admitting Need for Standards Historical Trauma & Toll Power & Privilege
Basic Needs (In)Security Breathe Eat Rest Take breaks	Basic Needs (In)Security Raise Awareness Campus-sponsored Pantries State-aided Clothing Closets Prioritizing Holistic Wellness	Systemic Basic Needs Inequities Historical Ignorance Patterns of Discrimination Geographies: Food Deserts

Figure 23.2 Modified sense of belonging critical socioecological model with intertwined levels

(Johnson, 2021), tied to deprivation of family support as they 'choose college over family' and, thus, may be excluded from trips, transitions, and traditions (e.g., orientation, study abroad, graduation) idealized by contemporary discourses of college and sense of belonging taking place inside the campus bubble.

A critical socioecological perspective on sense of belonging, like the one posited here, also interrogates the symbolic meaning of 'home' that historically is associated with the idea that one belongs in this world. This critical view intentionally draws attention to the complexity of the concept in ways that contest idealized visions of home as a place of comfort, acceptance, security, freedom, and attachment to significant others and unconditional love (Lahelma and Gordon, 2003). For some new majority students, home is often a dangerous and insecure place, a site of rejection, and a touchpoint of untreated trauma (Arnold, 2004, p.71). One trans woman of color said it succinctly in my study: "Home is now wherever I am... that former place called home is unsafe and I may likely never return". So, sense of belonging is not always about building 'family-like bonds' with campus personnel or 'making the campus feel like home', but rather about fostering positive, supportive, healthy relationships between staff and students in a campus climate that is welcoming, inclusive, safe, affirming, anti-racist, bias-free, and where they feel they belong.

Recap of the contribution

The profound and pervasive framing of sense of belonging as a social phenomenon resulting from individual behaviors or personal choices locates many students, especially URMs, outside the campus bubble. By campus bubble, I refer to the normative community of traditional students—whose experiences are often represented by the idealized image of a well-formed box, straight arrow, or bubble (see Figure 23.3). Although some equity-minded models acknowledge and affirm students' indigenous knowledges, complex economies of membership, and *discourses of decisions* (Strayhorn, 2015), far too many fail to incorporate institutional or broader societal and organizational currents that conspire to structure sense of belonging. The view advanced in this chapter builds upon Strayhorn (2019), positing a critical socioecological perspective that situates students within these broader intersections. For instance, some students, like JB and so many others, in my studies describe their hesitancy to connect or make friends due to difficulty finding those who share their interests, navigating unfamiliar campus spaces, and accessing learning supports necessary for their educational success. Let us not miss that some students have daily encounters with campus environments characterized by profound material and personal insecurity, threats of violence, harassment, and intimidation created by their precarity; institutions must protect against such threats by securing the safety and security of *all* students through formulation and implementation of appropriate policies, procedures, and protocols including, but not limited to, Title IX protections, anti-harassment, and anti-discrimination statements.

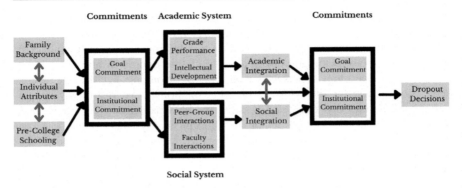

Figure 23.3 Traditional student retention model with boxes and arrows
Adapted from Tinto (1993)

Lastly, structural racism perpetuates unemployment, housing insecurity, and even school takeovers in densely populated urban centers, which reduces the likelihood that some new majority students will enroll in college. Even when they do enroll, without intervention, such students are less likely to encounter faculty and peers like them *or* to see themselves reflected in the curriculum, which can level or reduce their sense of belonging and, consequently, their academic performance and persistence. Classical explanations of sense of belonging are silent on these linkages. A critical socioecological perspective, however, acknowledges these relations and exposes how they provide group affiliation, recognition, and personal affirmation of worth to some while disadvantaging others. A socioecological perspective underscores how students' sense of belonging, in this case, can be boosted by institutions investing in recruiting diverse faculty, training instructors on inclusive critically conscious pedagogies, and revising curriculum to incorporate global perspectives.

A word of caution

It is important to note that a critical socioecological perspective need not entail or insist upon wholesale rejection of classical explanations—there is no need to throw out the baby with the bathwater, so to speak. Rather, a critical socioecological perspective's distinctive contribution goes beyond traditional hypotheses to establish the importance of organizational, institutional, and political considerations in the belonging project. In that way, it supplements rather than supplants prior postulations.

A critical socioecological perspective enhances our understanding of why and how the terms and conditions of human needs vary within and across people and groups in several ways. First, a critical perspective rejects the assumption of 'level playing fields', perfect hierarchies, and linearity as bearing little semblance to reality, especially for URMs in higher education. Second, this perspective suggests that classical belonging theory is limited because it does not explicitly account for the role of power, privilege, or structural (dis)advantage in the overall process. A critical view attempts to correct prior descriptions by making the implicit explicit and putting to words what is generally left unspoken. Third, a critical perspective challenges classical analyses viewing sense of belonging as purely personal exchange—it is social relations conditioned by broader institutional and societal forces.

Again, the goal of this chapter is not to generate a convincing theoretical alternative to classical analysis. Rather, the aim is to increase theoretical correspondence to reality by providing language for talking about these constructs, and, thus, improving accounts of (in)equality and sense of belonging that go beyond the strictures of classical paradigms where differences get touted as deficiencies and *structural* conditions masquerade as individual choices. This discussion allows for a more distinctly sociological explanation of belonging. I urge future researchers, practitioners, and policymakers to use it in their work to 'widen the aperture' on belonging and expand the campus bubble to include those in the new majority who have been pushed to the margins of main campus, the sidelines of scholarship, and the periphery of our critical gaze as educators.

Note

1 I use the term 'minoritized' to acknowledge and refer to the systematic subjugation, underrepresentation, subordination and oppression of people of color in some US social institutions such as colleges and schools, in keeping with others (Harper and Cole, 2012). It is used interchangeably with ethnic/racial 'minority' and 'ethnoracial minority'.

References

Anderman, L.H. and Freeman, T.M., 2004. Students' sense of belonging in school. In Maehr, M.L. and Pintrich, P.R. (ed), *Advances in Motivation and Achievement* (Vol. 13). Amsterdam: Elsevier. https://doi.org/10.1016/s0749-7423(03)13002-6

Arnold, K., 2004. *Homelessness, Citizenship, and Identity: The Uncanniness of Late Modernity*. New York: State University Press of New York.

Astin, A.W., 1997. *What Matters in College?* San Francisco, CA: Jossey-Bass.

Brady, S.T., Cohen, G.L., Jarvis, S.N. and Walton, G.M., 2020. A brief social-belonging intervention in college improves adult outcomes for black Americans. *Science Advances*, 6(18), pp.1–12. https://doi.org/https://doi.org/10.1126/sciadv.aay3689

Bui, K., 2002. First-generation college students at a four-year university: Background characteristics, reasons for pursuing higher education, and first-year experiences. *College Student Journal*, 36(1), pp.3–9.

Carales, V.D. and Nora, N., 2020. Finding place: Cognitive and psychosocial factors impacting Latina/o students' sense of belonging. *Journal of Student Affairs Research and Practice*. https://doi.org/https://doi.org/10.1080/19496591.2019.1662795

Cole, J. and Kinzie, J., 2021. *Sense of Belonging and the First-Year Experience*. Bloomington, IN: Center for Postsecondary Report, Indiana University.

Freeman, T.M., Anderman, L.H. and Jensen, J.M., 2007. Sense of belonging in college freshmen at the classroom and campus levels. *The Journal of Experimental Education*, 75(3), pp.203–220. https://doi.org/10.3200/jexe.75.3.203-220

George Mwangi, C.A., 2016. Exploring sense of belonging among Black international students at an HBCU. *Journal of International Students*, 6(4), pp.1015–1037. https://doi.org/10.32674/jis.v6i4.332

Guo, T.-C., and Cheng, Z.-C., 2016. Sense of belonging based on novel posting. *Online Information Review*, 40(2), pp.204–217. https://doi.org/10.1108/oir-06-2015-0198

Harper, M., and Cole, P., 2012. Member checking: Can benefits be gained similar to group therapy? *The Qualitative Report*, 17(2), pp.510–517. https://doi.org/10.46743/2160-3715/2012.2139

Hoffman, M., Richmond, J., Morrow, J. and Salomone, K., 2002. Investigating sense of belonging in first-year college students. *Journal of College Student Retention: Research, Theory and Practice*, 4(3), pp.227–256. https://doi.org/10.2190/dryc-cxq9-jq8v-ht4v

Johnson, R.M., 2021. The state of research on undergraduate youth formerly in foster care: A systematic review of the literature. *Journal of Diversity in Higher Education*, 14(1), pp.147–160. https://doi.org/10.1037/dhe0000150

Kuh, G.D., 2003. What we're learning about student engagement from NSSE. *Change*, 35 (2), pp.24–32. https://doi.org/10.1080/00091380309604090

Lahelma, E. and Gordon, T., 2003. Home as a physical, social, and mental space: Young people's reflections on leaving home. *Journal of Youth Studies*, 6(4), pp.377–390. https://doi.org/10.1080/1367626032000162104

Maslow, A.H., 1954. *Motivation and Personality*. New York: Harper and Row Publishers.

Ostrove, J.M. and Long, S.M., 2007. Social class and belonging: Implications for college adjustment. *The Review of Higher Education*, 30(4), pp.363–389. https://doi.org/10.1353/rhe.2007.0028

Rankin, S.R., 2006. LGBTA students on campus: Is higher education making the grade? *Journal of Gay and Lesbian Issues in Education*, 3(2/3), pp.111–117. https://doi.org/10.1300/j367v03n02_11

Strayhorn, T.L., 2021. Analyzing the short-term impact of a brief web-based intervention on first-year students' sense of belonging at an HBCU: A quasi-experimental study. *Innovative Higher Education*. https://doi.org/https://doi.org/10.1007/s10755-021-09559-5

Strayhorn, T.L., 2020a. Exploring the role of race in Black males' sense of belonging in medical school: A qualitative pilot study. *Medical Science Educator*, 30, pp.1383–1387. https://doi.org/10.1007/s40670-020-01103-y

Strayhorn, T.L., 2020b. Measuring the relation between sense of belonging, campus leadership, and academic achievement for African American students at historically Black colleges and universities (HBCUs): A 'gender equity' analysis. *Journal of Minority Achievement, Creativity, and Leadership*, 1(1), pp.94–118. https://doi.org/https://doi.org/10.5325/minoachicrealead.1.1.0094

Strayhorn, T.L., 2019. *College Students' Sense of Belonging: A Key to Educational Success for All Students* (2nd edn). New York: Routledge.

Strayhorn, T.L., 2015. Reframing academic advising for student success: From advisor to cultural navigator. *Journal of the National Academic Advising Association*, 35(1), pp.56–63. https://doi.org/10.12930/nacada-14-199

Strayhorn, T.L., 2012. *College Students' Sense of Belonging: A Key to Educational Success for All Students*. New York: Routledge.

Tinto, V., 1993. *Leaving College: Rethinking the Causes and Cures of Student Attrition* (2nd edn). Chicago, IL: University of Chicago Press.

US Department of Education, 2020. *The Condition of Education 2019.* Available at: https://nces.ed.gov/pubsearch/pubsinfo.asp?pubid=2019144 (accessed: 16 May 2021).

Walton, G.M., and Cohen, G.L., 2011. A brief social-belonging intervention improves academic and health outcomes of minority students. *Science*, 331(March), pp.1447–1451. https://doi.org/10.1126/science.1198364

Chapter 24

Valhalla and Nirvana

Views of Arnstein's ladder of citizen participation in further and higher education

Simon Varwell

Introduction

Higher education in 2022 remains in a period of unparalleled change, with COVID-19 causing "reduced engagement and disrupted learning opportunities" (Hill and Fitzgerald, 2020, p.6), but simultaneously a "significant (and perhaps, unexpected) influence on dialogue on the role of student partnership in institutional decision-making" (Hassan et al., 2020, p.1). Indeed,

> the challenges of the COVID-19 pandemic (and, yes, some opportunities) have shaped the 2020–21 year in ways that have revealed so much about the resilience and continuing importance of students and students' associations engaging as partners in quality.
>
> (sparqs, 2021, p.3)

Of course, universities and colleges are experiencing similar pressures to other public services where comparable debates about citizen participation began (Falanga, 2020; Moon, 2020). Therefore, there is merit in re-evaluating the role of students as partners through a lens of wider public engagement. I aim to do so using a classic tool for exploring how people shape the world around them: Sherry Arnstein's ladder of citizen participation (Arnstein, 1969). This ladder is an eight-rung scale, divided into three groups, ranging from manipulating stakeholders so they agree to pre-determined decisions, through to full citizen control. It has been adapted by Student Partnerships in Quality Scotland (Scotland's agency for student engagement; sparqs) (n.d.-a; Figure 24.1), adding a short narrative to explain each rung. It has been described as "a simple yet elegant characterization of the problems and prospects for achieving more meaningful participation of communities in the public decisions that affect them" (Lauria and Schively Slotterback, 2021, p.1). Since its development in 1960s American urban planning, it has "offered inspiration for a new practice of participation that centered people, communities and power" (ibid.) and features prominently in collections of diagrammatical frameworks for stakeholder engagement (Hussey, 2020; nonformality.org, 2011; Burns and Heywood, 2004, pp.49–71).

DOI: 10.4324/9781003271789-24

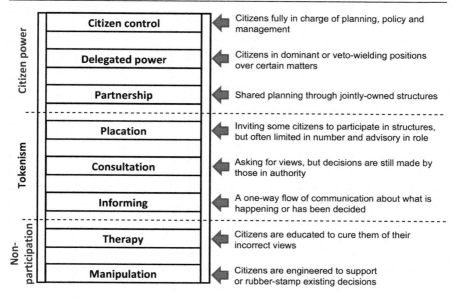

Figure 24.1 sparqs' version of Arnstein's ladder
sparqs (n.d.-a)

At sparqs we often use the ladder, and our above adaptation, to prompt staff and student reflections on partnership and engagement. While many models exist to benchmark or develop how students shape learning and quality (Varwell, 2021), Arnstein's ladder of citizen participation stands out due to its prominence within literature and practice. Hussey (2020, para. 1) points to "the emergence of 60 public participation models since its inception".

Although there is considerable literature addressing the ladder's value in assessing student engagement in higher education, little so far is from the pandemic era (Woods and Botcherby, 2021; Varwell, 2022a). This chapter's purpose, therefore, is to critically assess the value of Arnstein's iconic ladder for contemporary student engagement, through interviews with ten individuals in further and higher education who have used it in research or workshops. From these interviews and a literature review (Varwell, 2022b), there are lessons about partnership as the sector moves to a still-fragile near future, and about the ladder's efficacy for universities and colleges.

Literature review

Arnstein's ladder of citizen participation has shaped stakeholder participation in many sectors (Varwell, 2022b). This includes planning and design, where it originates (Schively Slotterback and Lauria, 2019; Lauria and Schively Slotterback, 2021; Gaber, 2021; Natarajan, 2019a; Natarajan, 2019b). It has also been researched or applied in housing (Cullen, 2005; Hall and Hickman, 2011); healthcare (Frankena et al., 2015; Nitsch et al., 2013; Marent et al., 2012; Dukhanin et al., 2018); and schools (Stelmach, 2016; Mavuso and Duku, 2014; Fletcher, 2005; Hart, 1992). The ladder is criticised for its simplicity (Tritter and McCallum, 2006), though it is mapped favourably against comparable typologies (Stewart, 2012). Arnstein's creation has inspired adaptations that add extra rungs (Prieto Martín, 2014) or axes (Romanin, 2013; Badham and Davies, 2007), convert the ladder to a wheel (Davidson, 1998; Varwell, 2022) or even re-imagine it as an A-style (de Leeuw, 2021) or X-style model (Hurlbert and Gupta, 2015).

Higher education, too, has a rich body of literature about the ladder exploring many aspects of the student experience, including three articles (Bovill and Bulley, 2011; Carey, 2018; Buckley, 2018) that prompted some of my interviews. Bovill and Bulley's adaptation presents a model for active student participation in curriculum design. Carey (2018, p.14) maps the ladder onto his own nested hierarchy of student engagement, highlighting the nature of the institution and the role of students at each of the eight rungs. Finally, Buckley (2018) compares Arnstein's original ladder with a model developed by Fielding (2012) that is in turn derived from Hart (1992).

There is notable application of Arnstein's ladder in Ireland's changing higher education sector, informing the creation of the National Student Engagement Programme (Collins et al., 2016, p.12) and reflection on institutional merger (Feeney et al., 2020). It has also been used to analyse student engagement in campus design in Australia (O'Rourke and Baldwin, 2016) and quality assurance in Zimbabwe (Jingura et al., 2018). Notably, however, there is minimal research on Arnstein within further education (Homer, 2019; Rudd et al., 2006).

Methodology

The interviews that informed my research were conducted online in summer 2021. Three interviews from literature were with authors who had written about Arnstein's ladder in higher education (Bovill and Bulley, 2011; Buckley, 2018; Carey, 2018), and sought to dig further into their analyses of Arnstein's ladder and understand more about the contexts for their research.

A further six interviews from practice involved individuals who experienced Arnstein's ladder in two types of workshops I have led in my work at sparqs. One was our Student Engagement Analysis Workshop (sparqs, n.d.-b), delivered in over a dozen institutions during sparqs' consultancy to Ireland's nascent National Student Engagement Programme (Collins et al., 2016) between 2016 and 2019 and then piloted in Scotland in 2019. The second was sparqs' contribution to the College Development Network's Governance Development Programme for members of Scottish college boards of management (sparqs, n.d.-c; College Development Network, n.d.). These interviews explored participants' views of Arnstein's ladder as a tool for reflecting on partnership within their role, and their sense of how partnership had recently developed especially during the pandemic.

The six represented a diversity of staff, student and governor roles, with a broad demographic spread including an equal gender split, two individuals from ethnic minorities, and at least one who self-identified in their interview as LGBT. Brief biographies of the six, plus the codes I use to refer to them throughout this chapter, are as follows.

- **P1: a non-clinical health service manager** who was recently a college board chair and university governor, and is now a students' association trustee.
- **P2: a legal professional** who was a current member of a college board of management.
- **P3: a recent HE arts graduate** who encountered the ladder at a student engagement analysis workshop.
- **P4: a senior learning and teaching manager** in higher education who engaged with the ladder in a student engagement analysis workshop.
- **P5: a quality officer** in an HE institution who participated in a student engagement analysis workshop in a similar previous institution.
- **P6: a national agency practitioner** who, when in a previous student officer role, attended a student engagement analysis workshop featuring the ladder.

sparqs' use of the ladder in the two workshop formats paused following COVID-19's disruption to our work, so these six interviewees' facilitated experience of the ladder occurred no later than 2019. Therefore, I shared a link in the interview to sparqs' version of the ladder (sparqs, n.d.-a; Figure 24.1) to root conversation, remind participants of the ladder's nuances, and "provide a common stimulus for each interviewee" (Newby, 2014, p.343). The six interviewees from practice seemed to appreciate this chance to re-engage with the ladder, with one stating "I've enjoyed the conversation because even just taking the time to talk about [the ladder] has been the thing that's been missing for me". Another said of their interview: "I think in a way it has sort of reinforced to me the power of [the ladder] as this really quite extraordinary tool".

Findings

Power and perceptions of Arnstein's ladder

My interviews revealed four themes in relation to Arnstein's ladder: the role of management; the place of partnership; equality and diversity; and a collectivised student voice. Before I explore them, it is worth noting that the ten interviewees overwhelmingly shared enthusiasm for the ladder and saw value in it. All, moreover, spoke of the importance of power to the ladder and the wider conversations it sparked about relationships between staff, students, management and governors. Power is central for Arnstein herself, who argues that "there is a critical difference between going through the empty ritual of participation and having the real power needed to affect the outcome of the process" (Arnstein, 1969, p.216). Indeed, interviewee Alex Buckley observed that the ladder was not merely a "neutral service improvement model" but "explicitly about power and empowering disempowered groups".

Positive general comments about the ladder concerned its simplicity and its value as a conversation starter. "I thought it was a really good talking point to show ranging opinions, without sort of sparking confrontational dialogue", stated P3, while P6 argued "it is a very informative way of thinking about where you are personally but also the structures that you work within". Philip Carey, an interviewee from literature, suggested that despite the criticisms of Arnstein "I think the simplicity of it actually is the reason why people still refer to it today, because it is such an easy metaphor to understand. And it's such a compelling metaphor: the idea of the ladder, the idea of climbing, the idea of evolution".

Similarly, Catherine Bovill stated in her interview that:

> if you start more with a blank sheet of paper I think it's harder sometimes to get to somewhere as quickly. And so even if people's responses are 'that model just doesn't do it for me, because it's missing x', you go 'right, okay, so why is x important?' We're in there, we have a discussion starting.

Some interviewees from practice even described how the ladder had impacted on their own work and thinking. P1 was inspired by their interview to incorporate a question about stakeholder engagement into a recruitment process they were leading at the time.

At the same time, many interviewees also criticised the ladder. P5 suggested that the ladder's more provocative language required careful treatment with some staff and management. Others highlighted the value (but simultaneously the extreme difficulty) of developing a means of truly objective measurement of engagement against the rungs. Interviewees proposed various improvements to the ladder, including aesthetic enhancements to sparqs' version (Figure 24.1), an associated card sort exercise and structural changes to move away from a linearity that many authors reject (Romanin, 2013; Badham and Davies, 2007; Davidson, 1998; de Leeuw, 2021; Hurlbert and Gupta, 2015). As P5 put it, "nothing ever is a linear journey, and you're probably going to be incorporating actually different rungs of the ladder at different times".

The role of management

Of the four themes, this underpinning concept of power perhaps most obviously connects to the role of management, due to decision-makers' power over cultures and structures of engagement. Indeed, management arguably have this power over not only students but other staff and governors. My two interviewees with experience of independent membership of institutional governing bodies, P1 and P2, both recognised management's power over board members (with the possible exception of chairs) which between them they attributed to independent members' unfamiliarity with the institution, the unpaid nature of board roles, perceived influence by management over members' activities and engagements with the institution, and a lack of buy-in by management to true partnership.

Some interviewees noted academic judgement as a factor in reinforcing perceptions of power over individual students and that this created a fear among students and their representatives about giving critical feedback. Philip Carey paraphrased this quandary as "how do I raise negative stuff to the people who are the originators of the negative stuff that is annoying the students I'm representing?" Alex Buckley suggested this was crucial to realising true partnership, arguing that "we have a particular culture of higher education where academic judgement is fundamental. So, yes, I guess to do it really radically, you would have to... really conceptualise how [learning and teaching] is even understood". This level of true partnership was described as 'Valhalla' by P6 and 'Nirvana' by Philip Carey, mirroring recent literature that speaks of "the 'unavoidable' dynamic" which "can be problematic for the implementation of collaborative or partnership dynamics in HE" (Symonds, 2021, p.3). This suggests a level of engagement that can be aspired to but never truly achieved without a transformed sector. Albeit that shouldn't stop us aspiring to it: as Philip Carey observed, "sometimes we get paralysed by the difficult to achieve, rather than seeing the difficult to achieve as something to aim for that will help us at least achieve something along the way".

My interviews and literature review consistently highlighted, therefore, the need for management to willingly cede power in order to change (perceived or actual) decision-making dynamics to enable truly effective engagement. Stelmach (2016) highlights in schools "the imperative of leadership in achieving high levels of parent participation" (p.284). P6 argued that "if you're trying to encourage an institution to move to some element of citizen power or partnership, then it's going to take a lot more culture change, and culture change is going to have to happen by ceding control".

That in turn links to comments about ideology, with many interviewees and literature demanding transparency about the motivations of those using Arnstein's ladder to develop participation. This is found in Stewart (2013), and in Buckley (2018) who argues that "the ideological values behind educational innovations colour their development and implementation" (Buckley, 2018, p.719). He further claims that "any literature on student participation in decision-making that substantially relies on the models of Arnstein or Fielding contains an ideological opposition to neoliberal approaches to higher education" (p.729). Similarly, Prieto Martín (2014) highlights "why" and "what for" as missing questions in community planning.

The use of the ladder can, however, help to reject accusations of neoliberalism in student engagement (Zepke, 2014, 2015) which are countered by Buckley (2018). Indeed, student engagement can be characterised at its most transformational as a firm challenge to neoliberal tendencies within institutional leadership (Dollinger and Mercer-Mapstone, 2009; Matthews et al., 2019), and is central to

Marxist models of education (Neary, 2020). There are arguably risks to such transparency, however, and Alex Buckley cautioned that:

> If you made that [Arnstein's positionality] explicit, then it would be a bit less useful as a mainstream tool because that would strike a lot of people who aren't in the industry of research, or like educational development, or the student movement, as quite radical.

Partnership... and beyond?

The role of management in shaping power dynamics depends, of course, on one's desired rung on Arnstein's ladder. Much literature, and some interviewees, suggested that for certain circumstances lower levels of engagement are more realistic or desirable. "Higher is not always better", argue Bovill and Bulley (2011, p.183), who further suggest that the highest levels of their adapted ladder "seems contrary to what we know about effective learning and teaching, to entirely remove any role for the expert tutor" (p.182). Cullen (2005, p.8) advocates a level beneath partnership in housing, and in health Nitsch et al. (2013) and Marent et al. (2012) are similarly sceptical.

Allied to such views is a supposed vagueness in definitions of partnership and student engagement generally (Ashwin and McVitty, 2015; Trowler, 2015; Leach, 2012). Indeed, P6 argued that partnership risks becoming ill-defined management-speak, and that the two higher rungs of delegated power and citizen control should feature in partnership". P5 even suggested that partnership could include elements of lower rungs; while P1 observed that "partnership has become one of those meaningless phrases that actually doesn't mean anything".

Interviewees were, however, clear about how partnership's placing in Arnstein's ladder highlighted the flaws of lower levels. Many described students sitting on committees (an example of Arnstein's placation) as ineffective and disillusioning, where meetings were rendered inaccessible or unwelcoming by management control. Moreover, even despite difficulties in defining partnership, interviewees could easily articulate what raises engagement from lower rungs towards more meaningful levels. Support and training for student representatives were mentioned, particularly in governance. P1, who had been a chair of a governing body, described one student member who "had great thoughts and great ideas – but she had no confidence" and in meetings "she wouldn't speak". P3 stated that partnership was "about empathy first, so it's coming from a place of understanding the relationship, and the dynamics, its purpose and the objectives of partnership" and described their recent representative role as "like marriage counselling between students and staff".

Other comments in the interviews highlighted the requirement to shift often deeply rooted power dynamics and, as stated earlier, for management to cede control, albeit through potentially small, experimental and incremental steps in either teaching or policy environments. P5 argued that "if you're at the beginning of your journey with student engagement, the first thing you probably do is say 'a student has to sign off on this'". Philip Carey described how he had converted meetings into workshops, stripping away "those rituals of the committee". Many interviewees, however, pointed to national policy as vital, with P6 arguing that the fundamental debate about student engagement

> needs to be something that changes through government policy. Agencies, students' unions and all of those bodies need to be a big part of effectively an exercise that lives and breathes that, because the problem is we're always going to be working in an enhancement space where everyone has a slightly different opinion of it.

The ladder as a tool of equality, diversity and liberation

Interviewees also observed that Arnstein's ladder has a capability to highlight inequalities and empower oppressed groups. This is an important consideration given the increasing emphasis placed on equality within contemporary tertiary education due to movements such as Black Lives Matter (Castillo-Montoya et al., 2019; Dancy et al., 2018), MeToo (Battaglia et al., 2019; Dolamore and Richards, 2020; Dey and Mendes, 2021) and campaigns to decolonise the curriculum (Saini and Begum, 2020; Arday and Mirza, 2018; Bhambra et al., 2018; Le Grange, 2016), many of which were raised by my interviewees.

Yet much literature argues that Arnstein's ladder insufficiently addresses stakeholder diversity and does not allow for nuance in how certain groups might, rightly or wrongly, be involved differently. Tritter and McCallum (2006) argue that Arnstein "fails to reflect the different forms of participation desired in health-related decision-making, or the range of users that exist" (p.162). They point to "invisible users" (p.162), a dynamic also explored by Frankena et al. (2015). Such criticism is unfair given the roots of Arnstein's research and practice in a highly racialised environment (Gaber, 2021) where "neither the have-nots nor the powerholders are homogeneous blocs" (Arnstein, 1969, p.217). Arnstein criticises the political orthodoxy of the day in that it broadly accepted the idea of citizen participation but failed to do so through a socially just lens:

> The applause is reduced to polite handclaps, however, when this principle is advocated by the have-not blacks, Mexican-Americans, Puerto Ricans, Indians, Eskimos,[1] and whites. And when the have-nots define participation as redistribution of power, the American consensus on the fundamental principle explodes into many shades of outright racial, ethnic, ideological, and political opposition.
>
> (p 216)

This powerfully echoes today's debates about race and gender, or scandals of historic abuses in religious and educational institutions. Indeed, Arnstein prophetically commended her typology to other sectors, proposing:

it could just as easily be illustrated in the church, currently facing demands for power from priests and laymen who seek to change its mission; colleges and universities which in some cases have become literal battlegrounds over the issue of student power; or public schools, city halls, and police departments (or big business which is likely to be next on the expanding list of targets).

(Arnstein, 1969, p.217)

There is less such criticism of the ladder among those who apply it in contexts of developing economies and poverty (Hart, 1992; Pétursdóttir, 2011), and my interviewees spoke of the ladder's value in highlighting and exploring issues of inequality. P3 stated that her reflections on the ladder as a woman of colour helped her realised that "historically, I've been very much at the very non-participation point", and that it "gives me the words and peripheral understanding of how I might have been taken advantage of in the past or been complacent of motives".

More positively, that same interviewee was inspired to use the ladder to further explore this issue:

I think I'll use it as a reference point in the future for when I'm advocating for more, like, under-represented groups in leadership positions, because I think it's a really useful tool and, like, viable, and just solid ground of research that I can use to explain where I'm coming from.

A number of interviewees discussed decolonisation of the curriculum as a topic for which the ladder presented a useful prism, highlighting both the importance of decolonisation and difficulties in defining it. Catherine Bovill described HIV-positive patients having to 'come out' in order to represent that demographic in committees. Other interviewees reflected on widening participation, using the ladder to illustrate how diverse voices could be used to inform decision-making through a richer range of views. P4 pointed to their engagement with the ladder through sparqs' facilitation as "the piece that really changed my practice most fundamentally and continues just to be how I think about doing things", describing instances where they had pressed for higher student engagement in policy processes relating to equality and inclusion, "even though sometimes that went beyond the scope of what we were technically required to do, on the basis that this was a whole institution partnership approach to bringing about cultural change".

For Burns and Heywood (2004) the link between diversity and engagement, and the challenge for decision-makers, is clear:

The extent to which institutions are prepared to allow diversity is a strong indicator of the extent to which local participation is real. If communities are able to construct their own plans and identify their own priorities, these will inevitably be different from area to area.

(p.7)

Collectivism and the sustainability of students' associations[2]

In the study of stakeholder engagement, an important consideration is the capacity for collective and not just individual input. The literature and interviews provided reassurance about tertiary education's strength on this, especially for the UK's well-developed context for students' associations (Brooks et al., 2015). Indeed, it has been observed that "students' unions on the whole are larger, more sophisticated and more effective in the UK than any comparable system in Europe or the US" (Day and Dickinson, 2018, p.55). In Scotland's colleges there is a commitment that students' associations "should be strengthened and become appropriately funded, autonomous and sustainable" (Griggs, 2012, p.38), with a resultant national framework (Developing College Students' Associations, 2021).

The idea of professionalised, resourced membership organisations within publicly funded providers distinguishes the further and higher education sectors from others. Unsurprisingly, the complex arena of planning and development features disparate stakeholder organisation where sustainability is a concern and policy is an obstacle to collectivism, for instance where "the organisation of the people could give way to demands that, to be met, would require the established relations with those in power to change. Not all governments are willing to negotiate this kind of innovation" (Choguill, 1996, p.435). The lack of professionalisation of stakeholder collectivism is noted in healthcare (Tritter and McCallum, 2006) and schools (Stelmach, 2016), with Stelmach (2016) and de Leeuw (2021) highlighting a lack of clarity in roles. Meanwhile Burns and Heywood (2004, p.7) call for community involvement to receive "far greater investment in administrative time, dedicated managerial support, and sustainable community development resources".

That is not to argue that students' associations are flawless in comparison, and it is perhaps due to interviewees' close involvement with them that they presented sophisticated observations about the organisations' supposed failings. Prominent among them was the perceived risk of students' associations and their officers not being truly representative. P1 spoke of a gap between the views of student officers and the experiences of student trustees of their association. P5 reported a continuing focus on social activities by their students' association and a failure to recognise the importance of quality enhancement activity. Students' association staff reporting to institutional managers was also identified as a problem by one interviewee. Meanwhile Alex Buckley highlighted the impact of varied students' association effectiveness:

> Some institutions have students' unions that function better, have better reach, so if you're in an institution where the students' union doesn't have great reach to the student population, then the idea that the best way to do it is collective empowerment via the students' union is less persuasive.

Furthermore, the breadth of activity in students' associations can cause challenges for new officers who, interviewees often noted, have a lot to learn across a wide range of responsibilities. Overall, though, the interviewees shared an optimism about student representative structures, and many felt that student bodies were respected and could, at least to an extent, share power. This relationship was summed up by P6, who said that

> students' union officers or students generally or staff in any given role can still disagree, can still fundamentally disagree and dissent on things, but they can still share a sense of power and strategy and vision.

P4 stated that they were always conscious of creating a space for engagement "that's structured in a way that's also respectful of their time, their other commitments". One consequence of this, they continued, was that on a major transformation "the students had more of an understanding of what was going on than some of the staff, because they had access to all of the working groups, and that wasn't shared below a very senior management level".

One interviewee from literature, Philip Carey, even attributed his reflections on representation and student voice as sparking his interest in Arnstein's applicability to higher education:

> I hear the voice in certain ways that represents, that replicates other voices I hear from students that come from evaluation or survey data or the sort of the more casual accidental stuff. And then that led me to think, well, actually that reminds me of stuff that I used to do in community development where we have the sort of consultation moving on to that higher level. So that's what really attracted me originally to Arnstein.

A number of interviewees also mentioned social and political changes as influences on the skills and experiences of student officers, a link explored by Hassan et al. (2020). Movements mentioned earlier like Black Lives Matter are one dimension, but my Irish interviewees spoke of the country's recent constitutional referendums in which many student officers gained campaigning experience, a point noted by Abrahams and Brooks (2019). One interviewee reflected: "If I think about some of the students' union presidents that we've had the pleasure to work with over the last few years, they were through those campaigns, so they understand how they can make things change, very quickly".

Albeit one interviewee argued that while that participation had been a good thing, "it didn't change the power dynamics of the country. It didn't change the way in which government works". Another contrasted this successful civic engagement by students with involvement in the pandemic response, where "suddenly it was totally kind of non-participation. I don't think there was even consultation, really, it was purely… we were being informed about things". They went on to draw a lesson for partnership within institutions from this perceived slide, observing:

I guess it shows that, you know, no matter where you are in the ladder it's not guaranteed, and it requires work and sustained effort and planning to make sure that you maintain the types of relationships that you want to maintain, and we can't just take them for granted. I can't just set up a committee and say 'we're done now'. We have to have a plan for how that's going to work and sustain itself into the future.

P4 identified initiatives on engagement sparked by the pandemic, including national working groups involving student leaders, impacting on government policy. While they noted that the pressure on student officers at a national level "must have been challenging", they nonetheless argued "fundamentally, we make better decisions at a policy level because they were… not just sitting around the table, they were contributing on an equal footing to everyone else in those discussions".

In contrast, another interviewee noted accelerated emergency decision-making in learning and teaching which excluded student leaders, articulating a risk as the sector returns to normal:

Whether that leads to a sense of, 'well, we didn't bother working with the students the last time we changed the assessment, so why should we bother this time?' So that would be a danger… And the question is, can we make sure that was just emergency mode?

Conclusions

Arnstein's ladder of citizen participation is "seminal" (Natarajan, 2019a, p.5) and "foundational" (Puskás et al., 2021, p.3), as evidenced by analysis across many sectors during a half-century shaped by multiple crises including COVID-19. For me, there are two standout features from my interviews and the literature relating to the ladder. The first is a recurring debate about the ladder's simplicity, with authors commending Arnstein's easily understood framework (Lauria and Schively Slotterback, 2021), others suggesting it is inadequate for complex contexts (Hurlbert and Gupta, 2015; Collins and Ison, 2009), and some doing both (Stewart, 2013; Bovill and Bulley, 2011).

The second feature is the importance of positionality and motivation to the discussions that the ladder can prompt. In introducing the ladder's purpose, Arnstein herself states that it "juxtaposes powerless citizens with the powerful in order to highlight the fundamental divisions between them" (Arnstein, 1969, p.217). The ladder can of course be manipulated for various objectives by those who seek to apply it: Buckley points out that student involvement can be advocated both by governments on the basis of "students as informed customers" (Buckley, 2018, p.720), and by student representatives as "a key element in the opposition to the implementation of neoliberal values" (p.720). This is a contradiction he further unpacked in his interview. He joins other authors (Stewart, 2013; Prieto Martín,

2014) and interviewees in urging consideration of the drivers and audiences for those who might lead the use of the ladder or equivalent tools.

Reflection on these two questions can help stakeholder engagement practitioners to clarify their own expectations of the ladder and consider more closely the ladder's purpose. Undertaking such reflection as a result of my research leads me to some reassuring observations about the strength of our sector, including the robustness of student engagement and representation. It also identifies opportunities and limitations in my research, which could enable highly relevant application of Arnstein's ladder in today's sector.

One practical lesson from this research is to frame the ladder's use around the above two questions of power dynamics and facilitator transparency, linking to interviewees' suggestions of an associated card sort exercise and a framework for creating an objective measure against the rungs. These suggested materials could be adapted for students, governors, academics, national practitioners and of course those senior managers whose perceived power would be redistributed. In turn this raises the idea of a structured toolkit to support the deployment of Arnstein's ladder in quality enhancement, student representative or academic development spaces, similar to existing guides in other sectors (Burns and Heywood, 2004; Cullen, 2005; Fletcher, 2005), which could even enable practitioners to develop adaptations to suit their own contexts, roles or subjects.

The four themes that emerged from my interviews, and the underpinning role of power throughout, demonstrate the value of Arnstein's ladder as a tool for reflecting on student engagement. More broadly, my literature review shows the ladder's importance for reflecting on citizen engagement in democratic society, especially given the upheaval of the pandemic. The ladder's application, however, requires time and willingness from decision-makers, and P6 summarised this challenge thus:

> I think the ladder is the way to have that conversation and say, 'listen, you know, how do you think people feel in this scenario? How do you democratise committee structures?' The only problem is: how do you even get those people into the room to discuss the ladder?

Of course, the interviews undertaken in this study were limited: the ten participants represented diverse experiences, but those in other roles, institutions or education sectors will reveal new insights into the ladder's contemporary applicability. Moreover, the world has changed considerably since much literature on Arnstein's ladder was published. Even relatively recent higher education publications on Arnstein inspiring my interviews from literature (Bovill and Bulley, 2011; Buckley, 2018; Carey, 2018) emerged before COVID-19, so further interviews could build on new research and experiences regarding what Arnstein can show a post-pandemic world.

That a simple tool developed by one practitioner from a single project over 50 years ago can have an "enduring relevance" (Stelmach, 2016, p.276) suggests that it has not been exhausted as a framework for researching stakeholder engagement.

The importance of students as partners has been highlighted during the pandemic (Ntem et al., 2020) and will be central to shaping our sector's uncertain future. Therefore tools like Arnstein's ladder of citizen participation are unlikely to diminish as valuable prisms and prompts for evaluating and advancing student engagement in a world where power dynamics and equality will remain central to our social discourse. I hope that both the suggestions and limitations in my conclusions can point to approaches for such evaluation and advancement.

Notes

1 The term Eskimo is "now considered unacceptable by many or even most Alaska Natives, largely since it is a colonial name imposed by non-Indigenous people" (Kaplan, n.d.). I retain the word in this quote, however, to provide an accurate citation, and to reflect the terminology used at the time even among those who, like Arnstein, were criticising such groups' exclusion. The term 'blacks' is similarly criticised today but also retained for accuracy.
2 The term 'students' association' is widely used in Scotland to describe the legally defined representative body for students at a university of college, and therefore is the default term in this chapter. 'Students' union' is more commonly used in England, Ireland and other sectors outwith Scotland, and refers to the same entity.

References

Abrahams, J. and Brooks, R., 2019. Higher education students as political actors: Evidence from England and Ireland. *Journal of Youth Studies*, 22(1), pp.108–123. https://doi.org/10.1080/13676261.2018.1484431

Arday, J. and Mirza, H.S. (eds), 2018. *Dismantling Race in Higher Education: Racism, Whiteness and Decolonising the Academy*. London: Palgrave Macmillan.

Arnstein, S., 1969. A ladder of citizen participation. *Journal of the American Institute of Planners*, 35(4), pp.216–224. https://doi.org/10.1080/01944366908977225

Ashwin, P. and McVitty, D., 2015. The meanings of student engagement: Implications for policies and practices. In: Curaj, A., *et al.* (eds) *The European Higher Education Area: Between Critical Reflections and Future Policies*. Cham: Springer. https://doi.org/10.1007/978-3-319-20877-0_23

Badham, D. and Davies, T., 2007. The active engagement of young people. In: Harrison, R., Benjamin, C., Curran, S. and Hunter, R. (eds) *Leading Work with Young People*. Thousand Oaks, CA: SAGE Publications.

Battaglia, J.E., Edley, P.P. and Newsom, V.A., 2019. Intersectional feminisms and sexual violence in the era of Me Too, Trump, and Kavanaugh. *Women & Language*, 42(1), pp.133–143.

Beesley, P. and Devonald, J., 2020. Partnership working in the face of a pandemic crisis impacting on social work placement provision in England. *Social Work Education*, 39(8), pp.1146–1153. https://doi.org/10.1080/02615479.2020.1825662

Bhambra, G.K., Gebrial, D. and Nisancioglu, K. 2018. *Decolonising the University*. London: Pluto Press. https://doi.org/10.1080/1070289x.2020.1753413

Bispo, J.P. and Morais, M.B., 2020. Community participation in the fight against COVID-19: Between utilitarianism and social justice. *Cadernos de Saúde Pública*, 36(8), pp.1–9.

Bovill, C. and Bulley, C.J., 2011. A model of active student participation in curriculum design: Exploring desirability and possibility. In: Rust, C. (ed) *Improving Student Learning (ISL) 18: Global Theories and Local Practices: Institutional, Disciplinary and Cultural Variations.* Oxford: Oxford Brookes University.

Brooks, R., Byford, K. and Sela, K., 2015. The changing role of students' unions within contemporary higher education. *Journal of Education Policy,* 30(2), pp.165–181. https://doi.org/10.1080/02680939.2014.924562

Buckley, A., 2018. The ideology of student engagement research. *Teaching in Higher Education,* 23(6), pp.718–732. https://doi.org/10.1080/13562517.2017.1414789

Burns, D. and Heywood, F., 2004. *Making Community Participation Meaningful: A Handbook for Development and Assessment.* Bristol: The Policy Press.

Carey, P., 2018. The impact of institutional culture, policy and process on student engagement in university decision-making. *Perspectives: Policy and Practice in Higher Education,* 22(1), pp.11–18. https://doi.org/10.1080/13603108.2016.1168754

Castillo-Montoya, M., Abreu, J. and Abad, A., 2019. Racially liberatory pedagogy: A Black Lives Matter approach to education. *International Journal of Qualitative Studies in Education,* 32(9), pp.1125–1145. https://doi.org/10.1080/09518398.2019.1645904

Choguill, M.B.G., 1996. A ladder of community participation for underdeveloped countries. *Habitat International,* 20(3), pp.431–444. https://doi.org/10.1016/0197-3975(96)00020-00023

College Development Network, n.d. *Governance.* Available at: www.cdn.ac.uk/governance/ (accessed: 28 August 2021).

Collins, K. and Ison, R., 2009. Jumping off Arnstein's ladder: Social learning as a new policy paradigm for climate change adaptation. *Environmental Policy and Governance,* 19(6), pp.358–373. https://doi.org/10.1002/eet.523

Collins, T., Gormley, B., Murray, J., O'Connor, B., Purser, L., O'Sullivan, D. and O'Brien, T., 2016. *Enhancing Student Engagement in Decision-Making: Report of the Working Group on Student Engagement in Irish Higher Education.* Higher Education Authority. Available at: www.thea.ie/contentFiles/HEA-IRC-Student-Engagement-Report-Apr2016-min.pdf (accessed: 16 May 2021).

Cullen, S., 2005. *Involving Users in Supported Housing: A Good Practice Guide.* London: Shelter.

Dancy, T., Edwards, K. and Earl Davis, J., 2018. Historically white universities and plantation politics: Anti-Blackness and higher education in the Black Lives Matter era. *Urban Education,* 53(2), pp.176–195. https://doi.org/10.1177/0042085918754328

Davidson, S., 1998. Spinning the wheel of empowerment. *Planning,* 1262(3), pp.14–15.

Day, M. and Dickinson, J., 2018. *David versus Goliath: The Past, Present and Future of Students' Unions in the UK.* Oxford: Higher Education Policy Institute.

de Leeuw, E., 2021. The rise of the consucrat. *International Journal of Health Policy and Management,* 10(4), pp.176–180. https://doi.org/10.34172/ijhpm.2020.36

Developing College Students' Associations, 2021. *Framework for the Development of Strong and Effective College Students' Associations.* Available at: www.dcsa.uk/resources/framework-for-the-development-of-strong-and-effective-college-students-associations (accessed: 5 September 2021).

Dey, A. and Mendes, K., 2021. "It started with this one post": #MeToo, India and higher education. *Journal of Gender Studies.* https://doi.org/10.1080/09589236.2021.1907552

Dolamore, S. and Richards, T.N., 2020. Assessing the organizational culture of higher education institutions in an era of #MeToo. *Public Administration Review,* 80(6), pp.1133–1137. https://doi.org/10.1111/puar.13179

Dollinger, M. and Mercer-Mapstone, L., 2009. What's in a name? Unpacking students' roles in higher education through neoliberal and social justice lenses. *Teaching and Learning Inquiry*, 7(2), pp.73–89. https://doi.org/10.20343/teachlearninqu.7.2.5

Dukhanin, V., Topazian, R. and DeCamp, M., 2018. Metrics and evaluation tools for patient engagement in healthcare organization- and system-level decision-making: A systematic review. *International Journal of Health Policy and Management*, 7(10), pp.889–903. https://doi.org/10.15171/ijhpm.2018.43

Falanga, R., 2020. *Citizen Participation during the COVID-19 Pandemic: Insights from Local Practice in European Cities*. Berlin: Friedrich-Ebert-Stiftung.

Feeney, S., Lillis, D. and Ramsey, L., 2020. Students as partners? Exploring student union engagement in the creation of technological universities in Ireland. *Irish Journal of Academic Practice*, 8(1), pp.1–13. https://doi.org/10.15173/ijsap.v4i1.3775

Fielding, M., 2012. Beyond student voice: Patterns of partnership and the demands of deep democracy. *Revista de Educación*, 359, pp.45–65. https://doi.org/10.1007/978-94-007-0805-1_5

Fletcher, A., 2005. *Meaningful Student Involvement: Guide to Students as Partners in School Change*. SoundOut.

Frankena, T.K., Naaldenberg, J., Cardol, M., Linehan, C. and van Schrojenstein Lantman-de Valk, H., 2015. Active involvement of people with intellectual disabilities in health research – A structured literature review. *Research in Developmental Disabilities*, 45, pp.271–283. https://doi.org/10.1016/j.ridd.2015.08.004

Gaber, J., 2021. Building "a ladder of citizen participation". In: Lauria, M. and Schively Slotterback, C. (eds) *Learning from Arnstein's ladder: From Citizen Participation to Public Engagement*. New York: Routledge. https://doi.org/10.4324/9780429290091-4

Griggs, R., 2012. *Report of the Review of Further Education Governance in Scotland*. Edinburgh: The Scottish Government. Available at: www.gov.scot/publications/report-review-further-education-governance-scotland/ (accessed: 8 September 2021).

Hall, R., 2020. Rallies and rent strikes: How students and staff are uniting against Covid chaos. Available at: www.theguardian.com/education/2020/oct/21/rallies-and-rent-strikes-how-students-and-staff-are-uniting-against-covid-chaos (accessed: 8 September 2021).

Hall, S. and Hickman, P., 2011. Resident participation in housing regeneration in France. *Housing Studies*, 26(6), pp.827–843. https://doi.org/10.1080/02673037.2011.593127

Hart, R., 1992. *Children's Participation: From Tokenism to Citizenship*. Florence: UNICEF.

Hassan, O., Scanlon, D., McDonald, C., Algeo, N., Corcráin, M.N., Jenkins, T., Kelly, S. and Whelan, S., 2020. Supporting student engagement and partnership in higher education decision-making during the pandemic: A reflection from the National Student Engagement Programme (NStEP). *All Ireland Journal of Higher Education*, 12(3), pp.1–9.

Hill, K. and Fitzgerald, R., 2020. Student perspectives of the impact of COVID-19 on learning. *All Ireland Journal of Higher Education*, 12(2), pp.1–9.

Homer, D., 2019. *The Rhetoric of Participation: Student Voice Initiatives in a College of Further Education – A Case Study*. Doctoral thesis, Bournemouth University.

Hurlbert, M. and Gupta, J., 2015. The split ladder of participation: A diagnostic, strategic, and evaluation tool to assess when participation is necessary. *Environmental Science & Policy*, 50, pp.100–113. https://doi.org/10.1016/j.envsci.2015.01.011

Hussey, S., 2020. *International Public Participation Models 1969–2020*. Available at: www.bangthetable.com/blog/international-public-participation-models/ (accessed: 29 August 2021).

Jingura, R., Muzinda, A., Munikwa, S. and Tapera. J., 2018. A model for enhancing student engagement within the context of higher education quality assurance. *Journal of Higher Education Management*, 32(2), pp.127–135.

Kaplan, L., n.d. Inuit or Eskimo: Which name to use? Available at: www.uaf.edu/anlc/resources/inuit_or_eskimo.php (accessed 5 September 2021).

Kung, M. and Zhu, D., 2022. What about my opposition!? The case of rural public hearing best practices during the COVID-19 pandemic. *Cities*, 120, p.103485. https://doi.org/10.1016/j.cities.2021.103485

Lauria, M. and Schively Slotterback, C.S. (eds), 2021. *Learning from Arnstein's ladder: From Citizen Participation to Public Engagement*. New York: Routledge.

Le Grange, L., 2016. Decolonising the university curriculum: Leading article. *South African Journal of Higher Education*, 30(2), pp.1–12. https://doi.org/10.20853/30-2-709

Leach, M., 2012. Bursting bubbles in higher education. Available at: https://wonkhe.com/blogs/bursting-bubbles-in-higher-education/ (accessed 4 September 2021).

Marent, B., Forster, R. and Nowak, P., 2012. Theorizing participation in health promotion: A literature review. *Social Theory & Health*, 10(2), pp.188–207. https://doi.org/10.1057/sth.2012.2

Matthews, K., Dwyer, A., Russell, S. and Enright, E., 2019. It is a complicated thing: Leaders' conceptions of students as partners in the neoliberal university. *Studies in Higher Education*, 44(12), 2196–2207. https://doi.org/10.1080/03075079.2018.1482268

Mavuso, M.P. and Duku, N., 2014. Participation of parents in school governance: A case study of two Eastern Cape schools: A view from below. *Mediterranean Journal of Social Sciences*, 5(3), pp.454–460. https://doi.org/10.5901/mjss.2014.v5n3p454

Moon, M.J., 2020. Fighting COVID-19 with agility, transparency, and participation: Wicked policy problems and new governance challenges. *Public Administration Review*, 80(4), pp.651–656. https://doi.org/10.1111/puar.13214

Natarajan, L., 2019a. Outlooks on participating people, plans & places 1. *Built Environment*, 45(1), pp.5–6. https://doi.org/10.2148/benv.45.1.5

Natarajan, L., 2019b. Realizing participation people, plans & places 2. *Built Environment*, 45(2), pp.141–142. https://doi.org/10.2148/benv.45.2.141

Neary, M., 2020. *Student as Producer: How do Revolutionary Teachers Teach?* Winchester: Zero Books.

Newby, P., 2014. *Research Methods for Education* (2nd edn). London: Routledge.

Nitsch, M., Waldherr, K., Denk, E., Griebler, U., Marent, B. and Forster, R., 2013. Participation by different stakeholders in participatory evaluation of health promotion: A literature review. *Evaluation and Program Planning*, 40, pp.42–54. https://doi.org/10.1016/j.evalprogplan.2013.04.006

nonformality.org, 2011. *Participation Models: Citizens, Youth, Online – A Chase through the Maze*. Available at: www.nonformality.org/wp-content/uploads/2011/07/Participation-Models-20110703.pdf (accessed: 25 August 2021).

Ntem, A. *et al.*, 2020. Students as partners in crisis? Student co-editors' perspectives on COVID-19, values, and the shift to virtual spaces. *International Journal for Students as Partners*, 4(2), pp.1–8.

O'Rourke, V. and Baldwin, C., 2016. Student engagement in placemaking at an Australian university campus. *Australian Planner*, 53(2), pp.103–116. https://doi.org/10.1080/07293682.2015.1135810

Pétursdóttir, S.D.D., 2011. *Technology Enabled Citizen Participation in Nairobi Slum Upgrades.* Masters dissertation, Reykjavik University.

Prieto Martín, P., 2014. *Participation schemas: A tool to characterize collaborative participation.* Paper presentation at PDD2014, Contemporary Difficulties and Future Prospects for Participatory and Deliberative Democracy, Newcastle, 11 July.

Puskás, N., Abunnasr, Y. and Naalbandian, S., 2021. Assessing deeper levels of participation in nature-based solutions in urban landscapes – A literature review of real-world cases. *Landscape and Urban Planning*, 210, pp.1–11. https://doi.org/10.1016/j.landurbplan.2021.104065

Romanin, A., 2013. *Influencing renewal: an Australian case study of tenant participation's influence on public housing renewal projects.* Masters thesis, Maastricht Graduate School of Governance.

Rudd, T., Colligan, F. and Naik, R., 2006. *Learner Voice: A Handbook from Futurelab.* Futurelab.

Saini, R. and Begum, N., 2020. Demarcation and definition: Explicating the meaning and scope of 'decolonisation' in the social and political sciences. *The Political Quarterly*, 91 (1), pp.217–221. https://doi.org/10.1111/1467-923x.12797

Schively Slotterback, C.S. and Lauria, M., 2019. Building a foundation for public engagement in planning: 50 years of impact, interpretation, and inspiration from Arnstein's ladder. *Journal of the American Planning Association*, 85(3), pp.183–187. https://doi.org/10.1080/01944363.2019.1616985

Scottish Funding Council for Further and Higher Education, 2021. *Coherence and Sustainability: A Review of Tertiary Education and Research.* Edinburgh: Scottish Funding Council.

Stelmach, B., 2016. Parents' participation on school councils analysed through Arnstein's ladder of participation. *School Leadership & Management*, 36, pp.271–291. https://doi.org/10.1080/13632434.2016.1247048

Stewart, E., 2013. What is the point of citizen participation in health care? *Journal of Health Services Research & Policy*, 18(2), pp.124–126. https://doi.org/10.1177/1355819613485670

Stewart, E., 2012. *Governance, Participation and Avoidance: Everyday Public Involvement in the Scottish NHS.* PhD thesis, University of Edinburgh.

Student Partnerships in Quality Scotland (sparqs), n.d.-a. *sparqs: A Ladder of Citizen Participation by Sherry R Arnstein (1969).* Available at: www.sparqs.ac.uk/upfiles/Arnstein%20Ladder%20Handout%20-%20sparqs.pdf (accessed: 28 August 2021).

Student Partnerships in Quality Scotland (sparqs), n.d.-b. *Student Engagement Analysis Workshop.* Available at: www.sparqs.ac.uk/institute.php?page=875 (accessed: 28 August 2021).

Student Partnerships in Quality Scotland (sparqs), n.d.-c. *Governance Development.* Available at: www.sparqs.ac.uk/institute.php?page=577 (accessed: 28 August 2021).

Student Partnerships in Quality Scotland (sparqs), 2021. *Celebrating Successful Partnerships in 2020–21: A Report Accompanying the sparqs Student Engagement Awards.* sparqs.

Symonds, E., 2021. An 'unavoidable' dynamic? Understanding the 'traditional' learner–teacher power relationship within a higher education context. *British Journal of*

Sociology of Education, 42(7), pp.1070–1085. https://doi.org/10.1080/01425692. 2021.1962246

Tritter, J.Q. and McCallum, A., 2006. The snakes and ladders of user involvement: Moving beyond Arnstein. *Health Policy*, 76(2), pp.156–168. https://doi.org/10.1016/j.healthp ol.2005.05.008

Trowler, V., 2015. Negotiating contestations and 'chaotic conceptions': Engaging 'non-traditional' students in higher education. *Higher Education Quarterly*, 69(3), pp.295–310. https://doi.org/10.1111/hequ.12071

Varwell, S., 2021. Models for exploring partnership: Introducing sparqs' student partnership staircase as a reflective tool for staff and students. *International Journal for Students as Partners*, 5(1), pp.107–123.

Varwell, S., 2022a. Partnership in pandemic: Re-imagining Arnstein's ladder of citizen participation for an era of emergency decision-making. *Journal of Educational Innovation, Partnership and Change*, 8(1). https://journals.studentengagement.org.uk/index. php/studentchangeagents/article/view/1076

Varwell, S., 2022b. A Literature Review of Arnstein's Ladder of Citizen Participation: Lessons for contemporary student engagement. *Exchanges: The Interdisciplinary Research Journal*, 10(1), pp.108–144. https://doi.org/10.31273/eirj.v10i1.1156

Woods, K. and Botcherby, P., 2021. Then & Now Arts at Warwick student project: Co-creation in the COVID-19 crisis. *Exchanges: The Interdisciplinary Research Journal*, 8 (4), pp.55–75. https://doi.org/10.31273/eirj.v8i4.797

Yeom, J.W., Jang, S.W., Ha, D.O. and Kang, S.W., 2021. Post COVID-19 visioning of urban comprehensive plan through citizen participation. *Journal of Korea Planning Association*, 56(1). https://doi.org/10.17208/jkpa.2021.02.56.1.156

Zepke, N., 2015. What future for student engagement in neoliberal times? *Higher Education*, 69(4), pp.693–704. https://doi.org/10.1007/s10734-014-9797-y

Zepke, N., 2014. Student engagement research in higher education: Questioning an academic orthdoxy. *Teaching in Higher Education*, 19(6), pp.697–708. https://doi.org/ 10.1080/13562517.2014.901956

So what and what next?

Concluding thoughts on advancing student engagement

Tom Lowe and Emily Parkin

Introduction

This edited collection builds on the work of *A Handbook for Student Engagement in Higher Education: Theory into Practice* (Lowe and El Hakim, 2020) to develop our student engagement thinking and practice in higher education. This collection offers support for those tasked with creating meaningful student engagement opportunities for students and staff in higher education. Only when we recognise and celebrate our diverse student bodies will we truly be able to ensure each student can succeed. Our organisations will require continuous and relentless development to adapt to ever changing priorities and contexts, yet a focus on student engagement in higher education will likely continue in the decades ahead.

Student engagement is important for educational developers, as it is important for students to work with staff to improve education. The process of engaging students in educational change brings a gigantic amount of learning and skills development for both parties, where dialogue, co-production and the resulting artefacts can make outstanding developments to the future of higher education. This book responds to the need to develop aspects of current and historic higher education, which are not suited to modern citizens' and society's needs. Students and staff within higher education need to have the values, attributes and problem-solving skills to reform education ourselves, before external forces try to change things for us. This chapter summarises the major discussions of this edited collection, outlining the key themes and areas for future research in the field.

Student engagement

This volume began by emphasising the need to problematise the now developed areas of student engagement practice and research, in order to help overcome the challenges faced in institutions. Although student engagement as a priority is accepted by many, the focus differs from university to university, as well as nation by nation. The successes of student engagement in educational development are clear, yet this publication was drawn together to discuss the challenges. Engaging students (and staff) together in developing education is not free of issues. Looking

DOI: 10.4324/9781003271789-25

forward, readers are encouraged to continue with critical reflection through asking who is engaging, how we are engaging and how sustainable our practices are. A major area where reflection is needed is research, as researching and evaluating students' engagement in higher education is continuing to gain support. But researching so many individuals' lives, within such complex institutions as universities, can push the variables through the roof! Austen, Pickering and Donnelly apply these questions to two major student engagement evaluation schemes used in a UK university, where the limitations were recognised as perhaps not the most useful means of creating judgements and findings on the student experience (Austen, Pickering and Donnelly, 2023). Questioning how we evaluate and research students' engagements is critical, especially while many of us find ourselves in settings where data is needed to justify our arguments. Yet the complexity must be remembered, that findings are not fixed and although some measures of evaluation are used *en masse* (such as national student experience surveys), they are not free of issues.

Conversations surrounding student engagement are often taken outside of the classroom, beyond the student–staff curriculum activities, to be perhaps addressed in the committee room. Sarah Bayless' chapter takes these critical discussions to where they belong, where perhaps all students engage – within the curriculum (Bayless, 2023). It important to return all conversations about student engagement to learning, as well as including students and staff on the ground in discussing the implications of policy and practice discussed in committees. Simplistic comments made around student outcomes targets and ideals of student–staff relationships are easy to support, yet when considering the thousands of students and staff included in such assumptions, the realities of how students and staff engage in the curriculum will naturally differ. It is clear that there is not one ideal measure for student engagement, as the measurable behavioural measures (such as attendance, response rates and wider learning analytics) do not tell us the full student engagement story. This takes us back to Bryson's (2014) edited collection, where his conclusion was that student engagement is like a black box, where all the information is within, yet it is complex and only able to be revealed through research and discussions with students.

Individuals matter

As individual university sectors in different nations differ, we must also remember that our individual students on our degree programmes are each wonderful individuals with their own learning preferences, motivations and stories. Fatima Umar's chapter reflecting upon her student journey in Pakistan does this, highlighting the change in roles and learning styles experienced by our students (Umar, 2023). It must be remembered that often many of our students join higher education from 'teach to the test' curriculum models (Freire, 1968), where the teacher is always right, and student voice is minimal. Additional focus is needed on how we change the culture from passive learners' part in a pre-determined structure of learning, to becoming contributing researchers, as Professor Mike Neary outlines in his work on students as producers (Neary, 2020).

It is important to remember that individual stories matter. The induction week, open day or first semester all offer opportunities to change this student–staff relationship, but this is not simple at scale when working with the great diversity of students. Institutions do this by preaching their commitment to inclusivity and championing of diversity, where working to improve our institution's, community's and curriculum's inclusivity will remain a constant enhancement theme. Because there is not one 'student experience', there are almost infinite students' experiences, and therefore perhaps infinite engagement journeys. Engaging students as partners and representatives in equality, diversity and inclusivity activity in universities is recommended, and celebrated, but the work is far from done. Maisha Islam's chapter demonstrates the considerable areas for development and factors that still cause exclusion for racially and religiously minoritised students, as well as how these students' engagement in supporting inclusivity is often overworked by institutions (Islam, 2023). This area of student engagement activity is perhaps the most urgent to critically reflect upon, to increase accessibility and not alienate students throughout the process of listening to the 'student voice'.

With any area for development in higher education, institutions commonly allocate a 'lead' for championing and writing strategies and policies. But who is responsible for student engagement development across a university? Is it those engaging students (wherever they sit), or perhaps 'Heads of Student Engagement' or 'Deans of Students', which are often new appointments cropping up across universities? Harriet Dunbar-Morris outlines the importance of strategic leaders in championing student engagement, where she draws upon an authentic leadership model (Dunbar-Morris, 2023). The importance of sharing, accessibility and values are explained, which can be used as a model for other leaders reading this publication, on how to act when engaging students on a strategic level. The committee student representatives are often over-relied upon at this level but Dunbar-Morris highlights other practices, which reach and create more engagement for the students involved. Looking ahead, the power-structured committee will likely be retained, but more innovative methods must be experimented with to increase accessibility for those student representatives who have often never been in a board room before!

Students as consumers

At the start of this section, Taylor Bunce, Rathbone and King share their research on a concerning move in student identity, away from learner or aspired partner, to a consumer of higher education (Taylor Bunce, Rathbone and King, 2023). This identity of transactional students is often used as a warning (and possible outcome) if staff do not engage students in the development of education, as alternatively a customer-orientated higher education will likely damage the system for all. Although *student as consumer* is becoming a reality in many tuition-fee funded nations, like England and the USA, recent research has found in lower-fee or no-fee charging higher education systems that students do not see themselves as consumers (Brooks, 2023). Charging students in any way for any part of their higher education will impact on engagement, learning and the relationship between students and the institution. These impacts are perhaps still playing out, and are often not considered when financial decisions instead of conversations about learning dominate institutions.

Student engagement in educational developments

As highlighted in the previous edited collection of this series (Lowe and El Hakim, 2020), there are now numerous practices to engage students in innovating education. Lowe and Lowe highlight several thematic considerations of these student participations, where students are asked to give time to roles such as student partners or student representatives, or to attend events additional to their core curriculum (Lowe and Lowe, 2023). Practical reflections are shared such as the benefits and barriers caused by attempts to make these 'student engagement practices' successful, such as reward, timing and language. The difficulty is often that staff are tasked with making these schemes successful, or the university wishes to engage large numbers. Steps are taken quickly to engage the majority, yet often these 'good will' motivations to create engagement can in fact create barriers for others. The advice would be not to assume practice as the norm and to continuously innovate and evaluate year on year. Talia Adams, Vice President of Lincoln University Students' Union (UK), follows on to highlight how we can create an ecosystem of student engagement opportunities across a university (Adams, 2023). Taking a pragmatic approach, as many of the chapters do, Adams gives a variety of case studies for engaging students, with a variety of methods and lengths of contact time for students. It is important that practice in engaging students in the development of education is not static, nor adopted at institutions from the literature just because they have been highly cited or celebrated. Individual universities, and courses within them, will have their own ideal solution for engaging students, and Adams highlights that within one university, a 'mixed methods' approach was most appropriate to ensure a diversity of perspectives.

However, it is not just about schemes of engagement with their timelines and operations. The individual student–staff conversations about education are critical to the success of any means of engagement. Katja Eftring and Torgny Roxå of Lund University (Sweden) discuss the subtlety of their student voice practices within their degree, where students and staff meet to discuss the student experience across the year (Eftring and Roxå, 2023). This chapter highlights the importance of buy-in for both students and staff in student voice activities, such as Student–Staff Liaison Committees attended by Student Academic Representatives. Eftring and Roxå also discuss the challenges for the students attending and how they must negotiate the meeting to keep it productive. Kate Walsh and Alison Jaquet's chapter complements this theme, where they importantly highlight the need for exploring staff engagement, concluding that staff training is needed to support student engagement across Australia, where culture change is needed to position students as vital contributors to university governance (Walsh and Jaquet, 2023). It is clear that student engagement takes time and that efforts are needed equally with staff, as well as students.

Looking ahead, the influence of individuals will make or break student engagement practices, where perhaps more work is needed in training staff, and not just students, to attend student representative meetings. The higher education sector has been celebrated for its student engagement and students as partners practice *en masse* (Blackstock, 2020; Mercer-Mapstone, and Clarke, 2018), yet these practices came under pressure during the global pandemic. Jim Dickinson reflects on the problems with student engagement during a global crisis (Dickinson, 2023). Universities and their change processes are often slow and therefore the urgent issues of the pandemic created difficulties in universities. Students were less engaged in the decisions made by universities which impacted sometimes the entire student bodies' assessment practices, access to campus and even the policing of student interaction. Although many universities have good records with engaging students' voices, these schemes were reliant upon large amounts of time. Importantly, student engagement in crisis needs to be planned for to prevent a destruction of student trust in their universities and breaking of partnership at the most critical moments.

Students as partners

Student–staff partnership initiatives at universities are often the most vibrant hubs of activity in student engagement in the development of education. Sophia Abbot leads the argument in this collection where students as partners is framed not as just a developmental activity, but the means for curriculum justice for historically marginalised students by creating meaningful opportunities for common understanding and representation of equity-seeking groups (Abbot, 2023). Alison Cook-Sather and Jia Yi Loh continue the case for student co-creation for student equity, arguing for enacting and embracing student agency in efforts to decolonise the university and racial justice (Cook-Sather and Loh, 2023). Yet as with other staff-reliant activities discussed in this collection, fostering partnership attitudes within the staffing body is critical for widespread adoption, to achieve partnership as a theme across whole institutions.

However, the power over these schemes often remains with university administrators and management committees. Jenny Marie and Stuart Sims discuss these tensions as areas for critical reflection, where the schemes which preach empowerment are often dominated in practice by the same barrier-enforcing structures which prevent engagement (Marie and Sims, 2023). That the power of senior staff and cultures positions us not to push too hard for change is well known by staff, but perhaps we are at risk of mis-selling these student engagement change programmes if the politics are not yet ready in our staffing structures. Sharing power is the key for authentic partnership, and it is important that staff are equally able to make changes and are not disempowered through the process of sharing responsibility and working together.

Positioning students as partners as opposed to consumers has been cited throughout this collection as beneficial for learning, belonging and the pedagogic relationship between students and staff. As the partnership aspiration becomes shared by more and more universities, the support to 'make' students partners in neoliberal universities has sometimes been adopted from the top, as opposed to developing at the grass-roots curriculum level. Tanya Lubicz-Nawrocka discusses to what extent universities really can make students partners in systems where marketisation is dominant (Lubicz-Nawrocka, 2023). Partnership has to have buy-in from both parties, based on shared values and activities, as does buy-in in other educational development activities discussed in this volume. For strategic leaders, supporting, funding and discussing the possibilities around students as partners can act as a catalyst, but forcing student–staff partnership will not likely create it. We cannot simply make students partners; we must nurture partnerships, taking time and real investment, if we wish to create a true culture shift in the institution.

The identity of students is discussed throughout this volume, where many of the students now entering higher education at the time of this publication would be described as 'Generation Z' (born from 1996 onwards). This generation of students have grown up in the digital age of fast consumption, mass availability of, and instant sharing of, knowledge. Students are surrounded by the media in their pocket, as opposed to being written down or on television. Students have also grown up in the shadow of the 2008 financial crash, international turmoil of dozens of conflicts, and a recognition of a climate change emergency. These students, arriving in university in the 2020s, will have lived through the COVID-19 pandemic and likely experienced some form of online learning or social distancing. Taking the assumption from previous generations that 'when I was a student, I learnt like this' is no longer acceptable, and Mollie Dollinger's chapter explores how we as university communities can overcome challenges to engaging Generation Z learners (Dollinger, 2023). Students are ever changing, therefore the purpose of student engagement in educational development is perhaps never completed.

Student engagement in the wider university

The student engagement approaches taken to develop learning are often focused on activities between academic staff and students, with the bulk of literature relating to learning and teaching enhancements. Madalene George's chapter highlights the need to focus equally on professional services, such as libraries, within our higher education communities (George, 2023). These more transactional or advisory services often do not have the high contact time that student–staff liaison meetings or research projects can be built upon. Therefore, reflecting on earlier chapters, flexibility is required in approaches to assess where student engagement practices may be deployed within professional services. Although many focus on customer service, services must be wary that the learning community does not end at their reception desk and partnership opportunities can be found through innovation and dialogue in professional services equally. If a focus upon student engagement starts and ends within the curriculum, student–staff relationships may be contradicted elsewhere in the academy, counteracting the work of academics when following practice such as co-design, student representation and partnership.

The human engagements offered by the modern university are indeed areas for exploration in student engagement, but there are other areas to explore that do not involve our students and staff personally. The physical estate of the modern university is continuously evolving to attract and benefit students – from sustainable practices, to classroom alterations, adoption of new technologies, and entire building works. These spaces *are* the university for many students and staff, where our movements throughout the campus are made accessible or hindered by design. Zachery Spire's chapter emphasizes the university estate in student engagement, where greater discussion is needed in regards to how our spaces impact on belonging, transition and attachment (Spire, 2023). Spaces can be daunting, but spaces can also be home, and sometimes a university buildings strategy dominated by an estate team can get distracted by aesthetics, rather than focusing on student engagement.

Student engagement research is defined by Trowler's (2010) literature review in three categories (emotional, cognitive and behavioural). In a digital age, the ability to measure behavioural engagement through participation and registers is available *en masse*, through education-adapted consumer management systems. Zoheir Beig's chapter gives an overview of these new student engagement systems which assess and predict students' pathways through a degree, as a means to support and evaluate (Beig, 2023). Student engagement became an area of research to improve learning (cognitive engagement), and has subsequently led to discussions around belonging (emotional engagement) as an outcome of engaging strategies. These technologies cannot yet measure emotional or cognitive engagement beyond surveys and grades, yet perhaps in a digital hyper-metric age for all workplaces, the university is prioritising too much digital engagement, and forgetting the individual story in the process.

But does researching and exploring student engagement go beyond the curriculum, into the extra-curricular space? Activities such as campus sport can be seen as just something for fun, for fitness, or even a distraction. However, the importance of recreational and competitive activities for students can mean everything for their personal experience. If a student remains and becomes fulfilled at university through any university network of friends via an activity, it must be valued, especially where institutions are focusing on belonging or retention. Maria Moxey's chapter highlights the importance of such activities, taking a Bourdieusian perspective on what sports team membership means for student engagement (Moxey, 2023). For students, the sporting opportunities are as much a part of the university as their degree programme, and if supported correctly, can be valued equally by university administrators as a support mechanism for student integration. This work is continued by Eddie Corr who draws together literature on employability, retention and student engagement to discuss the greater space of extra-curricular activities (Corr, 2023). Perhaps these are hidden elements of students' engagement, as they take place often indoors and in small areas of the university community. Corr argues that the sometimes perceived 'extra' can be seen as the 'extra' that does not matter, often not included in strategies. Corr argues for the hidden impact extra-curricular activity has on student engagement and success, where due to the nature of the staff supporting such schemes where academic research is not practiced, systematic research is not taking place and so this area may be under-valued.

Student engagement is not a single area of focus, as students engage in endless elements of the university and additionally beyond the curriculum throughout their student experience. Therefore, the target of 'all students being engaged' in whatever area of the university is difficult to achieve. In fact, it could be desirable to recognize that we have instead an ecosystem of student engagement in our universities, where we accept student preferences as long as students are aware and able to access opportunities and support when they require/desire it. The answer instead perhaps is to work on achieving a high student sense of belonging across a student population. Terrel Strayhorn addresses this term which draws considerable attention, where many have argued if a student has a high sense of belonging, they are more likely to succeed (Strayhorn, 2023). But do we define where students belong? Do they have to belong to the brand of the institutions or just their course? Or as Moxey outlines, could belonging be part of campus sport (Moxey, 2023)? Looking ahead, it has instead been argued that facilitating a sense of mattering is more valuable, particularly for professional services, to give maximum 'mattering' across a student journey (Gravett and Winstone, 2022).

Yet how do we make sense of all this? As highlighted in this volume, student engagement is a vast plethora of topics to explore, from physical to emotional, and including all elements of the curriculum and beyond. How does a university begin to strategise such areas of focus beyond the individual project, classroom or scheme? Simon Varwell offers a critical assessment of one model that has been tested by time and popularity, as a model to assess and compare staff and student ownership in the university. Although many institutions are keen and/or ready to share their education developments with students as partners, full power sharing is still not present in the most part. Arnstein's (1969) ladder offers a valuable framework to measure practice against, alongside several other models present in the field and referenced in this collection. Are student engagement conversations united by one framework? Can all of the areas of discussion within student engagement be summarised in one figure? Or is it better to let our discussions grow naturally, based on enthusiasm and need? Either way, it is clear that silos of activity are occurring in student engagement and, although there is good will, risks exist when the student, at the centre of the university, is sometimes exposed to every agenda at once without staff coordination.

Conclusion

It is clear from this edited collection and the continuing growing body of research that student engagement in higher education is evolving. Only by problematising, reflecting upon and critiquing our student engagement research and practice in the field will our engagements with students remain meaningful, student-centred and contemporary. Since 2009, the Researching, Advancing and Inspiring Student Engagement (RAISE) Network has welcomed students and staff internationally to have these discussions, as a free-to-join network of both in-person and online activities (RAISE, 2022). For example, its well-attended 2022 conference at the University of Lincoln (UK) discussed the student engagement issues which had been raised by the pandemic, with a greater shift to online teaching and support services. The network welcomes students and staff (both academic and professional services) to discuss and share practice on student engagement through activities such as an annual conference, several special interest groups, a journal and a reading group, to both advance and support student engagement internationally.

Looking ahead, it is clear that there still is a tension and risk that because we engaged students once in a decision or project, that we do not need to engage students again in educational developments. We must accept that our student body is ever changing and each individual student (and staff member) will have different needs and engagement preferences. We need to recognise and celebrate students as being in a position of power, as a mutual producer of knowledge, and move away from a didactic model of service and 'teach to test' pedagogies in higher education. Empowered by embracing difference and building equity in our providers, students can fully participate as partners who make change in our universities, to then go on to make change as citizens in wider society. Therefore, by empowering our students and staff to make better universities, we begin a process of making a better world. As degree education supports students to conduct research, define arguments and create solutions, meaningful student engagement opportunities can be part of this critical confidence-building process. Indeed, challenges persist when student engagement goes too far for some, and from some perspectives, students possibly demand too much. The question asked is, do we support the discussions to continue, or do we choose the balance sheet and conservatism, just keeping the gardens within the lines of the fences (university structures). Truly investing in the university by enabling experimentation can increase the impact we could collectively have on a more accessible learning experience. Structures that prevent progress and prevent student engagement should be questioned and need to be reshaped, to continue ensuring our universities support students, staff and wider society to succeed.

References

Abbot, S., 2023. Student–instructor partnerships for curricular justice. In: Lowe, T. (ed) *Advancing Student Engagement in Higher Education: Reflection, Critique and Challenge*. Abingdon: Routledge.

Adams, T., 2023. How to engage students in your educational developments: A student leader's view. In: Lowe, T. (ed) *Advancing Student Engagement in Higher Education: Reflection, Critique and Challenge*. Abingdon: Routledge.

Arnstein, S., 1969. A ladder of citizen participation. *Journal of the American Institute of Planners*, 35(4), pp.216–224. https://doi.org/10.1080/01944366908977225

Austen, L., Pickering, N. and Donnelly, A. 2023. Researching and evaluating student engagement: A methodological critique of data gathering approaches. In: Lowe, T. (ed) *Advancing Student Engagement in Higher Education: Reflection, Critique and Challenge*. Abingdon: Routledge.

Bayless, S., 2023. Challenges and tensions for student academic engagement practices in contemporary UK Higher Education. In: Lowe, T. (ed) *Advancing Student Engagement in Higher Education: Reflection, Critique and Challenge*. Abingdon: Routledge.

Beig, Z., 2023. Learning analytics in higher education: The ethics, the future, the students. In: Lowe, T. (ed) *Advancing Student Engagement in Higher Education: Reflection, Critique and Challenge*. Abingdon: Routledge.

Blackstock, D. 2020. Student engagement in hard work, but quality takes time. In: Lowe, T. and El-Hakim, Y. (eds) *A Handbook for Student Engagement in Higher Education*. Abingdon: Routledge.

Brooks, R., 2022. Students as consumers? The perspectives of students' union leaders across Europe. *Higher Education Quarterly*, 76(3), pp.626–637.

Bryson, C., 2014. Clarifying the concept of student engagement. In: Bryson, C. (ed) *Understanding and Developing Student Engagement*. Routledge: London.

Cook-Sather, A. and Loh, J.Y., 2023. Embracing student agentic engagement and enacting equity in higher education through co-creating learning and teaching. In: Lowe, T. (ed) *Advancing Student Engagement in Higher Education: Reflection, Critique and Challenge*. Abingdon: Routledge.

Corr, E., 2023. Recognising the hidden impact of extra-curricular activity on student engagement and success. In: Lowe, T. (ed) *Advancing Student Engagement in Higher Education: Reflection, Critique and Challenge*. Abingdon: Routledge.

Dickinson, J., 2023. The problem with student engagement during Covid-19. In: Lowe, T. (ed) *Advancing Student Engagement in Higher Education: Reflection, Critique and Challenge*. Abingdon: Routledge.

Dollinger, M., 2023. Critical challenges to support Generation Z learners. In: Lowe, T. (ed) *Advancing Student Engagement in Higher Education: Reflection, Critique and Challenge*. Abingdon: Routledge.

Dunbar-Morris, H., 2023. Authentic leadership for student engagement. In: Lowe, T. (ed) *Advancing Student Engagement in Higher Education: Reflection, Critique and Challenge*. Abingdon: Routledge.

Eftring, K. and Roxå, T. 2023. Student evaluation of courses – co-creation of meaning through conversations: Insights from the student perspective. In: Lowe, T. (ed) *Advancing Student Engagement in Higher Education: Reflection, Critique and Challenge*. Abingdon: Routledge.

Freire, P., 1968. *Pedagogy of the Oppressed*. London: Penguin Books.

George, M. 2023. Defining, delivering and evaluating student engagement in a professional service in higher education: A case study of a student engagement team in an academic library. In: Lowe, T. (ed) *Advancing Student Engagement in Higher Education: Reflection, Critique and Challenge*. Abingdon: Routledge.

Gravett, K. and Winstone, N.E., 2022. Making connections: Authenticity and alienation within students' relationships in higher education. *Higher Education Research and Development*, 41(2), pp.360–374.

Islam, M. 2023. Equality and diversity in our student engagement practice: Radical possibilities to reaching racial and religious equity in higher education. In: Lowe, T. (ed) *Advancing Student Engagement in Higher Education: Reflection, Critique and Challenge*. Abingdon: Routledge.

Lowe, C. and Lowe, T., 2023. Accessibility to student engagement opportunities: A focus on 'hard to reach' universities. In: Lowe, T. (ed) *Advancing Student Engagement in Higher Education: Reflection, Critique and Challenge*. Abingdon: Routledge.

Lowe, T. and El Hakim, Y. 2020. *A Handbook of Student Engagement: Theory into Practice*. Abingdon: Routledge.

Lubicz-Nawrocka, T. 2023. To what extent can we really make students partners in neoliberal universities? In: Lowe, T. (ed) *Advancing Student Engagement in Higher Education: Reflection, Critique and Challenge*. Abingdon: Routledge.

Marie, J. and Sims, S., 2023. Control, freedom and structure in student–staff partnerships. In: Lowe, T. (ed) *Advancing Student Engagement in Higher Education: Reflection, Critique and Challenge*. Abingdon: Routledge.

Mercer-Mapstone, L. and Clarke, A., 2018. A partnership approach to scaling up student–staff partnership at a large research-intensive university. *The Journal of Educational Innovation, Partnership and Change*, 4(1). https://doi.org/10.21100/jeipc.v4i1.741

Moxey, M., 2023. Placing sport at the heart of the university community: A critical reflection on sports club membership and what it means for student engagement from a Bourdieusian perspective. In: Lowe, T. (ed) *Advancing Student Engagement in Higher Education: Reflection, Critique and Challenge*. Abingdon: Routledge.

Neary, M., 2020. *Student as Producer: How Do Revolutionary Teachers Teach?* Aresford: John Hunt Publishing.

Quality Assurance Agency (QAA), 2022. *Expectations and Practices for Student Engagement*. Available at: www.qaa.ac.uk/quality-code/advice-and-guidance/student-engagement# (accessed: 21 August 2022).

Researching, Advancing and Inspiring Student Engagement (RAISE), 2022. *Researching, Advancing and Inspiring Student Engagement*. Available at: www.raise-network.com/ (accessed 18 September 2022).

Spire, Z., 2023. University estates: From spaces to places of student engagement. In: Lowe, T. (ed) *Advancing Student Engagement in Higher Education: Reflection, Critique and Challenge*. Abingdon: Routledge.

Strayhorn, T.L., 2023. Widening the aperture on college students' sense of belonging: A critical ecological perspective. In: Lowe, T. (ed) *Advancing Student Engagement in Higher Education: Reflection, Critique and Challenge*. Abingdon: Routledge.

Strayhorn, T.L., 2018. *College students' sense of belonging: A key to educational success for all students*. Abingdon: Routledge.

Taylor Bunce, L., Rathbone, C. and King, N., 2023. Students as consumers: A barrier for student engagement? In: Lowe, T. (ed) *Advancing Student Engagement in Higher Education: Reflection, Critique and Challenge*. Abingdon: Routledge.

Trowler, V., 2010. *Student Engagement Literature Review*. Available at: www.heacademy.ac.uk/system/files/studentengagementliteraturereview_1.pdf (accessed: 16 May 2021).

Umar, F., 2023. There is not one student experience: Our learner journeys as individuals. In: Lowe, T. (ed) *Advancing Student Engagement in Higher Education: Reflection, Critique and Challenge*. Abingdon: Routledge.

Varwell, S., 2023. Valhalla and Nirvana: Views of Arnstein's Ladder of Citizen Participation in further and higher education. In: Lowe, T. (ed) *Advancing Student Engagement in Higher Education: Reflection, Critique and Challenge*. Abingdon: Routledge.

Vuori, J., 2013. Student engagement: Buzzword or fuzzword? *Journal of Higher Education Policy and Management*, 36(5), pp.509–519. https://doi.org/10.1080/1360080x.2014.936094

Wagner, E. and Longanecker, D., 2016. Scaling student success with predictive analytics: Reflections after four years in the data trenches. *Change: The Magazine of Higher Learning*, 48(1), pp.52–59.

Walsh, K. and Jaquet, A., 2023. Towards inclusive student partnership: Challenges and opportunities for student engagement in the Australian context. In: Lowe, T. (ed) *Advancing Student Engagement in Higher Education: Reflection, Critique and Challenge*. Abingdon: Routledge.

Index